ALSO BY MARGOT PETERS

Charlotte Brontë: Style in the Novel
Unquiet Soul: A Biography of Charlotte Brontë
Bernard Shaw and the Actresses
Mrs. Pat: The Life of Mrs. Patrick Campbell
The House of Barrymore
Wild Justice (as Margret Pierce)
May Sarton: A Biography

Design for Living

Design for Living

alfred lunt and lynn fontanne

A BIOGRAPHY

Margot Peters

ALFRED A. KNOPF NEW YORK 2003

Frontispiece: Alfred Lunt and Lynn Fontanne as Tragedy and Comedy,
photographed by Edward Steichen

THIS IS A BORZOI BOOK PUBLISHED BY ALFRED A. KNOPF

Copyright © 2003 by Margot Peters
All rights reserved under International and Pan-American Copyright
Conventions. Published in the United States by Alfred A. Knopf,
a division of Random House, Inc., New York, and simultaneously
in Canada by Random House of Canada, Limited, Toronto.
Distributed by Random House, Inc., New York.
www.aaknopf.com

Knopf, Borzoi Books, and the colophon are registered trademarks
of Random House, Inc.

Owing to limitations of space, all acknowledgments for permission to reprint previously
published and unpublished material may be found following the index.

Library of Congress Cataloging-in-Publication Data
Peters, Margot.
Design for living : Alfred Lunt and Lynn Fontanne : a biography / Margot Peters. — 1st ed.
p.   cm.
"A Borzoi book."
ISBN 0-375-41117-8
1. Lunt, Alfred.   2. Fontanne, Lynn.   3. Actors — United States — Biography.   I. Title.
PN2287.L8 P48 2003
792'.028'092241 — dc21
{B}   2002192480

Manufactured in the United States of America

FIRST EDITION

For Joe Garton

A sense of style is the ultimate morality.

—Oliver Wendell Holmes

CONTENTS

ILLUSTRATIONS

ACKNOWLEDGMENTS

Some years ago, Lynn Nesbit, my agent, called to ask, "What about that Lunt and Fontanne biography you were going to write?" Thank you for jump-starting the project, Lynn. It had begun as a book about Ten Chimneys, suggested by Amy Henderson, a curator of the Smithsonian Portrait Gallery, who rekindled an interest in the Lunts that had taken root seriously in 1985 when I toured their Ten Chimneys estate with a Wisconsin Historical Society group. But then, my aspiring-actress mother had gone to Carroll because it was Alfred Lunt's college, so this biography has been germinating, really, for a lifetime.

I am grateful to the biographers of Alfred Lunt and Lynn Fontanne who have written before me. In 1958 George Freedley published a brief biography, *The Lunts,* "an illustrated study of their work, with a list of their appearances on stage and screen." Maurice Zolotow's colorful *Stagestruck* (1964) was based on extensive taped interviews with Lunt, Fontanne, and their contemporaries. Jared Brown's *The Fabulous Lunts* (1986) is a thorough, scholarly treatment of the famous acting couple. These books are invaluable resources for the study of Lunt and Fontanne and I am indebted to all three.

Many thanks to the staffs of the following libraries and collections: the Center for Film and Theatre Research at the Wisconsin Historical Society; the Billy Rose Theatre Collection at the Performing Arts Research Center of the New York Public Library, Lincoln Center; the Beinecke Rare Book and Manuscript Library, Yale University Library; the Harvard Theatre Collection; the Special Collections of the Houghton Library, Harvard; the Department of Manuscripts, the Henry E. Huntington Library; the Harry Ransom Humanities Research Center, the University of Texas at Austin; the Special Collections of the Hatcher Library, University of Michigan, Ann Arbor; and the Covent Garden Theatre Museum, London.

Special thanks to Harry Miller, Lisa Hinzman, and Maxine Fleckner Ducey (Center for Film and Theatre Research, Wisconsin Historical Society); Jeremy Megraw (New York Public Library Theatre Collection); Kathryn Beam (Hatcher Library); Fredric Woodbridge Wilson and Annette Fern (Harvard Theatre Collection); Hannah Frost (Harry Ransom Humanities Research Center); Thomas Ford (Houghton Library); Claire Hudson and Andrew Kirk (Covent Garden Theatre Museum); Gayle Barkley (Huntington Library); Patricia Willis (Beinecke Library); Kathryn Johnson (British Library); and Susan Baker (Waukesha Historical Society).

My gratitude to the following persons who granted permission to quote from unpublished material: Alan Brodie Representation for the Noël Coward estate (Noël Coward), Julie Gilbert (Edna Ferber), and Philip Langner (Lawrence and Theresa Helburn). Equal thanks to those granting permission to quote from published works: Crescent Dragon Wagon (Maurice Zolotow), Julie Gilbert (Edna Ferber), the Kurt Weill Foundation and the University of California Press (Kurt Weill and Lotte Lenya), Methuen Publishing Ltd. (Noël Coward's autobiographies), and the Orion Publishing Group Ltd. (Noël Coward's diaries).

To the many people who talked or wrote to me about Lunt and Fontanne, or otherwise offered assistance, my warm thanks: James Auer, Steven Bach, Arthur Bean Jr., Ronald Bowers, Joseph Broyles, Donald Buka, Clarence Bundy, Philip Byrd, Ronald Campbell, Montgomery Davis, Jane Doud, Gay Jordan Elwell, William Eppes, Carolyn Every, Catherine Gavigan, Claire Greene, John Hale, Joanna Harris, Stella Heintz, Bunny Raasch Hooten, Bruce Kellner, Harold Koeffler, Maurice Kurtz, Dan H. Laurence, Howard Lee Levine, Sydney Luria, John McMillan, William Manly, Barbara Martin, Faith Miracle, Michael Morrison, George Newill, Philip Nohl, Libbie Faulkner Nolan, Elliot Norton, Stuart Oderman, Christine Plichta, William Pronold, Bernard Ryan Jr., Verna Schmidt, Ruth Schudson, Lucille Shulberg Warner, and Charlotte Zolotow. To Margaret Whalen my thanks for putting her formidable Internet skills to work on Lunt and Fontanne.

Very special thanks to Ronald Bryden, Barry Day, Gloria Irwin, and Lucille Justin, all of them knowledgeable about Lunt and Fontanne and extremely generous with that knowledge. To Donald Seawell, Lunt and Fontanne's lawyer, my gratitude for his invaluable information and support.

My research in England was assisted by Sheridan Morley, Roger F. Fisher, Patricia Burnell, Terence Morgan, Richard Mangan, Muriel Pahlow, and Sir Donald and Diana Sinden. Mr. Fisher and Ms. Burnell were extraordinarily helpful with tracing Lynn Fontanne's family, and Mr. Fisher's unearthing of Lynn Fontanne's sisters' birth certificates a significant documentary contribution.

Thomas H. Garver interviewed on tape dozens of Genesee Depot area residents who worked for or otherwise knew the Lunts. The Ten Chimneys Foundation made his transcribed interviews available to me. I am indebted both to the foundation and to Mr. Garver's excellent work.

The young staff of Ten Chimneys has been a delight to work with. *Salut* to Christine Cross, Alice Kamps Curtin, Erika Kent, Virginia Thomas Malone, Nellie Martens Murphy, Terri Plewa, Amanda Schilling, former Vice President Sharon K. Kayne, and Acting President Sean Malone.

Peter Ridgway Jordan, my husband, lent his support, criticism, and research skills from the beginning—and found Lunt and Fontanne as brilliant, witty, and lovable as I did. "Mashed potatoes," darling.

I am also deeply grateful to Peter Jordan, Joseph Garton, and my former editor, Robert Gottlieb, whose continued support I treasure, for reading—and considerably improving—the biography in manuscript.

As always it has been a great pleasure to work with Victoria Wilson. I value her expertise, judgment, and enthusiasm for the acting profession, all of which make her the ideal editor for Lunt and Fontanne.

Listed in the Register of National Historic Places, restored and looking as though the Lunts just stepped out for a walk, Ten Chimneys opened to the public in May 2003. The estate's preservation is the work of the Madison businessman and theater enthusiast Joseph Garton. Knowing how deeply he cares about preserving the magic of Alfred Lunt and Lynn Fontanne, I gratefully dedicate this biography to him.

Design for Living

Critics called them the Fabulous Lunts, the Great Lunts, the Lustrous Lunts. The Magical Lunts. The Incomparable Lunts. The Infallible Lunts. Laurence Olivier called them the Celestials and the Glorious Beloved Supremes. Graham Robertson, a friend of Sarah Bernhardt's and Henry Irving's, enshrined them as the Ineffables. London dubbed them Duke and Duchess of the West End. In the States we called them the Aristocrats of the American Stage. For four shining decades of the twentieth century Alfred Lunt and Lynn Fontanne reigned as the most famous acting couple in the English-speaking theater.

"You both ennobled this world," said Kitty Carlisle Hart. Edna Ferber called the Lunts "a symbol for all that is fine, important, richly traditional and respected in the theatre." "Brilliant and heavenly artists," wrote John Gielgud. "I thank God," said Raymond Massey, "that I have had the privilege of working in the theatre for the many years that the Lunts have led it." Awed at Alfred's "God-given understanding" of the theater, Thornton Wilder called the Lunts "the Best Artists and Nicest Human Beings on my Country's Stage." "Absolutely superb," said Noël Coward. "The best acting possible. They are both incredible."

Coward also said that Alfred Lunt and Lynn Fontanne could not be captured in print. They were too strange, too possessed, too unlikely, to be nailed down by the written word. Taking Coward seriously, I still offer this exploration of the careers and private lives of two remarkable artists.

CHAPTER ONE

Lynn's Way: 1887–1919

Much of Alfred Lunt's early history Lynn Fontanne would learn from Alfred himself as well as from his mother, his half-siblings, his scrapbooks, his neighbors, and his childhood friends. Alfred would learn less about Lynn.

For one thing she came from across the pond. She was born on the wrong side of the tracks in a small Victorian house in Station Terrace, Snake's Lane, at Woodford Bridge in Essex, about ten miles northeast of London. He would not know her parents and seldom see her two sisters, Mai and Antoinette; meet few of her early friends and associates. And there was that British reserve: a cool customer, Lynn was less confessional than Alfred. One fact he would not learn till much later: Lillie Louise, renaming herself Lynn, was not born in 1892, as she claimed, but on December 6, 1887.

Lynn's father, Jules Pierre Antoine Fontanne, owned a typefounding business inherited from his father. Yet Fontanne was less a businessman than a would-be bon vivant. Lynn aspired to her father's imagined heights.

"I will be a mother," she said, "and have four children and twelve nursemaids."

She told everyone that her noble family had given up its title during the French Revolution. This was Fontanne fantasy; what was true was that her maternal great-grandmother came from a titled family in Ireland, though Lynn apparently did not know it.

Frances Ellen Thornley, Lynn's beautiful, dark-haired mother, resented her husband's impracticality. High-strung, her temper fueled by frustration and disappointment, she quarreled abusively with Jules. Lynn and her sisters often took shelter with their Irish grandmother, Sarah Ann Barnett, who lived nearby.

Lynn grew up poor one day, prosperous the next, but always in an atmosphere of fantasy. Her father read the girls Dickens, Tennyson, and Shakespeare. She memorized Shakespearean soliloquies, recited them in a voice that could "ring out like a bell." When the family moved for a time to the London suburb of Walthamstow, Lynn was often discovered missing from her bed. Antoinette knew where to find her: "She had climbed out of the window and was down the road where she had crept into the theatre to watch the performance." Taken to the Lyceum Theatre to see Henry Irving and Ellen Terry in *The Merchant of Venice,* Lynn stood up in the gallery and loudly recited the "quality of mercy" speech right along with London's reigning actress. Taken to *The Worst Man in London,* a thriller, she hid her face in her sister's lap, crying, "I never shall go on the stage—don't let me go on the stage!"

Frances and Jules Pierre Fontanne, seated. Standing, left to right: Lynn, Mai, Antoinette

Lynn Fontanne in 1899

It was perhaps on that visit that she saw Queen Victoria riding in a carriage. There was a sudden stir in the crowd and shouting and she rushed forward. A bobby caught her arm; she stared as the Queen rode by, and the Queen's great blue eyes stared straight ahead: a performer, just what Lynn wanted to be.

"I was a very noisy, happy, and exuberant child until I was eight," Lynn told Maurice Zolotow, the Lunts' first biographer, "and it was then my mother scolded me for being clumsy and I got to be self-conscious and lost all confidence."

When Lynn was in her teens, Jules Fontanne was called to the side of a dying French aunt. She left him some money; he promptly celebrated by taking his family to Paris. Strolling in the Bois de Boulogne, Antoinette complained that a man was following them. Jules accosted the stranger: "I demand to know, sir, why you are hounding my daughters!" The man explained that he was Wilfred de Glehn, an artist and a member of the British Royal Academy. He was struck by the girls' beauty. He begged permission to paint them.

Great luck for Lynn. All three girls had to work to support themselves (Jules spent his inheritance at a rapid clip); but though Antoinette was the raving beauty, Lynn became the favorite model of de Glehn and his wife, Jane. As Jane de Glehn's girl in *The Blue Coat* and Wilfred de Glehn's señorita in *The Spanish Mantilla,* Lynn hung in the Royal Academy. The money she earned modeling kept her in tea and buns while searching for acting jobs. More important, the de Glehn connection led to an introduction to the great Ellen Terry.

It was a September afternoon in 1905 when Lynn called at the small Georgian house at 215 King's Road, Chelsea. Ellen Terry was fifty-eight, three years parted from Henry Irving and the Lyceum Theatre (Irving would die that October), depressed about her failing memory and poor eyesight. Yet she still encouraged aspiring actresses who flocked to her: "her little circle of girls," Lady Duff Gordon described them, who "would gladly have laid down their lives for her sake."

Lynn was shown upstairs. Ellen was lying in bed wrapped in shawls, untidy fair hair falling about her shoulders. She gazed at the thin dark girl with the turned-in toes, gestured her forward. As Lynn knelt at the side of the low bed, Ellen put her hands on her shoulders and impulsively kissed her.

"Do something!" she commanded in a husky voice as the maid brought breakfast on a tray. Lynn took a deep breath. "The quality of mercy . . ." she began—Terry's most famous speech. Ellen laughed but she listened.

"I will give you lessons. I don't know exactly when or what hours, or how often, but mind, when I call for you, you must come at once. You must make no other engagements, not even in the evenings, for I may want you to work in the evenings."

Lynn had to receive Ellen's messages through a neighboring plumber in Down Street, where she lived in a shabby-chic room with no water but fan windows and an Adam fireplace. The lessons were sporadic, though one session working from Ellen's own annotated script of *King Lear* deeply impressed her. "Oh, my dear father," said Lynn as Cordelia. Ellen interrupted: "No, don't say it like that. You love him. You must say 'Oh, my deeeere father.' Now, no more instruction for Cordelia, for the whole understanding of the part lies in this line." She also gave her pupil a key that unlocked the spontaneous technique Lynn used all her

Ellen Terry, the great British actress and Lynn Fontanne's mentor

life: "Think of the *meaning* of what you are saying and let the words pour out of your mouth."

Ellen got Lynn a job in the chorus for the Christmas pantomime *Cinderella* at Drury Lane. She paid Lynn to read to her afternoons. She let Lynn take baths at King's Road. She invited her to her Elizabethan country house in Kent, paid her for odd jobs around the house, coached her in stage deportment. She pinned a bedsheet to the front of Lynn's dress and one to the back, then made her walk gracefully among the tangles. "Must get Lynn more money," Ellen reminded herself in her diary. "It's wicked. She is so intelligent."

But Ellen's attention was distracted by rehearsals of Shaw's *Captain Brassbound's Conversion,* where she fell impulsively in love with the thirty-three-year-old actor James Carew. She managed to get Lynn a walk-on in July 1906 at the Savoy, and before she took *Brassbound* to America she gave Lynn a miniature boxed set of Shakespeare as a keepsake and a letter of introduction to the actor-manager Herbert Beerbohm Tree. "That's all I'm going to be able to do for you," she told Lynn, kissing her. "If I helped you any more, it wouldn't be good for your character, for each one runs his own race."

In 1907 Lynn got another walk-on, in Booth Tarkington's *Monsieur Beaucaire* at the Lyric, under the name Viva Fontanne. Perhaps she thought calling herself "Viva" would boost confidence, for when not acting she was painfully shy. "I thought to myself, 'Why are you so shy? What makes you stiffen up as soon as you meet anyone?' " She answered herself: "It is because you are wondering what it is they think about you. Now, don't think that any more. Wonder what it is *you* think about *them*. And when you go into a restaurant, instead of dying when you go in, just . . . have a look, Lynnie, and see who's there instead of bothering whether they're looking at you." Slowly she began to gain more poise.

That fall of 1907 she used Ellen's letter of introduction to Beerbohm Tree, who was looking for schoolgirl types for his staging of Dickens's *Edwin Drood.* Rather hard of the great Tree to demand experience for a mere walk-on, and Lynn, with her new confidence, rebelled. "But how will you find girls this young with experience? And how will I get experience if you don't give me work?" Delighted, the eccentric Tree hired her, cautioning her to give her address to future managers not as unfashionable Pimlico, but as Belgravia.

ike many shy people, Lynn was a comic. Antoinette took her to parties where she "kept these men in their thirties in fits of laughter." When Tony was invited to dinner by three men one evening, she asked Lynn along for protection. Immediately attracted to the apprentice lawyer Edmund "Teddy" Byrne, Lynn launched into comic impersonations and wild tales of life backstage. Teddy laughed. When they found themselves alone in a cab together, he kissed her and Lynn kicked him in the shins. He was impressed. "Oh, he had a beautiful baritone voice," said Lynn, "and he stole my heart away."

Lynn was still sitting for artists like the de Glehns. "He'd be waiting for me to finish modeling in some Chelsea studio. He was tall and quite slim and he had a raincoat draped over his shoulders and he'd be lean-

ing on the Battersea bridge, waiting, looking down into the river."
Teddy would take her to her flat, where she'd change into an evening
dress she'd made herself, then on the town to the Cafe Royal, the Savoy
Grill, Rules, or Hatchetts. It was all glamorous and glorious and she
wanted to marry Teddy, but her career came first.

She longed for a London tour de force but, as Mrs. Patrick Camp-
bell quipped, was forced to tour. In 1909–1910 she played a
small role in Somerset Maugham's *Lady Frederick,* returned to
London in *Where Children Rule* at the Garrick, set out for the provinces
again as the maid Harriet Budgeon in *Mr. Preedy and the Countess.* In
June 1910 she was back in London in lodgings at 37 Lambs Conduit
Street in Holborn and writing to her mentor, who, now married to
James Carew, had been reduced to lecturing on Shakespeare:

> Dear Miss Terry,
> You will be pleased I am sure to hear that I have secured another
> engagement this time in London in *Billy's Bargain* at the Garrick
> to open on Thurs. the 23rd. It is only a tiny part in the first act—
> but I have never played in London before, so I am very delighted
> and excited about it. . . .
> > Yours affectionately,
> > Lynn. P.S. Let me come & *do* something for you.

Lynn had appeared in London before, but Lady Mulberry was her first
speaking part. She shook so badly she kept repeating, "I'm on the stage,
I'm on the stage, I'm on the stage" to calm herself.

Brother of George Grossmith, the famous Gilbert and Sullivan pat-
ter singer, Weedon Grossmith had directed *Mr. Preedy and the Countess,*
hired Lynn again for *Billy's Bargain,* and now engaged her as Harriet
Budgeon for a North American tour that played in Montreal, Washington, and came into New York at Nazimova's 39th Street Theater, where
it died after twenty-four performances. In February 1911 Lynn was
back in London playing in a one-act curtain raiser at the Criterion,
again directed by Grossmith. In January 1912 he cast her in *A Storm in
a Tea-Shop,* another curtain raiser, then engaged her on tour as an understudy. It was their last association, but Lynn learned much from this
multitalented man, even though—frustratingly—she'd still gained no
real recognition in London.

Though Teddy Byrne doubted Lynn could really act, in 1912 he introduced her to Lady Higson, whose at-homes attracted prominent theater people. There she met the producer J. E. Vedrenne and the actor-manager Dennis Eadie. Currently their London hit *Milestones* was the hottest ticket in town. They gave Lynn the part of the old maid Gertrude Rhead in their third touring company, which played villages not even on the map. She set off with the White Company in November 1912.

"Oh, places with only one train a day and you lived in cheap theatrical digs and ate awful food and it was all one-night stands, and I loved it, I loved it, I loved every moment of it, for experience was what I needed." She toured in *Milestones* six months, feeling at last that she was really acting. In three acts Gertrude Rhead ages from twenty-one to eighty: a great part for an actress of twenty-five to pull off. She could tell that audiences believed in her. When skeptical Teddy came to a performance in the Midlands he said in awe: "But you were good!"

Arnold Bennett and Edward Knoblock wrote *Milestones,* and Lynn went on to act in three other plays by Knoblock: *A War Committee, How to Get On,* and *My Lady's Dress,* with Gladys Cooper and Edith Evans. (John Gielgud believed Lynn and Edith Evans never got on: "Both *belles laides.*") Most important, she played Gertrude Rhead in a fall 1914 London revival of *Milestones.* It was her first significant London part.

Teddy, who had avoided introducing her to his family, now took her to meet his parents in Walthamstow. They got engaged; they might have married, but on June 28, 1914, Archduke Francis Ferdinand was assassinated in Sarajevo; major powers in Europe armed; England declared war against Germany in August. Lynn and Teddy decided to postpone marriage. She would also have to postpone fame. Though she was noticed in the *Times* ("Lynn Fontanne, who takes up the old-maid part . . . achieves the miracle of making as beautiful a thing of it as her predecessor"), London was focused on the coming conflict.

llen Terry had given Lynn a start, but an American actress propelled her directly to success. Laurette Taylor ("Greatest of them all!" said theater manager George C. Tyler) became an instant London celebrity in *Peg o' My Heart.* The Marchioness of Townsend

"Will you come and play with me in America?" the great actress Laurette Taylor asked Lynn.

gave Laurette a tea to which Lynn, courtesy of Lady Higson, was invited, still murmuring as she entered the room, "Don't worry what they're thinking about you, concentrate on what you think of them!" A crush of guests waited to meet the new star. Lady Higson urged her forward. Prim in a little hat with two velvet streamers down her back, Lynn recoiled. Instead she slipped into a chair, sipped a cup of tea. She was about to leave when miraculously the crowd around Laurette Taylor dissolved and their eyes locked across the room. "Why, she's as shy as I am!" thought Lynn. Impulsively she crossed the room and sat down next to the celebrity, teacup rattling in her hand.

"I'm an actress, just a little actress!"

"You are! What have you played in?"

"Milestones."

"I saw that. What part?"

"Gertrude."

"You mean you were that young woman and the middle-aged one and the old woman of eighty? What else have you done?"

"*My Lady's Dress.*"

"I saw that, you were wonderful! Will you come and play with me in America?"

"Boom! Just like that she asked me," said Lynn, believing that back in the States, Miss Taylor would forget her. A few months later she was driving an army canteen truck down in Devonshire when a cable arrived offering her a part in Taylor's next play at a hundred dollars a week, an unheard-of sum. Yet she discovered that getting a passport and an American visa in wartime was equally unheard of. "I got it finally by falling to my knees and crying and putting on a marvelous scene before a nice old gentleman in some office in Whitehall," said Lynn. A week later she sailed, courtesy of Laurette's husband, the playwright and director J. Hartley Manners. Teddy Byrne would be waiting for her after the war.

With *Peg o' My Heart* Hartley Manners had become a popular, though critically scorned, playwright. ("Poor Hartley," sighed Ethel Barrymore, "only the public likes his plays.") He intended to reintroduce Laurette to New York in his *Wooing of Eve.* It opened in Rochester, New York, in March 1916, with Lynn as Winifred, a weepy ingenue, but did poorly in Philadelphia, and Hartley decided to rush his *Harp of Life* into rehearsal. George C. Tyler eyed the scrawny import huddled in an oversized sweater.

"Gawd A'mighty! We got hundreds of girls in America who can play that part!"

"Not the way this one can," said Laurette firmly. "Hartley wrote it with her in mind."

Lynn was five feet six and weighed 102 pounds, yet her tummy stuck out. She was still insecure and had a raucous laugh. Her sex appeal was invisible. She didn't like America and was humiliated in shops by rude salesgirls who refused to understand about "vests" and "jumpers." She'd never had such a big part before—and opposite the Greatest of Them All. She was terrified of the short, squat, cigar-chomping Tyler.

And she believed her heart had been broken by the cablegram she'd just received: Teddy Byrne had died in action in France. He had left her all his money and possessions. She would not accept them; anonymously, through a lawyer, she transferred her claim to his sister in London. Edmund Byrne had been her first serious love. Losing him, she'd lost the chance of a normal life—husband, children, pretty home in the suburbs. She grieved for Teddy; but she hadn't truly wanted that normal life.

On opening night, November 27, 1916, at the Globe Theatre, New York, Lynn Fontanne triumphed. She played the shy eighteen-year-old Olive Hood, whose world is shattered when both her girlish mother (Laurette) and the man she loves betray her.

The feared Alexander Woollcott marveled at the skill of this "emaciated, gawky, astringent" actress. Guthrie McClintic was also at the opening of *The Harp of Life*. He had come for Laurette Taylor but found himself entranced by Lynn Fontanne. "She was a young woman, tall—dark—very thin and angular. She was also English, and she riveted your attention from the moment of her first entrance. Somewhere in the middle of the second act she had a brief emotional scene and so true was she—so touching and so vivid—that on her exit she brought the house down. During the entr'acte her name was on everybody's lips. The following day all the critics echoed the verdict of the opening-nighters. A new star was in the firmament."

Managers offered contracts, but Laurette advised her to accept only big roles. So Lynn stayed with the Taylor-Manners family. Hartley was British and kind, with charming manners and dark curls that fell over his forehead. Laurette was Irish, radiant, temperamental, fey, rude, imperious, and unfaithful to Hartley. She was generous enough not to mind that the *Times* considered Lynn's the outstanding performance of *The Harp of Life* after hers or that night after night Lynn's curtain call rang through the house.

Because she'd planned Lynn's triumph. And the young actress obviously worshiped her, took her advice about everything. "Bag o' bones," Laurette teased her, forced her to eat butter and cream, complained that she never gained an ounce, jealous of her thin elegance. Laurette issued orders: wear this, stand up straight, tuck in your tummy, turn out your toes. On weekends at the Mannerses' Connecticut place on Long Island Sound, Laurette would expound her theories of life, love, and acting, which of course was life. Absurd for Lynn still to be mourning Teddy Byrne! She'd never be a great actress without great love affairs to prime the emotional pump. She planted all kinds of eligible men in Lynn's way, but nothing happened. Her protégée seemed hopelessly naive. Yet what an actress! Particularly since she was devotedly copying Laurette's timing, mannerisms, and speech. And Lynn loved the theater with Laurette's passion. They were like sisters.

Frank Kemble-Cooper (a descendant of Sarah Siddons and John Philip Kemble) and Philip Merivale from the *Harp* company had also become "family." Joined by J. M. Kerrigan, a fine actor from Dublin's Abbey Theatre, they went into rehearsal in 1917 for Hartley's hastily written call to arms, *Out There.* In a battered straw hat, Lynn played the louche, slangy "Princess" Lizzie, who feeds her mother gin and ridicules her sister's patriotism: not a large role, but second billing to Laurette Taylor in a part written for her by Hartley Manners. *Out There* opened March 27 at the Globe Theatre. On April 6 President Woodrow Wilson finally declared war on Germany. *Out There*'s vehement patriotism appealed to the public, though with only eighty performances it hardly rivaled *Peg o' My Heart.*

Lynn stayed with her "family" for a revised *Wooing of Eve,* in which she was cast again as Winnie the weeper, required to burst into tears nineteen times in a single scene. But Lynn had grown as an actress; she wanted to make the unhappy bride comic and real. "I'm sure I can get good laughs, Hartley, if you'll let me do it." This time she burst into tears only once. After that she twisted her handkerchief, bit her lip, blew her nose—making the audience wait for something that didn't happen. Alfred Lunt, in the audience for a matinee, was impressed. "I can play any kind of a part and utterly loathe the word 'type,' " Lynn announced confidently in the press. Still, the play was not a success. One week after it closed Hartley Manners rushed *Happiness* into the Criterion, on New Year's Eve, 1917.

Lynn played a ditzy flapper mad about clothes, gossip, and sports cars. She delivered her lines in short, clipped sentences, "very fast, very brightly, giving an impression of a glass of sparkling champagne." And Laurette scored as usual. Unhappily, Hartley's play was not loved. *Happiness* was obviously a vehicle slung together for his wife, with stereotyped supporting characters and slipshod construction. Critics pointedly suggested that Laurette Taylor was wasting her talents in her husband's plays.

Laurette read the reviews. She might be "Greatest of Them All," but Nazimova was doing heavies like Ibsen and Strindberg; Ethel Barrymore had tackled *The Lady of the Camellias;* Mrs. Fiske was playing George Sand; and Constance Collier had scored with John and Lionel Barrymore in *Peter Ibbetson.* Laurette decided she'd try Shakespeare. Lynn read the reviews too, thought about other managements, yet agreed to play scenes from *The Taming of the Shrew, Romeo and Juliet,* and *The Merchant of Venice* for a special matinee at the Lyric.

The rehearsals forecast disaster. Laurette had never acted Shakespeare professionally; neither had her supporting cast. But Laurette didn't care: this would be Shakespeare *her* way. Hartley was supposedly in charge, but Laurette reduced him to a cipher. Rehearsals became ugly displays of temperament, indicating how insecure the star felt. Lynn began to dread the afternoon of April 5, 1918. Laurette "knew the plots but not the lines."

The Taming of the Shrew, Lynn as Bianca, went fairly well. Then Laurette appeared on a balcony as Juliet, only she didn't speak like Juliet. When she gazed into her lover's eyes and whispered, "Hello, Romeo," it was "goodbye, Juliet, from that moment on," said the young Helen Hayes; and the great Shakespearean actress Julia Marlowe was rumored to have fainted. The howling audience managed to pull itself together for the Portia and Nerissa scene: "How far that little candle throws his beams! / So shines a good deed in a naughty world." Lynn controlled the damage as long as she was onstage, but with Portia's "Go in, Nerissa" the scene went to pieces.

At the end Laurette appeared before the curtain. "Shakespeare has been crucified—so have I—long live Hartley Manners!" The eminent critic Burns Mantle forgave her: How many allegedly fine actresses would dare so much?

Lynn left Laurette's company, but they remained soul mates. "She was sometimes gauche, but so true," said Laurette. "While acting with her I forgot we were actresses."

What had Lynn learned from the Greatest of Them All? Confidence in her acting powers, certainly—especially in comedy. The freedom to reach inside and give herself to an audience without fear. The secret, too, that improvising won't ruin a play—though Lynn would never rely on that skill. Above all, the lesson of what it is to be a star. A star is capricious, self-centered, benevolent, rude, inspiring, impossible. Wherever she is is center stage. A play is written *for her.* And in return for stardom she gives herself utterly to her art.

Lynn Fontanne asked herself: Can I be a star?

She could be a leading lady, stepping next into *A Pair of Petticoats* by the British actor Cyril Harcourt as a replacement for Laura Hope Crews. In a season rocked by Lionel Barrymore in *The Copperhead,* John Barrymore in Tolstoy's *Redemption,* and Frank Bacon's enormous hit *Lightnin',* as well as by half a dozen popular war plays, nobody much noticed Lynn as a replacement in a poor play. George Tyler fumed, not over Lynn's capable performance but at rumors of a romance between her and Harcourt. Like Charles Frohman before him, Tyler tried to run his actors' lives, and Lynn was *his* discovery. On tour in Chicago, Lynn wired: THE MAN I MARRY WILL EITHER BE A MILLIONAIRE OR A *GOOD* PLAYWRIGHT.

Tyler had a play for Lynn in mind, if his hunch was good that an obscure *New York Times* journalist could rewrite the play *Among Those Present*. "I think we can skim through it if we add more comedy," he told George S. Kaufman, "and the way to do it is by building up a part I have in mind. I've got the perfect actress to play the part—a British kid named Lynn Fontanne." Kaufman asked when he needed the rewrite. "You got twelve hours, kid," said Tyler.

In twelve hours Kaufman transformed the conventional part of a society wife into a version of Franklin P. Adams's "Dulcinea," a fictional character whose platitudes Adams quoted regularly in his *New York Tribune* column. Reading the revision next morning, Tyler laughed out loud. Mrs. Glendinning was now a good-hearted creature who couldn't help expressing herself in deadly funny clichés.

The renamed *Someone in the House* opened at the Knickerbocker Theater September 9, 1918, with Lynn playing opposite Hassard (Bobby) Short. "I gave it everything I had and so did Bobby," said Lynn. "We ruined the play but we were funny."

Many critics agreed, the November *Vanity Fair* considering Lynn's empty-headed wife "the best bit of characterization that's been seen in these parts in many a day." But fate, in the form of the flu epidemic of 1918, had other plans. Public places emptied as Americans died by the thousands; Lynn and Bobby Short found themselves playing to empty seats. Kaufman sardonically suggested retitling the play *No One in the House,* or running ads "Avoid Crowds: See *Someone in the House.*" Desperate, he wrote thirty-five revisions—three more than the play had performances.

But Lynn Fontanne was now a Broadway leading lady and, according to John Corbin of the *Times,* "a notable young actress" of "extraordinary powers of personality." Kaufman was already thinking of writing his own play for her based on the "Dulcinea" character. Meanwhile, George Tyler called Lynn to rehearsals in New York at the New Amsterdam Theatre for *A Young Man's Fancy,* which he would take to Washington that summer of 1919 with a young actor named Alfred Lunt.

CHAPTER TWO

Alfred's Way: 1892–1919

When Lynn Fontanne was eight and reciting Shakespeare, three-year-old Alfred Lunt made an unofficial debut at one of his mother's tea parties at her Grand Avenue mansion in Milwaukee, descending the stairs as Cupid with a bow and arrow but minus Cupid's sash. The guests gasped. Hattie laughed adoringly.

Alfred Lunt Sr. had died in 1894, when his son was two. Hattie had also lost a daughter, Inez, who died at four. Now Hattie focused on Alfred—confiding in him, reading Tennyson and Dickens to him, playing him songs on the piano. Fortunately her lumberman husband had left money: $500,000 to his wife—the equivalent of millions today. To Alfred $30,000, most of it in trust until he turned twenty-one.

Hattie would rip through her husband's money in a few years.

Hattie adored the theater; she *was* theater with her flamboyant dresses and scarves, carrying voice, and tumultuous emotions. Alfred's first theater experience, at the age of three, was memorably bizarre. Hattie took him to the Davidson to see a company of German midgets called the Royal Lilliputians in the musical extravaganza *The Golden Horseshoe.* When one of the midgets seemed to explode into flames, Alfred screamed so loudly that Hattie rushed him to the lobby. There he screamed to go back inside. He watched the rest of the performance

Young Alfred and Hattie Lunt Sederholm

in rapture, clapping wildly at the finale when the scenery rose, creating the illusion of midgets descending into the sea.

Then Hattie met Carl Sederholm, a Swedish-born doctor. She married him in 1899, when she was twenty-seven and Alfred seven, breaking up their twosome. Alfred cried all night because she hadn't married his hero Buffalo Bill. Dr. Sederholm was a theater enthusiast and a talented pianist with a pleasing baritone, but Alfred resented the intruder. He chose to keep his dead father's name, Alfred Lunt.

Alfred was forced to grow up fast in the impractical Sederholm house. Hattie decided that her husband should treat his poorer patients free of charge. This left Sederholm chiefly her money to gamble on horses and prizefights. Then came the babies: Louise, Carl, and Karin. "How are the children?" Alfred would write from summer vacations on his aunt Achsah's farm near Neenah, as though they belonged to him and Hattie. *"Thousands of kisses for everybody.* Don't forget Karin. I am your loving son." He was less like a son than like a husband, worrying about the kids and the rapidly disappearing money.

Since Hattie was domestically occupied, he started going to matinees alone, taking the streetcar downtown to the elegant Pabst Theater on Water Street to see *Old Heidelberg* and *Trelawny of the*

"*Wells,*" or watching girls in tights from a ten-cent gallery seat at the Star burlesque house. ("Hang your clothes out the window!" shouted Hattie when he came home reeking of tobacco.) He preferred vaudeville and melodramas like *Bertha the Sewing Machine Girl* at the Bijou. But Shakespeare, bumps and grinds, divas, circus clowns, singing midgets—he adored them all.

When Alfred was nine the Conant family moved next door with their son Kenneth. Mr. Conant built the boys a miniature stage with side scenes, electric lights, and drop curtain. Now they could stage Shakespearean productions, dividing the parts between themselves and John Alexander, whose parents turned over a vacant top-floor room in their house to Alfred's enterprises. That year Alfred formed the "Lunt Stock Company's Wisconsin Theater, Alfred Lunt, Mgr." and presented *Rip Van Winkle, Parsifal, Twelfth Night, A Midsummer Night's Dream, Julius Caesar,* and *The Mikado* to the neighbors, including his sweetheart, Pauline Alexander. "I drew all my own characters and scenery—my God, I was fearless—and even tossed a few of King Arthur's knights into *Parsifal,* just to give my talent range."

As Alfred's collection of theater programs grew (a favorite was *L'Aiglon,* thrillingly autographed by Sarah Bernhardt), he did actually find time to attend school. Yet Alfred used his classrooms—at 17th District Number 1, the Milwaukee Academy, Carroll College Academy, and finally Carroll College itself—as stages.

"Alfred always stood up very straight," remembered his first-grade teacher, May Massee. "He was the first one the children would choose to read to them when they were reading out loud." Alfred had learned to keep one arm behind his back, hold the book well up, and before reading bow graciously left and right. He had a huge crush on Miss Massee and was always asking Hattie if he could bring her home.

At the private Milwaukee Academy, Alfred entered every declamation contest, sometimes with devastating results. "I wasn't good at all and I knew it. I was so ashamed of losing I once hid inside a cupboard for a whole day. I went through agonies, but I would do it every year, with the opposite of flying colors."

Success came at last with "I did not think to shed a tear"—Cardinal Wolsey's farewell from *Henry VIII.* "Well, I walked away with it, and I won the medal, and my [former] nurse, [Cassie] McNellis, rose to her feet and applauded wildly: 'And he's only twelve, he's only twelve!' "

He was only twelve that summer when he was stricken with acute appendicitis, developed peritonitis, then came down with scarlet fever in the hospital. Giving up a hopeless case, the doctor sent him home to Hattie. Legend is that Hattie told a local surgeon, "If Alfred dies, you die." The doctor operated on the kitchen table, removing the appendix and a kidney along with part of the supporting abdominal and back muscles. Alfred recovered, but slowly. All his life, despite his tremendous energy, he was prone to intestinal and kidney inflammation.

Sometime during this long recovery, Hattie announced that they could no longer afford the Grand Avenue mansion. To economize, they'd be selling the house and moving to the tiny village of Genesee Depot, twenty-seven miles west of Milwaukee. He could start the fall 1906 high-school semester at Carroll College Academy in Waukesha, commuting by the milk train locals called the Galloping Goose.

Though he'd miss his Milwaukee pals, the thought of moving did not devastate Alfred. He loved Genesee Depot, tucked into the rolling kettle moraine of southeastern Wisconsin. For years the family had taken the train out to Genesee for the day to picnic beneath the shade of tall oaks.

Yet Alfred seethed. He had a kind, generous, loving temperament, yet resented a mother and stepfather who had squandered his father's money. Pity Father hadn't left the thirty thousand to Hattie, the five hundred thousand to Alfred.

Still playing millionaire at Genesee Depot, Hattie again refused to let Sederholm charge his poor patients. Soon she was coaxing Alfred to dip into his trust fund. Alfred refused. Next was a drastic move to Finland, where the family could live cheaply with Carl Sederholm's relatives in the Swedish colony at Helsingfors (Helsinki). Finland thus became a large presence in Alfred's life: its lakes and forests, timbered buildings, vivid textiles, and short bright summers. He spoke Finnish to servants, Swedish to family and friends. He enjoyed his Swedish cousins, took countless photographs, sketched Scandinavian decor, sang Finnish folk music. His father had been Swedish; in Scandinavia he felt at home.

Finland was summer fun. In fall Alfred returned to Carroll College Academy, staying with friends in Waukesha. Back to school meant back to the boards: the Carroll Players staged full-dress plays for live audiences, unusual for a prep school. In 1907 Alfred, his hair framing his forehead in waves, appeared in *Private Secretary*, "the play that made all Waukesha laugh." Teaming with his friend Ray Weaver, he clowned in *Hit of New York*. He starred as Rip Van Winkle, the Mikado, Don Pedro, and Benedick in *Much Ado About Nothing*. He did readings, recitals, scenes from plays—anything to put him in front of an audience. Word spread beyond Waukesha about the extraordinary young actor.

In the summer of 1909 he returned to Helsingfors, where he shared a room at the Hotel Kemp with his stepfather. Waking to abnormal quiet one morning, he called out, then got up and gave Dr. Sederholm's bed a violent shake. "The saddest thing has happened," he wrote Kenneth Conant. "Father died suddenly in our hotel yesterday . . . Heart trouble. We were having such a good time and then this ending. Mother is to stay here this winter with the children. Poor soul!" Dr. Sederholm might have taken an overdose of sleeping pills. After all, he had squandered another man's fortune and the future may have looked bleak. At seventeen, having lost two fathers, Alfred stepped into the role of provider to Hattie and her children.

He sailed home on the *United States* in October, receiving a warm welcome at Carroll College Academy from Dr. Walter Lowrie Rankin and his daughter May Rankin, the inspired drama teacher who, discovering that Alfred could recite *Twelfth Night* from memory, had made him her protégé. He moved into a room at Mrs. Beggs's at 104 East Avenue at $3.50 a week, paid for, like his tuition, with interest from his trust. On the wall he hung posters of Christ and Ellen Terry.

He plunged into theater again—writing plays with his best friend, Ray Weaver, traveling with the Carroll and Beloit glee clubs, doing scenes from *Twelfth Night* and readings from the *Kalevala,* acting in *The Young Mrs. Winthrop* and *The Professor's Love Story.* Though he'd never laid eyes on him, he invented a Harry Lauder act in full Scots kit: "Audiences could not get enough of him." Life was not quite *all* theater. "Carroll 13, Laurence 5—Rah, Rah, Rah," he wrote Hattie, adding, "Oh, I would give anything to see the Finnish woods in Winter," and signing off, "Just *rooms* full of love to you and all the 'kids' with kisses by the millions."

But Hattie was no longer happy in Finland. Suddenly Dr. Sederholm's mother had turned "selfish." Alfred sent her money "borrowed out of the mining stocks." She replied in her dashing, nearly illegible hand: he was her "dearest of sons," her "best friend in the world." As for the plan, "Won't it be lovely darling if we can keep house and if necessary have two or three boys with us?" Buying a house was suddenly possible because Alfred had unexpectedly received money from his trust.

That June of 1910, after passing exams, Alfred sailed for Helsingfors on the *Empress of Ireland* to summer in Finland. Dr. Rankin, another father figure, died in August. "My best friend is gone," he wrote May Rankin in condolence. He was planning to return with Hattie and the children in mid-September, but Hattie's mother-in-law sped up the process. "Matilda told Mother to leave Sat. or she would have the police," Alfred wrote Ray Weaver. "Hurrah Hu-Ray," they managed to book third-class passage for September 3, and Alfred registered on time for his freshman semester at that "three-elm institution," Carroll College.

They moved into their new house at 101 Hartwell Avenue, with Alfred's closest friends, Ray and Andrew Weaver, as boarders. Hattie hoped for summer tourists as well, for in those days attractive Waukesha was known for its White Rock Mineral Springs. Yet Hattie didn't officially register as a landlady; and 101 Hartwell Avenue soon became known as "that weird household" on the hill.

Smoking cigarettes in a ten-inch holder, demanding breakfast in bed, ignoring a nest of squeaking mice in the couch, Hattie left running the place to Alfred. She also turned over Louise, Carl, and Karin to her competent but harassed son. "In God's name," he cried at the end of one frantic day, "please don't have any more children!" He was both mother and father now. There were no rules except those he laid down, just as there had been no rules when he was a child. Their financial situation deteriorated, Hattie spending as though the $500,000 were still intact. "We don't have one penny!" wailed Karin.

Alfred managed both studies and more acting. His comic impersonations made the reputation of Carroll's Men's Glee and Mandolin Club, which toured the state in 1910 and 1911, Alfred cracking up audiences with pieces like "Yiddish Theater," "The Fate of Yim Yohnson," and "Prunes." His Harry Lauder act more popular than ever, he distributed handbills promising that "Those who enjoy real rollicking fun of the most wholesome kind will find their demand satisfied."

Alfred always credited his success to May Rankin, who in his opinion was way ahead of Stanislavsky in her insistence that acting comes from inside. In turn, Alfred Lunt was May Rankin's dream pupil, the justification of her career. Discovering his genius, she urged him to leave Carroll after two years for her school, Emerson College of Oratory in Boston.

And so in the school year 1911–1912, Alfred redoubled his efforts. "Working like fury," he wrote Kenneth Conant the fall of 1911. He was studying Valentine for Shaw's *You Never Can Tell* and Consul Bernick for Ibsen's *Pillars of Society.* He was playing Caleb Plummer in *The Cricket on the Hearth* and making all the scenery. He had dropped French and was taking a voice course in "visible speech" so he'd be able to graduate from Emerson in one year.

After a tour with the rival Beloit Glee Club that spring of 1912 that had him breaking up audiences all the way to California, Alfred suddenly announced he was through with clowning and prepared Poe's "Tell-Tale Heart" for his tragic debut. "It was a faculty concert of the College of Music," remembered a fellow student,

> and Alfred was to reward us for listening to the piano numbers. . . . The black of the concert grand-piano and the black and white of Alfred's first dress-suit were melancholy and effective against the green [backdrop]. He was very tall and very slender then.
>
> He opened his mouth for the first word. The audience snickered. He rolled his eyes and made a tragic gesture. The audience chuckled audibly. He moaned "Oh, that eye!" and a burst of laughter drowned his next words. It was cataclysmic. Every sentence sent the audience into hysterics. Every time he groaned, "It beats, beats, beats," we went off into paroxysms of laughter. . . . Poor Alfred! He was crushed. He stayed home from school a week, refusing to see any of us. . . . He swore he would never be funny again as long as he lived. . . .

Yet Alfred was "a born slapstick comedian, a magnificent comedian."

Mia Stanton and Juliet Weeks were in love with him. He was a type of young man that women adore: tall, good-looking, shy, charming. Beautiful manners. Kind to children, animals, and adults. Smart, sensitive. Active, popular. Sophisticated—he smoked English Ovals. Enormously talented. And the biggest come-on of all: hard to get. His enormous energy he poured into the theater and outings with pals.

"Rehearsals all last week as usual and Friday night the [Beta Chi's]

Alfred Lunt and his best friend, Ray Bennett Weaver, at Carroll College

Beefsteak roast. . . . We walked out west of here about two miles down to the Indian mounds & I did have the jolliest time. Made a big fire & put flat stones on it to heat & afterwards taking 'em out & laying beefsteaks on them to fry & I can't tell you how good it tasted. Had potatoe salad, piles of sandwhiches, olives, pickles . . . & then later roasted marshmallows. It was a lovely evening and the *comet* [Halley's] was as plain as could be."

In those innocent years before World War I destroyed the givens of Western civilization, youth was permitted to develop slowly. Alfred's never having a date at Carroll would not have been an oddity; nor would, probably, the passionate poem he received from "Damon" to "Pythias." The feminine sensibilities he shared with Hattie—gossipy intimacy, interest in her clothes, exclamations of "Oh, mercy!"—might be attributed to a fatherless boy growing up close to an emotional mother who maddened and delighted him. "Dearest Beloved," he would write her, "You are my angel—my beautiful Aurora—Hattie dear—long may you shine. . . . I can't quite make up my mind just how I like you best—as a lover or a mother."

He was emotional, writing to the "one above all," Ray Weaver, "My heart leaps up when I behold my Raynbeau in the sky," yet at the same time describing a door opened by "the prettiest black haired . . . rosy cheeked, kissible lipped young lady that you ever laid eyes upon." Though it would be a relief, he couldn't fall in love: "The only women . . . I really care for are married & the other ones, tho' I dote on them & 'love' (in the other sense of the word) very dearly, never yet have quickened that very comical flame of matrimony within me."

Alfred left Carroll two months before his twentieth birthday. Though by now a sophisticated traveler, he did not have to tackle Boston alone. Unwilling to give up Alfred, Juliet and Mia were also transferring to Emerson.

In Boston, Alfred and Mia lodged with Juliet at the Weekses' Columbus Avenue house in the south end. Eyeing him as a potential son-in-law, Mr. Weeks insisted Alfred be their guest. "I wish they wouldn't do so much for me," he wrote Hattie nervously, "because I never can show my appreciation & besides do not deserve all this attention."

"Tomorrow I register at Emerson," he wrote Ray Weaver. "Ye Gods! I shake when I think of it." Yet he found both classes and students disappointing. Six days later, on his way to school, he passed the Castle Square Theater on Tremont, a year-round stock company now casting for *The Aviator.* Light broke. Why not get a real acting job?

John Craig, actor-manager, introduced him to the director George Henry Trader. Coincidentally, when Trader had been with the Pabst Stock Company in Milwaukee, Alfred had not only written him requesting a copy of a play Trader had written, but read it four times. Trader remembered. "Will you take five dollars a week?"

"I will."

He was cast in *The Aviator* as a U.S. deputy marshal and sheriff. "Not a particularly satisfying & grateful role," he wrote Weaver, "but it is an actual beginning & I shall 'go on' now if I die in the act. . . . Good luck to you Alfred—May heaven protect you. . . . I'm quite tickled."

During rehearsal week he lost his voice through sheer tension. He discovered that attending Emerson and rehearsing and performing a play a week at Castle Square was a killing grind.

I rise at 7:30 get my breakfast shave—clean up the dishes & then read my mail. Juliet knocks, we meet Mia & all walk to school (six blocks)—Chapel is out at 9:35 & I hurry over to the theater (another six blocks) & stand around until sometimes eleven & twelve (it is impossible to study or write there) and then hie me to lunch—I go to class (at school) at one fifteen & am out at two—Again hike to the theater & make-up (great practice) . . . until the third act call bell rings—go thru' my performance & am out at five o'clock or so—Hurry home (12 blocks or so—I hate to spend a nickel for car fare) wash up & then we all have supper. . . . I leave here at about eight—by the clock—for the theater & return & have my door locked at about eleven.

No wonder, as he told Hattie, he "went to sleep the minute I touched the bed last night & never budged until seven o'clock this morning." Still he found time to read Kipling, Dostoyevsky, Dickens, Gorky, Shaw, Ibsen, Balzac.

There was never enough rehearsal time, agony for a perfectionist. He couldn't catch his breath, let alone master a part. "Honestly Ray I don't know what ails me but I simply can't do a thing at the theater," he wrote during rehearsals for *The Man of the Hour*. ". . . I tried standing still, this morning, for five minutes & tried to give my lines naturally & easily but I couldn't. . . . Trader said this morning 'Now Lunt—remember the man in the last row in the gallery wants to hear—Keep your hands still! They'll look at them & miss what you're saying.' . . . Draw a moral from this poor struggling soul in Boston—'Take things easy.' . . . It doesn't pay to work one's self up to a bursting point before going out before an audience."

Alfred got his first (poor) review as Richard P. Roberts in *The Man of the Hour*—"I honestly am rotten in the part." Was the theater really for him after all? He attended classes sporadically at Emerson, kept up with the reading. He considered most of the Castle Square plays drivel and hated being cast "old" because of his height. In play after play he got character parts—sheriff, Indian, innkeeper, father, American consul, samurai, butler, judge, convict.

There were exceptions to the drivel: *Hamlet* (Alfred as the First Player), *She Stoops to Conquer* (the servant Jeremy), and *Othello* (Lodovico), the last a thrill because Trader let him copy stage business for the company from Edwin Booth's original prompt book. And Alfred saw as many touring actors in Boston as time and money allowed: George Arliss, Annie Russell, Maude Adams, Ruth Chatterton, Ina Claire, Wilton Lackaye, William Faversham. Above all, Minnie Maddern Fiske, "unquestionably the finest actress on the American stage & anyone interested in acting can't afford to miss her. . . . Such an example of repressed emotion you never saw before & you are just fairly swept off your feet, by it."

December 19, 1912, marked his ninety-sixth performance at Castle Square. Alfred ached to go home for Christmas to Hattie and the "Finns." He ached for Ray Weaver: "I just want to cry out & bring you here & never let you go again." But leaving was out of the question: he would play the Fiery Dragon in Castle Square's Christmas musical, *The Gingerbread Man.*

Alfred in his dressing room at the Castle Square Theater, Boston

To act or not to act, that was the question. The more he saw of the theater, the more it sickened him. "It's *cruel* . . . My God! Such a way to live!" And acting was so ephemeral. "What do we know of Irving, of Jefferson, after all. Very little. . . . They last but for a moment & are soon forgotten." Walking the night streets after Christmas, torn by indecision, Alfred met George Henry Trader and poured out his doubts. Trader was realistic. Alfred had "height, voice, appearance & understanding"—but success in the theater often depended on luck.

Alfred wrestled with his demons into the new year, 1913, and conquered. "Yes!" he wrote Weaver. "I have decided to remain on the stage—I battled & stormed & tore my little brain to pieces, wondering & worrying & debating & handed my decision in late last week. . . . I may not be altogether fitted for it. I have no voice, I have no 'weight,' I have little brilliance & force & worse of all that hellish lack of confidence which is oh so weak—but I do believe there is a great field to work in, unlimited when once the muck & grime is gone & tho' it will without doubt take years to get there I shall keep on."

Alfred would stay at the Castle Square Theater three years—1912 to 1915—acting in more than fifty plays. Evading Mia Stanton and Juliet Weeks, he moved out of the Weeks house into a series of rooms, sharing for a time with his friend Kenneth Conant. In February 1913 he was appointed assistant stage manager; his first play, Frederick Ballard's *Believe Me, Xantippe,* ran more than one hundred performances, and his salary was raised to twenty dollars a week.

He'd been borrowing money and selling a stickpin and watch so he could send Hattie five dollars a week, but in August 1913 Alfred Lunt turned twenty-one and came into his $30,000 inheritance. He promptly took one of the most important steps of his life: he bought three acres of the wooded land he loved just west of the village of Genesee Depot.

The next summer he drew on the interest to treat Hattie to a trip abroad. Hattie had Alfred to herself; he'd never seen her so happy. London, where they saw Mrs. Patrick Campbell in Shaw's *Pygmalion* and George Alexander in *An Ideal Husband,* but most thrillingly Nijinsky dancing *The Afternoon of a Faun,* Alfred wanting "to die there and then." France: Versailles, Fontainebleau, *Cyrano de Bergerac* at the Comédie-Française, Alfred sobbing during the last act. Brussels, Germany, and Russia, with its onion-domed churches and fabulous art galleries. Russia's contradictions fascinated Alfred: "Such confusion, such dirt, such misery, such wealth, such ignorance, such rotten systems of business & government, such intelligence, such artistic temperament all messed up together. . . ."

They arrived in Finland with no idea that Europe was on the brink of war. Since Finland was a Russian grand duchy, they were used to Russian soldiers, but this time the bank in Helsingfors shut its doors in their face, thousands of armed Cossacks clattered through the streets, and their hotel advised them to leave the country. They managed to crowd into a train for Tornio, get a boat to Sweden, hire a car to take them 150 miles to Boden, then a train to Stockholm. Mobilizing for war, Sweden seethed with refugees. The voyage home in crowded steerage on the *United States* completed their Finnish adventure.

Yet Finland was by no means a loss. Since buying the acres at Genesee, Alfred had dreamed of the house he'd build there. Finland had reinspired him. It would be a simple hunting lodge: "one enormous room with staircases" mounting to a walk-around gallery with doors leading to four bedrooms and bath, arched by a wood-beamed cathedral ceiling. That August Alfred started consulting a local builder. Hattie and the children had moved to 113 East Avenue in Waukesha after Alfred had left for Boston; she would stay there until the house was complete, taking in suitable boarders like the Bankes sisters, local artists. Meanwhile, Alfred returned to Boston for his last season at Castle Square Theater.

A new director, Al Roberts, released him from stage managing so he could act full-time. Boston critics were beginning to wake up to his skill and versatility. He won particular praise as the jealous husband in *The Ne'er-Do-Well,* "a man whose careful bearing is an attempt to veil the fires that increasingly smoulder beneath." But in fact he was sick of it all—memorizing new parts before he could forget the old, constant rehearsals and performances. Even before the English actress Gertrude Kingston singled him out to play New York in *The Cherry Orchard* for sixty dollars, one week guaranteed, he'd decided to leave Boston. But he didn't go to New York. He didn't feel ready for Broadway.

earing that Margaret Anglin's leading man was leaving the tour of her Broadway success *Beverly's Balance,* Alfred got in touch and was told to meet her in Chicago in June 1915. In the darkened theater Alfred chewed nail, confidence slipping away.

It did nothing for his morale when he was told to play scenes with Howard Lindsay, stage manager, while Miss Anglin critiqued from the house. He cringed, he crouched. He threw out his hip and minced, trying to conceal his lanky height. His voice—trace of Scandinavian accent and juvenile break—squeaked and scraped. "He was, in my opinion," said Lindsay, "the most hopeless aspirant I had ever seen or heard." Said Anglin afterward, "Make no mistake, Lindsay—that boy has quality. We will try him." Lindsay was forced to offer the hopeless Alfred Lunt fifty dollars a week. "Shades of Edwin Booth!" he wrote Weaver. "A *lead* with America's foremost actress! I can't believe my ears."

Feeling "dreadfully miscast," Alfred appeared as J. Courtland Redlaw in *Beverly's Balance* the first week in July—"I blush to make love to Miss Anglin"—then headed west on a series of one-night stands. From proud Hattie a wire on his birthday: HERE'S TO YOU BEST BELOVED RIGHT OVER A GLASS OF SPARKLING CHAMPAIGN SKALL SKALL FOR TWENTY THREE YEARS YOU HAVE BEEN THE HAPPINESS OF MY LIFE THE IRON OF MY SOUL . . . FERVENT LOVE MOTHER.

In Berkeley Anglin produced *Iphigenia in Aulis, Electra,* and *Medea* in the Greek Theater at the University of California. Alfred was carried away. "Oh, the spirit of it all. True art in the American Theater at last." Set on a stage 340 feet long, the stunning productions were directed by the distinguished actor Gustav von Seyffertitz and Anglin, with music by Walter Damrosch and a sixty-piece orchestra. Alfred played messengers and a reveler.

In rehearsals of *Medea,* Anglin objected that reveler Alfred was as decadent as apple pie. Defiantly, he reappeared nearly naked, with gilded hair and nipples, red fingernails and toes, his arms slung drunkenly over the shoulders of two similarly gilded youths. Anglin was sure they'd be arrested, Alfred sure he'd be noticed. To his amazement, the weather seemed to cooperate for the company's successes: clear and starry for *Iphigenia,* dark and foggy for *Electra,* threatening clouds for *Medea.*

Reaction was so enthusiastic that Anglin gave a repeat performance of *Iphigenia* on September 4, with Alfred playing the role of Achilles after one rehearsal. The young actor's physique was not exactly Greek, so Lindsay taught him how to hold up his head, fling back his shoulders, throw out his chest, and lock his knees. Loaded down with helmet, armor, shield, sword, and dagger, Alfred made a stunning

Casting couch? Alfred acted in vaudeville with the notorious British actress Lillie Langtry.
"She's brilliant beyond words—tho' cold as ice."

entrance, looking "about eight feet tall," but by the time he plodded across the endless stage into position for his first speech he felt like a midget. After the play, Howard Hull, Anglin's husband and manager, paying off Alfred for stepping in as Achilles, slipped a five-dollar bill into his hand. "This, I never told for years," said Alfred, "—out of shame for him—Miss Anglin would have been horrified."

Beverly's Balance went on the road again that fall and winter of 1915–1916, ranging from Calgary, Edmonton, Saskatoon, and Winnipeg to Sioux City, Fort Dodge, Des Moines, Cedar Rapids, Peoria, Springfield, Grand Rapids, and finally Boston. Meanwhile Hattie was driving Alfred mad:

> I asked you . . . to send me a daily account of the money you have spent & all the big receipts—It is absolutely necessary for you to do this for without it, I really do not know how I can manage

things—& we are again liable to go under. . . . You had $100 to
pay bills with . . . but you didn't & we still have to pay Cudahy's
$7.50 & Putney's $68. There was plenty for you to pay all those
bills in fact you'd have had $9.04 left over for the week's
expense. . . . Am glad you bought the shoes & suit. Hadn't you
better get the rest of the children's winter things right now & be
done with it. 2 pairs of underclothes apiece etc—But in heaven's
name write me about it. I imagine you are wild "I'd" & purple
while reading this & are growing extremely insulted & altogether furious—*but* as Gilbert says in the play "If things keep on
at this rate our little domestic shack will tumble to pieces. . . ."

Because "Miss Anglin is a genius," he had agreed to play Le Beau and
Jacques de Boys in her outdoor production of *As You Like It* at Forest
Park in St. Louis on June 4, 1916, with a cast of hundreds, including
the aging romantic actor Robert Mantell, the young Sydney Greenstreet, and Howard Lindsay. Rain canceled the show; the next evening
too was cold and rainy. Anglin appealed to the audience. Ten thousand
people roared they'd stick it out. The skies cleared and the cast took
their bows to wild applause.

In August Alfred was job hunting in New York when another sea-
soned actress tapped him to play opposite her in vaudeville in *Her Husband's Wife.* Laura Hope Crews (to be famous as Aunt Pittypat in *Gone
With the Wind*) adored charming Alfred Lunt who could learn his part
overnight. Alfred played vaudeville a week in Philadelphia, then in
Washington, where the satisfied Miss Crews passed him on to a more
notorious actress.

Lillie Langtry had been the mistress of King Edward VII and of so
many other royals that she had been nicknamed "the sport of kings."
Now, at sixty-three, she was a large, coarse woman whose acting ability
had not refined over the years. But Alfred was dazzled: "It was late
afternoon and I shall never forget her silhouette against the sky, exactly
as she looked in her early photographs. It was a beautiful profile. I must
admit that in the full light some of the aura was dissipated, but she was
still a handsome woman, rather big, with the bluest eyes I have ever
seen. She used to bead them with blue wax for the stage. Her hair was
browny gold, but the color she said, varied with her mood." As for
Langtry, she saw nothing incongruous about casting a twenty-four-
year-old as her lover.

Biographers of Alfred Lunt state categorically that both Laura Hope Crews and Lillie Langtry took him to bed. Possible, of course; but Alfred's clinical analysis of the Lily suggests not. "I adore her offstage, for there never was a woman as fascinating in conversation as she . . . *but* once the footlights hit her—she's a demon. I hate to act with her. . . . She's brilliant beyond words—tho' cold as ice." He assured jealous Hattie she was still first: "I have decided definitely to run home for a few days after New Orleans to help you move & to wallow in your lovely presence—Hattie, Hattie, you are a joy forever—as are our children. . . ."

Langtry played well to adoring audiences, walked through if the house applauded other acts enthusiastically. Her unprofessionalism angered Alfred, who never let a performance down. He had almost played out his six-month contract when Margaret Anglin asked him to join her for a revival of *Green Stockings*. Alfred wanted to get back to legitimate theater, yet was canny enough to bargain. GLADLY, he wired, BUT NOT FOR LESS THAN ONE HUNDRED DOLLARS A WEEK. Anglin called him ungrateful but paid his price.

Howard Lindsay had changed his mind about Alfred Lunt. He was a natural comic because he *thought* funny. As Colonel J. N. Smith, D.S.O., Alfred gave a performance, said Lindsay, that had "weight and maturity and dash." Anglin was so impressed that one night she urged him to take a solo curtain call. Forced to face the audience as himself, Alfred collapsed, and Lindsay saw the same scared kid who had auditioned in Chicago.

Though he would never stint a performance, Alfred was much occupied with Genesee that spring. Hattie had moved into the optimistically named Mon Repos, and he brimmed with advice:

Yes do enlarge the sewing room if it won't cost more than $50, but don't try to skimp on windows. . . . So glad to hear you've some hens sitting & that a couple of potatoes are in. . . . You must have the sewing room tiled exactly like the living-room with black plaster between—see? Use common red brick if you can't get more tile—I want the walls grey—curtains magenta—woodwork green (emerald)—white wicker furniture with brown & white stripe covering—a black rug & a yellow bird cage—I'm sure you'll like it—Don't you think the furniture on the balcony would be nice painted a sort of mauve?

Alfred's taste was exuberant. Mon Repos enthralled him like the toy theaters he'd loved as a child. If he had not chosen acting, interior decorating surely would have been his metier. He adored choosing fabrics, colors, antiques, curtains, rugs. Like George Washington with Mount Vernon, "he was involved in the daintiest questions of decor."

If not as an actor or interior designer, then Alfred had a future as a chef. Food had always been a passion. Now Hattie wanted to open a tea-room:

> I should serve coffee, tea, sandwiches & cake to begin with [he
> advised] & perhaps a little ice-cream—but this last is so expen-
> sive until you find out how it's going—Ham, minced ham,
> lettuce & mayonaise, peanut butter sandwiches—cream cheese,
> American cheese sandwiches too—at ten & fifteen cents, ought to
> be enough & some nice smooth looking cake—A little salad
> maybe—egg, shrimp or vegetable would be good—then your
> coffee & tea. . . . The place could be made most attractive. . . .

He returned to Genesee Depot in July, there being no jobs back east, paying Louise and Karin two dollars a week to help Hattie with house, garden, and hens. (The tearoom project had collapsed.) Fortunately Carl had a summer job, for Alfred got "so boiling mad" he could kill over that "great husky brute of a boy too God damn lazy" to take care of a beautiful place. "I leave Carl out of anything that has to do with *work* at Monrepos." He was perhaps a little jealous of Carl's easygoing charm.

Alfred himself had work in August—one week with the Pabst Stock Company, playing Trillo in the swashbuckling *The Pirate*. The pretty young British actress Cathleen Nesbitt had to play a scene opposite "tall gangly" Alfred during which he devoured a Spanish onion. "Oh, Alfred, couldn't it be a large apple?" pleaded Cathleen, eyes streaming. "The script says an onion," said Alfred. Milwaukee loved him, one critic declaring that he "walked away with first honors" in a portrayal that "stands out as one of the most perfect characterizations of the entire season." George Foster Platt, the director, offered him a role in *Romance and Arabella* that fall on Broadway—if the leading lady approved. She was Laura Hope Crews, and she did.

Alfred Lunt made his Broadway debut at the Harris Theatre on October 17, 1917, as Claude Estabrook, a Greenwich Village artist. Not a large part, but the *New York Sun* said, "Mr. Lunt has given us the most amusing character acting of the new season." Alfred particularly scored with some business he'd got from Mrs. Fiske in *Tess of the d'Urbervilles* when she calmly combed her hair after killing her lover. After his lovemaking with Laura Hope Crews, he combed his hair. "I didn't say a word. Just combing, combing, combing."

But the public didn't warm to William Hurlbut's whimsical comedy. "Not since I wrote you the wee short line to the effect that we are closing a week from to-day—have you heard from me," Alfred wrote Hattie, "—but to tell the truth I've been too heartsick to almost say my prayers. . . ." *Romance and Arabella* closed after twenty-nine performances, but not before Alexandra Carlisle, playing the lead in *The Country Cousin,* decided she wanted Lunt for the role of George Tewksbury Reynolds III on tour. "Oh, no, no, no, not the type," said George C. Tyler, the producer. But when Margaret Anglin recommended Alfred, he offered him the role.

Mr. Perkins, the Genesee Depot stationmaster and telegraph operator, relayed Tyler's wire over the phone, and Alfred dictated his reply: BE GLAD TO COME. SALARY TWO HUNDRED A WEEK.

Next day, Tyler: REPORT FOR REHEARSALS JUNE 17. ONE HUNDRED AND FIFTY DOLLARS ENTIRELY SATISFACTORY.

"But," said Alfred, "I asked for two hundred."

"Crazy, pricing yourself so high," snorted Mr. Perkins. "I wired him you'd take a hundred and fifty. You mighta lost the job."

Sure he'd saved Alfred's career, Perkins bought a scrapbook, labeled it "The Progress of Alfred Lunt in an Artistic Way," and began to collect clippings of the local wonder.

Alfred went down to rehearsals in Chicago with Ray Weaver. To get into the role of the privileged WASP he acquired calling cards engraved George Tewksbury Reynolds III, bought four suits at Marshall Field's, and had a solid gold cigarette case engraved GTR III. "You could buy a cigarette case from the five-and-dime!" said the horrified Weaver. "Who'd know the difference?"

"*I* would," said Alfred.

The Country Cousin toured that early spring, Alfred getting raves for his deft comedy as the Eastern snob who is reformed by a down-to-earth Midwestern young woman. Still, its author, Booth Tarkington, was skeptical when he came to Boston the first week of April 1918, and planned to catch only the first act at the Hollis Street Theater; but Alfred's entrance so dazzled the famous author of *Penrod* and *Seventeen* that he stayed for the whole play. "Lunt's got his own style; it's a gorgeous one," he wrote Tyler. ". . . Let me write a play for Lunt of my own kind . . . only keppa holt on Lunt so we can get him."

The tour frequently played to sold-out houses, gathering enthusiastic reviews. In November, when *The Country Cousin* arrived in Indianapolis, Tarkington's hometown, the playwright invited Alfred to lunch (artichokes with hollandaise sauce, lamb chops, and au gratin potatoes: Alfred never forgot it). Afterwards they disappeared upstairs into Tarkington's study. Hours later, a whoop brought Mrs. Tarkington running into the hall. Alfred was hurtling down the banister, shouting, "He's going to write a play for me! I'm made. I'm made."

Almost immediately, natural pessimism cooled the ecstasy. "Of course I am so upset & excited over the Tarkington play business I can hardly keep my feet on the ground but, mark my words, that I never hold from me the pretty little thought that the play may be no good & may not be accepted—oh that a hundred things may come up to prevent its ever going on but even so, it does show that some people are taking a little notice doesn't it."

CHAPTER THREE

Dulcy Marries Clarence: 1919-1922

In the summer of 1919 Lynn was sitting offstage at the New Amsterdam Theatre waiting to rehearse *A Young Man's Fancy* when a door opened, a young man entered, made her a bow, fell down three stairs, and landed at her feet. "Who was *that?*" she asked when he'd picked himself up and disappeared.

"Alfred Lunt," said Sidney Toler (to become famous as film's Charlie Chan). "He's going to be a great actor."

"Well," said George Kaufman all over town, "he certainly fell for her."

Lynn Fontanne and Alfred Lunt went to Washington as members of "George C. Tyler's Company of Brilliant Players." During rehearsals and rides through Rock Creek Park they discovered each other. Alfred was six feet two and slender, with mink-brown hair and penetrating brown eyes. Lynn had never met anyone so steeped in theater, so stagestruck. He seemed to know everything about acting, costumes, scenery, box office, directing. Yet he was tortured by doubts. "I'll never get it right," he'd moan. "Someone else should play the part."

"No, no, no. You'll be wonderful."

Yet he was practical too. He'd had to buy clothes for three plays, he told Tyler, "to look presentable in your productions in Washington.

Add to this the extreme high cost of living in Washington and I feel that I am justified in asking you for $200 a week." Tyler paid it.

Alfred understood Lynn's own doubts. Though admitting she could be "rather picturesque, in a gauche and angular way," she was still a plain girl who hid her shyness by playing the comic. What thrilled Alfred was that she was as gifted and crazy about the theater as he. "Lynn Fontanne is a joy to play with and a great artist," he wrote Hattie, "—you'd adore her." He made a pencil drawing of Lynn, then turned the paper over to write her name on the back as both "Fontanne" and "Fontaine," along with his mother's, Harriet Lunt Sederholm. Then he performed a bit of numerology on the letters to see if signs pointed to yes. He wanted them to; they did.

Lynn and Alfred did three plays together that summer to critical praise: *Made of Money, On the Hiring Line,* and *A Young Man's Fancy.* Despite a remarkable company that included Helen Hayes, Emily Stevens, and Glenn Hunter, the sweltering heat kept people away in droves. Disgusted, Tyler canceled the rest of the season and sent the company back to New York. He shipped Lynn out on the road in *Made of Money* and notified Alfred to report for rehearsals of Booth Tarkington's new play, *Clarence.*

Clarence "*is* a queer guy," Tarkington admitted to Alfred, who was sweating over the script, particularly the fact that Clarence plays the saxophone. But if that's the way Tarkington saw Clarence, by God, he'd learn the saxophone. Hattie had given him piano lessons as a child; he'd found a secondhand sax and an old German who tried to teach him the *William Tell* Overture. Back in Genesee Depot he jammed with Carl and Louise on ukulele and piano, though he couldn't get past the six opening bars. Alfred was profoundly musical, but his instrument was his voice.

The biggest problem, he was discovering, was Clarence himself—a shambling soldier in faded khaki who stoops and sags and blinks behind a large pair of spectacles. This was Harold Lloyd and Buster Keaton territory. But Clarence is a grub who is going to morph into a butterfly. Considering Lunt extraordinarily good-looking, Tarkington wanted to hold his "manly beauty" in reserve, to be revealed gradually. For Clarence isn't really an anonymous soldier but a famous entomologist with money in the bank and a laboratory. A Cinderella story, except that Clarence is his own fairy godmother—and everybody else's.

Tyler worried that Alfred Lunt was too eccentric to play a hero and that Clarence himself was too eccentric for audience sympathy. Tarkington worried that New York critics like Alexander Woollcott, Heywood Broun, and Burns Mantle would condemn him, as usual, for a simplistic plot. Tarkington didn't worry particularly that Lunt was taking over as director; he knew the actor had to work out his part his way, from the inside. Alfred worried mainly about playing the piano and the saxophone, which the cast heard shrieking and groaning backstage at all hours. With his pay—$300 a week—he was satisfied.

From his summer place in Kennebunkport, Maine, Booth Tarkington kept an eye on Alfred's progress. One problem remained. Lunt tended to signal Clarence's weirdness like a flagman at a crossing. Fatally wrong, warned Tarkington. *Clarence* is a modern play. "*No stress on points*—for any parts: just simple '*natural*' ways." Any consciousness on Clarence's part that he is amusing will kill the comedy. The "reality of him must outweigh the eccentricity."

Helen Hayes, fresh from success in *Dear Brutus* with William Gillette and cast now as young Cora, caused nobody a moment's worry. Tarkington had wanted her from the beginning: "This is the best girl or woman part I ever managed to write . . . and needs just that one young genius-person H.H. to play it." Helen was just eighteen but had been on the stage ten years and played fifty parts. Alfred had been on the stage seven years and played sixty-five parts. Tarkington shouldn't have worried.

Atlantic City loved *Clarence* and the company was ready to come into New York when the Actors' Equity Association shut down Broadway with a strike. Tarkington warned Alfred against joining Equity: "It's a harness." George M. Cohan, leader of Actors Fidelity, a splinter union loyal to the managers, Minnie Maddern Fiske, and E. H. Sothern agreed with Tarkington. Helen Hayes was so afraid of George Tyler she joined the Fidos. The majority, led by Frank Bacon, Ethel Barrymore, Marie Dressler, and Ed Wynn, supported the actors' cause. Both Alfred and Lynn joined Actors' Equity, though Alfred was bleakly certain that the strike had killed his chance on Broadway.

Exhausted and depressed, he took the train home to Genesee Depot, collapsed into bed, and was fed Wisconsin cream and butter by Hattie. Lynn was due to visit for two weeks, disturbing in itself since Hattie was violently jealous. Then too, he still hadn't got past bar six of *William Tell* on the saxophone. Doubts crowded in. Maybe Tarkington was right: he'd gotten big laughs in Atlantic City only because he ital-icized points instead of letting them happen. Must stop poaching those eyes, cracking that voice. Was his uniform too tight? Was he slicking his hair too flat? Just how much, at his entrance, should he give at the knees? Would *Clarence* be produced at all?

Because of mixed-up dates, Lynn found no Alfred to meet her train in Milwaukee. When she telephoned, he told her to take the next branch train to Genesee. He met her at the depot, laughingly showed her the few houses, Stag's Tavern, the two gas pumps at Harold Greene's garage, the old hotel, and the barn where people left their horse-and-buggies when they went into Milwaukee for the day. They walked the quarter-mile dirt road from the depot to Mon Repos. Not many Genesee citizens drove cars.

Alfred escorted her into the large living room with its fireplace and two-story vaulted ceiling, its red tile floor, emerald woodwork high-lighted with red trim, splashes of red, green, yellow, and white rugs, mammoth decorated Swedish chest, refectory table painted emerald and red, walls painted with scenes from the Finnish epic the *Kalevala.*

The woman some said could have been as great on the stage as her son entered, and the two actresses squared off. Lynn was rake-thin and elegant in a cloche hat and a suit that ended daringly two inches above her ankles. Hattie was handsome, stout, and swathed in bright scarves and shawls. Hattie swept her rival from head to toe. She disliked her on sight.

Lynn met "the Finns": Louise, nineteen, tall, blond, and Scandi-navian-looking like Alfred, with beautiful legs. Carl, eighteen, main skills hunting, drinking, and shooting pool at Stag's Tavern. Fourteen-year-old Karin, the wisest of the three. "I suppose it must have been a shock for [Lynn] to suddenly come into a family of happy lunatics, where the mother was like a sister and just as wild as the other children and all of us doing crazy things just for the sheer fun of it."

Louise and Karin moved in together to give Lynn a bedroom, while Alfred bunked downstairs in an alcove next to the piano. It takes a tough person to adjust to an environment as completely dominated as Mon Repos was by Alfred Lunt and Hattie Sederholm. But Lynn was tough. She had already done what only a handful of British actors then managed (or desired) to do: transplanted herself successfully to an alien country. If she could take America, she could take Hattie and the Finns. And Hattie was hard to take: coddling Alfred, telling family in-jokes, criticizing Lynn's wardrobe, cultivating deafness when Lynn spoke. Though Hattie *was* hard of hearing. Lynn got used to Alfred bawling *"Mothah! Mothah!"* through the house.

S TRIKE OVER. RETURN SOONEST POSSIBLE. REHEARSALS AT ONCE HUDSON THEATRE.

The *Clarence* cast assembled on September 6. They were a happy bunch: they believed in *Clarence.* Nothing depresses actors like a playwright handing them endless last-minute changes. Tarkington had written swiftly and surely. His confidence was catching.

In 1919 Clarence
*made Alfred Lunt
a star.*

But no one could have anticipated opening night. The end of the first act brought cries of "Lunt! Lunt! Lunt!" Act Two—Alfred shedding his ill-fitting uniform for an exquisitely tailored gray suit and making a bravura entrance playing the saxophone—raptured the audience to fever pitch and shouts for a speech. In Act Four comes the revelation that Clarence is an expert on coleoptera. Alfred delivered his impassioned speech on beetles rapid-fire, in sharp contrast with the hesitancy of his slack-kneed earlier self. He also used a technique that would become a Lunt trademark. Expecting an important letter, Alfred deliberately turned his long, elegant back to the audience. At the words "Your letter—didn't come" his shoulders slumped. When the letter was discovered a moment later, his shoulders lifted. Only then did he turn to speak his line. Lunt did not originate this technique ("I can hold an audience with my back as long as I like," said Mrs. Patrick Campbell in 1912), but he became famous for conveying emotion with body language—like Minnie Maddern Fiske, living a situation inside his skin rather than acting it.

With Cora's "Oh, Clarence!" the curtain came down and rose again before an audience gone wild—on their feet, cheering, shouting, stamping, tearing their programs into confetti to toss at the stage along with hats and handkerchiefs. The curtain came down, rose, fell, rose. Nobody wanted to let go of *Clarence.* The cast took twenty-five curtain calls before the audience reluctantly began filing up the aisles. "It was like Armistice Day!" said Helen Hayes's jubilant mother.

Clarence made a star of Helen Hayes. It reignited Booth Tarkington's playwriting career. As for Alfred: "Mr. Alfred Lunt . . . is extraordinary . . . perfectly flawless . . . irresistible," said the dazzled critic Alan Dale. "Mr. Lunt has made *Clarence* and *Clarence* in retaliation has made Mr. Lunt and there you are."

For Tarkington success was made sweeter by the fact that a fellow Midwesterner had been his inspiration. Eastern snobbery was potent. Alfred in these early years was slightly ashamed of his origins, precisely because he was devoted to Wisconsin; Tarkington had considered using a pen name for *Clarence* to get a fair hearing in New York. Their roots bonded them. "I should have worshipped Mr. Tarkington," said Alfred, "even if he hadn't written a play for me! He was, and still is, my idea of a great American gentleman."

With the reviews Tarkington saw that indeed he was no longer regional. He particularly relished Alexander Woollcott's about-face in

Helen Hayes fell in love with Alfred, and hated her rival Lynn Fontanne.

the *Times:* "Write it on the walls of the city, let the town crier proclaim it in the commons, shout it from the housetops that *Clarence* is a thoroughly delightful American comedy, which the world, his wife and their children will enjoy. It is as American as Huckleberry Finn or pumpkin pie. It is as delightful as any native comedy which has tried to lure the laughter of this community in the last 10 seasons."

Lynn had been touring in *Made of Money*. When she returned, she found Hattie in New York and every female in *Clarence* in love with Alfred. Obviously she had to protect her interest. Every night during the third act she would slip into the theater and head for his dressing room to wait for the end of the play. Mary Boland informed her only immoral women waited in men's dressing rooms. Elsie Mackay snubbed her. Helen Hayes, the most thoroughly smitten, writhed with jealousy. How could darling Alfred care for this "awkward, skinny creature" always wearing a hat "with dangling, bedraggled plumes"? No wonder the company got along so well, thought Helen: they reserved all their hatred for Lynn.

Asked in later years how she had "handled" the presence of other women in Alfred's life, Lynn replied coldly, "I didn't *handle* it at all. I didn't have anything to do with it." But she had dreaded running the gauntlet each night, daggers sticking between her shoulder blades.

Far more dangerous than mere actresses, however, was Hattie Sederholm. From childhood, Alfred had poured out his "love and longing" for his mother-lover: "Dear heart I love you desperately . . . love without end." Now Lynn insisted that he choose. Alfred could not. He was so tortured he fled to Philadelphia after one Saturday performance to hide from the problem. Lynn turned to Laurette Taylor, still her confidante. Laurette was blunt. "He'd make a terrible lover and a worse husband."

Was Laurette jealous of Alfred, as Lunt biographer Maurice Zolotow claims—or perceptive? At issue, surely, was not just Hattie's possessiveness but Alfred's doubts about his own sexuality. Heterosexual males may have possessive mothers but are not usually torn apart by them. It was safe for Alfred to adore Hattie because there was no question of sex. He clung to her because she deferred the question of his masculinity. She protected him. Still, ambivalence tortured him. He loved Lynn.

In January 1920 Hattie was still in town. Lynn thought it was all over; she hadn't heard from him for months. Then one day in February she picked up the phone. Alfred told her that Hattie was leaving for Genesee.

"Wait, wait right there. Don't go away. I'll be right over."

It was, said Lynn, the happiest day of her life. "Just having Alfred back in my arms was all I wanted."

No letters from Alfred to his mother survive between the years 1919 and 1941. Inconceivable that he stopped writing her, even though he had chosen Lynn. Perhaps they are lost. Perhaps Hattie was a bad loser and destroyed them.

Clarence ran for three hundred performances at the Hudson. Tyler had pulled Helen Hayes out of the cast—economics; you didn't waste two stars on one play. "I was torn from Alfred Lunt. . . . My last performance was heartbreaking . . . the last time that I would play that brilliant comedy with that congenial cast. The last time I would hear that glorious laughter flood the theatre. The last time I would hear Alfred play the saxophone so terribly."

In the spring of 1920 *Clarence* went on tour for a year, soon billed as "Alfred Lunt in *Clarence*." In Springfield, Illinois, where he saw his name blazed in lights for the first time, he wired Tyler in protest. "If you really feel that it makes you self-conscious, and as you put it, naked," replied Tyler, "I'll order that it shall never be done again. Of course lights are wonderfully illuminating." Alfred was forced to agree. And Booth Tarkington was writing him another play.

Meanwhile Tyler had rushed Lynn into Eugene O'Neill's *Chris,* hoping to capitalize on the success of *Beyond the Horizon* and make a star of Lynn Fontanne.

It didn't work—first, because the father is the main character; second, because O'Neill hadn't developed the daughter's part. Lynn had another objection to the play. O'Neill rhapsodized far too much about mothers. Given her own mother and Hattie Sederholm, she wasn't buying it. She confronted the moody playwright. Why didn't he write about the real thing? A bitter, scolding mother. A mother who would destroy her son before she'd give him up to another woman.

O'Neill looked at her with interest.

Chris opened in Atlantic City on March 1 to indifference. When Tyler desperately wired him to rewrite, O'Neill replied that his wife was ill. The play moved to Philadelphia, where Lynn was well received; but Tyler refused to risk it in New York. He had to be content with O'Neill's promise to someday "give you a real daughter and lover, flesh-and-blood people." A year later O'Neill did, but the Pulitzer Prize–winning *Anna Christie* made a star of Pauline Lord, not Lynn Fontanne.

At Laurette's urging, Lynn went to London to play in Hartley's costume melodrama *One Night in Rome.* She hated leaving Alfred, but as Laurette sensibly observed, they were touring separately anyway. The Garrick was packed with VIPs the night of April 29, 1920, but *One Night in Rome* was in immediate trouble. From the gallery came shouts of "We can't see!" With help, Laurette moved chairs and tables downstage.

Act Two began with Lynn and two other unfortunates playing a slow, wordy scene. The gallery stirred. "Go back to Ameriker!" someone shouted. "We don't want you 'ere!" The actors soldiered on, pelted with pieces of tile and pennies, then sneezing powder and a stink bomb. Meanwhile the stalls and pit were demanding British sportsmanship while the American ambassador slipped out a side door. The producer, C. B. Cochran, led Laurette onto the stage. "You shouldn't treat a scrubwoman this way!" she cried, burst into tears, and fled.

Mrs. Patrick Campbell and David Belasco were first backstage. "It's a shame," exclaimed Mrs. Pat. "They just don't like you this time."

Laurette and Hartley closed the Garrick for a week. Lynn had reunions with Antoinette, Wilfred and Jane de Glehn, and Beerbohm Tree. One day she lunched with Edward Knoblock, for whom she'd acted *Milestones* and *My Lady's Dress.* The story of Alfred poured out— the crises, the impediments, the uncertainties, the competition. There was only one solution, said Knoblock: she must act *only* with Alfred, tucking him firmly under her wing.

"Knoblock is awfully anxious for you to revive *My Lady's Dress,*" Lynn wrote Tyler. "I think well acted BY ME it would be a great success & Alfred Lunt in the man's part & you have a GREAT combination."

In London the actor A. E. Matthews proposed marriage to Lynn. "But I'm marrying Alfred Lunt," said Lynn. Matthews didn't know the name. Meanwhile, touring in *Clarence,* Alfred had fallen seriously enough for a young actress named Susan Westford to tell George Tyler that he "contemplated a matrimonial affair." (Susan sounds like a desperate attempt to escape marriage to Lynn.)

One Night in Rome reopened on May 3 with bobbies on hand in case of trouble. But the play didn't recover—Hartley's indifferent writing again—and closed after 104 performances. Who had caused the riot? Most probably a rival actress, Peggy O'Neill, who, with her boyfriend, had tried to guarantee Laurette exactly one *Night in Rome.*

On return, Lynn was handed a chance at stardom: the lead in the new comedy that George S. Kaufman, collaborating with Marc Connelly, had planned for her since 1918: *Dulcy.* Dulcy was "pure Kaufman: the bumbler, the little person, the innocent" who manages to outwit the smart guys and "ends up with love, power and above all, money."

Tyler had put together an excellent cast: Howard Lindsay as a campy screenwriter, Elliott Nugent (he would write *The Male Animal*) as the ad man, Gregory Kelly as Dulcy's brother; on Alfred's recommendation, Lindsay also was directing. Tyler and Kaufman thought so highly of Tarkington they decided to open in Indianapolis to get the benefit of his criticism. His big fear was theirs. Clichés like Dulcy's "No use crying over spilt milk" and "Let sleeping dogs lie" would have to be "explained in letters a foot high. 'Dulcy' is a character for semi-literary people. . . . The audience being commonplace won't be amused by commonplaces. . . ."

Dulcy, however, went with a bang, the actors taking at least twenty curtain calls. "The intelligent people in town were delighted with the play," said Tarkington, "and I should think it ought to have a success. I laughed until I cried over it. It seems to me I have seldom seen anything like so good a light comedy. It was beautifully acted too."

"I think we've got a hit!" said Marc Connelly.

"Indianapolis," replied Kaufman gloomily, "isn't Chicago."

But in Chicago at the Cort Theater on February 20 the audience began to laugh even before Dulcy bubbles into the room with her arms full of flowers. From there the play took off, Dulcy trying as the perfect wife to help her husband's business deals and creating chaos instead. People laughed so long and so often that the play ran overtime; the curtain calls seemed endless. Next day Percy Hammond in the *Tribune* loved the happy satire whose cast deserved "anthems and hat-waving," while Amy Leslie of the *News* proclaimed "LYNN FONTANNE SCORES TRIUMPH" in a play that was "caviar."

"We've done it!" said Connelly to Kaufman.

"Chicago," said Kaufman, "isn't New York."

Lynn had a wonderful time in Chicago, madly buying clothes and seeing a lot of the handsome British actor Leslie Howard, in Chicago playing in *Just Suppose.* Howard had his motherly looking wife, Ruth, with him, but that never stopped his attentions to other women, and he was utterly charmed by Lynn. Lynn reciprocated the feeling. "Lynn Fontanne wants me to return to New York and play with her," said Leslie; but he was a rather lazy actor, hard to pin down and wanting at this point to get back to England.

Just before *Dulcy* had its Midwest tryout, Alfred, playing *Clarence* in Boston, broke with George C. Tyler. Perhaps he couldn't see another hit ahead equal to his last, or wanted more money. Tyler replied evenly, yet his hurt was plain. What manager had stolen Lunt from him?

> When I say "steal from me" I mean it literally. Mr. Tarkington did not write *Clarence* for you until he had received my sanction and approval of the idea. From the moment you succeeded in it my mind was made up . . . I admit I didn't rush, but then you see I don't believe in rushing where the development of "stars" is concerned . . . I should have . . . drawn [a contract] up the very day you said "I will be the happiest man in the world if I can only make $300 a week." . . . What a fool I was! . . . I want to say that in leaving me as you do you are not proceeding even in the slightest manner differently from all the others—many of whom are now making vast sums of money. In the future, if I can be of service, you have but to let me know.

"Much disappointed about Alfred Lunt," Tarkington sympathized. "I'm sorry indeed about the separation." But Tarkington didn't intend letting Lunt go.

The *Dulcy* road company disbanded in May. Lynn joined Alfred for a fishing trip to a lake near Tomahawk in northern Wisconsin (she loved to fish). Back in New York she rented a third-floor room in a theatrical boardinghouse at 130 West Seventieth Street. Her landlady, a cheerful lady with untidy gray hair, was a physician who preferred theater people. Alfred was living downstairs in a basement front room with kitchen, bed, and two chairs—all he could afford, since ninety percent of his salary still went to Hattie and the Finns. Gimlet-eyed "Dr. Rounds" lived next to Alfred: no hanky-panky in *her* establishment. Asked many years later, "Did you and Alfred live together before you were married?" Lynn snapped, "None of your business. I mean that!" One might detect more regret than anger.

Into Dr. Rounds's boarding house that June—and into their lives—burst a young Brit with seventy-five dollars and a suitcase of play scripts. Noël Coward remembered Lynn from dance parties at the Ham and Bone Club in London, "a scraggy, friendly girl with intelligent brown eyes and a raucous laugh"; he hoped a fellow Brit might introduce him around and lend him the odd quid. She introduced him to Alfred. The three-way attraction was instant. Gay himself, Noël found Alfred "particularly attractive" but noted also that he and Lynn were

Alfred Lunt, Lynn Fontanne, and Noël Coward, their closest friend

courting, "to put it mildly." However, rumors persist that Lunt and Coward had an affair.

Lynn adored Noël, "a lovely companion!" He was twenty-one, thin and just under six feet, with sleek hair, a bony face, high cheekbones, and Chinese eyes. Almost twelve years older, Lynn mothered him, listening as he read them his plays—clever, she thought, though arrogant. She introduced him to Helen Hayes (Noël might distract her from Alfred); but Helen wasn't interested in either Noël or his plays. Then Lynn called Frank Crowninshield, the editor of *Vanity Fair.* Crowninshield bought Noël's short story "A Withered Nosegay." Not Broadway, but he could eat.

Alfred found Noël enchanting, worldly, a little sad. He could talk about his and Lynn's "happy delirium all the while we were with you"; camp their letdown at his departure: "We lie about like two ravished nuns—quivering & exhausted but oh so—*oh* SO—very very glad."

All three were frustrated: Lynn because she couldn't pin Alfred down to marriage, Alfred because she was trying, Noël because Broadway hadn't recognized that he could sing, dance, compose songs, write plays, act—anything it asked of him. They were three rockets waiting to go off. "From these shabby, congenial rooms, we projected ourselves into future eminence," wrote Noël.

> We discussed, the three of us, over delicatessen potato salad and dill pickles, our most secret dreams of success. Lynn and Alfred were to be married.
>
> That was the first plan. Then they were to become definitely idols of the public. That was the second plan. Then, all this being successfully accomplished, they were to act exclusively together.
>
> This was the third plan. It remained for me to supply the fourth, which was that when all three of us had become stars of sufficient magnitude to be able to count upon an individual following irrespective of each other, then, poised serenely upon that enviable plane of achievement, we would meet and act triumphantly together.

Lynn's behavior was often fey, but that summer her violent shifts from terror to elation over the New York opening of *Dulcy* catapulted her from tears one moment to hilarity the next. She couldn't stop being Dulcy, which meant she jabbered a great deal. Alfred and Noël tried distraction, prowling Chinatown, pacing out hot evenings in New York parks planning their triumphs, paying their nickels to see Lillian Gish, Richard Barthelmess, and Gloria Swanson in the silents, pressing their noses to the windows of antique shops that Alfred was dying to ransack. Some nights they'd walk Lynnie to the drugstore for a Coke to calm her jittery tum and briefly plug her mouth.

On the night of August 13 Alfred and Noël showed up at Lynn's dressing room at the Frazee Theatre an hour and a half before curtain, found her about to be sick, retreated and paced the streets. "We drifted in and out of soda fountains, consuming endless Coca-Colas and frosted chocolates, and behaving generally like anxious fathers expecting twins." At the sight of the first taxis depositing fares at the Frazee, Alfred began to shake. Condemned men, they crept into cheap seats in the back row. The theater was stifling. Alfred broke into a cold sweat.

And then Lynn swirled onto the stage in black velvet, arms full of gladioli, crying "Hello, everybody!" and they saw that she was in total

Lynn Fontanne achieved stardom in Dulcy *in 1921.*

command. By the second act, they'd stopped clutching each other and settled back to watch her triumph. The actress Alexander Woollcott had called "emaciated, gawky, astringent" was scarcely recognizable as the svelte, dark-haired, light-footed Dulcy. But it wasn't only the new glamour that she had invented for the part, it was Lynn's superb comic timing that carried the play. Inspiring gust after gust of laughter, she lured the audience into the palm of her hand. She won over the waspish, partisan, sentimental Woollcott as completely as she won the rest of the audience. At his typewriter that Sunday he described her as "an actress of extraordinary gifts. . . . She can do great things and perhaps she will."

Directing *Dulcy,* Howard Lindsay was perplexed by Lynn. He did not think her attractive: her legs were straight and "thin as toothpicks"; dancing lessons hadn't cured her toed-in walk. (One night George Tyler gave Lindsay a message: "Tell Lynn that when she sits on her husband's lap, her knees show." Lynn replied, "Tell Mr. Tyler I *have* no knees.") He also considered her a featherbrain. Night after night Lindsay would find Lynn standing in the wings, her hand on the doorknob, unconscious that the actors on stage were desperately ad-libbing as they waited for her appearance. Then one night they had dinner together. Lindsay was amazed to discover that Lynn was "an intelligence to be reckoned with." He realized that she was determined, shrewd, and aiming high. *Dulcy* was just the beginning.

Yet *Dulcy* was not quite to Fontanne what *Clarence* had been to Lunt. Booth Tarkington had few partisans in New York when Lunt delivered him his hit. Kaufman and Connelly were New Yorkers with friends in important places. No matter how brilliantly Lynn acted, it was the "new play by George Kaufman of the *Times*" that scored the showier hit. Then, too, it was harder for a woman than for a man to be comic: women were simply not allowed the range of behavior laughed at in men. For that reason, Dulcy was not quite so droll a character as Clarence; nor was Kaufman and Connelly's play as sound as *Clarence,* with its mellow humor and strong supporting parts.

Yet along with Pauline Lord in *Anna Christie,* young Katharine Cornell in *A Bill of Divorcement,* Eva Le Gallienne in *Liliom,* and Lenore Ulric in *Kiki,* Lynn Fontanne scored a triumph that season. *Dulcy* would run for 246 performances.

"Rich Lynnie will pay!" exulted Alfred and Noël. "Mother's bringing home the bacon." Still, Coward found it humiliating to borrow. During a severe financial dry spell he went round to Lynn's dressing room, found it full of well-wishers, was forced to pop the question in front of the crowd. Lynn was enthusiastically describing a bit of new business she'd added to the second act. "Darling, of course, don't be so silly," she said, digging into her purse and passing him a twenty without breaking her story. Three days later he paid her back.

Alfred was not a happy actor that fall of 1921. He wanted to play a serious part, but now Tarkington was offering him the romantic lead in *The Intimate Strangers,* an amiable comedy he'd written to lure the publicity-shy Maude Adams back to the stage. Adams declined the part and vanished again into obscurity, but a showier star stepped in: effervescent Billie Burke, the wife of Florenz Ziegfeld—no coincidence, since Ziegfeld was producing. Alfred knew *The Intimate Strangers* was not as good as *Clarence*. More to the point, he wasn't the star, though at the opening on November 8, Broadway welcomed Alfred back. "Alfred Lunt, recently of *Clarence* and much more avoirdupoiser than he was in those days," said Alan Dale in the *New York American,* "was an admirable foil for Miss Burke. A better and more satisfactory leading man could never have been secured. I had been wondering if Mr. Lunt was too good an actor to be in demand, and it was a pleasure to meet him again. Sometimes the actors who have achieved one success vanish curiously."

Alfred brooded over "admirable foil" and "vanish curiously," as well as Lynn's frank advice: "You worked too hard. Act being relaxed." He also brooded over "avoirdupoiser" and began to limit his breakfasts to black coffee and unbuttered Swedish rye bread. *The Intimate Strangers* lasted ninety-one performances, then toured—along with Miss Burke's maids, daughter, nursemaid, cook, chauffeur, and dogs.

On December 10, 1921, New York papers announced Alfred and Lynn's engagement: publicity, of course, but also an official notice that Alfred Lunt belonged to Lynn Fontanne. Bizarrely, Alfred claimed in the press that his real name was not Lunt but Ecklund. Uncontradicted stories began to circulate that he had been born in Sweden or Finland. The misinformation seems pointless, unless he was romantically trying to borrow Eklund, "oak grove" in Swedish. It must have been some very private joke.

The marriage would take place on May 27, 1922, after the *Dulcy* tour and during a break for *The Intimate Strangers.* Billie Burke remembers Alfred as so obsessed these months with his pending marriage that sometimes he forgot to eat. (Perhaps he was working on that avoirdupois.) He spent hours shopping for his trousseau, "stayed up late at night examining his new socks, shirts, and dressing gowns," nervously brought his purchases to her for approval.

He was also too distracted to give much attention to Booth Tarkington's proposal that he star in *Kunnel Blake,* a play commissioned, then refused, by Lionel Barrymore. Kunnel Blake, explained Tarkington, "has to have *remarkable* distinction of person or he's no go—and that is one of your assets—'not to your credit,' as people say, because it can't be acquired; what I mean is something a few people are born with." Despite Tarkington's great compliment, Alfred turned him down. The

Lunt-Tarkington collaboration was over, though each admired the other for the rest of their lives.

On May 26, 1922, a desperate Alfred turned to Lynn where they were sitting on a bench in Central Park. She was wearing a brown feathered hat and a nice brown dress which "suited him." "Let's get married," he said. "All right," she said. They took a taxi to City Hall and found Deputy City Clerk James McCormick willing to marry them. They'd forgotten they had to have witnesses. Two city clerk's employees obliged. The marriage license cost two dollars. Alfred came up empty, so "rich Lynnie" paid.

Continuing the comedy, they wired Hattie: HAVE MADE AN HONEST WOMAN OF LYNN and JUST THREW THE COFFEE POT AT ALFRED. They spent the afternoon at Coney Island, eating hot dogs and having their photograph taken. Sitting bolt upright, straw hat in hand, Alfred mimics the paralyzed stare of old daguerreotypes. Lynn rests her hand on his shoulder as she smiles down at him like an indulgent mother. For an impromptu wedding, bride and groom are dressed to the hilt.

Headlines too recognized Lynn's current "seniority" as an actor: "LYNN FONTANNE TO MARRY—Dulcy to Wed Alfred Lunt." This time fey Alfred reported his real name as Erklund and gave his age as twenty-eight. Lynn also admitted to twenty-eight; she was thirty-four.

"When we got back to Genesee Depot," said Lynn, "I found out from his family that Alfred was actually twenty-nine. I said to him, 'You lied on the marriage certificate.' He admitted it. But he never asked me whether *I* lied." But Alfred certainly *felt* Lynn's maturity. It helped keep alive something tender, vulnerable, and boyish in him.

The fact that Lynn was already well established in the theater didn't impress the family at all. They already had one of those. For the reserved young Englishwoman, living with Hattie (who also never admitted her age), Carl, and Karin in the big, boisterous house proved impossible. Louise had married John (Jack) Greene, whose family owned Brookhill, the big local dairy farm. (Alfred paid for her expensive wedding and complained.)

Karin gave Alfred four acres and a chicken coop that she owned north of the main house, with the understanding that Alfred would cancel Carl's gambling debts. Charles Dornbusch, a Chicago architect, charged a thousand dollars to convert the coop and feed room above

*Lynn and Alfred
photographed at Coney
Island on their wedding
day, May 26, 1922*

into two bedrooms and a living room and kitchen heated by brick corner fireplaces. With bright blue, red, and green motifs, the coop would become a fantasia on a Swedish cottage. That same year of their marriage Alfred and Lynn added a screen porch and front entry to the main house and bought forty more acres of rolling kettle moraine.

As for Hattie: "She was a bit niffy with me," said Lynn with British understatement, "but I finally turned on her and we had a good solid row." Lynn won. Truce was declared. But Hattie never forgave Lynn for taking Alfred away from her, and Lynn, underneath all the "darling, darling"s, never adored Hattie. "It must have been odd to be Queen of the American stage," said a friend, Enid Bagnold, "and to have a mother-in-law who was queen of a stage in a dream."

Only Lynn knew whether Alfred was a good lover—or whether they were lovers at all. Laurette said of her protégée: "Lynn was intensely ambitious. The core of her life was the theatre. It consumed all her passion. No man, not the most beautiful, the most intelligent, nor the richest in the world, could have found any left in her—unless he had been connected with the theatre." If that is true, Lynn gave Alfred not sexual passion but her passion for acting.

But many people said, suspected, or assumed both Alfred and Lynn were bisexual or gay. Lunt biographer Maurice Zolotow titled his first chapter "The Mystery of Their Marriage" and—though he didn't say it in print, since Lunt and Fontanne were still living—"never seemed to have the faintest doubt." Edna Ferber called Alfred and Lynn "double-gaited." The recent theater book *Changing Stages* treats Lunt and Fontanne as America's famous bisexual acting couple. Biographers of their theater contemporaries say flatly that the Lunts had a "white," or sexless, marriage. Lynn's words in old age tend to confirm an untraditional union: "We were friends right away. . . . I loved him utterly. We were in the same profession. We were like twins."

Yet no one has volunteered the names of their same-sex partners. Diana Sinden, the wife of the distinguished British actor Sir Donald Sinden, says Lynn propositioned her after dinner at Genesee Depot. Lynn would have been in her eighties, evidently no deterrent. What is unusual about the Lunts is that so many writers claim in print that they were gay or bisexual and yet no one is explicit.

What is certain is that Alfred and Lynn worked out a design for living to suit them both. There would be no children. ("Never had the time": Lynn.) There would be deep devotion—to each other, to the theater, to their Genesee Depot home. There would be close friendships, particularly the triangle kind that Lynn preferred: Lynn, Alfred, and a gay or indeterminately sexed male. Possessive, insecure, she would risk losing him to a man, never to a woman. There would be kindness and courtesy, loyalty and generosity. Above all, there would be passionate, total commitment to their work.

CHAPTER FOUR

Enter the Guardsman: 1922–1925

A lfred and Lynn took a second-floor apartment at 969 Lexington Avenue at Seventieth Street. Since Alfred wanted to furnish it slowly with antiques, their main purchases were an icebox and a bed. They ate off an orange crate, sitting on Biedermeier chairs. Lynn discovered that frugal Alfred bought only one pair of socks at a time. "Next time you come home with a dozen pairs or I'll divorce you!" When they were finally able to afford carpeting, they danced through the rooms barefoot.

Theatrical and literary New York regarded this new phenomenon, the Lunts, with affectionate curiosity. Howard Lindsay called them "the gayest, happiest couple New York had ever seen. They both loved to laugh." Noël Coward then and always pretended to be unable to define them: "It must be remembered that they are magic creatures and magic creatures are vulnerable in different ways from ordinary mortals. . . . Catching a moonbeam in your hand would be falling off a log compared with catching and holding the truth about the Lunts between the covers of a book." A magic person himself, Coward was always discreet.

Alfred and Lynn asked the struggling young writer Robert Sherwood to tea. Sherwood considered Alfred and Lynn "largely unaccountable"—"gifted grotesques, sure to shine in the sideshow but doomed never to achieve prominence in the Main Tent." Lunt had the stage personality of "a shy, repressed, neurotic young man with some kind of physical deformity." Fontanne was "a funny, gawky English girl who didn't care how ridiculous she looked as long as the laughs came quickly." All Broadway, said Sherwood, "felt sorry for this weird pair of fiancés." Certainly Clarence and Dulcy could only have married each other.

Laurette took the newlyweds under her wing. That autumn of 1922 she and Hartley moved into a neo-Gothic pile of red brick at 50 Riverside Drive looking northwest up the Hudson. At Laurette's Sunday suppers Alfred and Lynn could meet Jeanne Eagels, Jane Cowl, Gertrude Lawrence, John Barrymore, Douglas Fairbanks, Alla Nazimova, Alexander Woollcott. Laurette adored parlor games, though these days screening her movie version of *Peg o' My Heart* took precedence. (A guest asked Ethel Barrymore if she had ever seen *Peg*. "Oh, my dear," breathed Ethel, "one whole winter!") At the piano, Noël sang in a reedy, sophisticated voice for his supper.

The old star system seemed intact. Alfred met some of the very actors whose photographs he'd pasted in his scrapbook twenty years before. And that November 1922 a new star had blazed in the theatrical sky. John Barrymore's Hamlet was greeted as a triumph unequaled in the American theater of his generation, perhaps of the century. His fresh, radical, Freudian Hamlet seemed to herald a new era of theatrical superstars. And Barrymore was pure star: cutting Shakespeare to suit himself, dominating the spotlight, transfixing audiences with his gorgeous persona.

Yet the old star system was mortally wounded. Barrymore played a hundred and one performances of *Hamlet* to beat Edwin Booth's one hundred, then took the Super Chief for Hollywood. Too many actors would follow him. Movies were changing the theater irrevocably. Another change was the new dominance of the playwright. Popular plays presented the actor. With the coming of dramatists like Eugene O'Neill, Elmer Rice, Robert E. Sherwood, Sidney Howard, and S. N. Behrman, actors began to present plays.

Alfred deeply admired Barrymore, the one American actor, he thought, who spoke beautiful Shakespearean English. Apart from their enormous talents and excellence in comedy, however, no two actors could have been more different. Classically handsome, a womanizer, a heavy drinker, self-destructive, Barrymore was a reluctant actor. In the early days of creating a character he was a tireless perfectionist. Repeat performances bored him utterly. He fooled with the part, with the audience, with his fellow players. Tragically, he never respected his profession, nor the playgoers who idolized him. At forty-three he simply walked away.

The inevitable question after Barrymore: who now was the First Actor of the American stage? There were plenty of candidates: Paul Muni, Fredric March, Philip Merivale, Roland Young, James Gleason, Glenn Hunter, Joseph Schildkraut, Leslie Howard, Lee Tracy. And Alfred Lunt, who was acutely aware of the challenge.

That September 1922, for the princely sum of $600 a week, Alfred had appeared in the play *Banco* as the dissolute Count Alexandre de Lussac. Heywood Broun found Lunt "enormously clever and able" even while his eyes "grew weary of chasing gestures." In the *Times,* however, Alexander Woollcott rejoiced to see Lunt act "without the visible effort and fiddle-dee-dee mannerisms with which he has been hobbling himself," while Lunt impressed Percy Hammond of the *Tribune* as "preeminent among American players." And the young S. N. Behrman returned to *Banco* again and again:

> I was fascinated by Alfred's style and personality. . . . He captivated me. He had total command, not merely physically but mentally. You saw his brain digesting the lines and the situations and finding them funny. There was glee in his voice, in his expression, in his gestures. . . . I saw that Alfred changed his readings, changed his performance all the time, but he never changed his point of view, which was comedic. It was the comedy of intelligence. He was not always amused by the same things so that you got different facets almost at each performance.

There was no "comedy of intelligence" in the silent film Alfred made in 1923. Curiosity and money persuaded him to play a romantic hero in Distinctive Pictures Corporation's *Backbone.* The film was undistinctive. Alfred saw it once. He was quite good, but having to watch himself was agony: "I made a mess of things. I was so conscious of the camera . . . afraid to venture forth without the director's instructions." But his contract called for him to make another picture.

Escape from the cruel camera came with Laurette Taylor's invitation

Critics admired Alfred's romantic hero in the 1923 silent film Backbone,
but Alfred disliked acting before the camera.

to raise money for the Equity Players in *Sweet Nell of Old Drury.* For
nominal salaries Alfred would act Charles II to Laurette's Nell Gwynne,
with Lynn in the minor role of Lady Castlemaine. It was their first play
together since *A Young Man's Fancy* and their first on Broadway.
Because of this, they spent all their ready cash on costume jewelry to
make Lynn ravishing and insisted on endless rehearsals. To Laurette
they seemed possessed. *Her* genius was spontaneous; theirs, the capacity
for taking infinite pains. "Lynn and Alfred were untiring," said Laurette. "After rehearsing all day we would start again on individual
scenes after supper."

As the king's mistress, Laurette had a grand time peddling oranges
and tossing golden curls. Alfred, burdened with frills and a curly wig
that must have weighed twenty pounds, found less chance to exercise
his gifts, though he exuded a potent sensuality. Lynn, to the manner
born as Lady Castlemaine, played with a distinction that Laurette

couldn't equal. Even Hattie could be heard exclaiming, "Isn't she a *dream!*"

Dismissing the play as "gaudy rubbish," Alexander Woollcott declared in the *New York Herald* that "one performance stood out last evening as something of fine mettle, something true and shining. That was the performance of Lynn Fontanne as the frustrated and embittered Lady Castlemaine. . . . It might be noted in passing that she is growing beautiful."

Laurette saw it too: "She's the only woman I know that twenty pounds turned into a beauty." The pounds were courtesy of Alfred. A self-taught but gifted cook, he'd begun making Lynn caloric breakfasts of ham omelets, sweetbreads and biscuits, sausages and eggs. They had also begun to entertain at Lexington Avenue, their first dinner guest being the ever-hungry Noël, now living at the swank Ritz-Carlton in a room scarcely larger than a closet. For dinner parties they hired Louise Scott, a tall, beautiful black woman and a good cook. Soon she was bringing them breakfast in bed, mending, cleaning, and caring for Lynn's clothes.

An exacting job, because when she married Alfred, Lynn Fontanne had knelt at the altar of Beauty and taken a vow. Alfred was a frank aesthete: beauty in all forms moved him deeply. She would create a glamour that would be an integral part of their design for living. Alfred was distinguished, witty, divinely gifted, shy, moody, with a "vulnerability that was akin to a threatened heartbreak." She would be his ideal partner—sophisticated, poised, invulnerable because of her glamour.

Good clothes were crucial. After *Dulcy,* she'd begun to appear in tabloid fashion features, modeling gowns from her plays. Gone were the days of Lillian Russell curves: jazz-age flappers bound their breasts to look as boyish as possible; Lynn's thin was in. Her new image was sleek, sensual, feminine. She hadn't an ideal figure: short-waisted, a bit tummyish still. But as she said, "The neck and shoulders are what really matter. One's dressmaker can be relied on to do the rest."

She hadn't an ideal face, either, but it lent itself to glamorization: good bones; deep-set red-brown eyes gleaming beneath mushroom-cap lids enhanced with sweeping false eyelashes. Gleaming dark hair in waves framing her long face. She had a British complexion, pale and opaque, which she pampered with soap and cold water and a pat of face cream at night. Always conscious of her extra years, she concentrated on her throat, twisting her chin from side to side for twenty minutes a day or lying flat on her bed with her head hanging over the side. She did mild calisthenics, grew finicky over bowel regularity, and believed in plenty of catnaps. As the ultimate step, she began to think of herself as a beauty. Mind conquered any still-uncooperative matter. "Anyone who can't look beautiful when she has to look beautiful," Lynn would declare, "shouldn't be on the stage at all."

But beauty wasn't her only goal. "Married to perhaps the best actor of our time," said Howard Lindsay, "she had to become an actress to match him in every way. Again Miss Fontanne performed the miracle. Again it was a deliberate act, a personal achievement. . . . She had to travel to reach Lunt's stature. She made the journey." Not everyone would agree she arrived.

Lynn's new look dazzled audiences as she swept onstage in pink chiffon as Ann Jordan in *In Love with Love,* a romantic comedy that opened at the Ritz on August 6, 1923. As Noël said, "In *In Love with Love* she . . . began to be beautiful." Ann Jordan is not just flirtatious—Lynn had played that role before—but sexy. Sexiness was new for Lynn Fontanne. A year before, she couldn't have carried it off; now she used her hands and eyes and hips provocatively, and every critic noticed. In the year of Duse's farewell tour, Jane Cowl's triumphant Juliet, and Winifred Lenihan's Saint Joan, *In Love with Love* was not great theater, but Lynn played the slight comedy superbly.

As Lynn left the Ritz Theatre to tour in *In Love with Love,* Alfred moved in with John Drinkwater's *Robert E. Lee.* David Peel, a young Southern pacifist poet, was not a major role; yet the part demanded feeling and depth, and Alfred was intent on proving his versatility.

Robert E. Lee had opened at the Academy of Music in Richmond for an audience who couldn't understand the Northerners' Southern dialect. Discovering that the playing of "Dixie" moved him unutterably, Alfred spent a good deal of time onstage choking back tears. But in New York, Alfred Lunt was the play's only saving grace. Percy Hammond called him "as perfect as any Russian of the Moscow Art Theatre." Alexander Woollcott urged readers to go to the Ritz to see "a performance of distinguished beauty. That is the playing of Private David Peel by an actor whom chance had hitherto made known to this city only as a gay but highly mannered comedian. His name is Alfred Lunt and he is aflame in the new play." Despite Alfred's excellence, *Robert E. Lee* surrendered after 15 performances.

He went immediately into *Outward Bound,* Sutton Vane's allegory about seven people on a ship bound for an unexpected destination. The excellent cast included Beryl Mercer, Dudley Digges, J. M. Kerrigan, and Leslie Howard and Margalo Gillmore as the lovers. Alfred had the best part: Tom Prior, a drunken, self-loathing Oxford graduate who realizes the situation:

TOM: I am right, aren't I, Scrubby? . . .
SCRUBBY: Right about what, sir?
TOM: You—I—all of us on this boat.
SCRUBBY: What about all of us on this boat, sir?
TOM [*trembling with apprehension*]: We are—now answer me truthfully—we are all *dead, aren't we?*

After two hostile weeks in Atlantic City (Christmas holiday-makers weren't in the mood for dead men walking), the cast regrouped in Washington to save the New York opening. "Great fun altering play," said Leslie Howard wryly. "Which version do we play tonight? Do we know we're dead, or alive?" After an "utterly futile" rehearsal on January 7, 1924, Alfred and Leslie had a quick bite, then went to the theater with "much heart-pounding and jumping of nerves."

The Ritz audience, however, was "reduced to a jelly." More formally, John Corbin reported in the *Times* that people "sat breathless—thrilled and fascinated to the final curtain." For Heywood Broun in the *World* Alfred Lunt's performance was the standout. In Atlantic City the final curtain had stayed down to spare the actors boos and hisses. In New York the curtain stayed down to prolong the powerful spell woven by Alfred in the first act and sustained throughout.

"Lunt is one of those players who can present two strata of emotion at the same time," Helen Ormsbee would write.

There is a surface mood which may be humorous, stolid, sardonic; but beneath there is another layer, painful to the least touch. . . . The method is worth noting, for a more primitive impulse is to show how much the character suffers. This soon palls on the beholder—and so the artist's way is to suggest suffering by seeming to hide it. . . . [Thomas] Betterton "kept his Passion under and showed it most, as Fume smoaks most when stifled." With Alfred Lunt, in comedy or tragedy, there is a trace

Alfred (center) as Tom Prior in Outward Bound *(1924), with Lyonel Watts (left) and J. M. Kerrigan*

of something stifled and "smoaking." He can feel out the hidden turmoils which beset people.

Noël Coward came round to Alfred's dressing room—a new Noël, fresh from England, where, with Gertrude Lawrence, he'd been the hit of the 1923 season in his review *London Calling.* Success hadn't changed his mateyness with Alfred and Lynn. Pouring out his admiration for Alfred's performance (the first time he'd seen him act), he was amazed when his friend rolled his eyes and clutched his hair. Great performance? Noël had just witnessed the pit of his career! God, how he'd hammed it up and exploited every cheap trick in the book!

Noël could not comfort him. Over supper Alfred expanded the catalogue of his sins. Lynn listened unmoved. "Never mind, darling," she said, greedily forking scrambled eggs, "you gave a lovely performance last Wednesday matinée."

"Success of play seems assured," wrote Leslie Howard. "Both houses packed and apparently thrilled. Dined with Alfred, also Beryl Mercer and Charlotte G[reenwood]. Yes sir!" Howard usually had a preshow supper with Alfred, then dinner with Laurette and Hartley, where one met Marc Connelly, Gertrude Lawrence, Arthur Rubinstein, Zelda and Scott Fitzgerald—and Noël. Alfred and Leslie talked each other into taking Sunday drawing lessons "in a dirty studio atop the old Lincoln Arcade" with the well-known portraitist Clinton Peters, who, Leslie remembered, discoursed fervently on a shattered torso of Hercules.

Like John Barrymore, Leslie Howard faded fast in plays: he would, said his daughter, "begin to ponder why he was doing it, how bad his health was, and how ghastly it was anyway to work in the theatre at all." Alfred Lunt could have reinvented Tom Prior for two years without boredom, but to Leslie, his own part quickly seemed "hopeless and ineffectual." Besides, he wanted Alfred's role (which he got in the 1930 film). Anyway, audiences began to dwindle, and on May 10, 1924, *Outward Bound* closed. After the show Leslie, Kerrigan, and Aleck Woollcott went to Alfred and Lynn's, where Louise Scott had roasted a chicken. Alfred always carved, but Louise hovered behind him, fussing: "For chrissake, Mr. Lunt, now don't give no guests no wings!"

In 1919 Lawrence Langner, Philip Moeller, Helen Westley, Lee Simonson, Maurice Wertheim, and Theresa Helburn had banded together to form the Theatre Guild. Like the Moscow Art and Abbey Theatres, the Guild would present serious plays. Like its predecessor, the Washington Square Players, it would operate on subscriptions. Finding a home in the dim Garrick Theatre on Thirty-fifth Street, the Guild started looking for good actors—stressing that they couldn't pay much and would star no one, no matter how famous. Amazingly, good actors responded. After a shaky start, the Theatre Guild flourished with productions of Bernard Shaw's *Heartbreak House, Back to Methuselah, The Devil's Disciple,* and *Saint Joan;* Karel Capek's *R.U.R.;* Henrik Ibsen's *Peer Gynt;* and Elmer Rice's *The Adding Machine.*

Even though a New York production had flopped, the Theatre Guild had bought Ferenc Molnár's *The Guardsman* because Theresa Helburn had a gut feeling that the Hungarian comedy of marital sex games could succeed with the right cast. "Something told me the Lunts were perfect for it," said Helburn. "They were married and in love like the hero and heroine of *The Guardsman.* I believed their chemistry would make the play." No matter how vehemently she argued the case for these "brilliant actors," however, the board was skeptical. To them Lunt and Fontanne were Clarence and Dulcy. Only Helburn had seen Alfred's suave lecher in *Banco,* and none of them had seen the glamorous Lynn of *In Love with Love.*

Helburn persisted, cornering Alfred between performances of *Outward Bound.* Philip Moeller had created a sleek version of *The Guardsman.* Lunt and Fontanne were the only actors who could possibly play it. True, the Guild couldn't pay much, but what was money compared to art? Besides, the Guild had plans for two permanent companies presenting alternating plays in different theaters—an incredible opportunity for any actor. She appealed to his devotion, his conscience, his vision.

Though he was currently making $500 a week in *Outward Bound,* and Lynn had offers of $750, Alfred asked for copies of the play. That night he and Lynn began to read.

The Actress gazes out the window and ominously plays Chopin. Sure she desires another man, the Actor baits a trap by sending her roses from a royal Russian Guardsman. She is too pleased. Pretending to leave Vienna, her husband that evening calls on her as the Russian. She is attracted; they agree to meet that night at the opera. She does not yield—yet. The next day before the Guardsman calls, her husband appears. He cross-questions her; she is insulted. She sinks onto a couch and begins a novel. Flinging up the lid of his wardrobe trunk, he quickly pastes into place his Russian disguise and accent. He confronts her. She has been unfaithful!

ACTRESS: You came in at that door yesterday at exactly 16 minutes past six. At 17 minutes past six, I had recognized you. At 18 minutes past six, I was wondering whether I should laugh in your face— and at 19 minutes past six I had decided to play the comedy to the end.
ACTOR: That is not true.

Alfred and Lynn flung down the scripts. "We've found it!"

Yes, said Alfred, on reflection, they must do it. She would have an incredible triumph as the Actress. He did not mind playing second fiddle. Nonsense! *She* would do the play for *his* sake, the Actor being far the showier part. But could they manage on only $500 each a week? Probably, said Alfred—and think of eventually doing Shaw with the Guild, and Shakespeare. Alfred was dying to do Shaw.

But when he called Theresa Helburn the next morning, she corrected him. She expected *both* their services for $500 a week.

"She can't be serious," said Lynn when he hung up.

"And for each of your dresses," he said tragically, "only fifty dollars."

But because they did have devotion, conscience, and vision—and because the play was so right up their alley—they signed a contract with the Guild. They had agreed early in their marriage that they would keep their money separate and share all bills. Lynn now admitted she had $6,000 in the bank. They must go to Budapest to consult Molnár about the play and to buy her clothes.

In Budapest they searched for Ferenc Molnár (he was in Paris pursuing the actress Lili Darvas), Alfred making inquiries in Hungarian, which impressed Lynn until he admitted his Hungarian was really a Finnish dialect remembered from childhood. In Paris (Molnár had just left), they presented a letter of introduction from Noël to Captain Edward Molyneux, an Irish dress designer with ateliers in London and Paris. An aloof Molyneux agreed to do a few sketches. Disappointed, Lynn demanded to see Molyneux again.

"Captain Molyneux is an *artiste*," an assistant informed her. "He is *très occupé.*"

Lynn could deal with disdain. "Tell Captain Molyneux that Mr. Lunt and I too are artists and that we have changed our minds. We will go elsewhere."

At Paul Poiret, Lynn found the perfect gown for the opera scene, though Alfred insisted it must be white, not purple, velvet. White velvet slippers with rhinestone heels and a white velvet embroidered evening wrap for $1,000 completed the ensemble. She also bought a flowered black silk afternoon dress, a peach satin tea gown to wear with gold sandals with green rhinestone heels, and an apricot chiffon tea gown. She spent freely on jet, rhinestone, crystal, and turquoise earrings; pearl rings; ropes of pearls; fancy combs; and twenty bracelets.

For Alfred, the Guardsman's costume presented a tougher challenge. The stage tradition of disguise was ancient, but he fretted about the improbability of a wife not recognizing her husband. Philip Moeller's update had changed the Guardsman from an Austrian to an attaché at the Russian embassy. This suited Alfred, who'd long been fascinated by Slavs. He decided that his Russian must be the opposite of his Actor, a common matinee-idol type. He would give the Guardsman "a mysteriously ugly sex emanation"—a power that comes from brutality controlled by courtly manners.

In Paris he found and sketched a Cossack uniform. He wanted black against Lynn's white—black coat with silver epaulets worn over black pants and high Russian boots, a long red-lined black cape with Persian lamb collar, and a Russian hat. He added more details: mustache and short beard, outthrust lower lip, a gold earring, cropped hair.

Dead broke, they sailed home on August 25 and had to ask Lynn's friend Frank Crowninshield for a loan. "We couldn't even pay the rent." Alfred was generally thrifty; Lynn was not. (In Chicago after *Dulcy* closed, she'd spent so wildly on clothes that George Tyler had sent an escort back to New York.) Guilty about her extravagance, yet shrewd, Lynn sounded out Theresa Helburn about the possibility of reimbursement.

"If we run . . . ?"

"If we run *ten* weeks," said Helburn, "we will see what we can do."

They had not acted for a board before. Tiny, infallible Theresa Helburn was an executive director in the making and self-admittedly no lover of the human race. Lawrence Langner, a wealthy patent lawyer and a founder of the Washington Square Players, was considered inscrutable, chiefly because he never remembered names. The artist Lee Simonson had a black mustache and an explosive temper. ("Saw Lee," Helburn noted in her diary. "Fight.") Diplomatic, friendly Maurice Wertheim was a wealthy banker. With coal-black hair and clinging black dresses, the outspoken Helen Westley looked like the arresting actress she was. Philip Moeller, a playwright and director, was mercurial, reclusive, and smoked cigarettes in a long holder. "We had terrible hours with Philip," sighed Alfred.

Moeller's first words: "You can't play comedy in black."

"Listen, Mr. Moeller," said Lynn, "if the lines are worth reading you can play comedy inside a burlap bag, inside a closed piano—if they can hear you and the lines are good!"

Yet Alfred and Lynn discovered that Moeller's method of directing harmonized with their approach to a play: slow, meticulous, developing their characters experimentally and, in Alfred's case, intuitively;

reworking problems until they had solved them. Moeller did not really *try* to direct them—a good thing, for Alfred was a law unto himself. Instead he appeared onstage from time to time to make suggestions, which Lunt and Fontanne accepted or did not.

In *The Guardsman* Alfred and Lynn perfected a technique of "overlapping" that became their trademark. For instance, the Actress says, "Then the honor of this visit is due entirely to me. You don't care for music at all. I thought this afternoon you were fond of Chopin." Instead of waiting for "fond of Chopin," Alfred took his cue at "this afternoon." While Lynn raised her voice to project the rest of her line, Alfred broke in with his reply. They were acting the way people really talk, constantly interrupting each other.

Newsweek once described them rehearsing dialogue: "They sat facing each other on two hard-backed chairs, their legs interlocked, and played their lines back and forth with eyes fixed on each other's face. When one of them hit a line just a trifle off, the knees of the other would bang together—and the Lunts would start over. The result was an intimacy and shading and timing of performance beyond anything that audiences, critics or other actors could quite credit." Uncannily, both actors were entirely clear as long as the audience paid attention.

Still troubled by the husband-recognition factor, Alfred decided to test his Guardsman's disguise. In makeup and uniform, he walked into a neighborhood grocery whose owner knew him well and launched into a long argument in his Russian accent over a cut of meat. Alfred watched the man intensely, but the grocer showed not a trace of recognition; and he left, satisfied.

Still, they were unhappy with their acting, and Alfred asked Howard Lindsay to come to a rehearsal. He sat and watched a performance that was flawless yet "arid, without the juice of inner enjoyment." In their tiny dressing room, Lynn and Alfred clutched at him. What were they doing wrong? Just one thing, Lindsay told them. They weren't having fun.

Lynn exploded. How could they have fun with this crew of slavedrivers? Had he any idea how hard they worked for people who treated them like dirt? Suddenly she grabbed Alfred's arm. "Alfred, he's right!"

So now they were having fun, which made the slavedrivers' criticism harder to swallow. The Guild opened its plays cold, though it held a run-through performance the night before the premiere. After it, the board of managers summoned Alfred. His conception of the Guardsman was all wrong. He'd made the Russian black and saturnine and repulsive, completely lacking in charm and sex appeal. The Actress couldn't possibly be attracted to such a man; the audience would hate him. He must change his whole conception of the Guardsman before tomorrow night's opening.

It was Alfred's first run-in with the committee mind. "It's the cruellest thing anyone has ever done to me," he told Lynn, shattered. That night in bed he wept inconsolably at the wound to his artistic pride. It was Hattie all over again, telling him that with his slovenly diction he'd never be an actor. Toward morning he calmed down. He knew better.

The next evening, October 13, 1924, Alfred Lunt and Lynn Fontanne swept to triumph, ravishing the audience with their brilliant counterpoint. Years later, Theresa Helburn wrote proudly of the Theatre Guild, "What we wanted to do was to star the play and feature the players. And for over twenty years we succeeded in doing this."

Rot. *The Guardsman* established Lunt and Fontanne as indisputable stars. That night they marched triumphantly, as Robert Sherwood would say, into the Main Tent. They played to full houses at the Garrick Theatre for five weeks, then transferred to the Booth Theatre at Forty-fifth Street, where *The Guardsman* ran forty weeks. Writers all over Manhattan began to dream of plays they might create for Lunt and Fontanne to transmute into gold. They *made* the fortunes of the Theatre Guild.

Granted, *The Guardsman* fit Lunt and Fontanne like a glove. "The play really is the story of their marriage," says a Milwaukee theater director. "*They lived to act for each other,* just like the characters in the play."

Certainly the whole play can be taken as an act in the lives of a couple who can't stop faking emotion even when they're offstage. The Actress feigns sexual boredom; it's a game. The Actor responds histrionically. "Some day a soldier will come into her life, and I'll kill her, I'll kill her," he shouts, studying his thinning hairline in the mirror. Throwing themselves into the roles of seductress and seducer, they manage to entertain each other vastly for twenty-four hours. At the final curtain the Actress is again moodily playing Chopin, pondering the next camp stunt to keep them amused.

One thing is certain: everyone felt the physicality that Lunt and

Alfred Lunt and Lynn Fontanne made romantic comedy history in The Guardsman, *1924.*

Fontanne projected over the footlights. Many critics had pointed out Alfred's sexual attractiveness; he didn't much believe in it. Now in *The Guardsman* the great pretender prowled about the velvety, undulating Lynn like a tomcat in heat. If he was not her lover in private, he could magnificently act her lover onstage. From *The Guardsman* on, their sizzling sexuality onstage became a crucial component of their design for living. They projected a joyous yet knowing animal attraction, which was, however, meticulously planned and rehearsed. Brooks Atkinson called their technique "deliberate abandon."

Writing in the *New York Sun,* Alexander Woollcott recognized the importance of that sparkling first night: "They have youth and great gifts and the unmistakable attitude of ascent, and those who saw them last night bowing hand in hand for the first time, may well have been witnessing a moment in theatrical history. It is among the possibilities that we were seeing the first chapter in a partnership destined to be as distinguished as that of Henry Irving and Ellen Terry."

CHAPTER FIVE

Pure Gold: 1925–1929

awrence Langner's motto was: When in doubt, play Shaw. After Lunt and Fontanne's success in *The Guardsman,* there was no question of rotating actors in the principal roles. Alfred and Lynn would play Bluntschli and Raina in *Arms and the Man,* Shaw's genial spoof of military heroics. Guarding their golden geese, but always thrifty, the Guild raised the couple's weekly salaries to $300 each, $350 in theaters other than the Garrick. They could have acted anywhere. After *The Guardsman* every management in New York was after Lunt and Fontanne.

A uniform again for Alfred, and a luxurious mustache. Like the Guardsman, Bluntschli is an antihero, a pragmatist who carries chocolates in his cartridge belt and intends to get out of this Balkan war alive even if it means hiding in a Bulgarian lady's bedroom. Like Clarence, he is a diamond in the rough, revealed finally as a clever, worldly man with a fleet of prosperous hotels in Switzerland. Bluntschli was a part to sink teeth into, especially in the first act when the fleeing soldier invades Raina's bedroom by starlight and the sexual parrying begins.

Alfred took great pains to get his uniform in shape for his entry "in a deplorable plight, bespattered with mud and blood and snow, his belt and the strap of his revolver case keeping together the torn ruins of the

Bluntschli and Raina in Shaw's Arms and the Man, *1925*

blue of a Servian artillery officer." He let it flap for weeks on a clothes-line on the roof. Then he thwacked it with a rug beater until he produced "torn ruins." Jabbing his thumbs, Alfred smeared the cloth with his own blood.

How to convey the impression of utter exhaustion as he staggers into the lady's bedroom? He couldn't actually exhaust himself, yet he didn't simply want to counterfeit the effect. Lead in his boots, of course. His steps would drag, and when he collapsed onto Raina's bed, he would flop his feet over the edge and they would look absolutely dead.

Raina is dark and romantic, but Lynn was not particularly fond of her. Raina could be unconsciously ridiculous—boasting that her family washes once a week and owns the only library in Bulgaria. Lynn liked to be the knowing one. And, after the equality of *The Guardsman,* she thought her part decidedly inferior to Alfred's. Shaw had told the first London Raina that she could "wear extraordinary things if she wishes"; but the Guild still wouldn't pay Lynn a proper clothes allowance and she could hardly go out and spend another four thousand dollars.

They launched the 1925–26 season on September 14 in the beautiful new Guild Theatre on West Fifty-second Street and made *Arms and the Man* almost as great a success as *The Guardsman,* though Percy Hammond in the *Herald Tribune* confirmed Lynn's prejudice against the play: "Last night they did not divide the rewards of Shaw as equally as they did those subtleties of Molnár." Most critics pinned the gold on Alfred's chest. Howard Lindsay called his Bluntschli "cold, precise, hard, and one of the greatest performances any actor, American or British, has given in our time." Said Langner: "His Bluntschli was probably the finest this generation will see; the same part was originally played by Mansfield, and I doubt if it was played better. I have my acting heroes, and Alfred heads the list."

Shaw possessively followed the fortunes of his plays, writing Theresa Helburn: "I have seen a photograph of Raina and Bluntschli in which he is holding her in his arms in the bedroom scene. She would have screamed the house down and had him shot like a mad dog. Your producer has no *dull*icacy. Yah!" When the Lunts met the great man in London in 1929, GBS whipped out the offending photograph. "But," said Alfred, "I am only putting on her coat according to your directions." "Oh, in that case," Shaw is supposed to have said, "that is quite all right." But his stage directions say explicitly that Bluntschli "flings the cloak" at Raina; it's unlikely Shaw forgave Alfred's cuddling Raina into her cloak.

The Theatre Guild denied Lunt and Fontanne star billing, but their new $400-a-week 1926–27 contracts proved they were the Guild's premier attraction. As stars of New York's most exciting theater, they received enormous attention from the press and from New Yorkers who mattered. Harold Ross had recently launched *The New Yorker* magazine. Between its offices, the Algonquin Hotel, and the artist Neysa McMein's skylit studio on Fifty-seventh Street swirled the "beautiful" people: George Gershwin, Franklin P. Adams, Robert Benchley, Alice Duer Miller, George and Beatrice Kaufman, Marc Connelly, Moss Hart, Irving Berlin, Harpo Marx, Heywood Broun, Edna Ferber, Dorothy Parker, and Noël when he was in town. Directing traffic was Alexander

Alexander Woollcott

Woollcott—"the little New Jersey Nero," cracked Ferber, "who thinks his pinafore is a toga."

The in crowd terrified Helen Hayes, now in love (thank God, sighed Lynn) with the writer Charles MacArthur. "The big wind was Alexander Woollcott . . . the self-styled arbiter of protocol. He was always either bedazzled or contemptuous. There was nothing in between. He believed he was the center of the universe. . . ." Theresa Helburn was harsher. Woollcott was "a perpetual amateur in his approach to the arts. . . . His enthusiasms were unpredictable, ranging from 'going quietly mad' over third-rate sentimental fiction to waxing hysterical over Faulkner's *Sanctuary*. As a drama critic he could be not only malicious but quite unbelievably cruel. He could sacrifice his best friend for the sake of a quip, and sometimes did."

Alfred and Lynn took the beautiful people in stride. Alfred could match wits with any of them: Noël called him "quick as a knife with flashes of dreadful obtuseness." Lynn he considered "mentally slow with flashes of brilliant swiftness," a description she didn't quarrel with, though the idea of Lynn Fontanne as "mentally slow" is absurd. A Hirschfeld cartoon shows the famous Algonquin lunchers seated at the Round Table, Lynn and Alfred smiling at them from an adjacent but definitely separate table. They were as much a part of the group as they wanted to be, or as their work permitted. A young Moss Hart remembers walking into a party at the Kaufmans' and being struck speechless when Alfred Lunt cordially shook his hand. Alfred and Lynn dined at Edna Ferber's and drank cocktails at Neysa McMein's. But only Alexander Woollcott became a truly intimate friend. Alfred was enchanted to discover that Woollcott's first theater experience had been the Royal Lilliputians in *The Golden Horseshoe.*

Woollcott could be kind-cruel, sentimental-profane, petulant-generous, perceptive-silly. He was a cross-dresser in college and either born impotent or asexual. Thwarted desire exploded in bitchiness: "Hurt by nature before birth, Woollcott felt free to slash mercilessly." Those who accepted him won his absolute loyalty. Intimates were— intimate. Noël Coward addressed him as "Darly Acky-wacky-wacky-weeza-peeza," signing himself "love and wet kisses, Lady Vi." Lynn rated friends (1) Darling, (2) Darling Darling, or (3) Darling Darling Darling. Generally she reserved number 3 for Noël and Aleck.

Woollcott needed to dominate. Known as a matchmaker, he contradictorily hated couples sleeping together under his roof. Yet he kept hands off Alfred and Lynn, respecting their union as an artistic contract. He seemed equally fond of both and became their warm partisan in print, demonstrating that he appreciated not only third- but first-rate. They treasured his friendship jealously, hating to share him with others, as they almost inevitably had to do. "What are the chances of you being a little less surrounded?" Lynn would write him wistfully.

Lynn lost one friend during these early Theatre Guild years. Helen Hayes thought the rift might be about clothes: "As far back as I can remember [Lynn] always had authority and a wardrobe." Laurette Taylor never cared what she wore. Then Lynn began sweeping into Laurette's drawing room in couturier gowns—the new beautiful Lynn, glowing with the success of *The Guardsman* and pained by Laurette's careless clothes. "Showin' off, m'girl," thought Laurette, "to me, who wiped yer nose fer ya!" If Lynn became the center of attention, Laurette would growl, "Come off it, m'girl," or bluntly, "Shut up!" Lynn began leaving many of Laurette's parties in tears, Alfred stalking furiously behind her. "There's no reason to put up with such abuse, Lynn! We'll not go there again." One night after a particularly ugly scene, she left 50 Riverside Drive for good.

Few realized that Laurette at forty-two had begun to drink heavily; they only felt her tongue lashings. "Many of Laurette's friendships were destroyed," said her daughter Marguerite, "before those involved had any idea of what destroyed them." Laurette blamed Lynn for the break: Lynn had turned her back when Laurette's "broken soul" was "stumbling about" before her eyes. Hartley would die in 1928. Six years later, when Laurette managed a stage comeback, Lynn sent a huge bunch of violets and a beautiful purse. "They were six years too late," said Laurette. She never forgave Lynn for deserting her. "In later years I admired her technique, but she never again touched me as deeply as she did under Hartley's direction."

From 1926 to 1929, without Lynn, Alfred Lunt appeared for the Theatre Guild in *Juarez and Maximilian, Ned McCobb's Daughter, Marco Millions,* and *Volpone.* Without Alfred, Lynn appeared in *Pygmalion* and *Strange Interlude.* Together they acted *Goat Song, At Mrs. Beam's, The Brothers Karamazov, The Second Man, The Doctor's Dilemma,* and *Caprice.* They also toured *The Guardsman* and *The Second Man* and, in Chicago, added *Pygmalion* to their joint repertoire, Alfred playing Professor Higgins.

"Art theater, my foot," complained Lynn. "This isn't an art theater— it's a sweat shop!" She also deeply resented the Guild casting them in different plays.

The sweat shop had discovered, given Lunt and Fontanne's popularity, that it was growing out of its new 930-seat Guild Theatre. Meanwhile, it had established a distinguished permanent company, most of whom would appear regularly with Lunt and Fontanne: Helen Westley, Dudley Digges, Henry Travers, Ernest Cossart, Clare Eames, Margalo Gillmore, Glenn Anders, Tom Powers, Edward G. Robinson, Claude Rains, Earle Larimore, and Philip Loeb. Philip Moeller continued to direct most of the Lunt-Fontanne productions.

Reflecting the theater's new artistic seriousness, foreign playwrights had become chic. John Barrymore did Tolstoy's *Redemption;* Nazimova played Ibsen; Ethel Barrymore played Hauptmann's *Rose Bernd;* Eva Le Gallienne launched her Civic Repertory Theatre, playing Ibsen, Chekhov, and Molnár. People talked in hushed tones of Strindberg.

Franz Werfel's *Goat Song* was an obscure import about sex and politics, set in Hungary in the eighteenth century. Juvan is a fiery young intellectual who stirs the peasantry to revolt. Sexy Stanja is engaged to the brother of a creature half man, half goat. A symbol of the god-man, good-evil, spiritual-sensual in all of us? No one quite knew. *Goat Song* was romantic, murky, violent, earthy, perverse, and tragic. "The Lunts can do it," announced Helburn to an astonished board.

And Alfred and Lynn wanted to do it, an example not only of their courage as actors, but of the enthusiasm for experiment that the Guild inspired. Lee Simonson created moody, stylized sets, Jacob Ben-Ami choreographed forty supers charging about the stage as the clamoring masses. The ten-member cast included Blanche Yurka, Helen Westley, and Edward G. Robinson.

Goat Song intrigued and disgusted audiences for fifty-eight performances. Woollcott rhapsodized: "Alfred Lunt . . . as the dark bitter frustrated student leader of the uprising, trails clouds of the French revolution through the rich tapestry of the play. . . . Lynn Fontanne . . . as the scornful stricken Iphigenia in this altar piece, enters magnificently with him at last into one of the most beautiful colloquies of the modern theatre." Mrs. Vincent Astor canceled her subscription. Lynn defended *Goat Song* in the *Brooklyn Daily News:* "I think the confusion is caused by the noise of the mob. . . . Important lines are drowned out. . . . Though I must say I don't see why it is particularly necessary to understand a play." Some people considered *Goat Song* the best play the Guild had ever done.

That April 1926 they did a 180-degree turn in the light comedy *At Mrs. Beam's* as thieves who are trying to slip out of England with a load of lolly. Laura Pasquale is a Brazilian tigress, Joe Dermott a witty thief. This volatile combination explodes at the end of Act One with Joe driving Laura mad by the calm way he's going about their crime. She throws a book at him, followed by cushions, bananas, and her shoes. Joe laughs and pelts her with cakes. She hurls herself at him and they go over, rolling, kicking, and screaming. She straddles him, hauls off, and pastes him in the chops.

But Alfred got magnificently irritated in rehearsals because Lynn pulled her punches. "Goddammit, Lynn," he bellowed, "you're the rottenest actress I've ever worked with!" Furious, Lynn whirled him around and delivered a slap that rattled his molars. Alfred smiled. Lynn snarled that he could be a cold-blooded son-of-a-bitch. He did not disagree.

The violent simulated-sex scene lasted an astonishing twenty minutes. Philip Moeller helped choreograph it, but Alfred and Lynn cre-

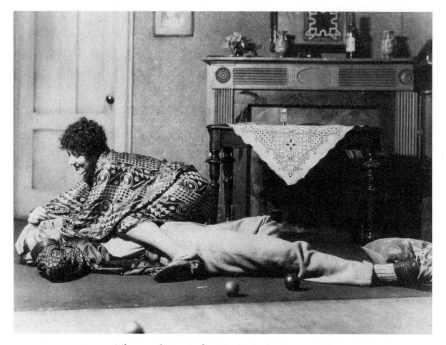

The wrestling match in At Mrs. Beam's, *1926*

ated the moves at home in their apartment. Their mayhem stopped the show. This was the Roaring Twenties, but the spectacle of lovers who are crooks wrestling each other to the floor was new. One satisfied customer saw *At Mrs. Beam's* forty-two times. After he bought his ninth ticket, the Guild refused to take his money.

Alfred and Lynn needed a break before a daunting 1926–27 Guild season, so they sailed for England in July. Their bank accounts were fairly stable, though Hattie's extravagance continued to drive Alfred wild. Then there was Carl, still living at home, still running up gambling debts which Alfred paid. Karin was gone. She'd tried a private college for one semester, then dropped out, perhaps feeling guilty that Alfred had to pay her tuition. Among the pals Carl invited to Genesee Depot was Alonzo Pawling, a rich kid from Milwaukee. Karin married him in 1925; a daughter, Suzanne, was born in 1926. As for Lynn's sisters, she blamed her bitter mother that they'd scattered far and wide: she to the States, Mai to New Zealand, Antoinette to France. But she wasn't helping them financially—yet.

On board was a dynamic young man with a perennial five-o'clock shadow. He would shortly become big on Broadway (and some people's favorite villain, including Laurence Olivier's, who would model his Richard III on him). Now he was simply fast-talking Jed Harris, out to book a good act. He enormously admired Lunt and Fontanne. He had just the play for them: Ferber and Kaufman's *The Royal Family,* modeled on the Barrymores. Alfred and Lynn must play the John and Ethel characters. They would hear from him back in New York.

They were on vacation, but seldom stopped thinking about the theater. In London Alfred bought a double-breasted lavender suit for his role as a jaded author in *The Second Man.* Lynn ransacked second-hand stores for Eliza Doolittle's battered hat, shabby boots, and ratty feather boa.

In Paris Alfred proudly introduced Lynn to Lillie Langtry, now seventy-three. The Jersey Lily notoriously disliked women.

"Well, well," stared Mrs. Langtry, "how on earth did you ever induce Alfred to marry *you*?"

"My dear lady," replied Lynn, "I chloroformed him, had the ceremony performed, and when he regained consciousness he was a married man."

Mrs. Langtry laughed and accepted Alfred's wife.

On August 31 Alfred and Lynn returned to go their separate ways at the Guild for the first time. Divide and conquer?

One view is that the Theatre Guild was afraid of Lunt and Fontanne's power. Control must remain where it belonged, with the board of managers. The Guild itself claimed that they were providing the Lunts with a variety of parts they couldn't play acting together. But economics surely entered into the decision to split Lunt and Fontanne. The Guild now had two acting companies and an alternating repertory system. Why waste two stars on one play when separately Lunt and Fontanne could draw?

So Alfred pasted on side whiskers and a beard as Maximilian, the futile emperor of Mexico (1864–67). Everyone thought they had a success until the dress rehearsal, when suddenly the elaborate period sets and costumes stifled the action of Franz Werfel's already ponderous tragedy. Critics called Alfred miscast, facile, and obvious. Many, however, considered *Juarez and Maximilian* an artistic success and Alfred's performance extraordinarily restrained and mature.

He was not miscast as Babe Callahan in *Ned McCobb's Daughter.* Leaping from the introverted emperor to the tough, quick-witted bootlegger was nothing for Alfred Lunt, though he went through his usual agonies of self-doubt. "Let someone do it who is good in the part," he'd say wildly.

Clare Eames was cast as Babe's wife. At rehearsals Alfred noticed that for a woman with children Clare was certainly flat-chested. "Why don't you go to Macy's basement," he suggested helpfully. "They've got all sorts of things to make you look more—you know." Clare bought a pair of falsies and immediately looked more motherly. During one performance, however, Alfred noted with horror that she had a large lump sitting on her shoulder. Striding across the stage, he threw his arms around her and managed to wrestle the falsie back into place. Clare thought he'd gone crazy.

Margalo Gillmore as a slut and Edward G. Robinson as a lawyer gave interesting performances; but Alfred walked away with the play. "Babe," enthused one critic, "is a man for you to meet." Babe was a violent role. Alfred liked violent roles.

While Alfred was bootlegging, Lynn was triumphing as Eliza Doolittle in *Pygmalion,* Shaw's surefire comedy about a Cockney flower girl turned into a lady by a professor of speech. Shaw had written Eliza in 1914 for his inamorata Mrs. Patrick Campbell as a joke to make the queen of snobs drop her *h*'s. Mrs. Pat had been forty-nine, too old for Eliza; then, too, she'd refused to be *really* low. Lynn played Eliza with vulgar energy and perfect comic timing, eclipsing Reginald Mason's acceptable Professor Higgins and making, said Charles Brackett in *The New Yorker,* "one's memory of Mrs. Patrick Campbell in the part seem like a faded cigarette-card."

Alfred and Lynn reunited in 1927 for *The Brothers Karamazov* in Jacques Copeau's superb adaptation. In a blond wig Lynn did not have much to do as Grushenka the prostitute, though Woollcott praised her as "animal, earthy, warm, absurd." Dmitri Karamazov, on the other hand, was a part to tear a cat in: "Dmitri leaps up with a sort of fury. He seems all at once as though he is drunk. His eyes become suddenly bloodshot." Another big violent role.

The distinguished French director and Alfred clashed at rehearsals. Copeau took himself very seriously and directed like a general with a battle plan. Lunt, he complained, was "un gosse." "Copeau could not altogether understand the fluidity of Lunt's inspiration," said Harold Clurman, the assistant director, "the spontaneous emotionalism that makes him so poignant an actor, even in comedy." Losing his temper,

Copeau would shout: "But I know the play; I've seen it performed for hundreds of audiences!"

"But not *American* audiences," Alfred would insist quietly.

Though he considered the sinner-saint Dmitri the most exhausting part he'd ever played, Alfred Lunt again took first honors. Percy Hammond: "exhilarating, exciting, overblown, unsexed and unkempt. He wrings your heart in pity and dazzles your mind by the brilliance of his work." Woollcott went farther: "I cannot imagine any player in the English speaking theatre—not even John Barrymore—approaching Alfred Lunt's realization of Dmitri."

Alfred and Lynn had moved into a triplex at 163 East Thirty-sixth Street, with terraces on two levels and a skylit studio where they rehearsed. Amenities included a fireplace with aluminum backing that glittered, a player piano, and six-foot silver candlesticks pounced on by Alfred in shops where a Chippendale chair or Meissen chandelier could be bought for twenty dollars. They had shelves built for three thousand books (Alfred had always been a big reader). Louise Scott still cooked for them—and cleaned, washed, and mended. Their concierge had a list of people from whom they would accept calls. Across the hall, by design or accident, lived Jed Harris, still pursuing his favorite actors. Alfred and Lynn were worn out with the Guild's punishing pace; they told Aleck Woollcott they were going with Harris.

Woollcott was horrified. The Theatre Guild stood for the best. How could they betray the cause? Why, *he* respected the Guild so much he even paid for his tickets! Professional suicide to leave. Besides, Harris was *vulgar.* Alfred and Lynn didn't agree. He'd been charming on the ship and given them a Bell and Howell movie camera. Woollcott retreated, with a plan. Shortly afterward, Lynn received a bouquet from "Jed Harris"—gaudy orchids, orange gladioli, flaming red roses crammed into a ghastly vase. "Oh, Alfred," exclaimed Lynn, recoiling, "we can't ever, *ever* do a play for that Jed Harris. He's . . . *squalid.*"

It is easy to tell Alfred Lunt from other American actors," said Woollcott. "He is the one who works." As attendance for *The Brothers Karamazov* dropped off, Alfred dug out his double-breasted lavender suit to play worldly, flippant Clark Storey in *The Second Man,* a first play by S. N. Behrman that Alfred and Lynn had recommended to the Guild.

Margalo Gillmore was cast as Monica Grey, in love with Clark

Storey; Lynn as a rich gray-haired widow of thirty-five. Kendall Frayne was the second female part—but with gowns by Hattie Carnegie. Behrman thought Lynn took it only for Alfred's sake: Kendall Frayne was "a perpetual exit."

Behrman fretted during rehearsals. Why was Lunt so "casual, only sporadically vital, and in the main, disinterested"? Even Miss Fontanne was walking through her part. Seeing his dismay, Lynn came to explain with a smile and squeeze of his hand. "I suppose it all sounds like nothing to you. You see, we're not thinking of the words now, just the movements, but I promise you—it'll be all right."

Watching from the balcony the night of April 11, Behrman realized: "I'd not had the remotest idea of what Lynn and Alfred could or would do. . . . I had written a line for her about [the scientist] who bored her: 'He never has anything interesting to say.' What I heard was: 'He never has anything interesting to say—never—never—never—never—never,' a perfectly graduated diminuendo of 'nevers' . . . faint with the claustrophobia of boredom."

From the first Alfred "had the audience mesmerized; he did what he wanted with it—made it laugh, made it listen." And Behrman was floored by the power of a climax he hadn't consciously written. Storey has been rejected by both Kendall Frayne and Monica Grey. Behrman had written: "He leaves the door, goes to the telephone." As acted by Alfred, that walk to the phone "shafted a light on the play and the character which I had not foreseen. It was a moment of self-confrontation, of complete awareness. Why hadn't he taken a chance? Why hadn't he tested himself? Perhaps he was better than the louse he knew himself to be? Alfred's eyes, when he picked up the telephone to get back what he didn't want, went insane. . . . He'd made Calvary out of an innocent stage direction." Alfred Lunt, decided Behrman, "was the luckiest thing that ever happened to me."

Critics emphatically agreed that Alfred Lunt had given "the most gorgeously invigorating comedy performance of the season." Some went further: Lunt was beyond question America's most gifted comedian.

As suave as Lowell Sherman, as dry and penetrating as Roland Young, as vehement as John Barrymore at his most volatile is Lunt. As authoritative as Bruce McRae is Lunt. As crisp and chipper as George M. Cohan is Lunt. As stubborn and forceful as James Rennie is Lunt. As honest as Leslie Howard is Lunt. As

romantic as Geoffrey Kerr is Lunt. As ironic as George Arliss is
Lunt. As debonair and offhand as the late Wallace Reid is
Lunt. . . . So marvellously versatile and adept is Lunt's perfor-
mance that he seems to be a whole repertory company in himself.

Only Alexander Woollcott had reservations. Lunt as a comedian, he
said, was "bidding for the laughter of us all, yet not quite enjoying it—
haunted, I think, by the ghost of an ancient dread. . . . I suspect that
some such spectre hovers near him whenever he plays in a comedy, and
the sound of laughter coming out of the dusk of a crowded auditorium—even when it is a laughter he himself has tried to beget—stirs in
his subconscious memory the uneasiness of a forgotten panic. . . . A
trace of awkwardness impairs all his performances in comedy." Woollcott preferred Lunt in "plays of pity and terror" like *Outward Bound,
Goat Song, Juarez and Maximilian,* or *The Brothers Karamazov,* believing
that laughter at his performance of "The Tell-Tale Heart" all those years
ago at Carroll College made him uneasy with all laughter.

The *Morning Telegraph* polled twelve drama critics to name the best
actor and actress of 1926–1927. Lynn ran against competition like Jane
Cowl, Ethel Barrymore, Blanche Yurka, and Ruth Gordon; Pauline
Lord won. But Alfred won hands down as best actor, confirming Woollcott's deepening conviction, as he accepted the award on the stage of
the Guild Theatre, that "the finest actor in the English-speaking world
today is Alfred Lunt." The critic Edgar Scott put it humorously:
"Things have now reached the point where Alfred Lunt, actor, is almost
too good to be allowed." With typical humility, Alfred called himself
"fussed about winning the award," claiming that the Guild company as
a whole should have been considered.

Flying high, the Theatre Guild now proposed to conquer America
by sending its companies on the road. In September Alfred and
Lynn opened a tour of *The Guardsman* and *The Second Man* in Cleveland. It was the first demonstration to the provinces of the dazzling,
joyous sophistication of their now expert teamwork. Audiences adored
them. It was the beginning of their long reign not only as Broadway
actors but as American stars. In Chicago they added *Pygmalion,* Alfred
playing a suave Henry Higgins, though he wasn't satisfied with his per-

formance until, one night, he sat up in bed and realized that Higgins must carry a green umbrella. And then it was back to New York for more Shaw.

The Doctor's Dilemma was repertory at its best, Alfred and Lynn surrounded by the elite of the Theatre Guild—Helen Westley, Baliol Holloway, Morris Carnovsky, Dudley Digges, Earle Larimore, and Henry Travers. As the artist Louis Dubedat, Alfred did not appear in two acts and only briefly in a third. Not what a typical Broadway leading man would put up with, but Alfred was delighted: "Oh, boy, he doesn't get in until the end of the second act—and then he has that marvelous death. . . . Boy, that's the dream." His dying speech (it reduced Theresa Helburn to tears every time) gave Alfred some of his most eloquent lines: "I believe in Michelangelo, I believe in Rembrandt, I believe in Velazquez. . . ."

Lynn won highest accolades as Jennifer, Dubedat's wife. Critics found her "better, truer and deeper" and praised the "humility of this all-conquering Jennifer." Woollcott was doubtful that anyone had acted Jennifer and Dubedat as well, or would again.

While *The Doctor's Dilemma* ran its one hundred performances, they separated again, Lynn to rehearse Eugene O'Neill's *Strange Interlude,* Alfred his *Marco Millions,* both to open in January 1928. O'Neill's satire on American capitalism was an ambitious and unwieldy play for the Guild to undertake: complicated sets, eleven scenes, and twenty-one actors playing thirty-two characters. Though O'Neill sat in the back of the theater during rehearsals, "I did not get to know him," said Alfred; "he was not an easy man to know."

Alfred solved two costume problems himself. He didn't like his thighs in blue tights on his first entrance, so he requested that the spot focus on his torso, leaving his legs in darkness. And he so hated the "Uncle Sam" costume that Lee Simonson designed for him in the last act that he tore it off during the dress rehearsal, stamped on it, and threw it into the orchestra pit.

Lawrence Langner remembered *Marco Millions* as warmly acclaimed by audiences and critics. He erred. Though George Freedley in *The Lunts* remembered the play as "brilliantly directed by Rouben Mamoulian and superbly designed by Lee Simonson," with Alfred's Marco Polo a tour de force, other critics, like Robert Littell in the *Post,* found it "surprisingly simple-minded, obvious and at times actually foolish." Percy Hammond in the *New York Herald Tribune* thought Alfred miscast, though "a resemblance of what Mr. O'Neill may have had in mind." For Woollcott, Marco was "a perfectly conceived and supremely competent performance, but it had only its one little moment of beauty in the first scene and it was marked by an almost hypnotic weariness, each line of the long role parting from him as if, although he was quite certain what the next might be, he had not quite decided whether to buck up and say it or just to curl up there on the Guild stage and take a good long nap." Alfred *was* so exhausted the first night he almost collapsed, but he recovered and played with his usual brilliance in what has proved to be not one of O'Neill's better plays.

Five hours and nine acts long after O'Neill agreed to cuts, *Strange Interlude* was a marathon test of audience acceptance of O'Neill as America's greatest playwright no matter what the pain. Part of the play's length came from O'Neill's using asides and soliloquies, part from his conviction, like Shaw's, that genius can't say too much. Langner agreed, judging *Strange Interlude* one of the great plays of all time. Curiously enough, Lynn had been an inspiration: "Remember during the production of *Chris* when you told me you wished someone would write a play exposing possessive mothers? This is it!"

The Guild had trouble casting the neurotic and, in those proto-Freudian days, unsympathetic Nina Leeds. Katharine Cornell, Pauline Lord, and Alice Brady turned down the part. Helburn and Langner prepared such long and complex arguments why Lynn should play Nina Leeds that they were chagrined when she jumped at it. O'Neill "did not cherish" the memory of Lynn in *Chris,* but accepted her, though he remained cold to her charm.

Not that Lynn was an O'Neill fan: "He's not as great as he's cracked up to be." But Alfred, realizing *Strange Interlude* was going to be the event of the season, insisted: "Even if it is a flop, it will be important and you will gain something by having played in it."

O'Neill was often difficult at rehearsals, expecting actors to do the impossible. "Play it as I wrote it!" he said bluntly when Lynn asked if she could make some cuts. "I did it anyway," said Lynn. "I cut, cut, cut, and nobody ever realized it." Alfred could also be difficult at rehearsals. "When I tell you that at a dress rehearsal of *Strange Interlude* I played a very difficult scene and played it for the first time I thought approaching what I wanted to do," Lynn complained to Kurt Weill years later, "Alfred who had never seen it before, after it was over came up on stage and all he said was 'Don't stand up during that scene.' This from the boy who has to be encouraged with the utmost tenderness and if given any criticism at all, it must be dealt him with kid gloves." She was comforted by O'Neill's telling her shortly before the opening, "You are so exactly right for the part that it might have been written for you." Audience and critics on opening night, January 30, 1928, agreed with O'Neill.

Sneering at *Strange Interlude* as "the *Abie's Irish Rose* of the pseudo-intelligentsia," Alexander Woollcott was banned opening night. Lynn had sent him the play in advance. Days before *Strange Interlude* opened, Woollcott's scathing attack appeared in *Vanity Fair.* (He was not responsible for the timing.) Outraged, the Guild demanded he not be allowed to review the play for the *World.* Woollcott resigned in a hissy fit and Dudley Nichols took his place. "Miss Fontanne was superb," he wrote, sounding Woollcottian. "The most was required of her and she gave to the brim at every demand. She was possessed of an inward power which broke through every restraint as radium shoots its glimmering particles through everything that would contain it."

Noël came to a performance and told Lynn, "In the seventh act you overacted, you groaned a bit too much"—then wished he'd kept his mouth shut. "Ten nights later she called me and said, 'You can come see it,' and I couldn't just see the seventh act, I had to sit through the whole boring thing from the beginning. And of course she had the seventh act down perfectly."

Alfred described the play as "a six-day bisexual race" and joked that "if *Strange Interlude* had had two more acts, I could have sued Lynn for desertion." Yet it astonished everyone by a run of 441 performances, suggesting either that there were plenty of pseudo-intellectuals in New York or that *Strange Interlude* was a great play. Alfred and Lynn never renounced their belief that the 1928 Pulitzer Prize winner was not.

What could Alfred possibly do with his time while *Strange Interlude* was still running and *Marco Millions* had closed? Shop for antiques? Read a book? Perfect a recipe? Relax?

Not when the Guild asked him to play Mosca, Volpone's parasite, in Stefan Zweig's adaptation of Ben Jonson's 1607 comedy. Furious with the slave drivers, Lynn flew to Alfred's rescue: he was exhausted, his voice was shot, doctors had ordered rest. From a corner of the room came a weak objection. Alfred didn't want to be rescued: he rather fancied playing Mosca.

In his element, Alfred pulled out all stops. Mosca means "fly" in Italian. He would be iridescent, buzzing, knowing, corrupt. Face painted white with a slash of red lips, wearing a red Harpo Marx wig, earrings, and gilded costume, he acrobatically covered the stage executing Volpone's orders.

Alfred played Mosca as homosexual, a salute to his gilded Roman youth in *Medea*. The *Telegram* called him "at times girlish." The night Noël was in the audience, Alfred made his message clearer. He played "sexy games with a basket of oranges and bananas"; then, at the end of Act Three, suddenly leaped across the stage, ripped back the covers, and jumped into bed with Volpone. Even though Volpone calls Mosca "my joy, my tickling, my delight," Dudley Digges was "blue in the face with fury." For days he refused to speak to Alfred. Noël laughed.

Yet, as usual, Lunt had stolen the show. "Primarily the evening is Alfred Lunt's," wrote Woollcott in the *World*: "time of his life . . . swift, sure, gleaming . . . outlandish insect . . . only one actor would enjoy and play it so well, the truant Barrymore . . . a feat: agile, artful, mocking, crafty."

Though she would not publish her memoir until 1960, Theresa Helburn had already assessed her chief assets. Dear Alfred was a perfect example of the actor's temperament:

Suicidal, desperate. Always giving up the stage during the rehearsal period—which was probably nothing but a need for encouragement, especially from Lynn. She was never lacking in confidence for a second. Angry perhaps, but coolly angry. Strong, sure, confident. . . . There is always something tortured in Alfred—something a little cruel in Lynn. How completely they supplemented and balanced each other. A calculating, brilliant and beautiful tigress married to a gentle lion with a thorn in his foot. Lynn is synthetic in more ways than one. She made herself into a beauty. She made herself into a lovely and seductive woman but it is, I fear, only an act—an act so skillful that she believes it herself.

Alfred never stops feeling. Lynn never stops watching, thinking, calculating. A perfect combination—Clarence and Dulcy. An adolescent dreamer and a teenage schemer. It is perhaps no accident that these two perfect impersonations were destined to come together.

Lawrence Langner and
Theresa Helburn,
directors of the Theatre
Guild, with Helen
Hayes in 1958

Lawrence Langner's account of these years has none of Helburn's dislike of Lynn. "There are many reasons for this 'Golden Era' of the Theatre Guild, as some of my friends have called it. The Alternating Repertory System was largely responsible for its success, for when you have such actors as Alfred Lunt, Lynn Fontanne, Dudley Digges and all the rest, you are like the owner of a magnificent orchestra, and whatever music the orchestra plays will be played much better than when you throw a group of artists together who barely know one another, and have no experience of playing together as a team."

Granted the quality of the Guild's acting company, still, if one subtracts the names Lunt and Fontanne from its roster, there would have been no Golden Era for Langner or Helburn to write about. In four years Lunt and Fontanne had done thirteen plays for the Guild, not counting tours—an incredible achievement.

Ring Lardner captured the magic of Alfred Lunt and Lynn Fontanne during these years in his "To Producers, Authors, Actors, Etc.":

You want to pack 'em in out front?
Hire Lynn Fontanne and Alfred Lunt.
Is wounding Joe Leblang* your plan?
Hire Alfred Lunt and Lynn Fontanne.
Wouldst have a smash, not just a bunt?
Sign Lynn Fontanne and Alfred Lunt.
The madam craves a Rolls sedan?
Get Alfred Lunt and Lynn Fontanne.

---

*Leblang-Gray was a theater ticket agency known both for scalping and for half-price rates for less popular plays. Lunt and Fontanne usually sold out.

CHAPTER SIX

Merger: 1928–1931

Yet the Guild found itself in difficulty at the peak of its Golden Age. "By spreading out over the country we strengthened the Theatre Guild," explained Langner, "but we weakened the Theatre Guild Acting Company. . . . It was impossible to send our Acting Company on tour and have them play in New York at the same time, so that while we gave our out-of-town subscribers our best actors during the season of 1928–1929, this left us with too thin a fare to provide proper sustenance to our New York members."

The Guild decided to hire more actors so it could alternate four plays in New York repertory. This plot failed when *Faust, Major Barbara,* and O'Neill's *Dynamo* flopped and Lunt and Fontanne's next play, *Caprice,* was so popular the Guild couldn't withdraw it. Playwrights were complaining, too, that alternating repertory didn't give their plays long enough runs. And actors began to bite the hand that underfed them. Edward G. Robinson, one of the Guild's key character actors, left because the board would not raise his salary twenty-five dollars a week.

Circumstances beyond the Guild's control also conspired against it. The stock market crash of October 1929 catapulted the nation into panic, then into the dark years of the Great Depression. And no one foresaw the impact that talkies would have on the theater. Talkies

Alfred and Lynn in Caprice *(1929). They never again acted separately onstage.*

demanded actors with voices. By 1930 the second Gold Rush was on. Talents like Spencer Tracy, Claudette Colbert, Clark Gable, Barbara Stanwyck, Cary Grant, Paul Muni, Lee Tracy, and Miriam Hopkins joined the stampede from Broadway to Hollywood. Claude Rains, Dudley Digges, and Henry Travers from the Guild would jump onto the wagon.

During most of the 1920s the road was healthy, vaudeville alive, and Broadway hosting over 250 productions each year. By 1930, Broadway theaters were closing, vaudeville was terminally ill, and the number of touring companies dwindling. Theater in New York would never be the same. It became known, after the title of a Hart-Kaufman play, as "the Fabulous Invalid." Not dying, but not well.

None of this yet affected Alfred and Lynn as they launched *Caprice* at the Guild Theatre on New Year's Eve 1928. Sil-Vara's play about the (not very serious) consequences of philandering took them back to

Vienna, scene of *The Guardsman;* back, too, to equal roles and the kind of comedy they charged like CO_2.

Alfred played Counsellor Albert von Echardt, torn between his son and his current mistress, Ilsa von Ilsen. Echardt wants them both. Ilsa solves the problem by telling the son she is his father's lover. The idealistic boy bolts and vons Echardt and Ilsen pick up their affair where they left it.

As the philanderer, Alfred looked distinguished with mustache, graying short-clipped hair, and a middle-aged paunch he'd deliberately acquired, though the cigar he smoked made him queasy. "Alfred Lunt, as Counsellor Von Echardt," said *The New Yorker,* "is so excellent that it's hard not to pass him by as an actor who just happens to be the exact type of Viennese man-of-the-world needed for the part. Yet with half a memory, one must realize that . . . here [is] a magnificent subjugation of personality to role."

Lynn had bought her gowns in Paris the summer before. The Guild had sprung $2,500 but, as Alfred groaned, "Twenty-five hundred wasn't even a drop in the bucket." Yet the gowns were worth it, especially the white silk with a cape lined with red satin over the derrière which she impudently flipped at Alfred as she exited. For *The New Yorker* the merit of the play was that it gave Lynn Fontanne "the opportunity for such lovely effervescent comedy as comes into the theatre only once in a blue moon. Her performance is champagne, and caviar, and a Viennese waltz all rolled into one."

Caprice was a milestone in Alfred and Lynn's careers. It was the first play that was sheer soufflé, with only Lunt and Fontanne's magic to prevent its collapse. In Ring Lardner's words, *Caprice* was a play

> *whose claim to wit*
> *Rests on one oft-repeated bit:*
> *The swilling, by a profligate*
> *Of sodium bicarbonate.*

"I doubt," said Burns Mantle, "if any other company in any other theatre in town could have saved it." *Caprice* was so unlike the usual Guild fare that critics puzzled at Helburn and Moeller investing so much effort in it. But this soufflé paid. Lawrence Langner called *Caprice* "the most joyous event in the Guild's eleventh season."

It was joyous for Lynn and Alfred. "Miss Fontanne and Mr. Lunt are a matchless pair of volatile comedians," said Brooks Atkinson. "*Caprice* lives in their style of walking, their toying with boutonnieres, and in their spontaneity with the lines and colloquies. . . . They have played similar parts before, but with no such effervescence and versatility as they summon in *Caprice*. Now they play with infinite subtlety, resource and drollery. . . ." *Caprice* simply was Lunt and Fontanne.

Caprice was important in another way. From now on, Alfred and Lynn would appear onstage only together. Asked years later when they'd decided to act as a team, Lynn said, "No, we never decided that," Alfred agreeing, "Never." Lynn went further: "Just because we work together is no reason we should be classed as a team." True that they began only by insisting on a clause in their contracts that they would always tour together; but remembering Lynn coaxing George C. Tyler—"With me and Alfred you have a GREAT COMBINATION"— it's hard to believe the merger just happened.

Becoming a combination had drawbacks for Lynn. Though she would always appear as Lynn Fontanne, she would merge linguistically into the phenomenon known as "the Lunts." (Some people would even forget how to pronounce her name, confusing it with Fontaine.) She would also commit herself to glamour. To counteract a certain androgyny about Alfred—tall, handsome, and distinguished though he was— she must be twice as feminine and bewitching. No Medea, no Lady Macbeth, no Mother Courage for Lynn Fontanne. No more Nina Leeds.

But Alfred had far more to lose from becoming a team. S. N. Behrman said that in only two actors was genius suggested the minute they stepped onstage: Alfred Lunt and Laurence Olivier. At this point, Alfred was unquestionably New York's First Actor. He had a greater range than Lynn: from comedy to tragedy, classics to contemporary— from Bluntschli to Dmitri to Babe Callahan to Marco to Clark Storey to Mosca. "Lynn is the lantern," said Constance Collier, "and Alfred the light within it." A soloist was choosing to become a duo pianist. Deploring the lack of Broadway male actors in 1957, the press agent Richard Maney wrote, "Lunt? He's indistinguishable from Lynn Fontanne"—surely the cruelest (and most untrue) thing ever said about a great actor.

In her heart Lynn knew what Alfred forfeited. After he died, she told Laurence Olivier, "rather sadly, that Alfred could have risen to the heights as a great actor, but becoming famous as 'The Lunts' and feeling obliged to choose plays with parts for both of them had prevented him from achieving that stature."

Certainly Alfred lacked star temperament. "It is the play that counts.

The actor doesn't matter a damn, or at least not a very big one." Then, too, it was practical to act with a spouse: "We rehearse at breakfast, at dinner, in taxi-cabs." And the "wounded lion" felt safe with Lynn, the tigress, who would protect him, validate his masculinity, be his "beard." In turn Alfred, with his distinction and male beauty, would validate her femininity. And Lynn would not have to be jealous. She intensely disliked Margalo Gillmore, Alfred's young Guild female lead. (Gillmore returned the feeling.)

Yet in show biz, marriage usually was death to romance. As one Guild subscriber so elegantly put it, "Husbands and wives should not be cast as lovers—It destroys the illusion—When a man snatches his own wife's hinder, it isn't exciting."

Married sex did not work on stage or screen for Laurence Olivier and Vivien Leigh, Elizabeth Taylor and Richard Burton, Tom Cruise and Nicole Kidman; and the Lunts would hear the criticism again. "Please don't tell me that I've been wrong all these years," Alfred wrote one critic, "and that love is done with mirrors." Djuna Barnes interviewed Alfred and Lynn "to prove that marriage is no hindrance to art"— reporting what they wanted her to say. "We rehearse together with the anxiety of matchmakers officiating at the marriage of our stage selves. We act as strangers who have known each other in a forgotten world. We are like duelists, fighting for an ideal, clasping hands when the duel is over, having learned to respect each other's fanaticism." Article after article probed the same theme.

And now husband and wife were signing on for good. Yet for most playgoers the Lunts' sex play *was* exciting—a testimony to the virtuosity of their artifice. Illusion remained intact. In the truest sense they were *playing*. Some playgoers actually preferred them as man and wife. "Isn't it nice, my dear," whispered a lady after a particularly hot love scene, "to know that they are married."

Then there was the view of one bitter actress. "How can any other actors hope to play together as well as Alfred and Lynn? They rehearse in bed!"

Their cook, Louise Scott, was arriving later each morning. Alfred and Lynn liked breakfast in bed. Louise was fatalistic: "I was a ten months baby, I was born late—and sir, I'm marked, *marked.*" Alfred finally dismissed her with a month's salary.

Louise took it badly. They were "blackguarding and scandalizing" her; she'd been working for "a pair of dirty hearts." She'd "scrubbed, mended, packed, darned, sewed, washed and ironed, cooked, raked and scraped, saved and pinched and stinched and fixed nice things"—all for "such an untidy pair" and a wife who "knew nothing about a house." She, who loved God and Jesus as a true Christian, had a final word for her slave drivers: "Repent!" Lynn filed the diatribe under "Touch Letters."

Lynn freely admitted that Alfred was the domestic half. "Is there any boss in your house?" she'd been asked by the *Brooklyn Daily News* in 1926, a splash of the rivers of print about the Lunt-Fontanne marriage that would pour from the presses for the next twenty-five years. "Alfred pays all the bills," replied Lynn. "He knows when there is a hole in the frying pan to be relined. He knows when there is a hole in a sheet to be mended. Come to think of it, he is the housekeeper. He knows everything."

Noël Coward called them the happiest married couple he knew. (He didn't know many.) Inevitably, though, there were quarrels, sometimes onstage. According to the producer Cheryl Crawford, Lynn slapped Alfred's face with her gloves harder than usual during a matinee of *Caprice.* Alfred swore at her under his breath. Lynn swore back. A moment later she was supposed to exit, then immediately return. She exited. Alfred poured himself bicarbonate of soda. No Lynn. He drained the glass slowly. No Lynn. He turned pale and began to shake with rage. No Lynn. Finally the stage manager rang down the curtain. He stopped Cheryl Crawford backstage. "Stay out of it, for God's sake! They're furious. Give them time to get over it."

To the public they were a miracle—as though no actors in history had made a go of married life. Alfred would solemnly credit their success to separate bank accounts. Lynn believed that too much analysis of a relationship was fatal, as were long separations. Alfred felt that their total immersion in the theater "gave them a habit of friendship which is continuous and pleasant." Alfred abhorred possessiveness. "I have *never* felt any jealousy. I cannot imagine myself in the awful role of a man who begins to tremble when his wife says she is going out for a walk down the avenue." Lynn could not say the same. Alfred averaged fifty "mash notes" a week, and some actress was always in love with him.

They ragged each other: "The way that man makes me work!" "And the *eternal* nagging of that woman!"

Both insisted they never felt smug about their marriage for a second.

"One walks across the street, an automobile skids, one walks no more. Marriage is just like that."

Alfred is suavely smoking a cigarette, Lynn lounging against cushions. They are playing to the reporter, their rapt audience of one.

aprice was also a milestone because it introduced Alfred Lunt to British audiences and returned Lynn to London as a star. Theatrical exchange was less common then. A few Americans had been welcomed in the West End, but British exports outnumbered imports. Willing to bet on the Lunts, the Guild in tandem with the British producer C. B. Cochran opened *Caprice* on June 4, 1929, at the St. James's Theatre.

Primed by Lynn with horror stories about the opening of *One Night in Rome,* Alfred was a wreck. He collared the wardrobe mistress.

"Do British audiences really boo a play they don't like?"

"Oh, sir, they boos something terrible. Don't you pay any attention. You just go right on talking, like as if you didn't 'ear it, sir."

"Do they really throw eggs?"

"Don't you mind an egg or two, sir. I'll get it off your clothes, sir. Don't you worry."

Waiting for her entrance, Lynn discovered that her knees were rattling like dry sticks. Then she swept onto the stage and immediately found her poise.

London audiences were at first confused by the Lunts' overlapping and by Alfred's back. (Lynn had a theory about that back: nervous Alfred turned away from the audience in emotional scenes so he could focus.) And Alfred refused to use a British accent. Yet by the end of the play the audience was marveling that they'd heard every word.

Critics gave the hometown favorite raves. Lynn Fontanne's very great talent, said James Agate in the *Times,* is "established before she opens her mouth." The *Daily Telegraph* rhapsodized: "Scintillating with humour, charming to look at and armed with a technique flawless and confident, Miss Fontanne uses her intelligence, talent and personal fascination to make an abject slave of each discerning playgoer." Alfred was content with *Punch*'s decision that he could not have played von Echardt better. In fact London was thoroughly conquered. The whole production was praised as distinguished and exquisitely balanced.

In the audience John Gielgud admired the pace of Lunt and Fontanne's overlapping dialogue. Lynn in a red dress reminded him of

Beatrice Lillie (Lynn would not have been amused). He was enormously impressed by Alfred's "sardonic and laid back" persona.

J. B. Priestley came to *Caprice* expecting to be bored. By the end of the first act he had completely capitulated to the Lunt and Fontanne spell.

Bernard Shaw came to a performance, laughed extravagantly, was asked by Helburn and Langner if he'd like to congratulate the Lunts on their acting in person. "It's not acting," said Shaw. "It's performing." He invited the Theatre Guild contingent to lunch at Adelphi Terrace, seating Alfred, Lynn, and Philip Moeller at his end of the table, where, indulging in a poached egg, he convulsed them with story after story. "He's all pink and white," exclaimed Lynn. "Looks as if he had been just scrubbed and rubbed. Ought to smell of soap and talcum. Generates ideas as fast as a clock can tick."

They saw Noël. Four years before, the incredible Mr. Coward had had five plays running simultaneously in London. Then had come the riot on the disastrous first night of *Sirocco*. But *Bitter Sweet* this year would revive his reputation. And of course he was still going to write that play for the three of them they'd talked about long ago in New York.

London loved the Lunts, the Lunts loved London. *Caprice* was the beginning of an ardent affair.

They returned to tour triumphantly in *Caprice* and rehearse another Behrman play, *Meteor*, with a lead written for Alfred as juicy as a rare steak. "The character," said Behrman, "was a young man with 'ghetto' vitality from the meanest background who pinned a grandiose name onto himself—Raphael Lord—and who persuaded himself that he had the gift of clairvoyance." Behrman followed the Lunts from Baltimore to Philadelphia and Boston, the company rehearsing *Meteor* between performances of *Caprice*.

Neither Fontanne nor Lunt liked *Meteor* as written, agreeing to act only if Behrman rewrote. "They won't like me in *Meteor*," said Alfred gloomily, meaning that Sam still wasn't getting it right. Rehearsing one afternoon in Boston's Hollis Street Theatre, Moeller threw down the script and burst into tears. Langner led him out of the theater. Moeller explained that if he hadn't had hysterics, Alfred would have.

By opening night in Boston, December 2, 1929, Behrman still hadn't written the final scene. Alfred prayed he'd be able to improvise something as he talked on the telephone, but in case he couldn't, he told the stage manager to bring down the curtain on the word "schlemiel." The curtain fell at the word, leaving a baffled audience. As usual, however, Alfred and Lynn, as Raphael Lord's disillusioned wife, saved the day. "We begin to wonder about the Theatre Guild," said the critic Francis Bellamy, "were it deprived of these two."

Meteor opened at the Guild Theatre in New York on December 23. In the wake of the stock market crash in October, audiences were not in the mood for a character study of a ruthless businessman. Then Alfred developed acute neuritis and the Guild suspended the play; he returned with his arm in a sling, but as severe pain continued, the Guild withdrew him, though Lynn continued to the end of the run in March. Langner considered *Meteor* a brilliant play that had lost itself when Behrman reduced it from four to three acts. Yet Lynn and Alfred weren't much in the mood for the play, either: only when they read of his suicide in the papers did they discover that their broker had embezzled their investments.

Not all their investments. They vacationed that April 1930 in Jamaica, then returned to Genesee Depot to rest. Instead they retackled the cottage, now painted red with white trim. Somehow they'd found time to scrub and shellac the floors and paint the main rooms ivory with yellow woodwork and every door outlined in bright blue. Alfred found a woodworker to make copies of traditional Swedish chairs, couch, and tall kitchen settle, then painted the furniture with Scandinavian designs. Lynn sewed red and white gingham curtains, bedcovers, and dressing-table flounces. (She called Alfred "Split Curtain" for suggesting splitting the fabric would save them money.) The decorator Syrie Maugham, wife of Somerset, had designed them a stunning white-on-white bedroom, but when she asked $1,000 for a carpet sewn of sheepskins, Alfred went to Chicago and got skins from the stockyard for $100.

Alfred set each of the flat rocks that made a path up to the house. He also constructed a garden built in the form of an amphitheater, with descending tiers of carrots, lettuces, sweet william, and radishes. Holding a parasol, Hattie would emerge from the main house in lipstick and high heels to pick parsley and zinnias.

Alfred had invited his secretary, Lawrence Farrell, out for six weeks' rest. "Six weeks' rest!" said Farrell. Farrell was short and trim with prematurely white hair and pink cheeks; gay. "I was given a pick and a shovel on arrival and I haven't put them down since." The place was crawling with workers: C. H. Fintel, "my Swedish sewer digger"; Chuck from Mukwonago making walls and laying stone; Mr. Grutz-macher and Eddie upstairs painting bedrooms. Lynn and Alfred worked beside them. Most nights they fell into bed at nine.

The brilliant Robert Edmond Jones came to Genesee to discuss sets for *Much Ado About Nothing,* which he would also direct. *Much Ado* would be their first Shakespeare, the parts of Beatrice and Benedick naturals for Lynn and Alfred. "It seemed as though Shake-speare must have imagined the Lunts before he started writing," said Theresa Helburn.

Unfortunately Jones was too innovative and *Much Ado* became "a pointless disaster." He flanked the stage with dressing rooms so that audiences could watch Lunt and Fontanne change costumes. Naturally audiences riveted on the Lunts, ignoring stage center. Jones realized his impossible staging, reversed, ended with a muddle. Sadly for the Lunts—they would be accused of being afraid of Shakespeare—*Much Ado* died on the road, the Guild announcing that the Lunts could not rehearse Shakespeare while playing *Elizabeth the Queen.*

Influenced by Lytton Strachey's best-selling *Elizabeth and Essex,* Maxwell Anderson had written a history play in blank verse. Lynn objected that Anderson was ignorant of facts known to every British schoolchild, but Alfred urged her to accept *Elizabeth.* Lynn wasn't satis-fied: she wanted a battle of the sexes between Elizabeth and Essex, con-flict and tenderness. Anderson promised to rewrite.

He didn't. The Philadelphia opening was a disaster. Langner and Helburn opted for closing immediately, but now Lynn wanted the play. The Lunts offered to produce *Elizabeth* themselves. Their faith per-suaded the Guild. Yet in city after city the play bombed. Finally they reached Baltimore in a heavy rainstorm. Anderson disappeared. Next morning he handed Moeller twelve pages of conflict and tenderness. He explained that he could write only when it rained.

Elizabeth the Queen opened at the Martin Beck on November 3, 1930. An exhausted curtain man raised and lowered the curtain seventeen times while Alfred, graceful in Essex's black tunic, and Lynn, in Eliza-beth's red wig and stiff robes, bowed to thunderous applause.

Critics raved about Fontanne's "miraculous reincarnation" of the Vir-gin Queen, with her ravaged white face, angry voice, and regal power.

She conveys cross-grained greatness, intellectual force betrayed
by abrupt seizures of mere womanly dependence and, most of all,
the inevitable loneliness of any high destiny. She is, by turns,
impressive, ardent, malicious and defenseless. She is coarse and
aristocratic, broad in good humor as in violence and, for all her
sharp ugliness and spinster's coquetry, so irresistibly magnetic
that we understand her sway over men's hearts and loyalties.

Wolcott Gibbs in *The New Yorker* dissented: "I was not bowled over
by Lynn Fontanne's characterization of Queen Elizabeth. . . . There was
no suggestion of age or eccentricity that I could detect and Miss
Fontanne's youthful voice did nothing to supply these qualities. . . . I
was oppressed by the feeling that the vocal strain of playing a particularly vocal queen was a little too heavy for her resources."

As for Essex, "Mr. Lunt does splendidly by everything." In the *World*
Robert Littell emphatically disagreed. "Mr. Lunt's mannerisms get in
the way of the character and trip it up. This is not Essex, one always
feels, not anything like him: it is a very good actor named Alfred Lunt
trying to do something that, in the nature of Lunt and Essex, he cannot
possibly do."

In December the *Theatre Guild Magazine* polled eight New York critics
to list the outstanding stage actors in America. The result:

1. Alfred Lunt
2. Lynn Fontanne
3. Eva Le Gallienne
4. Helen Hayes
5. Dudley Digges
6. Katharine Cornell
7. Ruth Gordon
8. Paul Muni
9. Tom Powers
10. Richard Bennett
11. Walter Huston
12. Alla Nazimova
13. Edward G. Robinson

That same month, Theresa Helburn received a passionate plea:

It's on my heart that the Lunts are destined for great things. It is obvious to me that they are slated to be the Irving and Terry of this generation—with Lunt, of course, a far finer actor than Irving was. A destiny which must be fulfilled.

I am so hoping that the Guild will be proud and bold in its use of them! . . . *Macbeth* is bound to come. Why not *Anthony* [sic] *and Cleopatra?* And the *Agamemnon* of Aeschylus. New York would be aghast at its splendor. . . . Or if you are afraid of that, Euripides' *Electra,* with Lunt the Orestes and Lynn the Electra.

Alfred could be by far the finest Othello of this generation in the English-speaking theatre. And Tartuffe, one of the fattest parts ever written. Or Tamburlaine, for that matter. And of course the Lunts will have to do *The Taming of the Shrew,* sooner or later, by popular demand. Eventually, why not now? And *Rosmersholm*—it can't fail, it's so well written—could be given its classic reinterpretation by the Lunts. *Monna Vanna* is sure fire theatre, and Alfred would have a part which he could build into something deeply moving. And Lynn will have to do Lady Teazle sooner or later.

You see, what I am begging you to do is to launch deliberately the magnificence which the Lunts have in them. They are the only actors in America whom you can count on absolutely and utterly. And if you do, you will make theatre history.

Now forgive me for presuming to advise you. But there hasn't been in a century such a combination of genius and opportunity—not on the English-speaking stage.

But this destiny depended on Lunt and Fontanne acting separately. *Elizabeth the Queen* played 147 performances in New York. The rest of the Guild's plays that season were artistic and financial disasters losing more than $180,000. In early spring 1931 the Lunts set off on tour to rave notices. In Chicago, Lynn's Elizabeth was hailed as "one of the great dramatic triumphs of our day." (Essex in Chicago nearly choked when, flinging himself upon Elizabeth's bosom, he half-swallowed one of her pearls.)

In Chicago they met with Irving Thalberg and Norma Shearer to settle details about the film of *The Guardsman* the Lunts would make for MGM that summer. Since Alfred's screen debut in *Backbone* in 1923, Lynn had appeared indifferently in *The Man Who Found Himself,* while Alfred had made *The Ragged Edge, Second Youth, Lovers in Quarantine,* and

Sally of the Sawdust. Directed by D. W. Griffith and starring W. C. Fields, only *Sally* was notable, and Griffith told Alfred he didn't like his close-ups. On the other hand, Louella Parsons considered Alfred big movie material. Neither Lunt nor Fontanne, however, considered themselves film actors. But in the midst of the Depression, MGM's $75,000 offer looked attractive.

"Now let's not have any stunt stuff," Alfred begged Thalberg. "No swimming or horseback riding or prize fighting or rolling down stairs." All they wanted was fidelity to the play and continuity in filming the story.

"No, no, no," said Thalberg soothingly. "You will find the pictures much more peaceful than the stage."

Society folk jammed Milwaukee's Pabst Theater for an April 22 "first night" of *Elizabeth the Queen*—no one more regal than Mrs. Sederholm with her snow-white hair and black lace gown with a gardenia corsage, totally eclipsing Karin in white taffeta and Louise in brown lace. It was Hattie's habit to stand at her seat and examine the audience critically through a lorgnette. Afterward in the lobby she formally received admirers of her son. Friends of Hattie's had insisted on giving Alfred and Lynn an opening-night dinner—unwelcome not only because of precurtain nerves but because Alfred had a temperature of 102. He spent the Milwaukee week in bed, Larry Farrell driving him to the theater, where he plied him with cold remedies and hot coffee.

One irritant was absent. Carl had left home, hoping to capitalize on his many afternoons at Stag's Tavern. Alfred was banking him as a pool sharp in New York. Carl did well: acting the country rube, he successfully relieved city sharks of their dollars. For a time he was ranked the number-three pool player in the United States. When word of his skill got round, however, he lost takers. Alfred kept on banking him.

For their Hollywood adventure Larry Farrell—secretary, valet, and business manager—rented them an apartment in Westwood, hired a cook, found them a used 1927 Ford and a chauffeur. On the Santa Fe Chief to Los Angeles, Alfred and Lynn read the movie script. They were nervous: Alfred would be thirty-nine this year; Lynn, forty-four—hardly the age to launch a Hollywood career, especially when the camera filmed old. Dining with young Ginger Rogers, on her way to

Hollywood to make three movies for Pathé, they plied her with questions about makeup, directors, scene shooting.

"Though they didn't try to call attention to themselves in any obvious manner," she recalled, "there was something electric about them, an aura of elegance that charged the atmosphere and set them apart. I guess you couldn't call Lynn Fontanne beautiful—her features were too irregular—but like all truly great actresses, she gave the impression of beauty. . . . Alfred Lunt was a nice enough looking man, but not a matinee idol. No, it wasn't looks that made them special; the Lunts projected an inner quality." By the end of dinner they were laughing and talking nonstop.

Arriving at MGM's gates, Alfred and Lynn were asked to show their passes. They didn't have passes and the gateman had never heard of *The Guardsman.* Alfred ordered the chauffeur to drive them home, their blackest opinion of Hollywood confirmed. Eventually Sidney Franklin, the director they had chosen, called to apologize and personally escort them through the gates. Stage and studio locked horns.

Sidney Franklin had seen *Elizabeth the Queen* and suggested *The Guardsman* begin with Elizabeth and Essex sparring as they come offstage removing their makeup. The Lunts agreed. But they were told that their technique of overlapping speeches was impossible for studio mikes to handle. They did it anyway. Then Alfred and Lynn insisted on rehearsing every scene of the play before it was shot—unheard of in Hollywood. Faced with the expertise of these actors, the cameras rolled sometimes as long as nine minutes (also unheard of). Retakes were relatively few. As a result, the film was shot in an incredible twenty-one days.

Thalberg refused to believe a prestige film could wrap that easily. Though he liked the rough cut of *The Guardsman,* he insisted on reshooting one scene. The Lunts dug in their heels. Watching the new rushes, Thalberg discovered that Alfred's left eyeball was rolling into the corner. "You did it on purpose to ruin the retakes," he charged. Alfred explained that his eye was weakened by the fatigue of reshooting. Thalberg ordered another take. Alfred went out and got his hair chopped off, settling the issue.

Alfred couldn't bear to watch the rushes, so Lynn did it for them. "Oh, it seems to be going well. In fact, you're wonderful, Alfred. Your voice, your manner, your timing—they all register beautifully. Of course, you could use a little more makeup to define your mouth—you look as if you have no lips. But that's trivial. You have such flair, such panache, it's just wonderful. But oh, Alfred, I am *dreadful.* I look scared to death, very plain and haggard with awful lines under my eyes—no shine in my hair—I look as if I'd been buried and dug up again. I'm terrible."

Alfred stared into space.

"I just can't face the camera tomorrow! Oh, Alfred, what shall I do?"

Said Alfred: "No lips?"

Alfred has lips onscreen, but far more strikingly, eyes. Outlined in black, they are in turn surprised, furious, suspicious, hurt, and amorous. His acting is so instinctive, so nervously agile that there seems to be no barrier between thought, motion, and speech, which pours out of him as a spontaneous reaction to the moment, his voice rising and falling with emotion. Occasionally, unused to the camera, he uses too much facial pantomime, and sometimes the camera is unflattering to them both. But the intuitive genius of his acting manages to get through.

Lynn is the opposite. Looking like a sleek black panther with half-closed lids and enigmatic smile, she poses gracefully and speaks deliberately in a modulated contralto. She is calculating, charming, devious, and in control. In the last scene, when she pulls her husband's head down on her breast, he is the eternal child, she the eternal madonna. *The Guardsman* is called the first version of "a joke that became central" to Hollywood romantic comedy: the male as weak, volatile, and hysteric; the female as "the figure of strength and solidity, the one who is cool, knowing, and 'potent.' " Arguably, Fontanne and Lunt's real and screen personas set the comic style for years to come.

Decades later, on a cruise, Lynn and Alfred saw *The Guardsman* again. "I knew exactly what I'd look like," said Lynn, "—a plain creature, a schoolmarm. Well! I didn't at all. I was a lush piece! . . . And Alfred was absolutely astounding. When people came up to speak to us afterward, I said, 'Yes, weren't we wonderful?' "

MGM chose a movie theater in San Bernardino for the preview. In those days studios based decisions on questionnaires filled out by gum-cracking audiences as they left the show. Furious, Lynn interrupted Thalberg's gloomy recital.

"But these are all written by children!"

"This is our audience," said Thalberg wearily.

Yet, "Our stay so far has been extraordinarily pleasant," Alfred wrote Maxwell Anderson. "Everyone is amazingly pleasant and helpful."

They saw old theater friends like Ina Claire, Roland Young (playing the Critic in the film), Laura Hope Crews, Lucille Watson, and Ivor Novello. (For Alfred the difference between East and West Coast dinners was that Hollywood served more avocados and less garlic.) They longed for the physical work of Broadway. Film, particularly for Alfred, was nerve-racking and exhausting. Still furious with the San Bernardino preview reaction, Lynn felt certain Hollywood didn't know how to market them.

The Guardsman turned out to be a modest financial and a definite artistic success. Though Maude Eburne as Mama couldn't touch Helen Westley's performance in the play, Roland Young's Critic was droll and knowing and ZaSu Pitts funny as the maid. Playing at the "refrigerated" Astor at Broadway and Forty-fifth, it drew large audiences and raves from New York critics. "If you don't see another picture—ever—you must see *The Guardsman*" (*American*). "The audience applauded as though Mr. Lunt were present in person" (*Times*). "Masterly work. Delightful, suave, mature, literate and humorous" (*World-Telegram*). In Hollywood both Lynn and Alfred were nominated for Academy Awards.

In Podunk, however, *The Guardsman* was too subtle to be popular, despite ads urging the public to try "The Blindfold Kissing Test: Can You Tell Who It Is?" And the notoriously married Lunts were decidedly not fan-mag types. Still, Hollywood liked to make a small quota of prestige movies, and offers started to arrive at Genesee Depot. Carl Laemmle of Universal Pictures wanted them to do *Tristan and Isolde* for $250,000. Thalberg offered them the incredible sum of $990,000 for a three-year contract, beginning with a film of *Elizabeth the Queen*.

Alfred was ready to make another film, finding the experience more positive than negative. Lynn was not. Besides, both wanted artistic control over their films. This desire for control had been responsible for "bad days" until the Lunts had persuaded the Guild they must act plays their way. In Hollywood, studio control was virtually absolute. Neither Laemmle nor Thalberg was about to yield it.

"TURN DOWN $925,000 OFFER," blared captions over photographs of Lunt and Fontanne in papers across the nation. Meanwhile, Universal Pictures received an immortal telegram:

WE CAN BE BOUGHT, MY DEAR MR. LAEMMLE, BUT WE CAN'T BE BORED.

CHAPTER SEVEN

A Good Depression: 1931–1933

Alfred and Lynn spent part of their Hollywood money installing an L-shaped (for Lunt) swimming pool north of the main house. Afternoons Alfred brought the workers coffee, tea, and cookies on a silver tray. Eventually Claggett Wilson would design a red and white bathhouse with dressing rooms and a copper cupola. A pump forced water up into the cupola for a shower. They called the pool the Mermaid Pavilion for the crowning decoration, a gift of Cecil Beaton. They also installed a roofed shelter known as the Cabana and a poolside patio, where they often lunched. Alfred liked to serve grilled steaks and tomatoes with scalloped potatoes and a hearty red wine.

During these years they hired Warren O'Brien, a professional photographer who had known Alfred since Carroll College, to photograph them breakfasting on the patio, picnicking under an apple tree, pouring tea under the arbor, sprawling against a haystack. A kid from the village accompanied these shoots so that if Lynn said, "Oh, we should have the old granite coffee pot," the assistant would run fetch it. The Lunts' quick change from bib overalls to evening dress amazed O'Brien. One of their favorite poses shows them walking away from the camera looking over their shoulders, swinging a basket between them. They called these rustic idylls "The Reapers" or "The Angelus" after the well-known paintings.

They wanted to record their developing estate; yet since they'd given up Hollywood they also wanted to preserve their images, first on home movie camera and now in professional photographs. O'Brien came year after year. The photographs, published in theater programs, made the Lunts' Wisconsin retreat famous and the Lunts themselves the theater's most photographed actors.

Their high living in the midst of the Depression shocked some residents of Genesee Depot. It also employed them. The village main street had been paved in 1928; the Lunts were now known as "the folks off the concrete." Paradoxically, while bread lines formed, banks closed, and a newly elected Franklin Delano Roosevelt told a desperate people they had nothing to fear but fear itself, the Lunts were living in luxury.

Two plays also helped them beat the Depression blues while giving delight to thousands of Americans who could still afford the theater.

Alfred and Lynn had intrigued Robert Sherwood since he'd met the "weird fiancés" back in 1919. He'd written a play called *The Road to Rome* for them, rejected by the Theatre Guild. Now he brought them another Lunt-Fontanne–tailored play. Alfred and Lynn immediately adored *Reunion in Vienna,* a third theatrical visit to the city romanticized as the capital of waltzes.

They also adored Bob Sherwood, all lanky six feet seven of him. He was shy, with an unsmiling laugh, a generous nature, and a habit, when tight, of singing "When the Red, Red Robin Comes Bob, Bob, Bobbin' Along." One of the most socially committed American playwrights, he'd come home gassed and wounded from a war that, he saw clearly, had neither saved the world for democracy nor guaranteed peace and prosperity. He was also one of the speediest of playwrights. In two weeks he'd written *Reunion* to relieve "apprehensions from which, with the help of God and a few Lunts, I have been attempting to escape."

Sherwood divides postwar Vienna into the venerable Hotel Lucher, where faded aristocrats gather to celebrate the hundredth birthday of Emperor Franz Josef, and the modern house of Vienna's most renowned psychiatrist, Anton Krug, and his beautiful wife, Elena. It is rumored that Archduke Rudolph Maximillian von Hapsburg, now a taxi driver in Nice, may slip into Austria for the party.

Elena and Rudolph have been lovers. Dare she go to the party, knowing they may meet again? Her supremely rational husband insists she cure nostalgia by taking a hard look at what ten years have done to her archduke.

Arriving at the Hotel Lucher in lederhosen and a feathered hat, Rudolph is as charming, mad, and irrepressible as ever. "Good evening, venerable strumpet," he shouts, whacking Frau Lucher's rump. "Still wearing the red flannel drawers?" He hoists her skirts. "Thank God, there's something in Vienna that hasn't been changed." Royal prerogative prevails:

RUDOLPH: I will occupy the Imperial Suite.
LUCHER: The Imperial Suite no longer exists.
RUDOLPH: Restore it!

The suspense of the ex-lovers' meeting is postponed until the middle of the second act. Elena enters in a clinging white gown.

ELENA *stares at* RUDOLPH's *back. He gazes at her image in the mirror. . . . After a few moments, he steps down from the chair, turns and confronts her. . . .* RUDOLPH *starts toward her, pauses, then walks around her.* ELENA *does not move, but her eyes follow him. . . . He is behind her. He reaches out to touch her, but doesn't touch her. He walks around, in front of her, stares at her, then slaps her face. He seizes her in his arms and kisses her, fiercely.*

Elena was almost a return to Lynn's Actress in *The Guardsman*, right down to the sleek white dress. She has a husband who doesn't much interest her and a lover who does. Yet Sherwood's woman is deeper. She respects her husband and is aware of the peril of waking the past. Then when she finds herself still enchanted with Rudolph, she has the courage both to go to bed with him and to say goodbye the next morning.

Alfred created an Archduke who was glamorous, coarse, arrogant, lustful, mad, witty, and above all regal. He slicked back his hair, emphasizing a noble brow. He applied a pencil-thin mustache. He added a dueling scar to his right cheek. He managed to be as ducal in shirttails as in dress uniform. He walked like a duke, poured brandy like a duke, received the homage of subjects like a duke. And he slapped Elena's face extravagantly and shockingly—like a duke.

At rehearsals Sherwood witnessed his love scenes spring to life as Lunt and Fontanne turned his stage directions into a ballet of primitive seduction. Elena in flowing white, Rudolph in white jacket and black

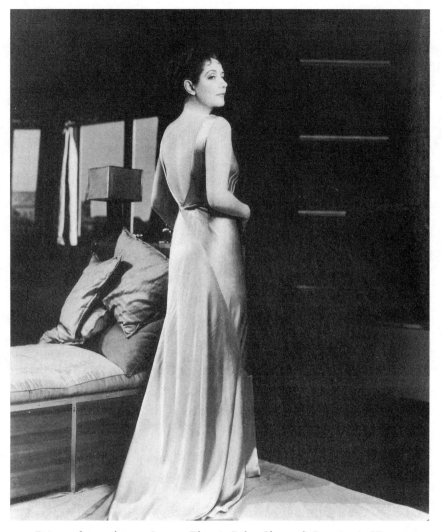

Epitome of stage glamour: Lynn as Elena in Robert Sherwood's Reunion in Vienna

trousers seated with his legs straddling her hips. Rudolph on a couch, Elena above him: suddenly she seizes his face, kisses him fiercely, slaps him, kisses him again. He pulls her down and she rolls over him, kissing him wildly. To the strains of the *Merry Widow* waltz, Rudolph shouts to his supporters, "Look at her! Look at her! She has been hitting me—hitting me with all the old strength! Show them how you did it, my darling!" Elena slaps him again, Rudolph kisses her gratefully, waltzes her into his bedroom, and slams the door.

Reunion in Vienna *(1931)*

Helen Hokinson immortalized the Lunts' *Reunion in Vienna* style in a famous *New Yorker* cartoon. A plump matron is trying to direct a local production with two young amateurs perched uncomfortably side by side on a sofa. "I think," says the director hopelessly to her assistant, "that this is where the Lunts *rolled.*"

"A queer thing," mused Sherwood, "that two such individualized and odd characters should have found in each other an extraordinary and flattering resemblance." They could fight "angrily and embarrassingly and pretty ludicrously" over a bit of business or the interpretation of a line. Yet in front of an audience they relied upon each other as unhesitatingly as the Flying Wallendas. "The thing above everything else that has made them harmonious and great, and a source of infinite entertainment to their public, and their friends, and themselves," concluded Sherwood, "is that they are both fundamentally hams."

Blissfully directed by Worthington Miner, *Reunion in Vienna* opened in New York at the Martin Beck Theatre on November 16, 1931, and was quaffed like champagne by an audience parched for gaiety, sparkle, and wit. Helen Westley played the cynical, cigar-smoking Frau Lucher. Henry Travers (to be remembered cinematically for his angel in *It's a Wonderful Life*) doddered lovably as Elena's browbeaten father-in-law and had a crucial line. The Archduke has stayed the night, breakfasted uproariously with Elena and old Krug, and left under escort for the Austrian border.

OLD KRUG: You know, Elena—I've never, in all my life, had so much fun!
ELENA: Neither have I.

Neither had the audience. Next morning, however, a gloomy Alfred phoned Sherwood.

"How's the press? Now don't be specific, Lynn and I never read reviews and we don't want to know, but in general—?"

"Well, the *Herald Tribune* is pretty bad. I guess the *Times* is a little better—"

"For God's sake," roared Alfred, "ignore the *Trib*! It's only a substitute critic who doesn't know what the hell he's talking about. Now, have you seen Gabriel in the *American*? 'An evening of the keenest interests and pleasures our present-day stage can afford.' Or listen to John Mason Brown in the *Post*: 'Mr. Sherwood's best play. . . . The Lunts sweep everything before them.' "

Before he hung up Alfred had quoted every reviewer in town.

Distinguished critic and Round Tabler Heywood Broun caught up to *Reunion in Vienna* belatedly. In the past, when asked "Who is our leading dramatist?" he'd grudgingly named Eugene O'Neill. *Reunion* converted him. It was, wrote Broun in the *World-Telegram,* "the best play written by a living American. . . . I see no reason why I should not make Robert E. Sherwood my own choice as the leading American dramatist." As for Lunt's Rudolph, Broun considered him "one of the most glamorous characters known to the modern theatre. After all, no man is a fool when he comprehends the precise nature and dimensions of his own particular sort of folly."

Gratifying to Sherwood, but his experience with the Theatre Guild had left him disillusioned when a board member told him he knew nothing about psychiatry and must revise the character Anton Krug. In the long run, the Guild lost the argument. Sherwood would eventually band together with other disenchanted writers like Maxwell Anderson and S. N. Behrman to form the Playwrights' Company.

More immediately, influenced by Sherwood's unhappy experience and having their own issues with Guild control, Alfred and Lynn decided to quit the Theatre Guild after the run of *Reunion in Vienna.* Another inspiration was perhaps Katharine Cornell, who had leased the Belasco Theater in 1931 and gone successfully into management.

Meanwhile, they played through June 1932 to SRO crowds. Soup-kitchen lines snaked around corners, but the longest line waited patiently outside the Martin Beck Theatre to buy tickets for Lunt and Fontanne. A heat wave bothered Alfred: "it's so awfully disconcerting to kiss Lynn all over everywhere when she's so wet." Yet the play went flawlessly, except for the night Alfred flung up Helen Westley's skirt to view the red knickers and discovered she wasn't wearing them. His next line—"Thank God, there's something in Vienna that hasn't been changed!"—stopped the show.

Woollcott saw the play for the fifth time and wrote the Lunts: "When your grandchildren (on whom you have not made a really effective start) gather at your rheumatic knees and ask you what you did during the great depression, you can tell them that you played *Reunion in Vienna* to crowded houses and enjoyed the whole depression enormously."

In 1933 Sidney Franklin, who had directed the Lunts in *The Guardsman,* directed John Barrymore and the English actress Diana Wynyard in MGM's film of *Reunion in Vienna.* Long-dead reviewers tell the tale. Compared to Lynn Fontanne's champagne, Diana Wynyard was tepid milk. Barrymore's shenanigans lent the film its only spark; but those who saw them both say there was no comparison between Lunt's Archduke and Barrymore's.

In 1929 Alfred and Lynn had hired Ben Perkins as overseer at Genesee. Ben never thought of the place as "Mon Repos": too damn many chores. He was tall and handsome, with curly brown hair. Everybody loved him. He was blessedly articulate, typing Alfred long letters about the farm when the Lunts were away.

Alfred once fired a plumber because he wouldn't talk to him on the job. He loved an audience, loved to gab. He chuckled over local names like Dingledine and Iona Kock. A Dingledine girl, asked about her sick grandmother, said, "Oh, she's failing beautifully." That was as good as

Ben Perkins drives Alfred's pride and joy, his new tractor.

the neighbor boy's sighing when his mother died, "Pity, she had a lot of work left in her."

Then there was Grandma Jones, who wore sun bonnets and made Lynn one every summer. Grandma Jones had a surpassingly ugly nephew whom she adored. One Christmas he planned to toss her a present as the freight train passed through the depot on Christmas Eve. That night there was a blinding blizzard. Grandma Jones struggled to the depot through knee-high drifts. Finally the engine emerged through the driving snow. A hand waved; she glimpsed the beloved ugly nephew and caught the parcel he threw into her arms. "What was in it?" Alfred is rocking with laughter. "His photograph in a gold frame."

Now, in the summer of 1932, they hired Carolyn Every, a local girl jobless because of the Depression. Carolyn's mother ran an old hotel in Genesee where Alfred liked to take friends like Larry Farrell and Aleck Woollcott to eat her famous hamburgers. Carolyn had taken piano lessons from Louise and knew Hattie, so it seemed natural to hire her as assistant cook, secretary to Lynn, and nanny to the dachshunds Elsa and Rudolph.

Carolyn had some bumpy times. She got hysterics when the stew wouldn't boil on the woodstove, upsetting Alfred: "We don't need *another* prima donna in this house!" She adjusted to Alfred's frugality: like the French he threw bones and scraps into a big pot on the stove to simmer. Then Alfred's instructions for coffee must be obeyed to the letter:

> Hills Brothers regular grind coffee and a granite open coffee pot. For 8 cups of coffee, in a bowl put 8 large tablespoons of coffee, plus one for the pot. Break a fresh egg into the coffee grounds, add cold water to moisten, mix well. Measure 8 cups cold tap water into coffee pot, bring to full boil. Put coffee-egg mixture into pot and immediately stir with a long-handled spoon. The mixture will foam up: continue stirring while removing pot from heat until foam is stirred down. Let it remain at very low simmer for 7 minutes. Pot cover on pot, plug spout with paper so as not to lose any fragrance. *Never let it boil.* The coffee should be clear, and as Hattie says, the same brown color as a new saddle.

He also taught her how to make *rödgröt*—mashing and straining raspberries and currants, boiling them with a little cornstarch, chilling, then serving the glorious crimson pudding with sugar and thick sweet cream. Never had she tasted anything so delicious.

"For a brief, magical time," said Carolyn, "I became a part of the Lunts' lives."

Hattie was "a feisty old bat." There'd been a quarrel about a brown wig. "Mother, you have marvelous white hair," cried Alfred, throwing the wig into the woodstove. Now she wore it pulled back in a bun topped with a bow. She wore fluttering scarves and pretended to hear what people said, with hilarious results. Once when she made a three-layer cake she forgot the baking powder. When the cakes came out of the oven flat as pancakes, she threw them on the floor and stomped on them, much to Carolyn's delight.

Alfred was high-strung, charming, and obsessive, "with a wonderful sense of humor." When upset, he pitched his voice an octave higher and talked staccato through his nose.

Lynn knew what she wanted and gave Carolyn firm and gracious orders. "Her word was law." Soon Carolyn's work included massage and manicures.

Carolyn considered the good-looking, prematurely white-haired Larry Farrell a New York snob because he patronized the locals. She was also uneasy because he was gay, as was Alfred's friend the scene designer and painter Claggett Wilson, who came to Genesee to help decorate the cottage. "I loved the Lunts but I wasn't crazy about some of their friends," she said.

She liked fat, owly Alexander Woollcott because he could laugh at himself. Alfred got up at five to make him a pot of coffee which Aleck drank slowly on the cottage porch in bright orange pajamas in full view of Hattie's cook Margaret in the main house. "That man, Mr. Woollcott," said Margaret, "looks exactly like a big Halloween pumpkin sitting there every morning." Then Aleck went back to bed. That summer he had a favorite joke. "When Alfred dies he must be buried in a grand tomb in his native metropolis. It will become known as 'the bier that made Milwaukee famous.' "

Although Alfred wrote Bob Sherwood, "I'm pretty fed up with most of mankind. . . . I wish I had the guts to stay here the rest of my life," it was time for the autumn tour of *Reunion in Vienna*. After a week's run in Milwaukee—"It was like acting for the movies, that terrible silence. You couldn't believe the curtain was up"—Ben Perkins drove Alfred, Lynn, Larry Farrell, Carolyn, and the dogs to Chicago.

Neither Lynn nor Alfred drove. The story is that Alfred drove once, caught sight of a circus billboard, and cut across three lanes of traffic to study it up close, after which Lynn said "Never again." Actually, the couple had been photographed in their new Model T Ford honeymooning in Tomahawk, Wisconsin, Alfred at the wheel, Lynn smiling serenely. Yet Alfred gladly gave up driving. When he was driving, they couldn't rehearse.

They had taken a large gloomy apartment in the Ambassador Hotel for the Chicago run and Alfred immediately got on the phone and ordered lamb chops, whitefish, chickens, choice vegetables and fruits, special breads. Carolyn quickly learned the touring routine: breakfast at eleven, dinner at five-thirty, a midnight supper. Her jobs were preparing meals and walking the dogs. Lynn at least was a delight to cook for; she never complained.

Reunion in Vienna opened at the Erlanger October 24 and Chicago went wild. The distinguished critic Ashton Stevens called Lunt and Fontanne's "suave presentation" the "most brilliant performance visible on the American stage this season or last." During the three-week run they played to sold-out crowds, pulling in $20,000 a week, tickets $2.75. Only the *Daily News* objected to Sherwood's erotic dialogue and Lunt's sexual body language, though quoting one respectable first-nighter: "This is outrageous but—ho ho—it—he he—certainly is—ha ha—funny."

Meanwhile Alfred and Lynn had wired their old playmate Noël Coward: CONTRACT WITH THEATRE GUILD UP IN JUNE WE SHALL BE FREE STOP WHAT ABOUT IT? Noël was vacationing as the only passenger on a small freighter. He wrote *Design for Living* on board.

Winding up their *Reunion* tour in Philadelphia, the Lunts moved into a New York penthouse apartment in a hotel on the corner of Park Avenue and Thirty-eighth Street. Again Alfred got on the phone to a good grocery. He taught Carolyn to make his favorite fillet of sole: "Fish have to be heavily peppered always, then lemon juice, butter, a smothering of sweet cream and twenty minutes under the broiler." Carolyn had noted that in every city Alfred knew just where to find fresh-baked brioche, coffee ice cream, the juicy oranges he liked for breakfast cold, sliced very thin and sprinkled with sugar. Sometimes late at night he'd make a batch of bread for next morning's breakfast.

Design for Living would open in Cleveland on New Year's Eve, 1932. Lynn spent the days studying the script, reading novels, getting fitted for costumes. Alfred was painting the Ten Commandments on canvas to complete the Scandinavian walls of the cottage living room. "If Adam and Eve look alike," said Lynn, "it's because I posed for both of them." Noël was constantly in and out. There are times when a trio can be more intimate than a couple. This was one of them.

Not that the trio always played in harmony. Alfred thought Noël kind—always kind. Lynn, however, had to brace for attacks that caught her off guard. Noël could turn on her, she didn't know why. As for Noël, Alfred could drive him wild. "I can't do it! Get someone else!" Once Alfred had jumped through all his hoops he'd be superb, but the process was maddening.

Publicity photo for Design for Living, *1933*

Other unspoken tensions roiled this trio. The theater world knew Noël was gay. He never spoke of it publicly, but neither did he refrain from pursuing men. He understood the Lunt-Fontanne masquerade (and knew they loved each other), but was faintly disdainful of their sexual reticence. Perhaps this is why he called them "Grandpa" and "Grandma," signing himself "Junior." He was junior, but the nicknames also mocked their conservatism.

As for rehearsals, Noël vented his feelings in a delicious send-up. Alfred is flagellating himself, Lynn snapping at Alfred because she can't remember her lines. Desperate, Noël turns the tables:

NOËL: I shall never, never be able to play this part . . . I'm wrong. I haven't got the feel of it—when I watch you—you're so meticulous, so superb it takes the ground from under my feet.

ALFRED AND LYNN: No. No. No.

NOËL: Yes. Yes. Let's get somebody else and I'll just direct. Honestly—I'm so wretched—I shall never—

ALFRED: You're *wonderful*—you're going to be better than you've ever been in your life.

LYNN: You're so fluid and assured. You're a *beautiful* actor.
NOËL: No. No. No.
ALFRED: Yes. Yes. Yes. I'm the one who's going to let the play down.
NOËL: No. No. No.
LYNN: No. No. No.
ALFRED: Yes. Yes. Yes. I'm awful.
LYNN: No, darling, no. It's me not knowing my lines.
NOËL: What does it matter about lines?
ALFRED: Let's go back and start all over again.

Each believed the other two impossible while considering him- or herself a model of reason.

One day when Noël came to inspect Lynn's costumes, Alfred called Carolyn into the big bedroom to admire a floor-length cape. "As I came in the door," said Carolyn, "she was regally striding away from us with her graceful, long steps, the velvet cape falling in rich folds down to the floor. She got to the other end of the room and gracefully swung around toward us. The cape was open and she was stark naked!"

Nudity was fashionable in the thirties, as were sheep-gland injections ("I've got ewe under my skin"). Noël was an ardent practitioner: when he stayed with the Lunts he would stroll through the kitchen stark naked and out to the pool. Dorothy Parker spent a whole weekend at Aleck's Neshobe Island wearing only a hat. Despite her passion for clothes, Lynn enjoyed displaying her body. In Hollywood during *The Guardsman* Sidney Franklin had shot Lynn from behind, naked from the waist up. When a telephone rang on cue, Lynn whirled around, displaying bare breasts. "Cut!" shouted a startled Franklin. "But," said Lynn innocently, "I was just turning toward the sound of the telephone."

In Chicago the Lunts had chatted with Ashton Stevens about undress. Alfred was still nervous in the shirttail scene in *Reunion,* though he wore white satin trunks under the short tail. ("They were *my* silk trunks," Lynn reminded him. "You owned none.") Yet if they ever played *Antony and Cleopatra,*

"I'm all for having Lynn play Cleo naked from the waist up."
"I'd—like—that!" drawled Lynn with a sultry, lazy laugh. "I think that on the stage one's body should, when needs be, be as visible as one's hands. . . . I would strip for any part that required it. . . . In fact, I think I should very much enjoy playing Lady

Godiva, with nothing but a not too abundant wig and a reliable horse."

"A black horse, of course, for high visibility," laughed Alfred.

At Genesee Lynn liked to swim nude. Workers hung around until Alfred nailed up a sign prohibiting the Mermaid Pavilion during Lynn's pool hours. Lynn didn't ask for the sign. Bill Pronold, a local high-school kid, worked for the Lunts summers. One day Lynn called Bill up to her bedroom, where she was sitting stark naked under a large hat. She eyed him in the mirror. "How do you like my new hat, Bill?" (Bill was speechless.) It was not an isolated incident. Lynn's favorite hour to try on hats for Alfred was at bedtime, when she would come out of her dressing room with nothing on and say, "Do you like my new hat?" ("I always think of the hat just before I put my nightgown on," she explained.) And Alfred would say either "Yes, very much" or "No, not at all" or "Maybe you should wear higher heels with it"—and presumably roll over and go to sleep.

Now Lynn flings back the velvet cape for Alfred, Carolyn, and Noël. "Look at me," she seems to be saying; "I am beautiful, desirable." "Well, *really,* Lynn!" booms Alfred in his deep, slightly cracked baritone. One senses Lynn's sexual frustration, preparing for a play about the joys of sex.

Dedicated to Alexander Woollcott, *Design for Living* explores the amorous escapades of an unconventional trio of artists—"magic people." Leo, a writer, and Otto, a painter, are both in love with Gilda, who loves them in return, yet marries a convenient husband. Sheridan Morley once asked Noël whether *Design for Living* was a comedy about three in a bed. "Yes, of course it is," said Coward. Early on the trio had discussed playing the entire comedy in a gigantic bed, until Alfred "suggested a few stage directions which, if followed faithfully, would have landed all three of us in gaol." Coward left out the bed, but an unashamed ménage à trois was shocking enough in the thirties. Today Coward's subtext is clearly visible. Otto and Leo are in love with each other, possibly more than with Gilda.

LEO [*haltingly*]: The—feeling I had for you—something very deep, I imagined it was, but it couldn't have been, could it?—now that it has died so easily?

OTTO: Thank God for each other, anyhow!

LEO: That's true. We'll get along, somehow—[*his voice breaks*]—together.

OTTO: [*struggling with his tears*]: Together—

It was a daring play for Noël the international celebrity to write. Because of his professional partnership with Gertrude Lawrence, he was classified in the public mind as a sophisticated "bachelor"; yet he'd had flings with men, including Prince George, Duke of Kent, and currently was in love with John ("Jack") C. Wilson, to whom he had turned over the management of his American business affairs.

It was also a daring play for Alfred to star in, though Americans those days were naive. If a man was married he *couldn't* be homosexual. Besides, Lynn would be onstage with him, flirting, seducing, confirming his heterosexuality. Yet they were aware they were dealing with a controversial play, a dark comedy that jeered at conventional morality. But they were brave and bold. Their fame, their charm, their genius, would save the day.

The hilarious trio in Design for Living

The *Design for Living* company left for Cleveland by train an hour before midnight on New Year's Eve. Noël was directing his own play; the publicity was enormous, advance ticket sales sensational. Dressed to the hilt, a crowd of 1,550 packed the Hanna Theatre for the world premiere on January 2, 1933—"perhaps the chief dramatic event of the year both in America and England."

Backstage the protagonists paced in an ecstasy of nerves. Lynn whirled on Noël venomously, realizing what a perilous first entrance he'd given her—balancing a tray of coffee cups. "I suppose," she hissed, "if your house in Kent were invaded you'd send your mother out to face the guns!" They clashed again onstage, Noël eyeing Lynn's décolletage. "Lynn," he hissed, "your tit is out. I'm going to walk off this stage." In the wings Lynn whirled on him. "Noël, how many times have I told you not to talk to me when I'm still learning new lines!"

For a week Cleveland applauded *Design for Living,* as did Philadelphia and Washington. But Noël discovered that no matter how warm the audiences, Alfred and Lynn insisted on rehashing the performance after the final curtain. They criticized each other brutally as they ripped up their own performances. Fed up with "Oh, Noëlly, I was *terrible* tonight!" Noël learned to counter with "Well, *I* was wonderful!" They seldom left the theater before two a.m. Yet Coward fully realized he was working with the greatest high comedians in the theater.

The New York opening on January 24 at the Ethel Barrymore Theatre glittered. Old friends George C. Tyler, Laurette Taylor, Helen Westley, S. N. Behrman. Theater folk like Sam Shubert, Lillian Gish, Judith Anderson, Tallulah Bankhead, Arthur Hopkins, Antoinette Perry, Philip Barry, Guthrie McClintic. Round Tablers Alexander Woollcott, the Kaufmans, and Neysa McMein. Irving Berlin, Jerome Kern, Oscar Hammerstein. Even Amelia Earhart, fresh from her triumph as the first woman to fly alone across the Atlantic. And Hattie, magnificent in black velvet, waving her cigarette holder, critiquing the crowd. In front of the theater mounted police curbed the mob.

Design for Living has the now-nostalgic elements of clever 1930s comedy. Witty dialogue. Silver lamé gowns. Tuxedos. A modern penthouse. Pajamas and robes. Lighting of cigarettes and pouring of booze. Hilarity. A backbone of defiance, ego, and sophistication. Its chief asset, however, was the "incomparable trio" Lunt, Fontanne, and Coward dazzling New York with a kind of comedy acting that Broadway, said John Mason Brown, hadn't seen in years.

Some critics read Coward's subtext correctly, though their references to the homosexual theme were tentative and oblique. Atkinson called *Design for Living* "decadent," John Anderson "unholy." Gilbert Gabriel observed that the gentlemen were quite "Attic" in their mutual admiration. *The New Yorker*'s Wolcott Gibbs speculated that if the play ran to a fourth act Gilda might find herself out of luck as Otto and Leo paired off. In *The New Republic* Stark Young faulted Coward for thinking a brainy, sensitive woman like Gilda could be satisfied with Leo and Otto. Coward had shirked his theme. On the other hand, Percy Hammond of the *Herald Tribune* denied that Mr. Lunt and Mr. Coward felt more for each other than "a fervent friendship, tinged a little with the bizarre."

Then in March came Hiram Motherwell's critique in the *Theatre Guild Magazine.* "Did any play ever have such a dull first ten minutes? Why am I enjoying it? Lynn Fontanne, of course. I am enjoying even dullness because it gives Miss Fontanne a chance to triumph over it. . . . And I can't take my eyes off Alfred Lunt. I feel that he never knows what he is going to do next. And I feel Miss Fontanne always knows. Which is the more fascinating?"

As for *Design for Living:* "Brittle farce, humane comedy, vaudeville blackout, stewing emotional melodrama, and also a serious something which the author is always trying to say and never quite gets said." If Lunt and Fontanne were really going to do *Antony and Cleopatra,* as rumored, they couldn't rely on Coward's cheap bag of tricks.

But Motherwell's review did not raise the outrage created by an attack on Lunt and Fontanne in *Vogue* that claimed their acting could not compare with Coward's. "Beside the young British dramatist's suave, polished yet emphatic acting, Lunt's florid style suggests a circus poster beside a Corot," while Fontanne's acting was judged inferior to her work in recent years.

Telegrams deluged Alfred's and Lynn's dressing rooms.

Alexander Woollcott: IF I ONLY HAD THE COURAGE TO SAY IT FIRST.

John Ringling: WILL YOU CO STAR WITH MARIE DRESSLER COAST PRODUCTION PRIVATE LIVES NEXT FALL.

Theresa Helburn and Lawrence Langner: READ VOGUE TODAY ABSOLUTELY DELIGHTED WE'VE ALL THOUGHT THE SAME THING FOR YEARS.

Irving Thalberg: WHY NOT RETURN TO US?

Katharine Cornell: AGREE HEARTILY WITH VOGUE REVIEW.

George M. Cohan: LONG LIVE VOGUE.

Condé Nast: PLEASE FORGIVE BUT MY PUBLICATIONS CANNOT RUN COUNTER TO PUBLIC OPINION.

WHAT AN OUTRAGE, wired George Jean Nathan—then, in his own review in *Vanity Fair,* took *Design for Living* apart line by line, proving that Coward's best gags were straight from vaudeville, his wit stale, his philosophy shallow as gin in a drained martini glass, his naughtiness juvenile. But what Nathan really hated was the play's subtext. "I can see in it little more than a pansy paraphrase of *Candida,* theatrically sensationalized with 'daring' gay allusions to hermaphrodites, 'gipsy queens,' men dressed as women, etc. and with various due references to 'predatory feminine carcasses' and to women as bitches."

In April the *American Spectator* published Nathan's *Design for Loving,* a play with Lord Derek, a hermaphrodite; the Duke of Mintington, his father, an onanist; the Duchess, his mother, a lesbian; Daphne, his sister, a flagellant—and so on down the line. Nathan's parody was surely the most virulent attack launched on Noël Coward to date.

Alfred had private critics. Ray Weaver, now a professor of speech at the University of Michigan, reminded him that, like Bernard Shaw, he had once championed theater as a church to replace superstition with humanism. Coward had corrupted him. "Oh, nothing of the kind," Alfred replied. "Ridiculous. Noël had no such influence on me."

Lee Simonson was blunter. "I found the play the nastiest I have ever seen—all the more repulsive because the nastiness was so deliberately arch and coy." Homosexuals he didn't mind, "but a demi-homo is the most disgusting of God's creatures, particularly when he is as cute about it as Leo is. Leo was the personification of the most loathing and revolting human being I have ever seen on any stage—no doubt a triumph of acting. But I prefer yours."

Home free, but Alfred would never again play a role like Otto.

Backstage stories about the run of *Design for Living* abound. How Alfred dragged Noël to the theater with an inflamed throat and fever of 103, arguing that if he wasn't in the hospital he had to go on. How Lynn became so rapt reading an account in a prop newspaper of a sailor who'd murdered his girlfriend that she missed Noël's cue three times. How one night Alfred and Noël borrowed each other's lines throughout the whole drunk scene without the audience noticing. High on audacity, they stumbled offstage arm-in-arm to meet a stone-faced Lynn. "Nothing either of you said was remotely interesting," she declared.

Instead of rehashing the play after the performance, Alfred slunk to the nearest movie house. Halfway through the film he discovered Noël sitting in the next row.

The drunk-scene exchange has been cited to prove that the roles of Leo and Otto are interchangeable. Not true. First of all, Noël gave himself the best lines. Then, too, Otto is more affectionate toward Gilda, as Alfred would be. And Otto is nakedly sincere. But chiefly, Coward would never cast himself as the fall guy. Otto is twice humiliated when he finds that Leo is sleeping with Gilda and when Leo and Gilda laugh hilariously at the memory of Leo trying to drown him in a bathtub—a joke that rubbed many the wrong way. Otto leaves: hurt, disillusioned. It's as though Coward pitted two London sophisticates against an American rube.

During the run, Noël, Lynn, and Alfred appeared in another arena, riding elephants at a performance of the Ringling Brothers Circus in Madison Square Garden. How this came about is uncertain, but it was a dream fulfilled for Alfred, who adored circuses, had wanted to be an acrobat, and, after a visit to Ringling Brothers in Norfolk, Virginia, had dashed into the hotel shouting, "Lynnie, Lynnie, they let me drive a stake!" Unannounced, their appearance oddly complemented their own three-ring circus at the Ethel Barrymore Theatre.

Allergic to long runs, Noël had signed on for strictly 135 performances and no tour. The friends parted, with a wire from Noël on May 23:

DARLING ALFRED DAINTY LYNN
NOW THE HOLIDAYS BEGIN
THREE SUPERB BUT WEARY HACKS
COMFORTABLY MAY RELAX
NO MORE NEED TO BOW OUR FACES
UNDER GULLYS GRIM GRIMACES
NO NEED NOW TO STRAIN AND HUSTLE
TIMING LAUGHS FOR ETHEL RUSSELL
NO MORE SLAPS TO KEEP THE CHIN UP
NO LONG TRAINS TO TRIP OUR LYNN UP
LET US THANK BENIGN JEHOVAH THAT
THE LONG LONG TRAIL IS OVER

"In *Design for Living*," said Noël, "we all three gave the worst per-formances of our careers every night together for four months and man-aged to be very good indeed." Almost immediately he began another play for the Lunts. Yet acting with dainty Lynn and darling Alfred had been rather harrowing, as had some of the reviews. He would take him-self out of *Point Valaine*.

CHAPTER EIGHT

London—a Flop—a Hit: 1933–1936

Alfred and Lynn retreated to Genesee Depot for the summer. Divorced from Alonzo Pawling, Karin had married George Bugbee, a childhood sweetheart. When he'd asked Alfred's permission to marry Karin, Alfred had flung up his hands. "I hope you know you are marrying into a family of damn *fools*!" At least only Hattie and Carl remained on the payroll, Alfred still banking Carl at New York pool tables. Living in a big, semi-isolated house just north of the Lunts, Louise and Jack Greene now had two children, Johnny and Priscilla (Pee-Gee). Jack was often gone, Louise often lonely, particularly since she didn't drive. Terrifying and fun, Hattie entertained her grandchildren at afternoon tea.

Woollcott came to Genesee in paralyzing heat. Alfred was deep into making raspberry, currant, and blackberry jelly. He was also constructing walls out of round stones he called "cherub bottoms," trimming trees, making fences, and taking lessons in landscape painting from an area artist, Emily Groom. Only horseback riding would lure Lynn away from the tough anagrams Aleck ("the goddamn son of a bitch") assigned her. Afraid The Wit found her slow-going, she worked hard to please him. Aleck lounged, dashed off gossipy letters, and forged ahead with his book of essays *While Rome Burns*. (It would become a best-seller.)

Flush with the financial success of *Reunion in Vienna* and *Design for Living,* Alfred and Lynn continued to expand their Wisconsin home, moving Hattie into the Swedish cottage (immediately dubbed the Hen House). In the next years the main house would undergo multiple expansions until, said Alfred, "Even the levels have levels." They had added stables, a pasture, a wine cellar, and the Studio, a building made of old squared fir logs from a Swedish house, with a sleeping loft reached by ladder, a Scandinavian fireplace, and a wrought-iron chandelier of bells designed by Alfred. It became a place to take guests for after-dinner champagne and whisky, to talk theater or read scripts until three in the morning. The Studio evolved into a think tank, to which visiting playwrights like Sherwood and Behrman were consigned until Lunt and Fontanne accepted what they'd written.

As major changes to the house were unfolding, Lynn and Alfred were leaving the country. Coward's new play wasn't ready, and memories of their hit *Caprice* persuaded them to take *Reunion in Vienna* to London. Before that Alfred wanted to show Lynn Copenhagen, Stockholm, Helsingfors, and Moscow, then trek to Egypt with Noël before opening at the Lyric on January 3, 1934. "In these days you either spend your money or lose it in a bank," Lynn explained.

They left Genesee Depot loaded with luggage ("Positively Russian. We cried, all the maids cried, somebody tried to give us a pie to eat in the train"), arriving in New York September 14 to stay with Aleck: "We would like to sleep together as usual if you don't mind or do you?"

They met with a Theatre Guild eager to recapture their stars and agreed that if O'Neill, Anderson, Sherwood, or Behrman came up with a play they liked, they'd seriously consider signing on again with the firm. Meanwhile, their passports were missing. "First they wouldn't believe we'd been born," complained Alfred, "then they didn't seem to care." On the 17th they sailed on the *Bremen*. "Our first real holiday in years," Alfred explained to reporters. Yes, they were keeping their Wisconsin retreat; "keeping the mortgage too."

With Larry Farrell solving all their travel problems, the vacation was a dream. This was pre–hell travel: leisurely promenades on ship deck, porters toting label-plastered trunks to the best hotels, deferential service, orchestras serenading behind potted palms—above all, no crowds. It helped, too, to be famous. And both were travelers: Lynn inexhaustible, Alfred burning with appreciation. He eagerly sketched furniture and designs for the developing main house. When he fell in love with a pair of tall, exquisitely painted Swedish stoves, he bought them (and much else) to ship back to Genesee.

Russia was best.

"Moscow has completely ruined us," Alfred wrote Aleck: the incomparable artists, the opera, the ballet, the vodka, the caviar. Instead of five days they stayed nearly two weeks to see Russian theater at its height, the Moscow Art Theater's production of *Dead Souls* "the most perfect thing I suppose ever done in the theater." Russia's respect for the play and the director thrilled him. Lynn was equally impressed by the discipline of actors nurtured by the system.

Alfred also appreciated Russian tact. At the Bolshoi, Lynn loosened her skirt after too much borscht and blinis. It fell off as she exited the third row and hundreds of stoic people watched her walk up the aisle showing "two bare legs in a pair of very short little pants." (A deliberate striptease?) And the Russians showered them with gifts; they might have walked off with Ivan the Terrible's crown. "It's bleak and it's dark and it's strange. God knows but we loved it."

A week in London to recast *Reunion in Vienna,* then off in November with good friend actor Romney Brent to meet Noël in Cairo. They lurched off on camels into the desert, accompanied by iron beds with box springs, gourmet food, and a French chef, returning by way of Rome, Perugia, Florence: "Never laughed so much, never." In Paris buying gowns for Lynn, they met Harpo Marx, persuaded him to go to Russia, and saw him off at the station "harp, wig, knives & all." In London they moved into a charming Chelsea house at 15 The Vale (four servants and a French cook for fifteen guineas a week) and plunged into rehearsals. For the first time, the multigifted Alfred directed a production.

If possible, London adored Lunt and Fontanne in *Reunion in Vienna* more than America. But Alfred and Lynn were suicidal. One first-nighter had shouted, "Louder!" and though the whole audience had screamed, "We think you're both marvelous!" they were sure they'd blown the show. Worse were reviews like Ivor Brown's in the *Observer:* "A good play? Probably; but one simply does not care." These superb artists "raise each other to an ecstasy of comic invention. . . . Fortunate any man who has a play Lunt-bestarred." In the *Sunday Times* James Agate bowed low: " 'No grave upon the earth shall clip in it / A pair so famous.' I shall declare la Fontanne and le Lunt to be the greatest pair of stage-players now living."

"I hope you will not be embittered or angered over the press here," Alfred wrote Bob Sherwood. "My only reason for being in the theater either as an actor or as a director of acting—is to project the author—not obscure or use him for my own purpose but to clarify & brighten whatever *he* wishes to say—If I have failed you in this then sock me baby & let's call it a day."

But Sherwood had pretty much lost interest in *Reunion* except as a Lunt success. "You can sum my whole career," he would say: "I was lucky to have the Lunts."

So Alfred and Lynn settled in to enjoy the run. They adjusted to London audiences, who called out their reactions. When Rudolph says, "You don't mind my talking about myself, do you?" a man in the gallery shouted "No, not at all." And one night as Rudolph waltzed Elena into the bedroom, an old gent jumped to his feet roaring, "Lecherous mountebank!" Unlike American audiences, Brits appreciated the story more than individual lines and would shush patrons whose laughter interfered with it.

The Lunts themselves took some getting used to. Coming upon Lynn backstage slapping Alfred's face, a reporter stopped dead, not recognizing a rehearsal. "Oh, don't worry," said Lynn, delivering another wallop. "He's used to it." Onstage, columnists noted, Lunt could sometimes be temperamental, but Fontanne was "always flawless." Curiosity about this marriage of two such brilliant artists flourished.

Early in 1934 the Theatre Guild offered Alfred and Lynn a production of *Antony and Cleopatra;* they turned it down. Shortly afterward Jack Wilson arrived in London to propose that the Lunts and Noël form a production company, with Wilson as business manager and producer. Transatlantic Productions would share profits: if Noël or Jack had a hit, the Lunts collected, and vice versa. A stunned Guild read the announcement in the papers, but it wasn't necessarily excluded from the Lunts' future plans. "I suppose you know that Noël, Alfred and I have gone into management with Jack Wilson as business advisor," Lynn wrote Aleck, "and the company will operate under his name. The arrangement is very nice because it leaves us all perfectly free, that is, if another management has a play that Noël or Alfred or I want to do, we can. It seems to us the best way of investing our money at the moment. We are reading scripts like mad. . . ."

America's top gossip relayed his news. Moscow had almost killed

Harpo. Robert Sherwood had expelled his wife, Mary, "from his bed and board." Incomprehensibly, Aleck's play *The Dark Tower* had failed. He and Edna Ferber were having "a pretty brawl." A "hulking young prodigy" named Orson Welles was touring with Kit Cornell, who was making money hand over fist. Woollcott signed himself "Duckey Dee," rivaling Lynn's "Lovey dovey mashed potatoes" yet not quite matching Noël's "Rabbit's Bottom."

In March, too, Alfred and Lynn made the acquaintance of a man who would become a treasured friend. Hamish ("Jamie") Hamilton, head of the British firm, introduced them to Graham Robertson—friend of Bernhardt, Duse, Irving, and Terry. Painted by Sargent as an exquisite young man-about-London, Robertson was an intimate of Swinburne and Rossetti, painted elegantly himself, collected William Blake and Pre-Raphaelite masterpieces. He wrote charming memoirs published by Hamish Hamilton. A bachelor of sixty-seven, he lived on an unspoiled country estate, Sandhills, in Surrey, attended by his devoted cook, Mrs. Cave, his man William, and a series of sheepdogs named Bob. He was as stagsstruck as the Lunts. The attraction was instant.

> You see—until I really spoke with you, I could not quite believe in you: you seemed too good to be true and I felt that either I must have dreamed you or come across you in some previous existence when you were playing a long run in Lyonesse or Atlantis. . . . I have loved the theatre all my life and perhaps I am ever so faintly able to appreciate the wonder of your work. You build up Perfection—and then so completely remove the scaffolding that many people can hardly see the art and talk airily about "charming natural acting."
>
> Natural! Bless their innocence.

"I don't wonder that you 'cannot imagine the Lunts,' " he wrote a friend:

> . . . They possess the power that Scots call "glamourie"—the art of making that that is not appear to be that that is. Lynn Fontanne is a plain middle-aged woman. What she allows you to see is a beautiful woman of twenty-nine or thirty, exquisitely graceful and of ineffable charm. Lunt is an ugly, common-looking man with a podgy, fat figure and a face like an uninter-

*The Lunts with their
adored Graham Robertson
at Sandhills*

esting potato. He allows you to perceive this for a
moment . . . but after that minute you only see a charming fairy
prince, elusive, annoying, outrageous, but wholly fascinating.
The two together have enough charm to devastate London.

The new trio exchanged dinners at the Savoy and at Graham's
Knightsbridge flat, and Alfred managed a trip to Sandhills alone in
June. Graham showed him the Pre-Raphaelite paintings, the flower
and vegetable gardens, the peach tree Ellen Terry planted, theatrical
memorabilia, the latest Bob. "You gave me one of the happiest days of
my life," wrote Alfred, "and I shall *never, Never, NEVER* forget it. . . ."
They dined with Sibyl Colefax, the famous celebrity collector; with
H. G. Wells; often with Noël. They met Rebecca West and James
Hilton, had Somerset Maugham for supper ("We are mad about him"),
and were invited to Adelphi Terrace by James Barrie: "shy and sweet and
sly and altogether adorable." They adored London and were adored and
celebrated in return.

When Lynn reminded him their last night at the Lyric, "You'll be
traveling in the morning," Alfred broke down and wept during the
tremendous ovation that exploded at the final curtain. They had now

played *Reunion in Vienna* over five hundred times and had thoroughly conquered London. Yet for them both, "our greatest joy has been Graham Robertson."

They sailed for the States on July 3 on the *Ile de France*. At Genesee Alfred grew bronzed getting in wood and vegetables (except string beans: "I can't grow good beans and it breaks my heart"), while Lynn had something of a nervous collapse. She wouldn't talk theater; instead had French lessons and bought an English saddle and a chestnut gelding with "a divine gait" who carried her around the expanding estate. They had two new bathrooms put in the house for guests. "I hope to God you'll come out some day, you little bugger, and enjoy it," Alfred wrote Noël. Lynn tried to lure Aleck back to Genesee: "You can emerge in a flowing negligee & join us in song & dance or anything in fact that you like."

But Aleck was busy entertaining at his eight-acre Neshobe Island in Lake Bomoseen, Vermont, to which he was trying to lure *them*. Lynn was so off theater that Alfred went east alone to Dobbs Ferry to see Ethel Barrymore, at her request, in a tryout of *Laura Garnett*. Fighting middle age and alcoholism, Ethel could not carry the play to New York. "It was very sad—She was like a great Christmas tree left standing in a back parlor—long after New Year's." (YOU USED TO LIKE ME, wired Ethel. I WONDER WHAT HAS HAPPENED.)

Perhaps Lynn didn't want to talk theater because they were both deeply disappointed in Noël's new play. How to tell their pal they didn't like their parts or that *Point Valaine* itself was melodramatic? Alfred's sister Karin read it and immediately had a miscarriage. "Everyone was delighted and feel it is a good omen," kidded Alfred.

Militantly avoiding anything gay, Noël had created the macho Russian Stefan, a sexual beast who snorts, grunts, and grabs his woman around the knees. Sultry Linda Valaine, a hotel owner, simmers in the tropical heat and flings back her dark hair. The talented young Louis Hayward, playing a British pilot with whom Linda falls in love, completed this heavy trio. "It will never run," said Alfred gloomily. He swore as he struggled to learn the accordion. "The saxophone was a cinch compared to this goddam thing." Johnny and Pee-Gee rolled on the floor with laughter every time he hit a wrong note.

On October 1 Claggett Wilson arrived for six months to hand-paint murals on the interiors of the expanding main house—and stayed two years. But *Point Valaine* had to be faced, and they reluctantly tore themselves away from the creation of their masterpiece, finally to be christened Ten Chimneys because of the many Swedish fireplaces throughout the main house and cottage.

They opened at the Colonial Theatre in Boston on Christmas Day, Noël directing. The mood was apprehensive. Rehearsals had not gone well. Gladys Calthrop's sets were too heavy to move easily and had to be changed at the last minute. Flooding the whole stage at dress rehearsal, the rain machine had to be scrapped. The friends snapped at each other irritably.

The audience expected a sophisticated Lunt-Fontanne-Coward production. What they got was Alfred as a waiter in a dirty white suit who spits in Lynn's face and makes animal noises, and Lynn playing a voluptuous, powerfully sexed woman. "When I played Linda Valaine, I imagined I had slept with ten different men in the previous year," she told the biographer Maurice Zolotow. She was furious when Noël suggested that "Alfred had rehearsed me in sex appeal. Actually Alfred has never rehearsed me in anything. I usually come through with a performance *in spite* of him."

Lynn did come through brilliantly, but Boston didn't want to imagine Miss Fontanne sleeping with ten different men. Waves of disbelief, then hostility broke across the footlights. For once Alfred's pessimism about a play was on target.

In Philadelphia he had a very bad moment on stage. He was standing on a huge rock about to leap to his death when the scenery disappeared, including the mattress which was to break his fall. He had no choice but to stand on his rock and wait for the curtain to fall, cursing the stage manager, who'd signaled a set change prematurely. After the play he bolted from the theater and paced the streets for hours before returning to the hotel to inform Lynn and Noël: "You have just witnessed the end of my theatrical career."

Point Valaine opened at the Ethel Barrymore Theatre on January 16, 1935—with Alfred. New York didn't like it any more than the provinces. Though Alfred told Lawrence Langner, "The play got panned, but we are doing a roaring trade," trade collapsed after seven weeks, handing Transatlantic Productions a big loss. Critics recoiled at

Alfred's Stefan: "part serf, part gorilla, part faun," with black hair "in a sinister triangle over his forehead" and "sinister, rolling eyes." Lynn fared better. "Undulating like a serpent," she immediately took charge of the play and through her "clairvoyant performance" gave it, according to Percy Hammond in the *Herald Tribune,* its only interest.

Alfred and Lynn chalked up *Point Valaine* as their only flop—privately. When Worthington Miner, director of *Reunion in Vienna,* admitted he found Coward's play sordid, Lynn rounded on him. "You are the first intelligent person of the theatre to feel this way. Have you lined up with the critics?" Then, as Alfred stood silent, she venomously ripped into Miner as a director. Lynn attacked out of blind loyalty, as she often did. The Lunts revealed their real feelings, however, by not pasting one review of *Point Valaine* in their theater scrapbook.

Coward had the final analysis. *Point Valaine* "was neither big enough for tragedy nor light enough for comedy; the characters were well drawn, but not one of them was either interesting or kind."

The scramble for a new play was on. Alfred turned down Sherwood's adaptation of *Tovarich*—"It wouldn't stretch me, I've done that before"—as well as the Guild's offer of Shaw's *Captain Brassbound's Conversion.* "I wish Bob would write one for us," Alfred wrote Graham Robertson, "—something with a lot of music & costumes & dash & go—something even with villains & a death scene—Lynn always gets so upset when I die on the stage & it's enormous fun for me."

Although the number of Broadway theaters continued to dwindle, 1935–36 would be the most successful season since 1928–29: Helen Hayes in *Victoria Regina,* Katharine Cornell as Juliet to Maurice Evans's Romeo, Leslie Howard and Humphrey Bogart in Sherwood's *The Petrified Forest,* the Theatre Guild's *Porgy and Bess,* Judith Anderson in *The Old Maid,* Jane Cowl in *The First Lady,* a young Margo and Burgess Meredith in *Winterset,* which would win the first award from the New York Drama Critics Circle.

Eager to recapture the Lunts, the Guild tempted them again with Shakespeare. *Much Ado About Nothing* had been canceled due to "lack of rehearsal time," Lunt and Fontanne were still talking about *Antony and Cleopatra* and *Macbeth,* but nothing had happened. Alfred had "a lovely idea for *Twelfth Night*"—his favorite Shakespeare—but thought this was not the time. Suspicion deepened that they were afraid of Shakespeare.

Others didn't care about Shakespeare, only that in these Depression

years that pitted rich against poor, capitalism against a visionary social-
ism, Lunt and Fontanne were wasting their genius in plays like *Design
for Living,* "one of the hollowest farragoes ever seen in the Western
Hemisphere." "Personally," Kyle Crichton, biographer of the Marx
brothers, had written in 1933 in an open letter to America's best actor,

> I should like to see you and Miss Fontanne in a good rousing
> proletarian drama . . . but even that isn't necessary. You can be as
> reactionary as you like if you will only promise to act in plays
> which are *about* something. . . . I am further convinced that a
> repertory theatre headed by Miss Fontanne and yourself would
> bring you the support of our finest playwrights, not to mention
> the new ones you would stimulate. . . . You have no financial
> worries; you are supreme on Broadway. All you have to worry
> about now is the fate of the American theatre itself and your
> place in history. A failure by Alfred Lunt in a great cause would
> be a triumph for the American stage. But you won't fail. The
> times are yours; they are made for you; all you need do is take
> advantage of them.

Seemingly, Alfred had ignored the appeal. And with Shakespeare,
Lunt and Fontanne compromised. Alfred was in the mood for music,
costumes, dash and go. *The Taming of the Shrew* fit that mood. After two
years they came back to the Guild on their terms. Transatlantic Productions shared profits; the Guild assumed production responsibilities.
Future plays were the choice of Lunt and Fontanne, not the Guild. And
no board member was to lay a finger on their conception of *The Taming
of the Shrew.* If Alfred and Lynn wanted midgets, acrobats, horses,
hounds, and bass drums, they would have them.

In 1887, the year Lynn was born, Ada Rehan and John Drew had
played their popular Kate and Petruchio for 137 consecutive performances at Daly's. Neither Alfred nor Lynn had seen the play since they
were children, so they came to Shakespeare's early comedy as though it
were a brand-new script. Both wanted their *Shrew* to be a bawdy
romp—as it must have been in Shakespeare's day. Since Shakespeare
provided no "business," the Lunts would do just what they liked—
Petruchio skipping rope with a string of sausages, Kate stuffing
oranges down her décolletage. Actors would interact with audience:
staring at latecomers, coughing at coughers, encouraging laughter.

Alfred and Lynn insisted on restoring the "Induction" in which Christopher Sly is tricked into believing he is a lord for whom a traveling band of players wishes to perform. This shifted the emphasis from the courting of Kate to the drama of actors performing a play. The entire cast doubled roles, playing not only Petruchio, Bianca, Tranio, and Baptista but actors performing for a drunken tinker. Missed cues, flubbed lines, wrong entrances, became as much of the plot as Petruchio's taming of the shrew. The play took on, said Lynn, "a fairy-tale quality like the Russian ballet, coupled with the naive, bawdy humor of the times."

At casting there was a young man who wanted to read every part from Tranio to the Widow. Alfred and Lynn didn't know what to do with him, only knew they must have him because of his obvious talent. Richard Whorf was signed on.

Alfred insisted that Claggett Wilson drop his paintbrush at Genesee to design the scenery and costumes. Wilson let himself go for Alfred's getups: barber pole–striped tights, knee-high laced boots, and (Alfred's suggestion) a rooster planted in his hat. For scenery Wilson painted good old-fashioned drops that absolutely delighted Alfred, though he worried how the New York press would react to their irreverent and original treatment of the Bard.

They opened in Pittsburgh at the Nixon Theatre on April 22, 1935, Alfred refusing to bring the *Shrew* to New York until problems had been ironed out on the road. Pittsburgh received the play with a roar, cheering for five minutes at the end of the first act. From Cincinnati to Toronto excitement built; again the Guild begged the Lunts to bring the production into New York. By now, however, neither Alfred nor Lynn would be denied their summer rest at Ten Chimneys, and the company disbanded on May 25. They'd worked terribly hard on the *Shrew* since March; Alfred was in a state of semi-exhaustion; Lynn in pain from a torn knee cartilage. The physical battles between Petruchio and Kate surpassed Lunt and Fontanne's brawling in *At Mrs. Beam's,* and they were nine years older.

Claggett Wilson also returned to Genesee to continue work on the interior of Ten Chimneys. In contrast to the bold reds, greens, yellows, and blues of the Cottage, Wilson worked in apricot, moss green, medium blues, pale yellows. For the walls of the great drawing room Alfred and Lynn had chosen biblical scenes. Although Catholic ceremony had made a vivid impression on Alfred when he was

Alfred and Lynn help Claggett Wilson paint a drawing-room wall at Ten Chimneys.

a child, neither he nor Lynn was conventionally religious. Religious decoration was traditionally Swedish, however, and Alfred copied motifs from Scandinavian houses and buildings. Biblical scenes were also dramatic. Visitors noted that the Old Testament figures looked rather like Alfred and Lynn.

Alfred sometimes climbed a ladder next to Wilson. More often he "went into the land," in one day picking a bushel of peas and twenty-nine quarts of raspberries and currants for *rödgröt*. He sat on his garden wall and picked off chipmunks with his rifle. "Don't tell Lynn," he warned Ben Perkins. "She feeds them on the patio."

After breakfast at their separate houses, Alfred and Hattie would stroll the property to discuss the dinner menu, served now at the main house when Alfred was creating a special dish. Hattie urged a plan. She was a good cook, her son a great cook. They must do a cookbook together. Alfred groaned and set about perfecting his Bombay Bisque and Roast Leg of Lamb with Coffee. "Pots and pans have been flying around these days."

They left for the East that August. Noël was making a Ben Hecht–Charles MacArthur film, *The Scoundrel,* on Long Island. Aleck was in the cast, so he invited Edna Ferber, George Jean Nathan (who'd publicly called Coward a pervert), and the Lunts to mingle as extras in a crowd scene. Then to Aleck's fabled Neshobe Island, where the beautiful crowd battered each other at croquet and whiled away nights at word games or poker. "Bitch delivered of a drab!" squeaked Aleck when he lost a hand. And all the while Alfred agonized over the New York opening of *Shrew.*

That September 30, 1935, first-nighters crowding into the Guild Theatre were handed a momentous playbill:

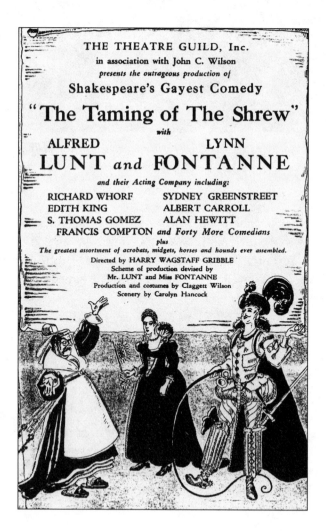

"It was the Lunts' somewhat radical notion that *The Shrew* needed gaiety and bounce," wrote *Time.*

> . . . In true Elizabethan style, the tale of Petruchio and his truculent bride Katharine is interrupted from time to time while tumbrils, a tenor, a troupe of midgets take the stage. Within the play itself, the Lunts have felt free to bring in any amount of extraneous horseplay that might add freshness and fun to their antic. Thus, as plain Kate, bonny Kate and sometimes Kate the curst, Miss Fontanne stalks about in a torn white gown with hair in her eyes, kicks people in the fundament, hurls bedding out a second-story window, rides a fake horse, makes an exit seated backward on a donkey. Whereas most actresses play the Paduan minx as though she were a frustrated psychopath, Miss Fontanne plays her as though she were a young filly simply spoiling for a good licking. Since for the past decade one of the most amusing specacles on the U.S. stage has been Mr. Lunt licking Miss Fontanne, their fantastic rowing in *The Taming of the Shrew* is something to see. Also something to see is the chariot at the finale, their quarrel mended, headed upward through a painted sky to further and more fabulous adventures.

First-nighters agreed that the funniest, most charming play now in Manhattan had been written in England three centuries ago.

Today *The Taming of the Shrew* does not always go down well with playgoers, many of whom consider Petruchio a chauvinist. Alfred Lunt, however, could never be a chauvinist. He injected depth and sensitivity into the swaggering role. G. B. Stern remembered that after Petruchio thoroughly thrashed Kate, who left the stage in tears, "Petruchio suddenly collapsed from sheer weariness and leaned exhausted against the door . . . by his complete surrender conveying how hatefully the masquerade had gone against the grain, and that he loved Kate, really loved her, but in carrying on in this abominable fashion until she capitulated lay their only hope of ultimate happiness."

As for Kate, "She is not written angrily enough to convince a modern audience," said Lynn, who decided to match Petruchio "with a shrew that is a shrew—a yowling, kicking, biting hellion projected into the play like a bat out of hell." *Esquire's* critic felt that Lynn's Kate

Kate and Petruchio in
The Taming of the
Shrew, *1935*

"remained unconquered, and that shortly after the curtain fell she would get revenge for hardships and humiliations by beating the hell out of her spouse." In conveying the equality of the sexes, Lunt and Fontanne gave their 1930s audience a thoroughly contemporary production. But then, there was always something aristocratic and dominant about Lynn, humble and beseeching about Alfred.

They had proved what they could do with their own production and company. People like Dickie Whorf, Alan Hewitt, Sydney Greenstreet,

Edith King, and Tommy Gomez would stay with them for years. Alfred was particularly fond of the enormous Sydney. In *Shrew* they began a game that continued over several productions. After a speech, Alfred or Sydney would take a step backward—one step only allowed. The game was to see who could get to the backdrop first. Needless to say, the audience wasn't in on the competition, and surely Lunt with more speeches won.

That fall Alfred agreed to join the Guild board if his duties did not interfere with performances. "I can learn a hell of a lot. . . . There are certain things, mostly financial, in the theater that I want to know about." This meant sitting down with people who had often frustrated him in the past. In part Alfred was conscripted to break three–three deadlocks between the opinionated directors. More importantly, the Guild recognized his broad theatrical talent. He received "a neat little check each week" and the power to vote and advise on play productions.

Privately Lynn was involved with a Christmas surprise for Aleck— nothing less than one of the Spanish capes that Graham Robertson wore so elegantly. Letters flew across the Atlantic. When she announced Graham was sending his very own cape, there was "a trenchant silence and Alfred said in a small voice: 'It's a shame to give it to Aleck.' "

"To Aleck it goes," cried Lynn, "and to nobody else. And nobody else will know and appreciate the beauty of it so fully." Still, Lynn hammered out a cape clause for Alfred:

1. That if we do a Spanish play Alfred is allowed to wear it.
2. That it is to be willed to us.
3. That [Aleck] wears it always in the evening.

Shrew played to full houses for two months, then to slightly smaller crowds. The Guild decided to send it on tour in January 1936 to Boston and Chicago before packing up the production. Ashton Stevens called Chicago's two-week booking "a crime" against show business and against the city, as hundreds were turned away from the box office. He marveled how Lunt and Fontanne's total belief in Shakespeare's "horseplay classic spreads out over the stage and affects a whole huge company of actors, from the superbly snorting Sly of Richard Whorf to the larded and bronchial Baptista of Sydney Greenstreet to the melodiously stylized Bianca of Dorothy Mathews to the four marvelous dwarfs. This is more than play-casting, it is spell casting. It justifies the use of the word magic."

Alfred and Lynn didn't object to the short Chicago run of "the old flapdoodle farce"—particularly since Lynn suffered bumps and bruises in almost every performance. And they were rehearsing a new play that was "passionately anti-war, marvelous theater and a very exciting story."

CHAPTER NINE

Idiot's Delight and Amphitryon: 1936–1938

Oh dear, now we are in for another war," Lynn had written Graham Robertson in October 1935, "and God knows what effect that will have on our being able to elude mines and torpedos and get to London for a season soon. Don't let England go to war, Graham, please! Write one of your beautiful letters to the Houses of Parliament and stop it all."

Most Americans would not recognize the catastrophe until Hitler swept through Poland in 1939 (or even then). Robert Sherwood, however, was acutely aware of the worldwide threat of fascism in Germany and Italy. Set in an Italian hotel in the former Austrian Alps "in any imminent year," his *Idiot's Delight* captures twenty-four hours in the lives of people trapped in the chaos of impending war. The hotel itself suggests "a vague kind of horror" in its sleek chrome impersonality (designed by Lee Simonson), as does the view from its windows of cold white mountain peaks and black firs. The roar of bombers from an army airport nearby drowns the four-piece orchestra's dismal rendition of "June in January."

Alfred had given Sherwood the idea for *Idiot's Delight.* "You could put us in Budapest this time—say a Chicago punk on his way to Bucharest to put in those old slot machines or a former 'barker' now managing a troupe of midgets—who meets the elegant fakiress between a couple of hot violins and a zimbalum. Easy! Bobby, you could do it on your ear."

The barker turned into Harry Van, a "thoughtful, lonely American vaudevillian promoter" who has shilled many things in his life, never quite honestly. Currently he is trying to sell his act, Les Blondes, from the Balkans to Geneva. Harry Van is kind, decent, intelligent, warm, funny, and sad—like Alfred Lunt. Yet:

"I never play myself in a part—at least I never mean to," said Alfred. "I pieced [Harry Van] together—accent, personality, appearance—from three people I used to know in vaudeville." He envisioned Van full of "forced bravado" and "eagerness to please," with a pasty face—"the look you see on men around Times Square who don't get out enough into the air—and black, shiny hair, slicked back around graying edges."

To make the role a challenge, Harry Van also sings, tap-dances, spiels, and wisecracks. At Nicky Blair's Paradise Restaurant in New York, the comic Milton Berle became acutely aware of a man who came to see his act night after night. Finally Berle asked the maître d' to send him to his dressing room. The man came, "sort of average-looking, hair getting a little thin on top."

"You must think I'm quite insane, coming here every night to watch you."

"Hey, watch it," said Berle. "People don't come to steal from me. That's my line of work."

The man explained that he was doing research for a play. "Oh, forgive me, my name is Alfred Lunt."

Alfred Lunt! Berle thought he had a fan—Lunt had a fan! Berle was so overwhelmed by the compliment that he signed on to work with Alfred for several weeks to teach him movements, timing, touches. Alfred sought out one of his heroines, Sophie Tucker, "the Last of the Red Hot Mamas," for voice lessons. Morgan Lewis taught him tap and soft-shoe. Alfred was like a man who'd never had a cocktail, said Lynn, then has four at once and discovers he's been a dipsomaniac all his life. The dance climax would come when Van, blowing kisses, is carried off by six blondes in ruffled purple short-shorts and green garters.

Harry Van also plays the piano, but Alfred refused to go that far. Lee Simonson rigged up a fake baby grand and set it against a stage flat representing a wall. Through a hole in that wall a professional pianist would do the playing as he watched Alfred's hands on the keyboard.

As for Lynn, "We've got to do it, Alfred," she'd said, eyes shining, "we really must do this, it's most interesting and exciting."

"How is your part?"

"I haven't come to it yet."

Lynn didn't mind that Irene (pronounced Ee-RAY-na) doesn't really make an impact until Act Two. "I like it better than any play I have ever been in and consider it by far Bob's best." She would play the adventuress Irene in a blond Garbo wig and sweeping black eyelashes, with a long cigarette holder (à la Hattie) as her main prop. The New York–based Russian designer Valentina (Nikolaevna Sania Schlee) designed the stunning costumes. "Ve must have blenty skink," declared Valentina. "Eet ees soch a Rooo-ssian vur."

Irene was a complex character: brash, unscrupulous, brave, disillusioned. She is the companion of an arms dealer, the dame who once slept with Harry Van at the Governor Bryan Hotel in Omaha, a woman who can say, "Oh, you must see this! It's superb!" when bombs rain from the sky.

Yet Lynn felt that Sherwood hadn't fully drawn her portrait. "She was like a paper cut-out," she complained. Sherwood encouraged her to fill in the details herself. After Lynn made Irene a Cockney with a phony Russian accent she felt more at home in the part—learning her accent from Princess Natasha Paley, whom Jack Wilson (to Noël's dismay) was courting. Whatever her complaints about her role, after *Shrew,* she told Graham, *Idiot's Delight* was for both of them "like lying on a feather bed and being served by William with some of that there cherry brandy." Alfred she considered "simply superb. Quite one of the best things he has ever done."

They chose Bretaigne Windust (from the cast of *Shrew*) as director because he would keep out of Alfred's way. Alfred intended *Idiot's Delight* to be actor-motivated, yet was himself the dominant figure at all times. Puffing one of his favorite Lucky Strikes, he directed the actors to stop concentrating on the text and start connecting with each other. They must talk gibberish, move only when they feel motivated. They must communicate by touch, look, and tone.

Alfred himself was an extremely tactile actor—leaning toward an actor as he listened intently, reaching out to brush a cheek with his fingertips, encircling a shoulder with his arm. He was also deeply musical, shaping a scene by nuances of forte, pianissimo, diminuendo. Once, Dickie Whorf recalled, he rehearsed them endlessly, then said, "Now let's try it an octave higher." Directing *Idiot's Delight,* he taught the large cast to interact by proximity, emotion, and pitch.

Again the Guild would bill the production as "Conceived and Super-

As Irene and Harry Van in Idiot's Delight, *1936*

vised by Mr. Lunt and Miss Fontanne." Yet how did Lynn like being directed by Alfred? "He irritated me," she said bluntly. "He showed off." Elliot Norton, a Boston theater critic for forty-eight years, remembered Lunt and Fontanne rehearsing. "Lynn Fontanne was brilliant in the sense that whereas Alfred did all the talking, all the theorizing, Lynn could listen. She understood how to put the character Alfred Lunt wanted on the stage—every intonation, phrase, facial expression, body movement." "I have great faith in Alfred," she once told Norton. But he could drive her crazy. "When he is directing he expects me to know it all. He tells me things over his shoulder—very cursory." He especially drove her crazy when he tried to direct her when they were being directed by someone else.

Most of the cast were from *Shrew,* the nucleus of the company the Lunts had gathered around them: Richard Whorf (revolutionary Marxist), Thomas Gomez (hotel owner), Sydney Greenstreet (German scientist), George Meader (waiter), Alan Hewitt (Italian officer). The lack of core actresses can be explained by both the predominance of male roles in most plays and Lynn's lack of enthusiasm for female competition.

The cast loved the play; Lunt and Fontanne loved it; Sherwood believed in it. Enter the Guild board, critical to the point of driving author and actors insane. Simonson and Langner did not think Sherwood could hang a war play on the slight shoulders of a shill's encounter with an adventuress. Bombers bound for Paris clashed with six blondes hoofing it to Irving Berlin's "Puttin' on the Ritz." Since surreal contrasts are exactly what gives *Idiot's Delight* its power, Sherwood fought back long and hard. Approaching a door behind which Bob was heatedly battling the board, Alfred stopped dead. "Oh, shit!" they heard him groan.

Alfred didn't back off; Sherwood didn't, either. Gradually the Guild realized that neither its presence nor its criticisms were welcome. This was Sherwood's play, but even more it was Lunt and Fontanne's: they were co-partners of Transatlantic Productions, they were wildly popular, they could walk away anytime. The Guild buttoned its lip.

Idiot's Delight opened out of town on March 9, 1936, at Washington's National Theater after a rocky final rehearsal where everything went wrong. Alfred finally called cast and crew onstage. "We will not give a performance tonight nor tomorrow night. We will not open this play until it is ready. We will stay here if it takes all day and all tomorrow night and we won't leave the theater until we get it right." Exhausted from coordinating bombs and machine-gun fire with Harry and Irene's last scene at the piano (ironically singing "Onward, Christian Soldiers"), the stagehands took heart and worked until the problems were solved at five-thirty the next morning.

Finally it was the first-nighters' belief that they were in for another magical Lunt-Fontanne experience that inspired cast and crew. "We gave a performance the like of which I, for one, have never been able to produce from the nerves of an opening night and everybody else tells me they felt the same," Lynn wrote Graham Robertson. "The consequence was that Bob's beautiful play went over with a bang. We took fifteen or sixteen curtain calls and the whole thing was a great triumph."

From Washington to Pittsburgh, where they were almost washed away. ("There are two weekends I don't play," said Cornelia Otis Skinner: "Easter Sunday and Pittsburgh.") The best account is Graham Robertson's:

The Great Flood arrived one evening. They heard it rush into the lower parts of the theatre, then all the lights went out and they had to get away as best they could. They escaped from Pittsburgh all right, but thought they had lost all their scenery, which was engulfed. Alfred suddenly became heroic and said: "We must open [in New York]. If we have no scenery we'll play without it," and became so worked up and over life-size at the idea of putting the whole thing over themselves with no aids from illusion that, when the rescued scenery did turn up just in time, he was quite disappointed. A very Alfredian touch—the eternal schoolboy.

They opened triumphantly at the Shubert on March 24. Hattie made an entrance in high heels and snug black gown, asking loudly, "*Idiot's Delight*—does that refer to the actors or the audience?" In a packed, excited house Milton Berle watched his pupil triumph with a father's pride. John Mason Brown in the *Post* gave Alfred his due:

> As for Mr. Lunt, he herewith takes his place among this depart-ment's favorite hoofers. He hurls himself ingratiatingly into his dance routines with a verve that is equalled only by his grace. He obviously enjoys spoofing the mannerisms of the floor-show artists. And every one enjoys him. But there is more than danc-ing to his performance. His hoofer is a deeply conceived creation. In spite of the gaiety he commands, he is poignantly projected and shows that Mr. Lunt has approached—and understood him—from within.

But *Idiot's Delight* was not just Lunt and Fontanne. The *Telegram* thought that Richard Whorf as the French Communist walked off with the honors. Sydney Greenstreet's Dr. Waldersee was also much admired, as was Barry Thomson's hotel social director and Bretaigne Windust's young Englishman. In the *Sun* Richard Lockridge declared *Idiot's Delight* "one of the best productions the Guild has given to any play"—not realizing how little the Guild had been involved. No won-der Alfred could say, "Theater is more alive than it's been for quite a while. Why—it's simply bursting with health and possibilities."

Again Alfred and Lynn found themselves apologizing to Sherwood for the reviews. "Hokum of the highest type," said *Time,* while *The Nation* deplored "gaudy situations" and "old gags"—missing the point that Harry Van *would* tell old gags. This negativism was partly due to the fact that before *Idiot's Delight* opened in New York, critics had split into Robert Sherwood and Maxwell Anderson camps. Anderson's poetic, exalted *Winterset* won the Drama Critics Circle Award in April to "howls and insults from the *Idiot's Delight* faction." Dedicated to

Harry Van hoofs it with Les Blondes in Idiot's Delight.

Lynn and Alfred, *Idiot's Delight* won the Pulitzer "as the drums of discontent were beating wildly." Among other things, Sherwood's drama was called "un-American" since its "only American character is a song-and-dance man accompanied by a moronic blonde."

"Dear Bob," wrote Alfred:

> . . . I didn't even cable after the awarding of the Pulitzer Prize as I didn't feel you genuinely cared whether you got it or not & personally I didn't give a Goddam—The award didn't affect business. . . . The public just knew it was good—all by its stupid little self—I wish I had the unselfishness to write you in detail all the splendid things people say—Nazimova has seen it twice & is coming again—Howard Lindsay broke down like a baby & cried his head off in the dressing room . . . Edna Ferber is still carrying on like mad over it—as is Alec. . . . Helen Hayes loved it and Ruth Gordon and Thornton Delehanty and, oh shit Bobby make out your own list—

That spring, depressed by their furnished apartment ("Each piece is a small mausoleum," said Ferber) and sure of a long run when *Idiot's Delight* reopened, Alfred and Lynn took a year's lease on an apartment at 130 East Seventy-fifth Street. Dickie Whorf, a talented watercolorist, helped Alfred paint Swedish polychrome trees, plants, and figures on citron-yellow walls. Claggett Wilson designed and painted Swedish Queen Anne furniture, as well as creating frost patterns on window-panes with Bon Ami. Lynn went out and bought a six-foot-six-by-five-foot bed—"and why not?" (Lynn often stressed that she and Alfred shared a bed.) She papered a small sitting room cinnamon brown, hung sulfur curtains, chose crystal light fixtures for the walls.

Edna Ferber described a Lunt-Fontanne midnight party for eight in the new apartment, with a Hungarian quintet accompanying a supper of sour-cream-and-caviar blinis, tiny lamb chops, julienne potatoes, salad, ice cream, and cake—"the orchestra playing anything we wanted to hear. It was divine." (Another Lunt dinner for only Ferber and Woollcott was a disaster. They were feuding—"Why would anyone call a dog a bitch when there's Edna Ferber around?"—and eventually didn't speak for nine years.)

Alfred was happy because Lynn now breakfasted in bed, something she couldn't bear to do in their former "hideous quarters." When they weren't decorating or reading plays or changing lines in *Idiot's Delight* or walking Elsa and Rudolph, they went to the movies. They were huge Gary Cooper fans.

Then Alfred's "Goddam kidney" began to act up again (a lifelong problem) and he took to his bed, though he'd "never had an ounce of talent for leisure." Bed gave him time to fret over physical and cosmetic decline: "my face does grow more & more like an old punching bag every day." They both looked forward to Woollcott's island in late August, gatherings that were "half orgy, half idyll."

Idiot's Delight reopened August 31 to standees, cheers, a dozen curtain calls, and Pearl Buck coming backstage to say she wanted to write them a play. Concerned that some critics had not understood Irene, Lynn had sent Sherwood new lines that made Irene, she argued, "less of a silhouette"—then used them without his consent. "I do hope you approve the little scene Lynn added to the play last night," Alfred wrote Bob. "If you don't, you're crazy!"

This high-handedness seems to contradict Alfred's insistence that "the actor is not a creative, but an interpretive artist. His one and only job is to work within the play, to translate the ideas of the author." Yet Alfred and Lynn sincerely believed they were working for the good of the play. As Alfred argued: "People who came back last night who were seeing the play for the second or third time, said they did not know why but the play seemed finer and clearer and more immediate than ever before." Tough on the authorial ego when actors improve a work, yet from all evidence the Lunts did improve *Idiot's Delight*. And, as Sherwood knew, they would be tinkering when the curtain fell on its last performance—and so would he.

Despite Helen Hayes's great performance in *Victoria Regina* and Kaufman and Hart's popular *You Can't Take It With You, Idiot's Delight* did the biggest business on Broadway that season of 1936–37. The year also featured a British invasion that would swell in coming years, with actors like Ralph Richardson, Robert Morley, Alec Guinness, Maurice Evans, Basil Rathbone, Charles Laughton, Ronald Colman, and Laurence Olivier storming American boards. John Gielgud's sublimely poetic Hamlet ran 132 performances this season (Leslie Howard's collapsed after 39). Emlyn Williams scored in his play *Night Must Fall,* Maurice Evans as Napoleon in *St. Helena.*

And Noël returned triumphantly in *Tonight at 8:30,* a series of short plays starring the Master, as he was now called, and Gertrude Lawrence. "*Family Album,* delightful," Lynn wrote Graham; "*Fumed Oak,* not so good except for the acting; but, *Astonished Heart!* What a lovely play and what perfect acting."

The British invasion emphasized what some historians call "the feminization of the American theater." At the turn of the century Richard Mansfield, Walter Hampden, William Gillette, Joseph Jefferson, James O'Neill, Maurice Barrymore, and Otis Skinner had dominated. They gave way to actresses like Laurette Taylor, Ethel Barrymore, Eva Le Gallienne, Nazimova, Helen Hayes, Katharine Cornell, and Lynn Fontanne. Though there were good actors on Broadway in 1936, talents like Tyrone Power, John Garfield, and Preston Foster would choose Hollywood. Alfred Lunt had few, if any, rivals. Moreover, he added to the feminization by teaming with Lynn Fontanne.

In contrast, British theater seethed with more male talent than it had ever known. "I have often wondered whether the comparative scarcity of American star actors does not spring from the very structure of their civilization," mused Peter Daubeny, British producer and friend of the Lunts. "England is a country, after all, where men are still dominant, and the women look up to them. Is it just a coincidence that England produces few enough good actresses, and any number of talented actors?" Alfred Lunt he considered "a class apart" among American actors.

In early February 1937 the *Idiot's Delight* company played Philadelphia on the first lap of a twenty-two-week tour that would take them from Boston to San Francisco. Everywhere full houses were "stricken with delight."

In Chicago in May Alfred and Lynn were to receive a distinguished-achievement award for their work in theater and service in the cause of peace. Alfred fretted over his speech. "I am inarticulate without an author to write some lines for me!" "Oh, please!" groaned Lynn. "That's what every actor says!"

When it came her turn to thank the committee for the award, however, Lynn froze. "I don't know what to say," she faltered. "I never made a speech before. I—I—I am bereft of speech without an author to write one for me." Alfred grinned wolfishly, then rose to speak.

"I can't think of anything appropriate to say," he began with a winning smile. "My mind is like one of those untidy sewing baskets, and strangely enough the only thing that keeps running through it is a recipe for roast lamb." The audience pulled out pencils. "Rub a leg of lamb with salt, pepper, and one-half teaspoon mustard, and roast. When it's half done, drain off the juices and add one cup of coffee and cream and sugar for basting, then finish roasting."

In Omaha the mayor announced that "five curses and three epithets" must be expurgated from *Idiot's Delight* before it opened at the Paramount. Irene's "She is lying in a cellar that has been wrecked by an air raid, and her firm young breasts are all mixed up with the bowels of a dismembered policeman, and the embryo from her womb is splattered against the face of a dead bishop" also had to go.

But Mayer Butler chiefly objected to Harry Van and Irene fornicating at the Governor Bryan Hotel in Omaha.

Idiot's Delight had been called un-American but not dirty. Alfred phoned Aleck. What about making cuts but denouncing them in a written statement? "If you play with cuts," shrieked Aleck, "I'll denounce you as unfit to be trusted with Sherwood's play or anybody else's!" He immediately branded it *Idiot's Delete.*

Lunt and Fontanne canceled the performance.

Uproar. Lynn got on the phone to Justice Felix Frankfurter of the

United States Supreme Court. A local bishop and an alderman said it was a shame to deny Omaha a Pulitzer play. The Drama League president expressed outrage. Mayor Butler hastily called Alfred to his office to apologize. "I saw *Sappho* when I was a child," said Alfred helpfully, trying to explain why this "ugly, vulgar play" did not shock him. The mayor swallowed that information; *Idiot's Delight* finally played to an enthusiastic full house. Afterward the fat mayor explained from the stage that he had only been trying to do his duty.

In Denver a packed house jeered Omaha's stupidity. After the play Alfred read Mayor Butler's speech to hoots, catcalls, and tumultuous applause for the Lunts' having taught Cowtown a lesson. They triumphantly boarded the train for California.

Naturally Alfred and Lynn had been rehearsing a new play since early April. "You couldn't be with the Lunts without rehearsing," said Behrman. Now Sam had adapted a translation of *Amphitryon 38* by Jean Giraudoux, a telling (for the thirty-eighth time, Giraudoux estimated) of the myth of Jupiter descending from Olympus to seduce the faithful wife of the Greek general Amphitryon. Like *The Guardsman* (and many of their comedies), *Amphitryon 38* puts fidelity to the test. Behrman was keen to work with the Lunts again. As Sherwood quipped, with a debt to Ring Lardner:

> *If you want a play to run many a munt*
> *Get Lynn Fontanne and Alfred Lunt.*

On a metaphysical level, Lunt and Fontanne had also inspired Giraudoux. Their very existence as an acting couple was "to impel the dramatist towards the most gripping and the most serious of the conflicts to be found in life and on the stage, the conflict made necessary on this earth by the co-existence, unavoidable and yet undesirable, of those embodiments of brotherly hate, man and woman." When Lynn and Alfred asked him to write them a play, he scribbled two lines:

DELILAH: What is Samson like? What type is he?
NURSE: The type you hate.

Lunt-Fontanne creativity took over immediately. Alfred thought Giraudoux's setting boring. Why not raise the curtain on Jupiter and

S. N. Behrman (seated), adapter of Giraudoux's Amphitryon 38, *with Lynn, Alfred, and John C. Wilson, their partner in Transatlantic Productions*

Mercury (Richard Whorf) lying on their stomachs, gazing down on Earth from a cloud? Their heads would be their own; their naked backs, legs, and buttocks courtesy of the scene designer. Behrman loved the idea.

Alfred is confident one day, tortured the next. He rushes into a rehearsal, distraught. "Ladies and gentlemen, it is impossible for me to play this role, so we cannot go on with this play. Please consider the production canceled. Speak to the company manager and pick up your checks. I can't go on. I can't find the green umbrella." He turns and is gone.

Lynn sits quietly down near the footlights. "Don't worry," she tells the stunned company. "We'll go on, and he will find it."

Rehearsals proceed. Half an hour later, Alfred re-enters, arm up-flung. "Don't worry. I've found it. We'll start again at the beginning of the act."

Lynn would be fifty-two at the end of the run of *Amphitryon 38* in 1939, yet as Alkmena she had never looked so radiant. Somehow the Lunts had shifted chronological gears. In early photos Lynn looks older than Alfred. Sometime about 1930 the balance changed. Before he was thirty-eight, Alfred's sleeked-back hair was sprinkled with gray. His sensual mouth drooped; lines from nose to mouth deepened. His face went south, though he still looked incredibly distinguished, and onstage, with the help of his black valet, Jules Johnson, could look almost anything.

In contrast Lynn kept getting younger. Her eyebrows arched higher, her lips curled more triumphantly, her cheekbones resculpted themselves, her nose tilted, her black eyelashes flew up like birds. The famous chin line held; the hair appeared, if anything, darker. "If this keeps on," said Woollcott, "people will think she's Alfred's daughter." She made up for an hour and a half before every performance. For Alkmena she slathered zinc ointment on her arms so she'd look like a Greek statue. ("What lovely arms!" sighed a woman in the audience. "Yes, but are they her own?" whispered her companion.) In flowing chiffon Grecian gowns by Valentina, Lynn glowed. "Ravishing!" said the critics.

Of course in *Amphitryon* Alfred too was gorgeous, tall and godlike, with naked thighs and silvery locks and a long beard that was a "firework of golden curls." ("I look like I've swallowed Shirley Temple," he complained.)

San Francisco's Curran Theater hosted the world premiere on June 23, 1937. Theresa Helburn and Lawrence and Armina Langner represented the Guild, for the first time sponsoring a West Coast opening. As for Behrman, he never enjoyed an out-of-town opening more. "Oh, yes," Eugene O'Neill told him, "it's the best audience in the world. They come to enjoy themselves. Singular motive, isn't it?"

Yet the critics said plainly that *Amphitryon 38* needed work: with anyone but the Lunts it would close in a night. Behrman was ready to revise, yet Lunt and Fontanne took over. Behrman marveled how, in the coming days, the scenes between Jupiter and Alkmena underwent "the tiniest capillary changes," intensifying the synergy between them. He credited this to Alfred's musical sense, which tuned him in to the subtlest shifts in emphasis and tone. *Amphitryon* came to the Shubert in New York as a test of Lunt and Fontanne's power to turn sophisticated French dialogue into a hit.

Theatre Arts magazine came to a rehearsal in October. Clutching her script and chewing gum, Lynn wears a wide-brimmed hat and blue-rimmed glasses. Alfred strides the stage in a dark business suit and tie. "All right, let's get going!" But Alfred and Dickie Whorf can't resist horseplay. Lynn rebukes them by making a regal entrance. Alfred settles down.

By now there are so many versions of *Amphitryon* that everybody's confused. "Try the Los Angeles opening. No, that didn't work. How about the third night in San Francisco?" Alfred and Lynn have been rehearsing at home; constantly changing lines and business. Now he crosses too early, before his cue. They do it again, changing Behrman's lines once more. The scene between Alkmena and Leda still doesn't jell. "It's very bad. It's got to be completely rearranged!" Stage carpenters begin to hammer relentlessly. The tempo of Alan Hewitt's speech is wrong. "Don't think of the meaning of the words," cries Alfred. "It doesn't matter what you're saying. Try it just repeating: 'You son of a bitch, you son of a bitch!'" The hammering crescendos. "Come on, Berrie," shouts Alfred, "let's get out of here!"

The good news is that crabby George Jean Nathan thinks the show will flop. The cast perks up. Some first-nighters pay $100 for a seat.

At the last run-through the Guild board is present. Alfred and Lynn are still worried about the end of Act Two, but this time it goes so well they fall into each other's arms. Chomping a cigar, Langner strides down the aisle. "We think you should hit it harder," he announces. Alfred comes over the footlights. "Playing high comedy to you is like feeding soufflé to a horse!"

Amphitryon 38 did not flop. "It was a brilliant opening, such as [the

Jupiter and Alkmena in
Amphitryon 38
(1937)

Guild subscribers] have never bestirred themselves to before," Lynn wrote Noël triumphantly. She dismissed critics who found the play shallow and talky:

> They are as naive, as unworldly, straight-laced and prejudiced
> in their particular way as a small New England village.
> Gone are the Woollcotts, Hammonds, Benchleys; and your
> John Mason Brown has long since ceased to know what he is
> writing about. Some of them complained that it is a bed-room
> farce . . . of course it is, one of the great classic bed-room farces
> of all times . . . ! The best answer to them all is your box-office,
> and at the moment (fingers crossed and rattlings of rosaries!) so
> is ours!!

Critics did agree that this was Lunt-Fontanne 38—"spirited Aphrodisiantics, urbanely conducted infidelities." But Giraudoux's play was more intellectual than audiences expected: a conversation between an immortal god and a mortal woman who gets the better of him. Gods propose; woman disposes. Brooks Atkinson caught the spirit—"exultantly outrageous, elegantly wicked, superbly acted"—as did Woollcott: "an enchanting and iridescent piece which shows [the Lunts] at the top of their bent."

Giraudoux came to the opening—"all charm, gentle, very handsome, very quiet, and extremely kind," according to Lynn; "formidable," according to Behrman. Afterward the Lunts took him home and watched him devour almost the whole Virginia ham Noël had sent as a good-luck gift. What Giraudoux perhaps did not say then was that Alfred Lunt's playing of Jupiter had been revelatory, "possibly more satisfying" than the great French actor Louis Jouvet's.

Fifty-five years old, John Barrymore came to see "the matchless Lunts" with ambitious Elaine Jacobs, his fourth wife:

> Lynn Fontanne and Alfred Lunt were one hundred per cent the-
> atre and John's admiration for them was boundless. Their magic
> not only threw us into a spell but reawakened my dream and
> ruined the rest of our lives. The tale of Alkmena and Jupiter had
> always served as a model, indeed a prophecy of my life with
> John—parallel to our history and also played by an acting couple
> whose dedication and brilliance I had always dreamed of emulat-

ing. As we sat and watched the play, I felt the old gnawing. As Great as the Lunts were—and still are—I was married to John Barrymore. . . . What a Jupiter he would have made! As for Alkmena, I had much to learn, but I had to start somewhere and the top had always seemed the perfect place. Together we would make theatrical history.

Barrymore and Elaine did make theatrical history of a sort. Two years later she persuaded him to return to the stage in a bad play, *My Dear Children.* Barrymore was ill, alcoholic, prematurely senile. Some wept to see the great actor self-destruct; others admired the fluttering rags of genius. Alfred was horrified, impressed, and sad.

In November Jupiter and Alkmena made the covers of *Life* and *Time.* While still playing *Amphitryon,* Alfred and Lynn called rehearsals of Chekhov's *The Sea Gull*—a study in frustration and futility that was perfect for Alfred, less so for Lynn. The translator was Stark Young, critic, novelist, and "Darling." Both Alfred and Lynn wanted to get away from "one obvious Lunt-Fontanne vehicle after another" and were waiting until a new, exciting, and serious play came along.

Meanwhile, Alfred was writing his architect, Charles Dornbush. "I think that if we connected the garage and the house, using the present kitchen perhaps for a dining-room, and putting the kitchen on the ground with butler's pantry up-stairs, dumb-waiter, etc. something very interesting might come out. . . . I hate to be so fussy but after all we are changing it for the last time and I think it will have to last until our old age. . . . I know God damned well it will!!!"

His attention to detail, as on the stage, was staggering:

I have made a tiny change in the cupboard . . . (see enclosed plans). There are certain things in the kitchen I wish you'd think about. . . . These things always bother a cook. Where to put pot covers? . . . Where to hang dish towels to dry etc.?

Where to SCREW the meat grinder? Can you use white tile in back & at sides of kitchen stove? And do you have a deep cupboard where we can keep breakfast trays. . . . You need 2'3" for trays.

Write me & I'll try to be clearer another time. *The Sea Gull* is too much for me.

Rehearsing a Chekhovian drama about impermanence and disintegration while in Europe the thud of fascist boots grew louder, Alfred and Lynn were stubbornly building their own estate.

CHAPTER TEN

Searching: 1938–1940

Alfred and Lynn opened *The Sea Gull* in Baltimore in March 1938. "Why," groused Thomas Gomez, "should all of us have to work for two and a half hours or even three on this tiny play when only two characters are needed—not even scenery. The curtain simply rises. . . . Says Teacher: 'Masha, why do you always wear black?' Masha: 'Because Constantine shot himself.' There you are. We could all go home." In a spirit of mischief he kept telling Lynn that her last act line was "In the long winter evenings we always lay blotto" instead of "play lotto." "Terrible thing to say to an actress," wailed Alfred, "as, of course, she could never get it out of her head."

Woollcott had come down for a rehearsal. "I have never seen anything better anywhere. They have never done anything so good. It can never be so good again, I expect, as it was in that stripped, unadorned, hair-trigger performance." Alfred himself always preferred rehearsals to the actual performance.

Lynn played Irina Arkadina, the vain actress; Alfred, Trigorin, the fashionable writer. Richard Whorf as Irina's son, Constantine, and Sydney Greenstreet as her brother, Peter Sorin, had hefty roles. Unlike most Lunt-Fontanne vehicles, *The Sea Gull* also had two strong parts for young actresses. Margaret Webster, the daughter of British actors Ben

Webster and May Whitty, played the bitter Masha. Uta Hagen was Nina, the country girl dazzled by Trigorin and shot down like a gull.

After a week in Boston, they returned to New York, where Lynn and Alfred read in a gossip column that they'd separated. They traced the mischief to the afternoon their cab had stopped, windows down, at a red light. They'd been rehearsing.

TRIGORIN: Let me be free!

ARKADINA: Have control over yourself! [*Violently*] Are you so enthralled?

A fan had called to report a breakup.

Firmly married, they opened March 28 at the Shubert. Richard Lockridge in the *Sun* underlined why this time Alfred and Lynn had avoided another obvious Lunt-Fontanne vehicle: "There have been times when a reviewer might discharge his full duty, and come disconcertingly close to exhausting his subject, by recording simply that Alfred Lunt and Lynn Fontanne had opened their booth again, and were doing lively business at the old stand. No such comfortable device, it is invigorating to report, will do for last evening's considerable event. . . . The Lunts have done nothing they should be prouder of."

Acting Trigorin in blond hair and beard, Alfred was praised as "uncommonly varied" and his central monologue as "a brilliant exercise." Lynn soon became aware how much audiences considered her "Mrs. Lunt." When Trigorin tells Irina he's in love with young Nina, their sympathy suddenly shifted to her, as though Alfred were actually betraying her. Richard Whorf was praised for his nervous brilliance and Uta Hagen, in her New York debut, for her "aching, utterly moving, intensity." New York was finally seeing "a human Chekhov."

Then there was the *Times:*

It seems to this observer that Mr. Lunt and especially Miss Fontanne remain brightly on the surface of an introspective play. . . . For Chekhov is pure expression; it is limpid and translucent. Within the structure of this play egotists are walking through life blind to hands that stretch out to them and deaf to tender speaking. It is the tragedy of indifference. As the vain, selfish actress, Miss Fontanne cheapens the part considerably by overacting and by gaudily wigging it. As Trigorin, Mr. Lunt has

*Trigorin and Madame
Arkadina in* The Sea
Gull, *1938*

the invaluable gift of making the lines sound as if he had just
invented them on the spur of the moment. But he, too, seems a
little obtuse to the spiritual solitude of the play as a whole.

Audiences could see the literal half of *The Sea Gull* at the Shubert,
Brooks Atkinson concluded. The genius half was missing.

Alfred and Lynn were used to having plays criticized as unworthy of
them—not vice versa. It was some years before they felt friendly toward
Brooks Atkinson.

They played *The Sea Gull* five weeks in New York. "Our souls get
stronger every day," said Alfred. At they same time they were preparing
Amphitryon 38 for London. They could hardly spend the whole summer
in Genesee with their house still under construction, and they wanted
to look for new plays abroad.

Today is the Great Day when the Lunts open in *Amphitryon*," Graham Robertson told a friend. ". . . The divine ones have, as usual,
had their ineffable noses hard on the grindstone during the last
few days, and our meetings have mostly taken the form of a rapturous
moment or two on the telephone."

They opened at the Lyric on May 17, 1938, to a tremendous welcome.

At the end the audience "tore up their seats." "Bravo! Speech! Speech!" Alfred stepped forward. "Louder! Louder!" The pessimist heard "Lousy! Lousy!" "Welcome! Welcome!" He heard "Rotten! Rotten!" When they shouted, "Why have you stayed away so long?" he finally understood.

Critics raved: "Divinely matched" . . . "their playing together is the most fascinating thing of its kind" . . . "amazing duet of intelligence and gaiety" . . . "shimmers from first to last" . . . "Never in our time have partners in acting played into each other's hands with tact more exquisite."

The *Times* did have a reservation:

Miss Fontanne's performance is so good in its own kind, so rich in intelligence and high spirits, that it is not even ungrateful to imagine . . . it might be even better than it is—more spectacularly brilliant, warmer, more passionate, in a word, more human, with a kind of ironic pathos that Miss Fontanne's lightness of touch excludes. But that lightness of touch is faultlessly used, and one might not be aware that anything was being sacrificed by it if Mr. Alfred Lunt were not there to prove, in the glancing humour and the passionate intent of his Jupiter, that comedy may, in this piece, be carried farther and deeper than Miss Fontanne carries it.

The British critic and novelist Charles Morgan, on the other hand, congratulated Lynn for knowing her place. "Miss Fontanne acts faultlessly within certain definite limitations; these limitations are self-imposed, deliberately and discreetly chosen. . . . Mr. Lunt is the sun, she the moon! The loveliest of all her accomplishments is that she recognises it."

As for Graham's reaction:

Well the Great Night is over—and magnificently over. . . . Of course, before it began, the Great Ones were in their usual state of despair and complete prostration, which doesn't help the rest of their devoted little company very much.

In fact, I believe the play actually began thus:

[JUPITER *and* MERCURY, *in their birthday suits and visibly quaking, recline high in air upon a thunder cloud, over the edge of which they peer*]

JUPITER [*in a hollow whisper*]: How do you feel?
MERCURY [*ditto*]: Feel? I feel that I've lost my voice. Supposing
I can't speak?
JUPITER: You must speak. I'm going to be sick. . . .
MERCURY: You can't be sick! There goes the curtain. [*Curtain
rises*]
JUPITER [*apparently apostrophising himself*]: Oh God—we're off.

Two minutes later the house was roaring with delight, Graham
deciding that London was "getting the Lunts at their very best this
time. . . . Their art is their own, impossible to imitate or reproduce.
And even so was Irving's, and Sarah Bernhardt."

Graham found Alfred and Lynn as "simple, kindly, and affectionate
as ever." They went on to Noël's studio for an intimate supper. (Graham
had been apprehensive about meeting the legendary Coward until Lynn
said, "He is not in the least like what you think he is and you will like
him very much.") This night was "all happiness." Lynn and Alfred even
forgot to say they'd given the worst performance of their lives.

On May 29 the Adorables visited Sandhills, which they explored in
wind and rain. Jupiter-like, Alfred stroked the cat, who immediately
produced four kittens; he passed the barn and big Sarah the sow
dropped nine piglets. Alfred was being temperamental. He must give
up acting in cold New York. London audiences reached out; each night
he went to the theater with joy. A quiet day in Surrey, but Graham
believed that the Lunts liked to be quiet. Surely Noël's Goldenhurst in
Kent, swarming with theater folk, had tired them out.

The effusive Graham could also coolly analyze the couple:

They are strange and wonderful personalities—very difficult to
understand until you realize that they are not two but one personality. Each is the other's complement. Together they are marvellous, their artistry amazing. Apart they are oddly ineffectual,
Alfred a vaguely wandering soul who looks at you like a lost dog
who is afraid of being washed; Lynn (like "Maud") splendidly
null—a sort of highly intellectual ice maiden. Alfred's genius
illuminates Lynn; Lynn's strong brain and well-balanced judgment keep Alfred within bounds and bring him back to earth
when he soars skyward. I love them both, but the Alfred-Lynn
combination is the real person, not the component parts.

Lynn, too, could claim they were one person. Refusing to come without Alfred to England, she explained: "I really don't care about travelling so far without him, much as I long to see you all. And then, I am sure people feel as if they are talking to half a person when they talk to either one of us without the other."

As two distinct personalities they went to Noël's supper party to meet the Duke and Duchess of Kent. Noël was chummy with royals, not only as the Duke of Kent's former boyfriend but as a great fan of the monarchy. Supper at Noël's usually meant "a sandwich and a seat on the floor," but that night white-gloved servants moved among the guests—though everyone did end up on the floor. Lynn decided that she was still very Brit, still in sympathy with Edward VIII, now the Duke of Windsor, who in 1936 had given up the throne for the woman he loved. "Isn't it strange what a fuss is made about that sort of thing? I never can understand it."

On July 14, Queen Mary appeared in the Royal Box, panicking Jupiter and Mercury on their cloud because they were sure Her Majesty would stalk out of the theater when she heard the ribald lines. Instead she rocked with laughter and led the applause throughout.

People had thought them mad to export their entire company and scenery for an eight-week run. But with sold-out houses they'd actually made money—even though they had chiefly brought *Amphitryon* to London for Graham. "This may sound bizarre and extravagant," said Woollcott, "but it's the God's truth."

On July 17, the last night, Lynn gave Bessie Porter, her dresser, a big tip and hugged her goodbye. London gave the Lunts a tumultuous send-off, the Lyric leaping to its feet shouting as if it would never let them go. Yes, the British valued Lunt and Fontanne's artistry, perhaps more than Americans. Yet with Britain edging closer to war, the very presence of Alfred with one of their own may have suggested a support which as yet America hadn't offered.

They retreated to Sandhills for quiet, though when they visited Robert Sherwood nearby at his estate, Great Enton, they found the house "crammed with the usual crowd that always collects round Bob." Graham was shy and protested he didn't really know Sherwood. "You are fond of Bob," said Alfred. "If you are fond of him you do know him."

"Anyhow the hush and peace of Sandhills seemed intensified when we got back. The guests seemed really rested, Alfred wandering vaguely about the house and garden in his old grey dressing-gown, murmuring: 'I'm so happy. I don't believe I was ever so happy before'— like a small boy just home for the holidays. And now it's all over, and a farewell telegram announced the departure of the divinities from our shores."

They went to Sweden ("much too exciting"), then on to Hotel Bellevue in Hango, Finland: "a scream—tawdry, slightly soiled, with a dance band and water closet but the beds are comfortable and the beach and weather perfect." The Guild was proposing six weeks in New York when they returned, but "I can't bear the thought of that city just yet," Alfred wrote Warren Munsell, the business manager. "For God sake let's go on tour—London spoiled us dreadfully! And if we can't manage *Idiot's Delight* in the south—well we can't! . . . I'm getting old and weary, Warren—But what concerns me most is the Guild season! It looks awfully thin—Nor have we got a new play either, thank you very much. . . . Does it mean the Radio?"

So they toured with *The Sea Gull, Idiot's Delight,* and *Amphitryon 38.* In Pittsburgh a seventeen-year-old actor named Donald Buka read for them; they turned him down, then wired him to join them in Chicago, though Alfred asked, "What shall we do with him?" Buka became a curtain runner, a callboy, and a shrewd observer of Lunt and Fontanne during the two years he acted in their company:

The Lunts gave their company tough love. Actors had better know their lines for the first rehearsal "or there was hell to pay." Lynn called a Lunt tour "a concentration camp." It was. "Once in our hands," said Alfred, "you're in the hands of the Gestapo." Alfred could be stingy: in Kansas City an actor wanted fifty dollars more a week; he was sent home. Alfred felt deep friendship for Sydney Greenstreet, known in the company as "Mr. G-String" or even "Up Your Ass Mabel." Sydney hated train sleepers, so the Lunts always asked him to ride with them if they had a car. Richard Whorf was "ever present."

Finally Buka was given the part of Auguste, the waiter, in *Idiot's Delight.* Before his first performance he confessed to feeling "all cottony inside." "Donald," said Alfred, "when I go on without butterflies I'll know I'm dead."

At other times the great actor could be less than sympathetic. In

Kansas City they played *Idiot's Delight* in a huge auditorium with three other events going on simultaneously. At the brush-up rehearsal the cast was distracted, loose. Alfred strode to a café table and swept crockery onto the floor. "I don't have to open this show!" he roared. "I can close it in a minute!" He stormed past Lynn where she was sitting at a little table, tended by Auguste. "Oh, Alfred, that was very good," she murmured. "And you didn't break the good glasses."

Most fascinating to Buka was Lunt and Fontanne's imaginary child. It is often said that plays were the Lunts' children: "No mother could take care of her babies more conscientiously than the Lunts take care of their plays." Evidently plays were not enough. With Woollcott and Coward they kept up the fantasy that they had a son who lived in London with a governess named Miss Prinn. Sometimes the child was a daughter, Winnie. To Woollcott Alfred also wrote of "Albert Putnam, my grandson." Their company knew of this game; perhaps it's not far-fetched to wonder if Edward Albee used it in *Who's Afraid of Virginia Woolf?*

Lynn was begging Aleck to come to Genesee for Christmas—"Hattie doesn't bother us much." A few company members who couldn't get home would be there. "We sat around and watched them perform," said a nephew, "and my mother instructed me to rave about Alfred's Christmas cookies." Claggett Wilson and Gustav Eckstein were also guests—twenty for Christmas dinner.

The remarkable Dr. Eckstein was a naturalist and writer who kept canaries, in his Cincinnati laboratory, that answered to their names. Drawn by Eckstein's brilliance, celebrities made pilgrimages to Cincinnati, John Barrymore happily emerging from his laboratory brushing canary droppings from his suit. Woollcott read Eckstein's book on canaries and became a friend, which meant that George Kaufman, Ruth Gordon, Noël, Harpo Marx, and Bob Sherwood were also buddies. Gus had become an intimate of Alfred and Lynn's—another triangle. He came often to Genesee, exchanged letters, phone calls. One Christmas the Lunts gave him a car.

Aleck, who called their refusing an invitation to Bomoseen "completely foul and offensive and infuriating," did not come. Still, they had a wonderful Christmas. Yet Karin called Louise and Jack Greene "a tragic topic." They were too swept up in the Lunt glamour, were not very good parents to Pee-Gee and Johnny, who had to call them by their first names. When Lynn and Alfred were away, Louise did not make herself popular with the workmen by bossing them as though she owned the place. She seemed displaced, at a loss to be herself.

Ben Perkins was in the middle of the whirlwind. "[Your family] have had me on the ropes many times these years," he once wrote Alfred. He blamed the women's dependence. "They have always had you to lean on and have never been entirely on their own. They think of everything in terms of you. Whenever they are hurt, they want to get even through you." When Louise, for instance, was insulted by the local butcher, she told Alfred to stop buying meat for the dogs because Mr. Torhorst might poison it—creating hard feelings everywhere. The family was jealous when Alfred said he bought a new Chevy because Ben was wild about it.

Aloof from family quarrels, Carl was there with his new wife, Patricia. Possibly the courtly gambler was going to settle down. He now traveled selling a molasses supplement for cow feed and had bought a house in nearby Mukwonago. Carl and Pat never came to Ten Chimneys uninvited. People never heard Carl either brag about Alfred or speak against him.

Delighted to have the family together, Alfred flew about on skis, baked pies, and roasted a twenty-six-pound turkey. Louise and Karin "sang Christmas carols softly in high sweet sopranos with their heads together." Gus Eckstein and Lynn wandered over snowy fields, Elsa the dachshund in her arms, Gus "discoursing beautifully."

Alfred's sister Louise with her husband, Jack Greene

"I love Genesee," he wrote in gratitude. "I wrote small spots of the present manuscript in Genesee, when I was supposed to be napping, and, each time I come on such a spot in the revision, it says something about the fireplace, or the lazy chair, or the feel of the linen on the bed, with, downstairs, yourself and Alfred. . . . I love you."

Alfred and I are touring so long and oft in lieu of a new play" became the theme of 1939. "We don't seem to like anything that we have read for two years and don't intend to waste anybody's money and do something just because it's new." The Guild sent scripts, producers sent scripts, playwrights sent scripts. Alfred's response to one was pretty much his response to all: "I have read *Turn Again Home* and found a lot of it very interesting but it does need a deal of work. . . . The author assumes you know his people and what they've done up to the rise of the Act I curtain. And I'm awfully sick of the word dream and the word star. Just count the number of times he uses them and for why? . . . Mr. Callaghan is surely talented but it'll take something more than *Turn Again Home* to make me sit up and want to work."

Edna Ferber wanted to do a play about Saratoga with George Kaufman, who agreed only if they built it specifically for the Lunts. But Alfred and Lynn weren't interested, Lynn "very difficult."

They were offered *Life with Father.* "A producer always starts trying to get Alfred Lunt and Lynn Fontanne for his play and he is eventually happy to finish up with anybody of the stage," said Oscar Serlin, producer of Howard Lindsay and Russel Crouse's play. Alfred and Lynn read the script. "I've been seducing you in the theater for fifteen years," Alfred said. "Here's a chance to marry, settle down, and have children. I think it's about time."

"After all these years," said Lynn, "I don't think I'd want to spend every evening wondering whether or nor you're going to get baptized. No, thank you very much."

Lynn would have spent many evenings wondering. *Life with Father* broke Broadway records with 3,224 performances.

Guthrie McClintic once planned an all-star *Three Sisters* with Alfred as Vershinin and Lynn as Olga, but Alfred refused to let Lynn play a less important part than Ruth Gordon's or Katharine Cornell's. Now McClintic offered them an all-star *Candida,* with Cornell as Candida and Burgess Meredith as the young poet Marchbanks. Alfred would play the Reverend Morell and Lynn the small but interesting part of

Miss Proserpine Garnett, his brisk secretary. Lynn was not amused. She was as big a star as Cornell.

"Lynn," said Guthrie, "you would make a superb Candida—but, you see, Kit couldn't play Proserpine."

"No, thank you very much."

Lynn had thrown out the red wig and was doing her own hair, but still *The Sea Gull* wasn't drawing. "Well to hell with them," she wrote Aleck. "Kit had to make *The Barretts* pay for *Romeo and Juliet.*" Next day there were great reviews, but still they dropped Chekhov.

According to Sam Behrman, *Idiot's Delight* "used to be entirely Alfred's play, Lynn struggling with a part which she didn't like and could never find the right way of playing. Now . . . it's her play instead of Alfred's." Lynn used to say, "There must be a right way of playing it—there always is a right way—but I can't find it." But on this tour she had. In Austin, Texas, the audience yelled "Yippee!" at the curtain. When the cast walked into the auditorium in Waco, workers were shoveling manure from a rodeo, but after *Amphitryon* Wacoans threw cowboy hats onto the stage. In San Antonio, Larry Farrell had to add four hundred chairs—"You have never seen such audiences, never!" (In Houston, however, a patron was heard saying, "I like to see all this acting but you can give me Mickey Mouse anytime.") Alfred became an authority on Texas chili parlors.

In Little Rock they were joined by the New York theater writer Morton Eustis. He found the Lunts "drenched alternately in gloom and elation." Little Rock was dry; there wasn't a bright light in town; the high-school auditorium where they were to play was out in the sticks. Alfred and Eustis wandered the empty streets. "It's going to be okay," Larry promised, but "I don't believe it," groaned Alfred, "I don't believe it!"

Every seat was filled. "I wouldn't have believed it," said Alfred.

"Alfred always goes on like this," said Lynn, "and the worst of it is, though I should know better by this time, I always believe him."

Alfred was contentious.

"I'm always wrong," smiled Lynn.

Alfred was always on the brink of catastrophe: "I never closed an eye all last night!"

"Nonsense. You were snoring."

Yet underneath all the pyrotechnics, Eustis sensed a humble man.

Then on through the South: Memphis, Chattanooga, Atlanta. Chattanooga sold out for a week, Atlanta sold out with standees. Lynn and Alfred were so elated that they stayed up until three a.m. restaging a scene in *Idiot's Delight*. Eustis left them with four more weeks of one-night stands ahead.

Uta Hagen had left the company:

"Jo [José Ferrer] wants to marry me and I want to marry him."

"You'll have to speak to Mr. Lunt about that," said Lynn coldly.

Alfred shot his voice an octave. "It's the height of unprofessionalism to leave a tour!"

Hagen left and a young red-haired actress named Thelma Schnee took her place. Lynn found her "promising" yet "eccentric and peculiar." (Schnee would make a hit as Bessie Watty with Ethel Barrymore in *The Corn Is Green*.) But Lynn resented Hagen's leaving. Laurence Olivier, too, had left the New York cast of Katharine Cornell's *No Time for Comedy*—"in love or some God damn nonsense. . . . Olivier and Uta Hagen should be grafted into Siamese Twins and branded UNFIT," she told Aleck, who explained that Olivier actually had played beyond his contract. The "God damn nonsense" was Vivien Leigh.

Montgomery, Birmingham, New Orleans, Nashville, the Midwest. In St. Louis the movie of *Idiot's Delight* with Clark Gable and Norma Shearer was playing down the street. (If the Lunts saw it, their reaction doesn't survive.) Only for Minneapolis, Madison, and Milwaukee would they play *The Sea Gull*. Their trust was rewarded.

Throughout the tour the Lunts were accompanied by their personal staff, always difficult to keep track of, though many stayed loyally for years. Carolyn Every had left to be married; the actress Jackie Paige replaced her as secretary. Lynn still had Agnes and also a black maid, Alma. Larry Farrell had been promoted to business manager. Charles Bowden, a Harvard graduate who would become Tennessee Williams's producer, acted minor roles and functioned as Alfred's dresser and valet. Chuck and Larry were close. In the next years Renee Orsell and Charva Chester, a lesbian couple, would join the company as Lynn's secretary and assistant stage manager, respectively. Obviously Alfred and Lynn were comfortable with homosexuals.

That winter Claggett Wilson had returned to Genesee Depot to decorate the entrance hall with symbols of hospitality. A woman offers a cordial. Tea and crumpets suggest waiting delights. A maid supplies fresh bedding. A Swedish coffee urn steams. Alfred would greet guests in the large "arrival court," Lynn float down the spiral staircase as guests gazed up in anticipation.

In early spring of 1939 Ten Chimneys finally was finished. Czechoslovakian chandeliers sparkled over the entrance hall and dining-room table. Air-conditioning was installed against humid summers. A big modern kitchen with stainless-steel sinks welcomed Alfred—"Prettiest kitchen in the world—yes sir the world!" (On the back of a cupboard panel Mr. Meticulous listed the location and wattage of every single lightbulb in the house.) He'd vowed to spend not a penny more than $36,000 for the remodeling, but they had actually paid almost twice that amount.

John Hale Jr. had worked for two years with his father, John Sr., and Claggett Wilson, painting for fifty-five cents an hour. John was the "straight-line man," decorating furniture and walls with narrow bands of gold-leaf paint. Clagg had designed the furniture and had it made, unfinished, in New York. He painted the floral designs, John the rest, applying twelve to fourteen coats of paint to the top of a table or chest, rubbing the surface with pumice stone and water between coats to produce a satiny glow.

"Alfred was hands on with all aspects of the house and garden," said John. "Lynn was not. Lynn walked around in gardens, Alfred went down on his knees and pulled weeds, hoed. He'd also grab a brush and paint right along with me."

The Lunts treated John like a son. He in turn admired Lynn's beautiful hands and was impressed that she ordered two dozen pairs of black and brown gloves from Saks at a time. Alfred's deep laugh could be heard throughout the house. There was "something different about his eyes—penetrating, but one eye not straight." He could listen to Alfred talk for hours: "Oh, that voice!" He treasured Clagg Wilson's March 26, 1939, telegram: LUNTS WILD ABOUT WHOLE HOUSE NOT ONE SINGLE FAULT. CONGRATULATIONS TO ALL THREE OF US.

Claggett Wilson was a stage scenery designer. Ten Chimneys itself was a series of sets against which Lunt and Fontanne could act out their design for living. Since they could not survive away from the theater, they created private stages. The Flirtation Room, its many doors suggesting a French farce. The drawing room with "Noël's" Steinway painted by Clagg Wilson and walls decorated with Clagg's biblical scenes. The dining room, furniture, carpet, and ceiling designed by Wilson and Alfred. The Belasco Room, furnished with the libidinous actor-manager's own casting couch. Some people might object to the riot of velvet and gilt and crystal, but "we adore it," Alfred wrote Aleck. Ten Chimneys was "about the gayest house" he'd ever seen: every room a stage set and "you could play anything from *Trojan Women* to *Dear Brutus* on the grounds."

Some did object. Kurt Weill wrote to his wife, Lotte Lenya, "And if you see Alfred's house, love it, he is so proud of it. It's awful in parts. Done by a fairy."

In the Cottage Alfred had used Minnesota Mining Company gold Christmas tape to decorate white woodwork. It looked like gold leaf, that's what mattered. The look of the main house was achieved in the same spirit: faux marble, faux Directoire, lines shaded to look like molding, panels painted to look like doors—completely and delightfully stagy. And if one takes into account blackamoors supporting tables, figures holding lamps and vases, faces in paintings and on china, and the many busts, figurines, and statues as well as the dozens of people Claggett Wilson had painted on walls, the Lunts were surrounded by a cast of hundreds even when alone. Truly they had a *horror vacui.*

They named the first bedroom upstairs the Helen Hayes Room. Lynn created hangings for all the beds, sweeping them into a crown above the headboards. Noël's Room had white chenille and a corner fireplace. A bath with a bird theme connected Noël's to another bedroom with vibrant flowered wallpaper that would become Larry's (Olivier's) Room, though Aleck considered it his.

Edna Ferber loved visiting. "A wonderful night's sleep. Raining a soft lovely rain. . . . Lynn . . . playing solitaire and calmly waiting, she said, for a movement. Alfred cooking creme vichyssoise in the kitchen. A walk up the road and down a pleasant lane. Lunch, and the day slipped by. Listened to some Viennese waltzes on the phonograph in the studio after dinner. Alfred gay and amusing. I shall hate to leave."

Lynn had what she'd always wanted: an English estate. Gardens, stable, studio, woods, a pond (it would dry up), and a country house in which to entertain guests for weekends. Ten Chimneys had "that certain Genesee quoi" that would draw and entrance theater people of all ages.

Its completion coincided with what, in retrospect, may be considered the height of Lunt's and Fontanne's careers. It had been twenty years since Alfred became a star in *Clarence,* eighteen since *Dulcy* made Lynn's name. They had their own repertory company, their own

Edna Ferber loved visiting Genesee Depot.

Transatlantic Productions, the Theatre Guild. They played (usually) to packed houses. Their acting had matured to a dynamic counterpoint of wit, charm, vitality, and sophistication. They were perhaps the most respected actors in the profession.

Though Aleck called the estate "Lynnbottom," Lynn was not as content as Alfred. To Noël she complained that her idea of fun wasn't staying at the Depot all summer. She wanted to see more people, to travel. Alfred was a regular slave driver—too much work, too little play. But Alfred loved getting up at daybreak, hoeing the garden, pruning trees, clearing brush. Behrman understood the difference between them. "Well, bake, dig, cook but don't bore Lynn with your agricultural and culinary achievements."

While Lynn was solitary, Alfred had the company of an area artists' colony. Edward Harris Heth, a writer whose novel *Any Number Can Play* had been filmed with Clark Gable, lived on fourteen acres nearby with his partner, William Chauncey, a potter. Gentle and generous, Heth loved the countryside as ardently as Alfred. He also loved to cook (jams and pickles a specialty), and the two traded recipes. Heth's circle included Karl Priebe, a Milwaukee artist. Emily Groom lived in the area. A congenial group for Alfred: they visited Ten Chimneys quite often.

These people were thoroughly content with southeastern Wisconsin, while Lynn was still insecure about the Midwest. Bob Sherwood and Moss Hart had estates in England and upstate New York. Kit Cornell would hew a fantastic $500,000 retreat out of the Hudson River palisades, besides owning a house on Martha's Vineyard. When a property came up for sale near them, Lynn would naively beg their friend John Mason Brown to buy it. But he was quite content in the East.

Yet friends loved Genesee Depot. Sydney Greenstreet came. (His mentally ill wife, Dorothy, was at a sanitarium nearby; he visited often.) Ben Perkins observed that it took ten minutes for the enormous Sydney to huff his way up the circular staircase.

Aleck sent a gift of a dozen white birches, then came with his movie camera to record the transformed house and comfort Alfred, who'd had two teeth pulled. (Alfred's New York dentist always scheduled him after his other patients because he made such a fuss.)

"The more I think of your place the better I like it," Aleck wrote from Lake Bomoseen, "and after considerable gastric meditation I have come to the conclusion that you set the best table I know in America. The Charlie Bracketts, Joe Alsop in Washington, and the Ted Roosevelts on Long Island are the other entries for the benison of my approval."

Alfred smiled. At 255 pounds, Aleck was a prime gourmand. ("Rancor was Woollcott's only form of exercise," said Marc Connelly.) Alfred had created for his friend Fraises Alexander: molded French ice cream coated with raspberry ice and glazed with a sauce of crushed strawberries, sugar, grated orange peel, and Cointreau. It rivaled the Brandy Alexander created in Woollcott's name. On this visit Alfred plied Aleck with Bombay bisque, cardamom bread, and maple-syrup dumplings. If he and Lynnie couldn't find a play, maybe he'd publish that damned cookbook.

On September 3, 1939, two days after Hitler invaded Poland, Great Britain and France declared war on Nazi Germany.

Noël telephoned from London.

"Well, my darlings, it may be a long time before Rabbit's Bottom

Alfred pulls a loaf of his famous Swedish cardamom bread from the oven.

sees Grandpa and Grandma again. Think of me, think of old England. I am thinking of you."

Idiot's Delight had become reality.

Lynn and Alfred took a bottle of champagne and walked hand in hand to the Studio. Alfred popped the cork. They toasted England, Noël, Graham, their many other English friends, their cherished London audiences. They finished the bottle in silence. Alfred locked the door behind them. "We will not open the Studio until Noëlly is with us again," they said.

In the next years Lynn's frustration and rage grew as America under the influence of isolationists like William Randolph Hearst, Henry Ford, and Charles Lindbergh campaigned against Roosevelt and U.S. involvement in Europe. She grew ashamed to look English friends in the face as America shirked a moral commitment to her country she felt it must make.

Many of the Lunts' friends were passionate Anglophiles. In 1940, though suffering heart disease, Aleck would campaign for Roosevelt. Behrman had deep feeling for Britain. Sherwood, who owned an English country house, became a trusted Roosevelt assistant. Difficult to explain to her sister Antoinette, to Bessie Porter, to Jamie and Yvonne Hamilton that most Americans considered World War II none of their business.

Because the University of Wisconsin asked them to inaugurate its new theater and they thought *The Taming of the Shrew* would be just the ticket, they decided to go "whoopsing across the country" in a revival, opening in Washington, heading west to Los Angeles, playing Christmas in Tulsa, winding up back East in January 1940.

Their auditions at the Guild Theatre in New York were not publicized, but word got out and Fifty-second Street between Seventh and Eighth Avenues looked like a Cecil B. DeMille mob scene. Alfred drove up in a taxi with Sydney Greenstreet and Dickie Whorf and shouted to the crowd. "Ladies and gentlemen, I deeply regret this, but there are only four parts that Miss Fontanne and I are auditioning. There are two women's parts and there are two men's parts." They didn't have to audition anyone without an appointment, but tenderhearted Alfred couldn't turn anyone away. As Lynn interviewed for the part of Bianca, the line wound through the corridor and out into the street.

On October 9 they christened the sleek new Union Theater with a bang-up *Shrew,* then after the performance joined a receiving line to shake hands and autograph programs. Ben had driven Hattie to Madison for the event: "It was a night of triumph for Mrs. Harriet Sederholm. . . . Looking enough like Queen Victoria to have stepped out of the cast of *Victoria Regina,* Mrs. Sederholm was one of the most striking figures in the assemblage of fashionable guests. Her white hair worn high in the manner of the noted English queen, Mrs. Sederholm wore a modified mantilla of black Chantilly lace and a simple black gown, its low square neckline outlined in fine lace." As her son-in-law George Bugbee had learned when he took her to a circus, Hattie got more attention than acrobats and clowns.

Attending the Union Theater opening, Lee Simonson, Stark Young, and S. N. Behrman were struck by the impossibility. Lunt and Fontanne had brought their 1936 *Shrew* to the pitch of perfection. Yet here was *Shrew* again, far better than before, with a bang-up new entrance for Lynn. She came on dressed in hunting clothes and carrying a blunderbuss. Aiming skyward, she fired. A big bird fell at her feet, convulsing the audience. Young and Behrman went home to tackle their typewriters.

Unluckily for them, Bob Sherwood, fresh from a second Pulitzer for *Abe Lincoln in Illinois,* was drafting his friends a new play. Edna Ferber had been so right about Sherwood: "All you have to do to succeed is get away from the Algonquin for two years," she'd told him.

On this tour the Guild touted Lunt and Fontanne's company as "by far the most accomplished group of actors in the country." Guthrie McClintic disagreed, claiming that Katharine Cornell as a manager had "assembled casts that few have equaled and none surpassed." Indeed, a list including Leslie Howard, Franchot Tone, Burgess Meredith, Margalo Gillmore, Ruth Gordon, Ralph Richardson, Edith Evans, Mildred Natwick, Brenda Forbes, Basil Rathbone, Laurence Olivier, and Orson Welles is unbeatable. But none of these actors formed a permanent company for Cornell. What is notable is that she could and did act with other major names. Lunt and Fontanne may have had the most accomplished group, but they were the stars.

The Lunts treated newcomers to that group (males at least) like family—Cameron Mitchell, Donald Buka, William Le Massena, Robert Downing. Reflecting the family atmosphere, Downing began editing the *Luntanne Tatler,* a gossipy weekly with the motto "The troupe, the whole troupe and nothing but the troupe." It featured "Tattle Tales," "Season's Quiz" ("In what town did Sydney Greenstreet talk to the wrong blonde?"), paragraphs on favorite people and what the critics said. When they weren't playing matinees Alfred would go off to burlesque shows with the guys. "We'll have a nice cup of tea," Lynn would say firmly to the actresses.

The Nazi-Soviet nonaggression pact in August sickened the whole company. Then on November 30 Russia bombed Helsinki— Alfred's Helsingfors, where he had spent summers as a boy and young man, where his stepfather had died, where he had introduced Lynn to the beauties of Finland.

That December in San Francisco, defying Alfred's black mood, Lynn made a dramatic entrance into his dressing room at the Geary Theatre swathed in sables. "Alfred, it's so dear of you. Dickie and I shopped at Gump's and look what you bought me for Christmas!" Alfred retaliated the next day, dropping a bill for a new tractor onto her dressing table.

They kept up the holiday spirit, partying in Los Angeles with Joan Crawford, Charlie Chaplin, and Bette Davis. At Christmas they threw the whole company a bash in Fort Worth, Texas, with daiquiris, turkey, Christmas pudding, and champagne. Even more festive was a celebration on the train of a British victory, with one of the company jumping up and singing "Rule, Britannia," then everyone joining in with World War I songs like "Tipperary," "Pack Up Your Troubles," "Mademoiselle from Armentières"—ending tearfully with "God Save the King."

Alfred was thinking of Finland. After almost two years away from New York, therefore, they decided to bring *Shrew* into the Alvin Theatre to play a week of benefits for the Finnish Relief Fund. After the second performance, on February 6, 1940, Alfred stepped before the curtain to announce that the first night had netted $3,032. Then Herbert Hoover, chairman of the Fund, rose to thank Lunt and Fontanne for an unprecedented week of benefit performances. Good cause aside (the Lunts raised $25,000), their *Shrew* was welcomed back as great entertainment, "infinitely better by the entire company than at the end of the New York run," praised Langner, though Brooks Atkinson called this lily too gilded for his taste.

"The blaze of excitement and warm affection from the audience was wonderful," Lynn wrote Graham, "as the American theater is nothing like so personal as the English. But every night was like opening night in London."

Meanwhile Bob Sherwood, riveted by a Christmas broadcast from Helsinki, had been charging ahead with his play for the Lunts, depending on talks with Alfred for much of his information about Finland. He swore to complete the second draft on February 10, 1940, the day Lynn and Alfred were leaving for Genesee. When he came backstage with the manuscript tucked under his arm, he met Stark Young similarly equipped. Both felt like "suitors caught bringing flowers to the same girl."

Lynn finished Sherwood's script, called *Revelation,* by Harrisburg. At 3 a.m. Alfred telegraphed him that she was wild about the play and wanted to do it immediately. On February 12 Sherwood called Ten Chimneys. Alfred was so crazy about it that he wanted to stage and direct and had already summoned Dickie Whorf to talk sets. Elated, Sherwood caught a train for Wisconsin.

CHAPTER ELEVEN

There Shall Be No Night: 1940–1942

He arrived with flowers for Lynn and sat down immediately with Whorf's scene sketches, which he thought excellent. The Lunts forgot they were exhausted from the *Shrew* tour: there was laughter and toasts. Sherwood had remarried, but Madeline seldom came to Ten Chimneys, so that it was just Lynn and the men as usual. "Dined too well," Sherwood noted in his diary. "To bed late."

On February 14 he announced production; the play, now titled *There Shall Be No Night,* went into rehearsal March 2 even though everyone was saying it needed drastic cutting. The story was simple. Russia invades Finland. Dr. Kaarlo Valkonen, a Nobel-winning neurologist, deplores war. His son, Erik, and Erik's fiancée, Kaatri, are already fighting on the front. The Russians close in. Valkonen tries to persuade his American wife, Miranda, to leave the country. She refuses. Word comes that Erik has been killed. The antiwar doctor picks up a gun and goes off to certain death, leaving his wife to face the enemy as Uncle Waldemar at the piano plays a Finnish folk tune.

Tragic, yet *There Shall Be No Night* throbbed with optimism. Kaatri is pregnant; there will be new life. Miranda and Uncle Waldemar have guns and ammunition; they'll go down fighting. And when he is asked, "But how can you deny that the light is going out—it's going fast—

Robert Sherwood, Alfred, and Lynn go over the script of There Shall Be No Night *(1940).*

everywhere?" Valkonen replies: "It is just beginning to burn with a healthy flame." Anguished about the fate of Finland and Europe, Sherwood had unashamedly written *There Shall Be No Night* as propaganda to end what he considered his country's suicidal isolationism. Valkonen's decision to fight must be America's.

Sydney Greenstreet played melancholy Uncle Waldemar ("There's been too much Sibelius in his life"), Dickie Whorf a CBS representative in Finland to broadcast a talk by Dr. Valkonen. A problem was the son, Erik. Donald Buka desperately wanted the part, but was too young and finally was let go, taking with him letters of recommendation and Lynn's advice, "Donald, I don't want you going to have a beer at Ralph's Bar. That's where the losers go. I want you to go to Sardi's. It's good for you to associate with the best."

Arriving on time to audition for Erik, a young man in a gray flannel Brooks Brothers suit and polished shoes sauntered across the stage, bent over Lynn's hand, and kissed it. "Look what the wind blew in!" murmured Alfred. He gave the young man a long look, walked over to Lynn, and said, "That's the boy." Lynn studied him. "Yes," she said, "I guess that's the boy."

The Lunts silently hired Montgomery Clift on the spot, but sent him away only with encouragement. He'd just been fired without explanation from *Life With Father*—the dark, nervous, rake-thin young man could never play a comic juvenile. Now—sure he'd lost the part of Erik Valkonen—he walked into a barbershop and recklessly demanded a butch. Lunt and Fontanne hired him sheared.

Here was a son more real than their boy in London tended by Miss Prinn. Alfred immediately recognized a natural actor, an actor who— like himself—was able to spin thought behind action and words. But everyone in the company adored Monty, particularly Phyllis Thaxter, a new ingenue. And William Le Massena.

As for Monty Clift, he worshiped the Lunts for their glamour, animal vitality, and sheer passion for acting. Being in the hands of "the Gestapo" thrilled the sensitive and insecure young actor. He loved the discipline, loved the fact that Alfred never wasted a moment once rehearsals began. He admired his meticulous shaping of subtexts, working until not a word or expression failed to hit its mark.

Lynn, Montgomery Clift, and Alfred in There Shall Be No Night. *Clift worshiped Alfred and copied his style.*

He began slavishly imitating Alfred's style. Lunt's great gift was persuading an audience that he spoke and reacted on the spur of the moment. The technique was highly calculated, like the Lunt-Fontanne overlapping. He would hesitate—seemingly at a loss—stumble a little, then rush into speech, tumbling words over each other. In moments of emotion he pitched his voice higher. He took pauses during which he reached out to actors. Soon Montgomery Clift sounded exactly like Alfred Lunt. Since in this play he was Alfred's son, he got away with it.

He considered Alfred Lunt a genius like Laurette Taylor, and listened wide-eyed to his creed: "Don't work for money—don't work for fame. Work to be good at what you do. It's the quality of the work that is important, not the salary or size of your billing. And if you're good at what you do, you damn well know you can be a helluva lot better. You must never stop working. There are only glimmers of perfection in acting and they are always astonishing. But creation is a mystery and the end result is acceptance only if you don't see the work behind it."

Gradually Alfred and Lynn realized that Monty was a confused young man agonizing about his sexuality—pretending to be as attracted to Phyllis Thaxter as she was to him, hating the pretense. Alfred cared so much about Monty that he warned him against homosexuality, a public route he had rigorously shunned. Being gay could ruin his career. "Noël Coward's an exception. You can't ordinarily be a pansy in the theater and survive." Clift listened to the warning from an actor who was obviously tortured himself. But he couldn't change. What he did absorb was Alfred's artistry: "Alfred taught me how to select. Acting is an accumulation of subtle details. And the details of Alfred Lunt's performances were like the observations of a great novelist—like Samuel Butler or Marcel Proust."

At rehearsals Sherwood discovered that his writing was "very sloppy. . . . Awful repetition. Lynn wonderful, & Alfred." He accepted Lynn's suggestion that scene 3 end with the coffee Mrs. Valkonen has made going cold. Watching a rehearsal, John Wharton of the Playwrights' Company reflected that along with every successful actor's technical skill, good looks, and personality, Lunt and Fontanne had "something more. Playing together they could, by some mysterious magic, bring a scene to life in a way that no one ever quite understood." They were doing it now: turning a discussion about coffee into a moving reconciliation between husband and wife.

Alfred was directing the play "exquisitely. . . . The quality of gentle people is being brought out so well—people who love and respect each other." Greenstreet, Whorf, and Clift were outstanding; Lunt and Fontanne playing with great simplicity, force, and conviction. During rehearsals the war in Finland ended, yet the story of Finland's three months of resistance was more current than ever, with Denmark and Norway in the Nazis' way.

There Shall Be No Night came into the Alvin Theatre in New York on April 29, 1940—three and a half months after Sherwood typed the first word. When he slipped into the Alvin at the end of the first scene of Act Two the place was vibrating with success.

At the post-theater party they accepted congratulations from the Herbert Bayard Swopes, Averell Harrimans, Gladys Swarthout, Harold Ross, Helen Hayes, Jack and Natasha Wilson, Valentina, Fredric March and Florence Eldridge, George and Beatrice Kaufman, Ruth Gordon, and Edna Ferber. Noël, too, was at the party, "sweet, dear and very serious." He had wept throughout the play.

Inevitably critics found that Robert Sherwood had written too fast. Yet *There Shall Be No Night* was an important play. As for the acting: "If Mr. Sherwood's craftsmanship is often uncertain," said Brooks Atkinson in the *Times,* "the Lunts' is unexceptionable. Aroused by the sincerity of their playing, they and their associates are acting it beautifully. Mr. Lunt, who was fooling with Shakespeare a while ago, looks the part of Dr. Valkonen straight in the face and acts it with impersonal sobriety and understanding, not forgetting to speak the contemplative passages with driving precision. As Mrs. Valkonen, Miss Fontanne plays with a light touch in the early scenes and a gallantry in the later ones that round out a completely articulate character. This is one of her finest characterizations." *There Shall Be No Night,* said Atkinson, "honors the theatre."

Aleck came to a performance, bolted afterwards to Lynn's dressing room in tears. "She tactfully shooed people out so that I might have a little decent quiet for a good cry. But if she counted on being allowed to stay and enjoy the spectacle herself she was in error. I threw her out and wept noisily amid her costumes."

Charlie Chaplin telegraphed: INTENDED TO COME AROUND AFTER-WARDS BUT WE WERE TOO DEEPLY MOVED BY THE PLAY AND YOUR MEMORABLE PERFORMANCES. IT IS A SHAFT OF LIGHT SHINING THROUGH THE SOMBRE SKIES.

Eleanor Roosevelt came to a performance—"an experience I shall never forget"—and wrote in her newspaper column, "My Day":

Robert E. Sherwood has written a remarkable play in *There Shall Be No Night.* Of course, Alfred Lunt and Lynn Fontanne give a performance so perfect that I felt I was living in this portrayal on the stage. The rest of the cast is so good that we finished the evening feeling that we had actually been through every experience in that Finnish family's existence, which tragically enough, is now part of the life of so many other people. May God grant that if such dark hours should ever come to us, we may acquit ourselves as well!

Inevitably, *There Shall Be No Night* roused violent antagonisms. The Communist *Daily Worker* branded Sherwood "the stooge of the imperialist war mongers," and the *Daily Mirror* accused him of exploiting the Finnish situation to incite militarism. Declaring that "Warmongers Capture Alvin Theatre," a group called the Theatre Arts Committee distributed leaflets asking audiences to sign peace petitions. In May, in

Alfred, Richard Whorf, Lynn, Elizabeth Fraser, Montgomery Clift, and Sydney Greenstreet in There Shall Be No Night

the midst of the controversy, Germany overran Belgium and the Netherlands, broke into France, and swept to the English Channel. Alfred began to make curtain speeches in support of resisting military aggression—an idea that, said Atkinson, had become "an understatement of reality now."

It was this sense that they were doing something important, not only for the theater, but for democracy and freedom, that drove Lunt and Fontanne to new heights in *There Shall Be No Night.* Audiences felt their sense of mission as well as their transcendent artistry and responded passionately night after night. Lynn called it the most satisfying play she had ever done. As for Alfred, he had "never been so happy in a play or loved one so much as this."

Wanting to devote more energy to the war cause, Alfred wrote Helburn and Langner:

> It is with considerable regret that I must tender my resignation as a director of the Theatre Guild—Even if the Board was functioning as a whole (and I enjoyed that enormously) I should have to resign—as I feel I have not the time nor energy to give it what I should. . . . I would like to slip away as quietly as possible— You will understand I know.

In Genesee Lynn organized a "Knittin' for Britain" society. She kept a British Relief Fund tin can in her dressing room and rattled it in autograph hunters' faces until they gave. In July 1940 she and Alfred broadcast a scene from the play for the benefit of the Red Cross. Lynn made a thousand dollars for the American Theater Wing's British Relief Fund by advertising her "lily white hands" for Pacquins hand cream. Then, on October 13, Lynn broadcast a poem by her friend the novelist and short-story writer Alice Duer Miller called "The White Cliffs of Dover." By popular demand, she repeated the broadcast two weeks later, would read the poem again on tour in Vancouver, Canada (other programming suspended for her half-hour), perform it with the Cleveland Orchestra, and finally record it in 1941 for NBC and Victor Records.

Beginning "I have loved England dearly and deeply," Miller's "White Cliffs" tells the story of an American woman married to an Englishman. Johnny goes to France; Susan stays with Johnny's mother in Devon; Susan gives birth to a son. Susan longs for the United States to help desperate England; finally help comes, though too late for Johnny.

The Victor recording is one of relatively few surviving performances of Lynn Fontanne. Her voice is a strong contralto. Though she pronounces "hour" *ahr,* "cast" *cahst,* and "were" *wear,* she does not have an overpowering British accent. Her vowels are pure, with few if any diphthongs. Her diction is perfect. She often drops her voice at the end of lines. She reads fast. She sounds tough, strong, clear, and supremely unsentimental. It was precisely this unsentimentality that brought her audiences to tears when, for instance, Englishmen uncover their heads at the sight of the Yanks, or when she concludes:

> *I am American bred.*
> *I have seen much to hate here, much to forgive.*
> *But in a world where England is finished and dead*
> *I do not wish to live.*

That July 1940 they took a deserved break on Aleck's Neshobe Island.

Aleck himself needed rest. In March 1939 *The New Yorker* had published a vitriolic three-part profile of Woollcoot by Wolcott Gibbs (the Lunts loyally canceled their subscription). That same year Hart and Kaufman's *The Man Who Came to Dinner,* with its uproariously acid portrait of Woollcott as Sheridan Whiteside, had been an enormous hit, flooding Aleck with publicity. Though Monty Woolley created "his" part, Aleck headed a third company on the West Coast. ("You can take it from me," he admitted, "I was pretty lousy.") Soon acting, violent socializing, and gourmandizing sent him to the hospital with a severe heart attack. He recuperated on Neshobe, surrounded by visitors.

As they'd been depicted by Hirschfeld sitting a little apart from the Algonquin Round Tablers, Alfred and Lynn stayed at the larger house when visiting Aleck. "The Lunts will occupy my house on top of the hill," he once wrote publisher Harold Guinzberg, one of the original shareholders in the island. "Perhaps you could arrange a design for living with them."

This time guests included Noël, the Ted Roosevelts, Vincent Sheean and his wife, Dinah (niece of the actress Maxine Elliott), and Ethel Barrymore, with her "morose gaiety." Lynn was impressed by the vivacious Dinah: "I like her as I like few women." She and Alfred were full of plans to bring Michael Redgrave's wife, Rachel Kempson, and their babies, Vanessa and Lynn, over to the States for safety. Lynn Redgrave had been named for Lynn Fontanne.

With France's surrender, Britain had been left to fight on alone. That July Germany launched its Luftwaffe to bomb the island into submission. Sherwood, Lynn, and Alfred (and the White House) had already decided that the message of *There Shall Be No Night* must be spread cross-country with a tour.

An odd time, then, for a quarrel with Edna Ferber, who had been so shocked by Lynn's statement that she hoped England would give Bermuda to the Germans so that the United States would know what war means that Ferber felt "as though I were an alien in my own country [and] was ill as a result." She recovered enough to beg them to campaign for Roosevelt: the Lunts were "important not only as the two leading names in the acting profession" but for all that was respected in the theater.

Alfred replied as always that actors had no place in politics. Their audiences comprised Democrats and Republicans: the theater must unite, not divide. "I reject most of your letter, Alfred," replied Ferber, "because I know you so well." Of course with *There Shall Be No Night* the Lunts had already taken on the isolationists—chiefly Republicans.

"That horrible, horrible Lindbergh," raged Lynn, less diplomatic than Alfred. "What a dreadful traitor to his country. And that dreadful Kathleen Norris, whom I have known for years. . . . I suppose with a country of this size we could hardly hope to escape our Quislings. . . . They are either fools or knaves and in either case a washout. It eliminates 50% of your friends, doesn't it? And that's O.K. with me. . . . From now on I neither speak to them nor acknowledge that they are alive, no matter where I meet them."

FDR was re-elected (the Lunts were invited but unable to attend the inauguration ceremonies), and that November the company left on its twelve-thousand-mile tour, including two Canadian provinces. Aleck met the train with hot cider and doughnuts as it halted for ten minutes near Bomoseen—but, as he told Graham, "if there is a troupe in the world that doesn't need feeding it's that one. Nor cheering, either. At least Lynn and Alfred feel as never before that they are engaged in something worth doing. This play lets them say every night what is in their hearts so that nightly they are refreshed and renewed."

From the Ottawa and Toronto performances Bob Sherwood donated his percentage and Lynn and Alfred their salaries, as well as fifty percent of all Canadian profits to the British cause—down payment on a Spitfire.

They ran into pockets of resistance to *There Shall Be No Night*—picketing in Philadelphia, poor reviews in Chicago, which, Alfred told Sherwood, was "notoriously anti-war, and I believe to a great extent anti-British." The most bizarre attempt to undermine the play was a letter sent to Washington's *Post* and *Evening Star,* supposedly from Genesee:

My dear friend,
I find that I must ask a favor of you, and, if you can do this favor, it would help us all.
When our show *There Shall Be No Night* comes to Washington, would it be asking too much to just forget writing a review? Or if you can't do that, just give us a very small notice—an unfavorable one. Of course, I would want you to consult your managing editor about this.
I trust that you will understand my feelings in this matter as we are not at all eager to continue in this play. . . .
If you can do this favor it will mean so much, and I thought it kinder to give you my honest opinion. I shall be very grateful.
                                                    Yours sincerely,
                                                    Lynn Fontanne

No sabotage could turn away audiences: they played to sold-out houses everywhere.

A dream tour, Alfred called it, which broke on May 3, 1941, to give cast and stars a rest. That month the Lunts strenuously observed their nineteenth wedding anniversary:

First of all, Alfred kissed me good morning and said, "This is our wedding day. I have a surprise dinner for you tonight." So I went down to MY cellar and brought out a surprise bottle of Château d'Yquem. We had a grand dinner and drank the whole bottle. The next day we turned on the radio and a voice boomed forth, "And it is also the wedding anniversary of Alfred Lunt and Lynn Fontanne." We were very surprised but felt their head for figures was probably better than ours, and so we celebrated again—

brought out another bottle of wine and had a wonderful time.
The next day we had a letter from that old black Louise, our first
cook. . . . She congratulated us on our anniversary and said she
would always remember the date as it was her sister's birthday.
We felt that that was more than authentic and so we celebrated
again—did ourselves up brown. The following day was the sink-
ing of the *Bismarck* which seemed to me an even better excuse
than any, and so now we are rather tired, chastened, and on the
wagon. . . .

In June Alfred and Lynn left for Canada on a fishing trip with Carl,
who indeed had settled down with Pat and had a son, Alexander (Alex
was born with a deformed ear and jaw; Alfred paid for the operations),
and Carl's friend Archie Koeffler. Archie's wife, Katherine, came along
to keep Lynn company. Every morning Lynn went out in the boat with
Alfred, Archie, and Carl and fished all day, leaving Katherine alone in
the cabin.

On return they were presented with Doctor of Letters degrees by the
University of Wisconsin—"rather amusing, considering that we can
hardly spell." Bob and Madeline Sherwood came to see them through
the ordeal. They found that Alfred had already been drawn into another
war effort: directing Maxwell Anderson's antifascist drama *Candle in the
Wind,* starring Helen Hayes as an American actress in occupied Paris.

Acting Anderson's *Elizabeth the Queen* twenty-one years before,
Alfred and Lynn had been full of advice. As director (for the first time
not acting himself), Alfred was all over *Candle in the Wind.* To Max
Anderson:

[Franchot] Tone would be superb of course & so would [Cedric]
Hardwick[e]—as the Emperor. . . . By all means let's have Kurt
Weill's wife [Lotte Lenya] in the play—She's an awfully nice
person and I should think a good actress. . . . Eric[h] Von Stro-
heim is in *Arsenic & Old Lace* and doubt if you could get him—
He'd be alright as a last resort but he's so awfully common in his
speech. . . . I'm sure you're right about [Paul] Muni, also—He
certainly is a fine actor but grossly miscast as Raoul—He'd probably be too timid to play Erfurt—He could if he weren't afraid &
hated the Nazis ENOUGH. All people from Hollywood seem so
frightened. . . . Ray Massey would be better . . . or even [Oscar]
Homolka or Conrad Veidt. It needs someone with real sting.

I've talked to Jo [Mielziner] & I've written him—I do hope he doesn't mind all my suggestions. I've stuck my nose into scenery for so many years I can't seem to resist. . . . It seems to me, that the play should have (and God knows has) the inescapable, hypnotic sound and effect of the thumping of a great clock—persistent obstinate—and through it now & then a great burst of chimes. This sounds Goddam arty and so much poop—but maybe I can make myself clearer sometime.

Wish we could find a plumpish peasantish type for that mother. . . . I can see that character so clearly—in a four buttoned dark suit, black cotton stockings & gloves—a small plush hat—black shiny shoes with a strap—a little white showing at her throat—with a small gold brooch—and she carries quite a large soft bag—she also keeps dabbing the right corner of her mouth with a tightly rolled handkerchief. It is so—isn't it?

After a visit from Laurence Olivier—"burnt black . . . excellent health . . . too fat . . . dieting now"—Alfred and Lynn cut their Genesee stay short, arriving in New York July 21 for a blissful weekend at Kit and Guthrie's island house at Martha's Vineyard. Rehearsals began August 19; Alfred "wearing crepe." He was having particular trouble with an actor who had personality but no technique: "That man doesn't even know how to lift his ass off one chair and put it down on another."

Theresa Helburn later analyzed the difference between Alfred and Lynn as directors. "Lynn could always tell the actor exactly what to do and how. Alfred could and would only suggest gently, tentatively, with a great sense of the actor's sensitivity, which was his own, and a real humility. Lynn sensed the actor's weakness and her method was more a strength-giving one—where Alfred's was a stimulating of the actor to develop his own performance from within." She noted with less approval that Alfred was directing Helen Hayes as Lynn would have played the part.

Candle in the Wind opened at the Colonial in Boston September 15, 1941, Alfred "nervous as a cat" and Helen Hayes in despair over Anderson's unwillingness to make changes. Max was the playwright who wrote best when it rained; evidently Boston was dry. Alfred would have cheerfully rewritten for him, but instead was going mad over the reluctant playwright.

Candle in the Wind came into New York on October 22, 1941, where it ran for ninety-five performances, then toured. Burns Mantle in the

Daily News said that "Alfred Lunt directed the play in something of the impressively serious mood and convincing realism he used with Sherwood's *There Shall Be No Night.* But in this instance he has permitted a kind of dull gray monotony to settle over the telling of the story which smothers it with set rather than human speeches." In general, critics felt Lunt's direction was overreverent. Woollcott thought Anderson had written a bad play.

Lynn had her own opinion. *Candle in the Wind*

flopped and the awful part of it is that it need not have. It was an excellent script. It needed a little toning down here and there. . . . The end of the play we knew would never go at all. Alfred made various suggestions to Max and I made one that everybody thought was good, but Max simply could not write it. He seemed plunged into a sort of elephantine lethargy—nearly drove Alfred insane—and then finally did nothing at all. The minute Alfred's back was turned . . . [the Guild and Playwrights'] did some rearranging, took themselves into New York and had a terrible flop and served them damned well right.

Alfred had asked $2,000 for directing plus two percent of the gross receipts; he donated half that sum to the Actors' Fund. "They certainly left me holding the bag with *Candle in the Wind,*" he wrote Jack Wilson. To Langner: "I thought possibly a miracle would happen but apparently nothing of the kind passed its way—which only goes to prove that actors never pulled a play through yet. . . . I wanted to get out of the damned thing in Baltimore but like a fool didn't. It serves me bloody well right! Well . . . it's knocked out any desire in me to do anything in the theater again for a long, long time to come. We have got a nice place in the country and I think I can make it fairly profitable. I can raise my own raspberries in Genesee, which is a damned sight more fun, thank you, than in New York."

Alfred had not been around to take the flak. GOOD LUCK GOOD LUCK GOOD LUCK, he'd wired the Playwrights' Company on opening night from Norfolk, Virginia, back on tour with *There Shall Be No Night.*

Though sold-out houses loved it, political events finally doomed Sherwood's play. In 1941 Finland joined Germany in fighting the USSR. "What else can Finland do?" asked Alfred. ". . . Since the Germans helped them out in 1917 it's obvious they'd welcome them once again. They prefer Fascism to Communism." Then on December 7 Japan's First Air Fleet bombed Pearl Harbor and America at last declared war against the Axis powers. With Russia now a U.S. ally, the anti-Russian theme of *There Shall Be No Night* became an embarrassment. Under pressure from the White House and after a meeting with the Playwrights Company, Sherwood announced he would withdraw his play. Alfred was devastated: never before had he been so deeply involved in a drama. They had intended to tour it into February 1942, then reopen on Broadway.

There Shall Be No Night, Alfred wrote Theresa Helburn, "has been the greatest privilege and experience of my life in the theater. It can never come about again. I should like now to get a shooting job if possible (and I don't mean movies) and I shall make every effort in that direction."

The company gave its last performance December 18 in Rochester, Minnesota, then left for Genesee Depot, where the Lunts threw the cast a farewell party and distributed gifts. To their adored Monty Clift they gave a photograph of themselves signed "From your real parents."

Alfred and Lynn gave each other cows—two Jerseys named Lily and Sugar after Langtry and her husband Sir Hugo "Sugar" de Bathe. They became the stars of Ten Chimneys. "Alfred is blissful making the butter," Lynn told Graham, "we have cottage cheese too—we love having them. . . . Sugar was taken off to a rendezvous with what Alfred calls her bull-friend if we get a cow-calf we shall call her Ellen [Terry]—Nell—for short." Skeptics like the Greenes, who owned the large dairy Brookhill Farm, didn't think the Lunts could sell their milk and butter. "Your mother is the best friend we have in this," Ben Perkins wrote Alfred. "She is as thrilled as anyone with the whole idea. It seems to me she is more in keeping with your ideas, from Roosevelt down."

Since letters often didn't get through, Alfred had been sending LOVE LOVE LOVE cables to Graham (Lynn was sending monthly food hampers) and that New Year's Eve wired him that he was thinking of him while having Graham's favorite supper—lobster and a bottle of beer. They were blissfully snowed in at twenty-four below zero on their first New Year's Eve in their completed house. Next day there was skiing and tobogganing.

Aleck dropped in for twenty-four hours, strangely angelic since his heart attack. "I think," said Lynn, "it is that he was just about to leave us all for a long time and realised acutely how much he loved us. . . .

There are occasional flashes of the old devil but it's mostly a rather chastened little boy infinitely tender and lovable."

The talk, of course, was "What play now?" They wanted to avoid politics. "We want to do an hilarious comedy next but, even better, a musical—a review. We could do all the sketches, talk a few songs—take it on a grand tour . . . spot all the camps and naval bases." They would have played *There Shall Be No Night* for the duration; since that was impossible, they wanted to make audiences laugh.

CHAPTER TWELVE

A Very Good War: 1942–1945

Twenty-five years before, Alfred had played *The Pirate* in Milwaukee summer stock. Still thinking of touring military bases, he asked Sam Behrman to rework the play as another *Taming of the Shrew* with stunts, dance, magic tricks, and music. Perhaps Behrman suggested Kurt Weill for the music. At any rate a flurry of negotiations began that February 1942, thoroughly discussed by Weill and Lenya, who was touring with Helen Hayes in *Candle in the Wind.*

Alfred went to the Milwaukee opening of *Candle* on February 24 and had Ben Perkins drive Lenya to Ten Chimneys, where Helen Hayes was staying four days. (Lynn had left for New York; there was still rivalry between them.) "They [the Lunts] have nothing and are dying to find a show," Lenya told Weill, adding Helen's opinion of Alfred: "He is really very dumm, doesn't know anything what's going on in the world and is just a good actor. I am sure that's true. If you talk to them just be very sure and dont treat them too carefully. He hasn't got much mind of his own and you can talk him into anything."

Alfred soon joined Lynn in New York, where they became deeply involved in the Stage Door Canteen, sponsored by the American Theatre Wing. Entertainers like Al Jolson, Sophie Tucker, Benny

Goodman, and Count Basie performed for American servicemen, who were served coffee and doughnuts by Helen Hayes, Katharine Cornell, and Tallulah Bankhead while others did the lindy hop with Ethel Merman, Kitty Carlisle, and Julie Haydon. Three thousand to four thousand servicemen and -women poured into the basement of the 44th Street Theatre nightly.

Sleeves rolled, Alfred was "chief cook and bottle washer of the American Theatre Wing." He did everything from talk to GIs to spread sandwiches to carry out trash. "He's the only man who succeeded in putting glamour into garbage," said Kit Cornell. In the 1943 movie *Stage Door Canteen,* Alfred and Lynn in cameos are outshone by Cornell, reciting Juliet's balcony speech to a soldier, and by Katharine Hepburn, ending the film with a call to arms. One can sense their modesty, Lynn in an absurd hat that ties under her chin (relic of *Idiot's Delight?*), Alfred lurking shyly behind her. "I suppose Alfred and I will come out looking like a couple of crepe bags," said Lynn resignedly. The movie netted more than a million dollars for Allied causes. Few worked harder at the Canteen than Lunt and Fontanne, who called it "my pride and joy and the center of my life."

Then in April Alfred agreed to give two cooking classes a week for the Theatre Wing at their offices at 730 Fifth Avenue. If Alfred was nervous before a performance, he was a basket case before his first class, sleeplessly rehearsing recipes and one-liners like "There are many superb cooks who, for some unaccountable reason, serve the most appalling breakfasts" and "The perfectly poached egg should resemble a veiled bride swooning away on a mattress of toast."

In white chef's hat and apron, Alfred did a breakfast for an in crowd of forty-seven that included John Mason Brown, Antoinette Perry, and Mrs. William Randolph Hearst. Alfred started simply with Sunday breakfast—scrambled eggs, fish, bacon, potatoes, and fruit. But when the flame (unnoticed) went out under his famous Swedish brew he had to admit, "This is the lousiest coffee I've ever tasted."

Over the next weeks the class learned the mysteries of Norwegian fish balls, Tipsy Parson, And the Priest Fainted (lots of garlic), and Oysters and Sole in Lobster Sauce. Alfred's cooking was rich and buttery, full of cream, wines, egg yolks; fragrant with spices; heavy on beef, veal, sausages, tongue, kidneys. He cooked as he acted—wholeheartedly—and for the same reasons. Watching Alfred cook, said Herman Shumlin, "was like watching a performance."

Negotiations with Weill went on as Behrman labored on the script. Weill thought *The Pirate* could make a million. Lenya agreed: "First it's an interesting job for you, 2nd the Lunts! . . . I hope Alfred is not too stupid." Weill lunched with Behrman and Alfred, observing the actor's near-hysteria when Sam suggested Lenya would rather be at home than on the road: "No, no, she wouldn't leave the show! An actor should never leave a show!"

Then on April 11 Alfred called to say the whole deal was off, because the Guild insisted on producing *The Pirate* and he and Lynn refused to work with the Guild. "The Lunts are awful fakers," Weill wrote Lenya. ". . . I wanted them to come to that concert (it would have shown them what could be done with *The Pirate*), but they are soooo busy with the Canteen, and it is soooo wonderful at the Canteen and so on—just ver-logenes Gequatsche [twaddle packed with lies]."

Weill blew hot and cold. One day Lunt was "a great theatre tal-ent . . . ideal for this type of play." Two days later he was furious because Behrman hinted Alfred didn't want to pay him royalties (it was Behrman who didn't want to pay him royalties). He was gratified when the actor loved his idea of black musicians and dancers, then reverted to insult:

> [Sam] has finished rewriting and sent a script to the Lunts.
> Alfred called him up and said, he didn't think it was improved.
> Then Sam, for the first time, got furious and told them that is all
> he can do and they can take it or leave it. Half an hour later
> Alfred called back and said he had read it again and thinks now
> it is very good. They are absolutely awful, those two old fakers,
> and she is definitely the greatest bitch I've ever seen. . . . She was
> tired, soooo "overworked," had to eat dinner early and lie down
> an hour before a radio rehearsal. And he is so dumb and so ego-
> centric! He reminds me of [Otto] Klemperer all the time—the
> same fake voice and the same stupid chicken-eyes. . . . Life is too
> short to be bossed around by two old hams. . . .

Lynn wrote an apology for Alfred to Weill. "Berrie should know Alfred of old. His sledge hammer way of criticizing. . . . [Also] Alfred is always perfectly sure that anything he has to do with is not very good and as he has had so much to do with this play, he feels he is criticizing himself more than Berrie and was therefore freer about it even than usual. . . . He just felt that the play was a little too cut and dried. Our best wishes to you and dear Mrs. Weill."

On May 14 Weill had a talk with Jack Wilson, who was sure the Lunts really wanted him. "But he warned me: working with the Lunts is hell, they are just thinking of themselves, nothing else counts, they consider everybody just at their service, they treated Bob exactly the way they are treating Sam—but the results are worth it."

The collaboration fell through, chiefly because Behrman didn't want the play billed as a musical. And the Lunts recoiled from Weill's hostility (partly homophobic? Weill admired Helen Hayes and Gertrude Lawrence, couldn't stand "that female impersonator Cornell," dismissed Lynn as a bitch and Ten Chimneys as "fairy"). "We wanted Kurt Weill for the music," Lynn told Aleck, "but, even before signing the contract, he has exhibited such signs of trouble that we have decided not to make the difficult days of production more difficult by having him."

In the end the Guild, the Playwrights' Production Company, and Transatlantic Productions all shared *The Pirate*. Back in Genesee Depot that May for the spring planting, Alfred and Lynn huddled with Behrman and John Wilson over tea. (Lynn forbade Behrman to view their herd wearing a red sweater that would enrage the bull, but all he found were four mild cows.) Charva Chester and Renee Orsell were also in residence, and in June the composer Herbert Kingsley and the designer Lemuel Ayers joined them—one big happy family, smiled Lynn.

But their former family—the Lunt Repertory Company they cherished—had broken up. Richard Whorf, Sydney Greenstreet, Thomas Gomez, and Cameron Mitchell had gone to Hollywood, where Sydney made a hit as the suave Gutman in *The Maltese Falcon* and Gomez (one of the few actors who didn't imitate Alfred, said Ruth Gordon, but "is a genius on his own") became a reliable heavy. "I hate to see Dicky go up the movie spout like that because I doubt if he will ever be a successful picture actor," said Lynn, but Sydney's loss hit them hardest: "He is really brilliant in every kind of acting—comedy, tragedy, the whole gamut."

His bulk at least was replaced by Jack Smart, radio's "Fat Man," who became J. Scott Smart when the Lunts told him "Jack Smart" had no class. The fey British comedian Estelle Winwood also joined the cast. As Serafin, a wandering entertainer, Alfred learned to break an egg that turned into a rabbit and expertly fake walking a tightrope between balconies. And the "divine colored people in the cast" were an "honor and a pleasure" to work with.

Lynn always called it Alfred's play, considering the romantic wife, Manuela, "a very dull girl" except they'd "snipped a bit off her here and put a bit on her there." And *The Pirate* wasn't even a play but a show. They were still wrestling with the script when they premiered in Madison, Wisconsin, at the Union Theater on September 13, 1941. Instead of the planned three-week tour, they spent three months on the road— each day prying big words out of the script "mostly over Behrman's dead body." Though Madison and Chicago loved it, Lunt and Fontanne were gloomily certain they had a flop on their hands. Trouble developed in Boston with less than enthusiastic reviews and with Jack Smart, playing the important role of Manuela's husband, Pedro.

Though Lynn said, "I get more from Jack's eyes than I get from anybody's," Jack complained she kept changing lines on him, while the Lunts complained that Smart was "a soft, kind little fellow with no menace at all." By the time the revamped *Pirate* came into New York, Alan Reed had replaced Smart as Pedro—"though that part, I'm afraid, will always wait for Sydney Greenstreet."

Visiting New York, Jamie Hamilton had his first taste of Alfred in the throes. "I shall never learn this damned part!" he groaned, throwing himself full-length on the sofa. "Why will Sam write such difficult stuff? It's worse than Shakespeare." The next time Hamilton saw him, Alfred was bubbling with enthusiasm. Graham Robertson wasn't worried. Having read the script, he thought Serafin fit Alfred "like a skintight suit" yet left him free "to play about and enjoy himself."

They opened with éclat at the Martin Beck on November 27, 1942. "The Lunts are in it up to their necks," wrote Louis Kronenberger in *PM*. ". . . To get by with such fol-de-rol, you must have one of two things: a first-rate musical comedy score, or a lady and gentleman from Genesee Depot, Wisc." Said Lewis Nicholls in the *Times:* "Anything that serves to return the Lunts to Broadway is an occasion for rejoicing. . . . [*The Pirate*] is flamboyant and bizarre, and it gives the Lunts an opportunity for burlesque thus far unparalleled in their combined career."

Playing the young lovers, Alfred was fifty, Lynn almost fifty-five. (From Noël on Alfred's fiftieth: HALF A CENTURY HAS SPED / OVER GRANDPA'S SILVER HEAD / SILVER HAIR IS GRANDPA'S SORROW / HERE

TODAY—BLACK TOMORROW.) Many thought Lynn had never looked more beautiful. Amazed, they found they had a hit.

Alfred and Jack Wilson directed and staged the production. "Jack has become very dear to us," Lynn told Noël. "He has a definite talent for directing and . . . was excellent on the script altogether and I suppose it is a great tribute to his ability and his kindness and tact that we have come out of this long, tortuous readying of the play more devoted than ever. He is the only person in the world who is quite free to come in around half-past five, when we are having our dinner." Yet Jack was drinking heavily, his alcoholism fueled by the break with Noël and marriage to Natasha.

In 1940 Alfred had won *Variety*'s poll of drama critics for best performance for *There Shall Be No Night,* sharing the honor with Barry Fitzgerald in *Juno and the Paycock.* (*There Shall Be No Night* won Sherwood his third Pulitzer.) In 1943 *Variety* named him best performer for *The Pirate.* In May that year the Drama League of New York awarded both Lynn and Alfred for the best performances of the season. (Tallulah Bankhead also won *Variety*'s poll for best performance for Thornton Wilder's Pulitzer Prize–winning *The Skin of Our Teeth.* Wilder had offered the play first to the Lunts, who said they couldn't make head or tail of it.)

A beloved friend did not share their triumph. On January 23, 1943, Aleck was doing a CBS radio program when he scrawled on a sheet of paper "I AM SICK." He was rushed to Roosevelt Hospital, where he died that night at fifty-six of a massive heart attack and cerebral hemorrhage. His obituary made front pages across America. Lynn and Alfred were devastated. They'd visited Neshobe Island the previous summer—"our strange disturbing time together"—and just recently he'd come for breakfast and stayed the whole day. Curiously, they are not listed among those attending his memorial on January 28 when he was eulogized as "a passionate defender of good causes, the enemy of whited sepulchers, of hypocrisy and sham, who died with his boots on, fighting." Lynn and Alfred could speak only of "our dreadful loss."

They donated a substantial amount of their profits from *The Pirate* to their pet Stage Door Canteen. Yet Lynn had higher ambitions. She and Alfred had seen Noël's war film *In Which We Serve.* "I feel . . . as if I had gone through a great, terrifying and wonderful experience and it has left me very changed and set apart and with a deeper longing than ever to come to England." Since Britain's 1939 entry into the war, she had seen the English people as sanctified by their suffering and courage. After Noël's film, she realized she must go to England now, or not go again. "Both Alfred and I feel that we will never be able to look any of you in the eye unless we do. . . ."

So that when she became ill and they canceled their tour of *The Pirate* a week early, they immediately plunged into plans not only to bring *There Shall Be No Night* to England but to stay there until the end of the war.

They knew what wartime Britain was like, not only from the media but from friends like Jane de Glehn, who wrote that her studio near Battersea Bridge was a heap of dust. Noël's studio had taken a hit. Bessie Porter, Lynn's dresser, wrote of no coffee, meat, or tea, of turning ragged sheets sides to middle. Living in a garret flat, Antoinette regularly got "shaken up like dice in a box," and Bessie had gotten "bounced out of bed up to the ceiling by a bomb."

They knew too what they were leaving. They now had four cows—Lily, Sugar, Ellen, and Rose (Ellen, said Ben, "is going to stop people thinking of Lana Turner"). They had homing pigeons, Franklin the horse, chickens, and pigs. They butchered and carried on dairy and farm operations. Moreover, Ben sent them fruit, meat, vegetables, butter, and eggs from the farm weekly: they ate like kings. They would be

Alfred serves lunch to farm workers.

deserting Broadway for who knew how many years. They'd be subletting their New York apartment. And Hattie was now eighty-one.

"It's something we've wanted to do—something I had to do," Alfred, who once described himself as "all arse and no character!," wrote his mother.

> Ever since war broke out I've sneaked around, knowing I wasn't doing enough—no matter what I did. . . . I couldn't get into the navy or the army but even so I felt silly—and then this opportunity came and my head is high. For one thing it may do away with my double chin. If we can help the Anglo-American relations that's dandy with us—at least they have living proof that an English girl and an American can get on damned well. Right before them they can see it—married over 20 years in a profession in which marriage at best is supposed to last not more than five.

They sailed with Larry Farrell and five pounds of butter on September 3, 1943, on a small Portuguese boat that was two days plowing out into the Atlantic. Their private bath smelled like "a very old New England Boiled Dinner" and there were 125 children on board whom Alfred did not wish to meet again. They tossed about for nineteen days before reaching Lisbon, "an enchanting city" where they were wined and dined before flying to London to be met by H. M. Tennent's managing genius, Hugh (Binkie) Beaumont, and settled into a suite at the Savoy. The next day they began casting *There Shall Be No Night*. Their appearance in London was quickly dubbed "the theatrical event of the year."

Sherwood had changed the locale of the play to Greece, currently occupied by Germany, and the family name to Vlachos. They missed Monty Clift (currently doing an Alfred Lunt imitation on Broadway in *The Skin of Our Teeth*) but found Terence Morgan, "a wonderful boy, very good looking and a beautiful actor," for the son. Muriel Pahlow was cast as Eleni, his sweetheart. She remembers Binkie Beaumont sending her to Lunt and Fontanne, who asked, "Would you like to do it?"—no read-through or rehearsal. Frederick Lloyd played the uncle, "so like Sydney Greenstreet that we hardly miss him at all."

They viewed their first air raid from the window of the toilet in their hotel suite. "We saw the searchlights pin one plane and the Aac Aac's go up for it, then we saw it hit, a big red glow appear in it but it didn't come down. . . . Presently, there was a terrible sound like thunder. Alfred and I turned to each other and said, 'What's that?' then about half a beat later we said, 'A bomb' at which we beat it out of the 'lu' [loo] and then flew right back again in time to see another airoplane pinned in the searchlights. . . . It's the most exciting and wonderful sight and somehow not at all frightening."

London itself was a stage set designed by Bosch: a beautiful curve of blond Regency façades sheared off behind; the soaring arch of a gutted church; iron area railings missing, converted to scrap metal. But Londoners themselves were cheerful, brave, and determined. Lynn had never seen Antoinette looking so well: "not silly any more at all." Sunburnt and triumphant, Noël was back from entertaining troops at lonely outposts in the Far East. "Personally," said Lynn, "I'd rather have a Bren gun in my hand than a piano and a mike."

They found Sandhills and Graham Robertson the same. "We had a delightful day," said Graham, "—at least I had—and they put up a wonderful performance of keen enjoyment. They are more entrancing than ever, and our five years' separation seemed to fade away and leave us as though we had parted yesterday." Graham presented Lynn with an antique beryl necklace and Alfred with a walking stick that had belonged to David Garrick.

They returned to London to rehearse for the tour of *There Shall Be No Night*. In awe of the Lunts, Muriel Pahlow found Alfred amusing and quirky, Lynn elegant and helpful. If Alfred gave her a direction that confused her, Lynn would put an arm around her and murmur, "Well, you know what he means." Muriel found Alfred incredibly meticulous. In one scene he covered his face with his hand—not, apparently, a simple gesture. "What do you think, Lynn? Would my right hand be better, or my left?" He experimented at length with both hands. They conferred: the left. One day Alfred took Terence Morgan aside. "I was watching a young couple necking on the bus. The muscles in his back were so expressive when he was cuddling her. I want you to get all that passion and sex into your back."

There Shall Be No Night opened in Liverpool November 1, then moved on to the northern cities—"a tremendous success so far, sold out in fact and with much praise for play and cast."

But it was a tough tour. Crowded, freezing trains—Alfred huddled under two overcoats and a blanket. Icy theaters—in Aberdeen Lynn wore her mink throughout the performances. A meal in Manchester consisted of a baked potato stuffed with mashed potatoes served with a dried-egg potato omelette and a side of french fries. Flu. "And the W.C.—Jesus!" Worse, the army kept yanking away actors and in Edinburgh they had to hand over the actor playing Dickie Whorf's old role to the police as a deserter. In Leeds Terence Morgan sprained his ankle chasing Muriel Pahlow. "As long as you can talk you can act," said Alfred, and hired a doctor to show Morgan how to walk with a sprain. Yet in every theater there were flowers and a bottle of hard-to-get scotch in their dressing room and the enthusiasm of their audiences was incredible. Grateful playgoers would show up at the stage door with half a dozen eggs, three oranges, a lamb kidney.

They opened to a sold-out run on December 15 at the Aldwych— "thrilling for us beyond words . . . they screamed & yelled & cheered their blessed heads off—quite hair raising and very satisfactory." Binkie Beaumont came round to their dressing room and, with other friends and well-wishers, unashamedly wept. "It was the most amazing experience I have ever had," said Binkie. "I had never seen a dress-room after a triumphal first night turned into a wake."

London audiences, many in uniform, "seemed to weep more than anyone had ever wept at *There Shall Be No Night,*" said Alfred. "And the Lord knows," added Lynn, "we drenched many a theater with that play all over America and Canada." They speculated that the British crowded to the play because it gave them a chance to cry, emotion the stiff upper lip tabooed in public.

Some critics faulted the play: Sherwood was not content to let the audience feel but had to lecture. Lunt and Fontanne, however, were accepted with open arms. Lynn Fontanne, wrote James Agate in the *Sunday Times,* is "a brilliant comedienne, a mistress of the art of insinuation, extremely skilled in that hoodwinkery of quietism of which Duse was the arch exponent." On the other hand, Alfred Lunt "works by accomplishment rather than implication. His fun is brilliant; his pathos is open and declared, and at times almost unbearable."

In the *Observer* Beverly Baxter focused on one scene. After the son announces he's joining the army, he walks off, leaving Karilo Vlachos alone onstage. Alfred slowly lowered himself into a chair, his back to the audience. Then, reluctantly, he made an awkward stretching movement as if racked with pain. "I don't know any other actor who could have achieved so much with so little."

They were proud to walk from the Aldwych to the Savoy in the blackout without flashlights. Proud to volunteer as air-raid wardens in the Strand, Alfred also emptying bedpans anonymously at St. George's Hospital. Proud to greet General Patton backstage. "Alfred was so overcome by Patton that he almost went down on his knees." A great crowd had gathered at the stage door. When Patton threw open the door he was silhouetted against the light and the roar that burst from the crowd rolled from Shaftesbury Avenue into Piccadilly Circus.

Proud every night to risk annihilation.

A buzz bomb hit very near. I was on the stage and he was in the wings waiting for his cue when the smash came. I found myself somehow on the other side of the stage. The scenery was bucking like sails in a high wind, things were falling. I looked for Alfred. There he was, pushing a canvas wall up with one hand and starting to make his entrance. Then I saw the fire curtain coming down and heard him shout in that metallic voice he gets when he is excited, "Take it up! Take it!" Like a shot it went up and then he turned to me and curious as it may seem, the precise line he had to speak in the script at that moment was, "Are you all right, darling?"

Well, neither of us ever had such applause as came up when he finished saying that. The audience, which had sat as silent as the grave all during the crashing—audiences never walk, much less run, for exits during blasts—burst right out in cheers and stood up and kept on and on, really holding up the play much longer than the buzz bomb. . . .

Terence Morgan had been blown out of the theater by the blast. Brushing down his uniform and smoothing his hair, he also made his entrance on cue to cheers. By Binkie's watch, the demonstration lasted a full minute. "Now you'll know how to say that line," he told Alfred after the performance. "I knew something good would come out of the war."

German raids were heavy early in 1944. The play had become theatre verité, lines and action from *There Shall Be No Night* reflecting the battle outside. "The enemy is not far away," said Alfred, and the Aldwych would vibrate from a detonation. "Listen," he said in his final scene.

"What you hear now—this terrible sound that fills the earth—it is the death rattle." Was he speaking as Karilo Vlachos or directly to the audiences as Alfred Lunt? When in the last scene Lynn picked up a rifle and deliberately began loading it, tension would burst into sobs or cheers, every member of the audience knowing personally the meaning of resistance.

Lynn's sangfroid onstage was particularly admired. She seemed totally oblivious to bombs, ack-acks, and sirens, never flickering an eyelid. "We were afraid of the bombs," Alfred admitted. Yet "it wasn't fear of death but fear of separation. There was the terror of being apart when something happened."

Sometimes *no* flying bombs were just as bad: "There is something strange in the air these days," Alfred wrote that spring, "a kind of restlessness hangs over everyone & that dreadful question forever ringing out 'When will it happen? When will it begin?'—no fright in it, you know, just a gentle anxiety. It's like getting to a station hours too early for your train—with nothing to read." They noticed fewer uniforms in the audience. Did it mean a big push was coming soon?

Tension was broken one night as they stepped off the train from Windsor, where they'd given a performance for their friend the Very Reverend Albert Victor Baillie, Dean. Overhead they saw a V-2, then felt a terrifying silence as its motor cut. Seconds later debris hurled skyward with a roar—a close escape. When they returned to the Savoy they found every window blown out of their suite. Alfred reassured a worried Hattie: "We are much safer in [the raids], than, for instance, little Billy Roth is riding with his father on the binder. All we do is to go to a shelter & stay there until the 'all clear'—as snug as can be." Alfred read Dickens voraciously in the Savoy shelters, while Lynn devoured Jane Austen and played solitaire.

Giving eight performances a week, as well as special matinees for the Greek Red Cross and Allied troops and hospitals, Lynn and Alfred had little time for socializing, yet they were emphatically the nucleus of what Graham Robertson called "the Inner Brotherhood." Defined by their love and respect for Graham, this Inner Brotherhood included Jamie Hamilton, Noël, Robert Sherwood, and the theatrical producer Peter Daubeny. (Aleck had been a member.) It would expand to include playwright Terence Rattigan and actors John Gielgud and Laurence Olivier.

Laurence Olivier and Vivien Leigh, close friends of the Lunts, 1939

Olivier had first "seen and worshiped" Lunt and Fontanne in 1929 in *Caprice*. Now Alfred and Lynn saw Larry and Vivien Leigh often as a couple, though Vivien was not considered Inner Brotherhood. "We had a heavenly week-end with Larry Olivier & Vivien Leigh," Alfred wrote Hattie, "—the nicest I do believe we ever had. Delicious food & such a warm sweet cottage—fires in every room & a beautiful countryside to look out on. They have but one maid but Vivien is a perfect house-keeper & we had the old pre-war breakfast in bed, lunch, tea & dinner as though the house has 6 servants."

Another weekend with Larry and Viv was even happier: "I had a high old time as their garden was full of weeds & I did go to it. They have an instrument over here called a Dutch Hoe which is a wizard for top weeding & we must get one to take back. . . ." When they could yank Alfred away from weeds, the couples dined with Bob Sherwood, who had a play in mind for the four of them. He described the roles for the Lunts—"Perfect," said everyone. He began sketching the Oliviers' roles. "Oh," interrupted Lynn, "Larry and Vivien wouldn't be suited for those parts at all."

Their wider circle included Henry ("Chips") Channon, American-born Conservative member of Parliament. "The Pope is almost as charming as Alfred—could one say more of a man?" Chips wrote Lynn. Ivor Novello, Winifred Ashton (the writer Clemence Dane), and Lady Sibyl Colefax also belonged. The most important member was Hugh Beaumont.

There is some truth in the statement that there were two London managements during these years, one straight, Albery, and one gay. Binkie had moved in, commercially and domestically, with H. M. Tennent; when Tennent died, Binkie became known in the West End as the Boss. Binkie had first met Lynn and Alfred during the run of *Amphitryon 38,* promptly inviting them to dinner at his house in Lord North Street. Nicknamed Hotel Paradisio, it was notorious for galas for stars like Tallulah Bankhead, Mary Martin, and Katharine Hepburn, and as a place where handsome young actors met male angels. Binkie was dark, shrewd, elegant, and given to phrases like "Too *bijou,* my dear." Chips Channon called him "that Steel Eros."

Binkie's sexual persuasion was perhaps attractive to the Lunts, but more important would have been Noël's connection with Tennent and the fact that Binkie had the sharpest eye for talent in town. The Tennent system was based on stars. Edith Evans declared she'd rather be out of work than play for anyone else but Binkie. Now Tennent had rolled out the red carpet for Alfred and Lynn.

Defying the destruction, London that spring bloomed with laburnum, lilacs, primroses, and bluebells. The big push Londoners were feeling in the air came on June 6, 1944—D day, the storming of the Normandy beaches. "It seems incredible that it is taking place less than a hundred miles away—as far as Chicago is from Genesee." At the same time a desperate Germany was launching thousands of flying bombs ("doodlebugs") at London. Binkie begged his stars to take a taxi from the Savoy to the Aldwych; they refused. On June 30 when they arrived for a matinee, they found the theater bombed.

They felt strangely relieved. Sales had fallen off. The play, said Alfred, had suddenly become "too close" to be enjoyed by cast or audience. Lynn called it "a boon and a blessing": little sleep and the constant wail of sirens during performances had exhausted her. They fled to

Ivor Novello's Redroofs in Berkshire for peace and quiet and stayed more than three weeks, breaking for a weekend with Larry and Vivien, lunch with the Dean of Windsor at the castle, and a drive into Maidenhead to see *Gone With the Wind*—"superb picture."

Dark, beautiful, a thorough romantic, Novello was an enormously successful actor, manager, dramatist, and composer. His "Keep the Home Fires Burning" had inspired the doughboys of World War I; he had recently set a record as author, composer, and leading man in four successive musicals at Drury Lane. During their stay at Redroofs Alfred and Lynn so admired the lilacs that Novello immediately sat down at the piano and composed the song hit of 1945–46, "We'll Gather Lilacs."

Even at Redroofs, however, Alfred managed to drum up pressures. "One or two items distress me," he wrote George Bugbee, closely involved with Ten Chimneys since he and Karin had moved from Cleveland to Chicago. "Hat must pay the telephone & electric bills— that was thoroughly understood." Little had changed since he was a young actor worrying about Hattie's carelessness except the amount of the check he enclosed to cover expenses: two thousand dollars instead of five. "We long to be home," he added. "Lynn gets so homesick." He was sick of war: "I hope they wipe the bloody [German] race off the face of the earth."

vor Novello suggested they meet Terence Rattigan, whose new comedy had been turned down by Gertrude Lawrence. Rattigan was enchanted by Alfred and Lynn, who stood for everything in the theater he most admired, including success. They agreed to do his comedy. Alfred would direct and had a few suggestions. . . .

Rattigan was launched into the madhouse of perfecting that Sherwood and Behrman knew so well. Olivia was the chief character in *Less Than Kind*. Even though Alfred told Rattigan, "Sometimes Lynn has the play, and sometimes it's my play," he immediately began pressuring Rattigan to turn the unlikable Sir John Fletcher into the lovable focus of the plot. And the title must be changed to *Love in Idleness*. "I didn't realize," said the dazed playwright, "that he was asking me to write a new play. But he was right. In the end I wrote a far better play because of his suggestions. But at the time it was rather a trying experience."

Rattigan thought both Lynn and Alfred jealous of Brian Nissen, playing the teenage boy, Michael, a part Alfred ruthlessly pared down.

He was also ruthless with Brian at rehearsals. "Alfred's way of rehearsing him is to take him over three lines in three hours, finally reducing him to tears and hysteria. It is hard to see whether he will be good or not, but I am willing to bet that if he survives the next two months he is going to become the best juvenile actor on the English stage."

They were still touring with *There Shall Be No Night.* Alfred admitted to Graham that Rattigan's play "must be acted with the touch of a feather duster and I feel nothing so much as like an old iron shovel." They finally closed *No Night* in early November in Blackpool on "the very day it was announced the last German had been driven out of Greece. Most dramatic & a fitting day to end our tour." A few days later they were back in London rehearsing for the new tour, to begin in Liverpool November 26.

Liverpool adored *Love in Idleness;* critics were cool. Cautious Binkie ("secret as a snake," the director Peter Hall called him) sent fellow investor Noël to the provinces to check out the situation. Noël was scathing. They mustn't dream of taking the play to London.

Perhaps Alfred and Lynn understood that the Master was jealous of the younger playwright, who in turn rather despised Coward, "with his patriotic films and his private homosexuality." At any rate, Noël's ploy didn't work: the Lunts assured Rattigan they loved his play and told Binkie they must do it. If they hadn't, Binkie might have taken Noël's word and canceled.

Love in Idleness opened at the Lyric Theatre December 20, 1944. Curtain time in London was now 5 p.m. so playgoers could hurry home just as the blackout descended. Still, there was such a dense fog that Alfred was sure the house would be empty. Backstage Lynn comforted a terrified Antoinette, cast in the small part of Lady Markham, while Alfred groaned that he knew he was about to give the worst performance of his life. But the Lyric rippled with delight from first curtain to last.

"Mr. Alfred Lunt and Miss Lynn Fontanne are accepted players of comedy, and with their consummate art they made the performance of Mr. Terence Rattigan's *Love in Idleness* a riot of laughter at the Lyric Theatre last night," said the *Daily Mail* the next day. James Agate, dean of London critics, thought Lunt and Fontanne "superb in the first act and good in the second; if their performances crumbled away at the end it was merely because the comedy had lost its sincerity." In the *Observer,* Beverly Baxter bowed low: "I just don't believe they can be as good as they seem. It isn't possible."

"Lynn's performance is absolutely bewitching," Alfred wrote Theresa Helburn. ". . . I sit in the wings and chuckle like an old fool. Her telephone speech at the opening is a triumph but then so are all of her scenes and she looks a dream." Lynn's costumes were by Edward Molyneux, the designer who had once snubbed her in Paris. On this visit, seeing her at a party, he had literally dropped to his knees and crawled across the floor begging forgiveness. For the telephone speech she wore a sheer pink chiffon negligee. The temperature inside the theater was the same as outside. One by one the audience would remove their coats. If Miss Fontanne could take it, so could they.

Still, they were determined to go home in May. Lynn was more homesick than Alfred, especially after visits from Stanley Phenus ("Stag") in uniform, worried about his wife and tavern back at the Depot. Yet they'd had a "marvellous, wondrous" Christmas with Larry and Vivien, and their Savoy sitting room was packed with gifts— pheasants, grouse, George II silver, Wedgwood china, Bristol glass. "My god but people are sweet here," Alfred wrote George. "You have no idea how good they are."

That winter and spring of 1945 the wonderful audiences, a general feeling that the end of the war must be near, and Alfred and Lynn's great social success created one of the happiest times of their lives. They were frantically busy—a secret visit to the Royal Palace of Westminster to perform *Love in Idleness* for people who had worked on anti-V2 devices; Sunday troop matinees; Alfred washing dishes at a charity hospital and making three hundred waffles at a crack at the canteen; eight regular performances—yet they managed time for friends and VIPs.

A last weekend with Larry and Vivien. Dinner with Lady Cholmondeley, with Cecil Beaton, with the Greek ambassador, with Anthony Eden. Dinner at Chips Channon's in Belgrave Square with the Duchess of Kent, Lady Juliet Duff, the Duchess of Westminster, and Sibyl Colefax. Lunch on Nelson's old flagship, *Victory*. A lunch at the Ritz given them by Sir Campbell Stuart attended by Honorables, duchesses, and dukes. Gala at the English Speaking Union and a Russian Ball ("a tatty mess").

More intimate were dinners at their Savoy suite with John Gielgud and Peter Daubeny. At first sight, said Daubeny, Alfred "gave the impression of a collie, a sophisticated collie perhaps, but a collie nevertheless; any moment now, one thought, he would knock off the table a delicate piece of Meissen with one stroke of his long faithful tail. Then gradually I came to see that with this apparently shaggy air went an extraordinary delicacy both of movement and of mind, a rippling sense of fun, charm, humour, and almost all those subtle virtues which God has denied even the most brilliant of dogs."

Or the dinner Alfred made for Noël, Gielgud, Channon, Joyce Carey, and Lynn at Terence Rattigan's digs in the Albany: pâté, mushroom soup, corned beef hash with poached eggs, tomato aspic, lemon meringue pie. "I did the whole damn thing on a two-burner electric stove. . . . Chips and Terry later awarded me the Cordon Bleu, which consisted of an old blue dressing-gown sash of Terry's with an enormous jewel affair they had found at some costumier's and a great scroll with ribbons, seals and God knows what."

Rattigan, Channon, Gielgud, Novello, Noël, Binkie, and Winifred Ashton were homosexual. Being intimate with such a circle of artistic peers was surely central to Alfred and Lynn's happy experience in England. They had much more social life than they had in America. As Marlene Dietrich famously remarked, "In Europe it doesn't matter what you are, it only matters if you're charming." In England, even in wartime, the Lunts could relax more completely than they could at home.

The King and Queen and lesser royals appeared at *Love in Idleness* in the royal box. But the biggest thrill was Winston Churchill, who came to the Lyric the night before he left for the Yalta Conference. Alfred and Lynn could hear the cheering in the street, then the prime minister walked down the aisle to his front-row seat, flashing his famous V-for-Victory sign. Alfred had a moment onstage when, as the cabinet minister, he pulled out a cigar. Cheers erupted that went on for five minutes as Churchill stood and waved to the crowd. A few days later Alfred unwrapped an enormous Corona with Churchill's signature on the band: "my great gift—a cigar from Mr. Churchill. . . . I'll carry it about to my dying day."

Germany surrendered unconditionally on May 7, 1945. VE day bells rang out as war-weary Londoners surged into the hot sunshine.

That night [wrote Lynn] all the lovely buildings were flood-lighted: Big Ben, Westminster, the National Gallery, all the government buildings, Buckingham Palace. . . . The darkness hid the scars, and London was bathed in such beauty that one stood weeping to see it. Big Ben was especially beautiful; the floodlights made him disappear in vapour around the base so that he looked like a sturdy, honest ghost. The people walked the streets in an orderly fashion, some singing and dancing, nothing rowdy. Young couples who had been walking the streets all day lay asleep in doorways looking very childish and innocent.

Everyone crowded into Winifred Ashton's house in Tavistock Street, where they listened to broadcasts by King George VI and Generals Eisenhower and Montgomery. At Buckingham Palace, when the King and Queen appeared on the balcony, the crowd roared itself hoarse.

Once they'd experienced London's fighting spirit, Alfred and Lynn had known England would pull through. "The theatre is a measure of a nation's virility," the critic Beverly Nichols wrote. "If it's true," agreed Alfred, "this is the greatest period in English history. Look at what we've seen since we came over." Olivier's Richard III, Gielgud's Hamlet, *Love for Love, Heartbreak House, A Month in the Country, A Midsummer Night's Dream,* Robert Helpmann's ballet—"and that's only the beginning of the list." "And all of it," said Lynn, "in the fifth year of the war,

Alfred and Lynn acted Love in Idleness *(later retitled* O Mistress Mine*) in 1944 for American troops in Europe.*

against every conceivable difficulty. . . . And all of it a success—a howling commercial success. The British are certainly a pretty remarkable people." For the Lunts, if theater was alive and well, the country must be too.

Love in Idleness ran for six months, until June 23. The ban on civilian traveling prevented their return to the United States, so they decided to tour the "Foxhole Circuit" of USO camp shows in France and Germany. The last night of the play there was a huge farewell party for them at the Savoy, the entire cast in uniform. They left the next day for Paris, exhausted and triumphant.

"If you can keep your head and concentrate on your performance while bombs are crashing all around you," said Alfred in retrospect, "then you can call yourself an actor. We wouldn't have missed it for the world. You could say that we had a very good war."

CHAPTER THIRTEEN

Comfy Laurels: 1946–1951

The opening of Lunt and Fontanne in Rattigan's retitled *O Mistress Mine* at the Empire Theatre on January 23, 1946, lit up Broadway. Theatergoers attended not so much a play as a celebration of the Lunts' return after three long years. The A-bomb had been dropped, World War II was over, people craved the laughter and glamour that nobody could generate like Lunt and Fontanne. Backstage after the show they greeted friends and fans outside dressing rooms bursting with flowers, after hours of embraces staggering back to their apartment, where Alfred was too exhausted to produce anything but cornflakes for their supper.

"Sitting in a theater watching and listening to the Lunts," said veteran playgoer and theater scholar Dan H. Laurence,

> was the nearest I've ever come to knowing what heaven will be like. Their performing was synchronized to perfection, blending her regal stature with his loose-limbed amble. Most people remember them for their vocal delivery, which both in pitch and timbre and the tempo of delivery, was unforgettable; but it is the eyes that I found most thrilling and dramatically effective: startlingly wide at one moment, directly in communication, then

*In their longest-running play,
1944–1949,* O Mistress
Mine

side-glanced unexpectedly, narrowing to unblinking slits. Thinking of Hayes, Cornell, and Bankhead, only the latter's Regina in
The Little Foxes sticks in my memory, and Ethel Barrymore's *The
Corn Is Green;* but I can remember dozens of Lynn Fontanne's
great moments, and there wasn't a single actor in all the years
from the 1930s to the 1950s who could hold a candle to Alfred
Lunt. What a smoothie.

Vernon Rice, *New York Post:* "The Lunts could stand with their faces
to the wall reciting the alphabet in pig latin and if they wanted me to
laugh, I'd laugh. If it were tears they were after, I'd shed them. Just
putty in their hands, that's me."

Dorothy Kilgallen, *Journal-American:* "If I had a magically elastic
bankroll I would send everyone in the city of New York (yes, and
Brooklyn too!) to see Alfred Lunt and Lynn Fontanne in *O Mistress
Mine.*"

Robert Garland, *Journal-American:* "Here is where you read another rave review. You cannot help it. I cannot help it. I would not help it if I could. This is our big little world of makebelieve at its most professional. This is Broadway at its most beguiling."

Which was the more celestial player—Lunt or Fontanne? Some thought Fontanne dominated with her unforgettable laugh, her assured yet light comic touch. Her first scene, lying on a couch in a negligee making phone calls to society friends, brought down the house, as did the scene in which Lunt lies on the couch, his legs on her lap, and she erotically runs her fingers up his trousers. "Lunt works a bit harder for his laughs," said Howard Barnes in the *Herald Tribune,* "but he does not fail to get them. His timing is immaculate and his pantomime . . . in the top bracket of acting."

But most critics concentrated on Lunt and Fontanne's interplay: "that peculiar alternation of frank physical passion and raucous amusement at it which is practically their trademark in the theatre . . . the queer fits of abstraction, when one or other of the stars seems to be overtaken by a terrible boredom." Their verbal dueling entranced John Mason Brown: "A cat could not have more fun with catnip than they do with the lines they speak. They do not hammer them; they play with them. They pounce on them, toss them in the air, pull them earthward, romp with them, and roll on them. They know how to hold a sentence back, and then send it scurrying to its conclusion. They never miss the meaningful or explosive word, and never overstress it."

Anticipating criticism of the play, Alfred had made a first-night speech, hoping that *O Mistress Mine* would help keep alive a spirit of laughter "in an angry and suspicious world." He did not disarm the critics. As Tallulah Bankhead once remarked, "There is less here than meets the eye." *O Mistress Mine,* decided *Time,* wasn't "worth a toy locomotive's toot." *The New Yorker* called it "impalpable." Brooks Atkinson dismissed it as "rubbish." Most writers about the theater have followed suit, whipping Lunt and Fontanne for wasting their gifts.

Lawrence Langner disagreed. *O Mistress Mine,* he argued, "was a far better play than the critics here admitted it to be." Rattigan—who would write *The Winslow Boy, Separate Tables, The Deep Blue Sea,* and *The Browning Version*—was hardly a featherweight. For 1945 *O Mistress Mine* was fairly sophisticated: an unmarried couple living together; a pain-in-the-ass son full of left-wing ideas; ideological and oedipal battles between the mistress's son and the rich, conservative lover.

Back in 1930 the Theatre Guild had badly wanted Lynn and Alfred to do O'Neill's *Mourning Becomes Electra.* They chose *Reunion in Vienna* instead—and how grateful audiences had been! Critics who deplored *O Mistress Mine* were asking the Lunts not to play their biggest success, which ran 452 performances on Broadway, saved the Theatre Guild's 1945–46 season, gave Rattigan his first American hit, made everybody a great deal of money, and ravished audiences. Rather much to ask.

Not that Alfred and Lynn weren't thinking of serious plays. Alfred was aware that Cornell was doing *Antigone,* that Laurette Taylor was making a triumphant return in *The Glass Menagerie.* Ward Morehouse had interviewed the Lunts in London, and between questions like "Do you think we should retire?" and "Do you think we've changed?" both had insisted, "We want so much to have our own company."

Langner had jumped at the idea. "Needless to say the idea of doing a Repertory Theatre with you would be just completely wonderful. . . . What do you think of *Love in Idleness, The Guardsman,* and *He Who Gets Slapped* as a starter, or possibly throw in an Ibsen play or something from Shakespeare? . . . I don't know what's the matter with the modern writers, but they certainly don't seem to be writing the plays now." The Guild had been staging musicals like *Oklahoma!* and *Carousel* to stay in the black.

But Alfred and Lynn had old grievances with the Guild about Shakespeare. First they canceled *As You Like It;* then *Twelfth Night,* Alfred's favorite. He had sketched a production based on what he considered the key to the play: Viola's first line, "What country, friends, is this?" Then he read in the papers of a Guild *Twelfth Night* with Helen Hayes and Maurice Evans. According to Lynn, Richard Whorf had already designed sets for *Macbeth* when the Guild asked Evans to do it, then pretended Evans had pestered them for a production—"downright stupidity . . . that they should risk offending us, who are at the moment their only golden egg." (The Guild did not do an Evans *Macbeth;* it waited vainly for the Lunts.) Now Turgenev's *A Month in the Country* tempted them. Meanwhile, at the sold-out Empire Theatre, said Lynn, "We are just a couple of hot cakes."

The hot cakes could be temperamental.

"Why were you glaring at me so when I was standing near the fireplace?"

"Because a few days ago you had asked me to stand somewhere farther away. I was trying to cue you into telling me with your eyes just where to move."

"Stand upstage, upstage, and get that great moon of a face of yours out of MY light."

Alfred grinned. They were at each other all the time. Sam and Bella Spewack soon would write *Kiss Me, Kate* based on the battling Lunts.

They also did radio broadcasts that season of *The Guardsman, Elizabeth the Queen, The Brothers Karamazov, Strange Interlude*—and didn't like it at all. "Why do it?" asked Edith Evans, and Lynn found herself explaining that they hadn't made any money in England even as she was showing off a smashing new hat and sable scarf Alfred had given her for Christmas—irony not lost on Edith.

It had been a glorious Christmas at Genesee with the family and Binkie Beaumont and Terence Rattigan—smorgasbörd, and "everybody got rather drunk and very happy." A typical Ten Chimneys spread included Prague ham, tongue, ham and salmon in jelly, sausages, liver pâté, herring and sardines, meatballs, fish balls in sherry lobster sauce, cold trout, mushrooms and eggs in custard, cheeses, smoked turkey, crudités, four kinds of salads and breads, accompanied by aquavit, beer, martinis, and punch. Wrote Rattigan in thanks: "My weekend at Genesee I shall always remember as one of the pleasantest, most exciting and most wildly lavish weekends of my life."

They played until July 13 to sold-out houses, then returned to Genesee with Larry Farrell and Chuck Bowden, who would work on the farm for eight weeks, and Lisa, a dachshund presented to Lynn by the cast—"more trouble than ten children." Lisa wasn't yet housebroken, and Lynn didn't tell Alfred when she came into heat, "as he is on the hysterical side over nothing, you know." Alfred got up at five a.m. to run the separator, bottle milk, and make cottage cheese. He kept the milk room and pigpens spotless, put up batches of wild plum jelly, and made butter in a white coat and apron. They now had ducks. Ben and his wife, Gertrude, had moved into a stone house built for them by the Lunts at the northern edge of their estate.

Hattie and Alfred still talked recipes, still joked and sparred. Every Mother's Day Alfred sent her telegrams in doggerel:

> DEAR LITTLE GRAY HAIRED MOTHER O' MINE
> SITTING THERE ON THE END OF YOUR SPINE
> THINK WHAT YOU DID WITH SUCH APLOMB
> JUST ADDED ONE MORE FOR THE ATOM BOMB.

A special visitor that summer was their British producer friend Peter Daubeny.

Jules Johnson and Ben Perkins

Alfred collects him at Milwaukee, Ben driving the Cadillac. As they drive through Genesee, lounging figures come to attention, almost salute. "Sound your horn, Benny," says Alfred as they turn into a wooded drive. The white, green-shuttered house sprawls before them "like a two-star hotel," says Alfred. Youthful in blue jeans, Lynn bursts out of the house. "Darling! Darling! Darling!" Daubeny feels "surrounded and defended by love."

Back from the war, Stag is reopening his tavern.

"Fine," says Lynn. "What time shall we go?"

Alfred gives her a surprised, hurt stare. "Well, you know, it's a bar—and everything."

Whispered conference. Lynn wins but decides she'll ask Louise to meet them there.

On the walk to Stag's Tavern they exclaim at the brightness of the stars. Says Lynn firmly, "I think they hang lower in this part of the country." Alfred and Peter stop and stare. Lynn begins to ripple with laughter; they join in. "My God," gasps Alfred, "that's your best so far!"

The next morning Alfred appears in Peter's room with a breakfast tray. He is wearing a frilly white apron and enjoys its effect on his guest. The rest of the morning he's invisible doing chores, while Lynn and Peter walk, returning to find him planning lunch like Patton planning a siege. What will storm their senses: a cheese soufflé, pâté-stuffed eggs in aspic? Then he asks abruptly, "Do you like trifle?"

Daubeny admits fondness for the English dessert.

"There you are, Lynn. This is your moment!"

Delighted, Lynn seizes a calendar. She seldom cooks, but has mastered the trifle. "Now," she says, pencil raised, "what night shall be trifle night?"

Back to New York in September, with *O Mistrees Mine* sold out until January 1947, the line at the box office longer than opening week a year before. They continued to alter the text and business of Rattigan's play, informing him after the changes. "Certainly Rattigan had far less to do with his play than Lunt and Miss Fontanne," critics noted. "They should get credit for authorship."

After coaching him for three weeks at Ten Chimneys, they were happy with young Dick Van Patten, playing Lynn's son, Michael. Marlon Brando had auditioned for the role. According to Brando, he had displayed his contempt for the stars by scornfully reciting "Hickory Dickory Dock." The Lunts didn't remember "Hickory Dickory Dock," only that Brando looked twenty-two and they wanted an actor who looked sixteen; so they politely turned him down and he thanked them for hearing him. Though Van Patten sassed Alfred in front of the cast and once tried to fight him, it was love. Van Patten said the Lunts were "the best actors I've ever known"; they called him "a beautiful actor."

Their East Seventy-fifth Street apartment had become a meeting place for Brits. Jamie and Yvonne Hamilton, Larry ("the child is killing himself") and Vivien ("fatter and oh, so lovely"), John Gielgud, Ivor Novello, Peter Daubeny, the composer Richard Addinsell, Edith Evans, Binkie Beaumont, Terence Rattigan, Edward Molyneux, Beatrice Lillie, Cecil Beaton—and Noël. Iced champagne flowed as Alfred served up steak with sauce béarnaise and sole *à ma tante Marie* with mushroom purée ("It is to die!"). Their mainstay in the kitchen now, however, was a good Scandinavian cook—"Alfred is blissful."

Joyce Grenfell spent a happy evening seated between Alfred and Larry Olivier. "A.L. has the nicest manners and I think a divine sense of humour, and he flatters me by appearing to listen." Passing through their bedroom, she was "very touched somehow by the sight of Lynn's white nightie (unpressed) and scruffy little red bed-slippers on one side of the bed and Alfred's white pajamas and similarly worn bed-slippers on the other side of the bed." Suddenly the Divinities were human.

British visitors reminded them that England was still suffering shortages and rationing. Discovering that Graham Robertson missed chocolates, Lynn launched a stream of gifts that in the next five years swelled to a flood of parcels to English friends. Because New Zealand wasn't rationing meat and fats, Lynn paid her sister Mai to ship steaks, suet, and fat drippings to England—fifty-two hampers one Christmas alone. From Sherry's in New York they sent rice, hams, canned chickens, fruit juice, flour, jams. From the Canadian firm Marshall Ellis Ltd. they shipped scotch whisky, pâté, fruitcakes, sausage, maple syrup, cooking oil, canned fruit, tea, and Christmas puddings. They sent towels, sheets, silk stockings, warm underwear, slippers, gloves, scarves, hot-water bottles, coats, soap flakes. When the actress Diana Wynyard needed new false eyelashes, Lynn sent false eyelashes. When the beloved old actress Madge Titheradge needed cortisone, Lynn sent cortisone. She also sent sympathy: "Just a quick line," she wrote Bessie Porter, "because I've been thinking about your varicose veins." In addition, she continued to make Antoinette, Mai, and Bessie weekly allowances of one to three pounds.

Lunt gifts occasionally caused annoyance—customs often held shipped packages so that recipients had to send someone to meet the boat; Renee Orsell's follow-up letters when acknowledgments were delayed might seem like demands for thanks. But most friends were deeply grateful for Lynn's incredible generosity, not least because it came from one of their own.

Outraged that Valentina and Mainbocher were now charging $1,000 for an evening dress, war-wise Lynn, an expert dressmaker, had begun designing and making her own clothes.

Meanwhile, Alfred was cutting and pasting toy theaters. He had always been passionate about scenic design: "Whenever he hears some one is going to do a play he immediately designs the sets for it." In London, overcome with nostalgia for "the unaffected pleasures of my childhood," he had bought antique miniatures; hearing of his passion, fans had also brought gifts of toy theaters to the stage door. Putting them together was a major project. "I worked my Goddam head off over it," up to the neck "in glue and spit for weeks, weeks"—constructing stagings of famous old melodramas like *The Forty Thieves, Uncle Tom's Cabin,* and *Oliver Twist.* In December the Museum of the City of New York exhibited twenty-five of his collection of sixty, which further required his designing illuminated glass-fronted shadow boxes.

"Why I'm doing it, I can't tell you, except that it's out and out pure theater, the very essence of theater!" Included in the widely publicized exhibit was Alfred's own toy theater. He studied his youthful creation of *Parsifal.* "I look at it now and it seems done by someone else. As indeed it was, indeed it was."

Unfortunately the exhibit coincided with an attack of severe abdominal pain. Unable to pinpoint the trouble, his doctor ordered rest. Alfred would not leave *O Mistress Mine.* He did quit radio broadcasting and teaching drama classes for ex-GIs, turned down offers to direct on Broadway. Eventually X rays revealed a large stone in his remaining kidney, and on January 11, 1947, he was operated on at St. Luke's Hospital. *O Mistress Mine* closed and Karin came to New York to comfort Lynn, who was totally in control.

Although Lynn and Alfred liked to believe they were twins, they could be separated. Alfred went to concerts and opera, tastes Lynn did not share. (Listening to a singer one evening at the Raymond Masseys' home, Lynn was heard to exclaim, "I hate music!") Now Lynn went to the theater to see *Joan of Lorraine, Annie Get Your Gun,* and Helen Hayes in *Happy Birthday.* "Poor darling," Lynn wrote Sibyl Colefax, "had to strive to the breaking point to hide the poverty and vulgarity of the play."

Noël came to visit, "very distinguished and more solid looking," and christened their spinet by playing songs from his new *Peace in Our Time.* Wearing tight black satin with a long V back or a silk suit, she let Edward Molyneux take her to parties for Noël at Neysa McMein's and Gilbert Miller's. "I designed both of them and had them made by an unimportant little tailor at about a third the price of Mainbocher and Valentina and I must say that I looked more chic than I have done for years . . . thin as a pencil."

Alfred "escaped from Dachau" in early February. He "goes for walks now," Lynn wrote Graham, "and today he said for the first time he feels less operated on. We even had people to dinner the other night and he sat up until twelve o'clock. . . . When I tried to urge him [to go to bed], he said, 'No. Go away. I'm having a lovely time.' "

By February 24 Alfred and Lynn were back as the hottest ticket on Broadway. Yet Alfred still wasn't well. He had gout; the doctor ordered him to restrict his diet (doom) and cut out drinking. A martini now consisted of water and an olive—except at Pipe Night at the Players Club on May 5, honoring Alfred. When Howard Lindsay introduced him as "America's most distinguished actor," the whole room rose to cheer. Guests included Walter Hampden, John Gielgud, and—bravely for 1947—Paul Robeson, the great black singer. Alfred's talk, said John Mason Brown, was "modest, gay, witty and moving" and won another standing ovation. "I left the Players proud of him," Brown wrote Lynn, who stayed home because women were barred, "proud of that club, and proud of the theatre."

They celebrated their twenty-fifth wedding anniversary that May 26, 1947, "quietly unconcerned, without fanfare," dining at the home of the pianist Victor Wittgenstein. They ended the run of *O Mistress Mine* on May 31 and fled to Genesee to rest, at the same time booking passage on the *Queen Elizabeth* for June 11, mainly because Lynn wanted new costumes from Molyneux for the 1947–48 tour of *O Mistress Mine*. In the end Alfred refused to travel. He was more interested in the new dairy and greenhouse, he still felt under par, and their income tax was "nothing short of stunning."

Despite the great success of *O Mistress Mine,* they were concerned about money. They spent lavishly—on Ten Chimneys, hired help, food, wine, antiques, clothes, gifts, charity, each other. They had refused lucrative movie and radio jobs, preferring to take their plays to England for Graham to see. Lynn was nearing sixty; Alfred was fifty-five. "I have just discovered that we haven't saved one cent in the last five years," she wrote Antoinette, ". . . so as we are now no longer young and our future is mostly behind us, we are going to start [saving] like mad so that we can live in comfort more or less when we are old."

That summer they turned down a revival of *The Guardsman.* A tougher decision was Bob Sherwood's new play, *The Twilight.* Lynn was blunt: "no story, no situations, no drama, no tears, and not enough laughter to cover." His career declining, Sherwood was hurt and angry. He had always found Lynn tougher than Alfred: trying to write dialogue for both, he learned "you concentrate on good lines for Lynn." Now Alfred tried to heal the wound: "I can only tell you that it is sickening to us both that we have doubts of *The Twilight. . . .* We have always been happier in your plays than any others, and that includes Shaw and Shakespeare, and I do hope the next one we do will be yours. . . . This is most depressing and I wish I never had to put these words on paper. . . . I only wish Madeline were with you that she might call us filthy names you never even heard of."

The friendship survived.

Noël came for a week, "terribly happy about the success of his new play," and they talked about the new Sir Laurence and Lady Olivier. "He and she are so beautiful that knighthood, instead of being an absurd and rather dubious honour, seems to come in flower again with them," sighed Lynn. (When Ralph Richardson was knighted before him, Olivier had stormed, "I should have been the fucking knight!")

Hattie was never happy during Noël's visits. She complained that strange things went on. She suspected Noël had a crush on Lynn. Perhaps she deliberately avoided the truth.

Alfred felt rested by the time they opened at the Selwyn in Chicago in November and would have toured O Mistress Mine into the summer of 1948, but in April he was ill again:

> It's been a perfectly hideous experience. . . . We love San Fran-
> cisco. We were sold out here completely for the four weeks, and
> then this God damned thing had to happen. I played on Thurs-
> day night with a temperature of 103 and, as it didn't kill me, I
> thought of course I could continue. But by Friday morning I
> couldn't budge from the bed. . . .
>
> It has been such a fabulously successful season, it seems a
> shame to end up in this sordid manner. I couldn't be more deeply
> depressed and humiliated.

Alfred recovered with penicillin, but they cut short the tour in May in Seattle, returning for six weeks in Genesee, then leaving for England July 16. To the end Alfred was defiant about Rattigan's play. O Mistress Mine was their biggest moneymaker. They never played to an empty seat, yet the play never got a good review.

The critics rankled. Hard to believe Alfred would have taken ill during the runs of Idiot's Delight or There Shall Be No Night—plays he believed in. Very possibly the constant carping of critics about O Mistress Mine ulcerated him, creating an agony of innards and conscience. Certainly he was sick when he and Lynn were passed over for Arthur Miller's Death of a Salesman. "Why didn't they ask us to do it?" he would lament—justifiably, for he would have played Willie Loman superbly. It is less easy to imagine Lynn willing to shed her false eyelashes and Molyneux gowns; still, she had worn aprons and made coffee in There Shall Be No Night. No one, however, saw Death of a Salesman for Lunt and Fontanne, least of all Arthur Miller, who preferred leftish Group Theatre graduates.

That summer of 1948 in England they stayed again at the Savoy but saw less than planned of Graham because there were so many friends and Lynn needed Paris dresses. Graham Robertson did not live out the year. "My Lady," his faithful servant William wrote Lynn in December, "I cannot allow Christmas to pass without writing to thank you for your beautiful and comforting letter. . . . I do indeed find consolation and always shall do in feeling that I did everything I possibly could for the comfort and happiness of our dearly beloved Master." A cherished friend, as well as a lifeline to England's artistic past, was gone.

If Lunt and Fontanne had now gotten serious with Brecht or Beckett or Williams, they might have salvaged their reputation with critics grinding their teeth in frustration. "Golly, what they could do if they selected a script as subtle and skillful as they are!" lamented Brooks Atkinson. "For instance, something written with literary distinction." Alfred would have been superb in Brecht or Beckett—despairing, grungy, spiritual, sardonic. But actors are much more flexible as far as age goes than actresses. At sixty-two, Lynn was not about to be relegated to character parts. Only in plays tailored for the Lunts could she still play a sexually desirable woman. And, said Alfred, "I hate Brecht."

Actually, voices like Bertolt Brecht and Samuel Beckett hadn't arrived on Broadway, which vibrated to blockbuster musicals like *Annie Get Your Gun; Call Me Mister; Finian's Rainbow; High Button Shoes; Brigadoon; Kiss Me, Kate; Gentlemen Prefer Blondes* (the Lunts owned five percent); and *South Pacific.* True, Lunt and Fontanne could have played classic revivals. They preferred, however, the challenge of creating a hit from a dubious play. As Lynn told Noël, his *Blithe Spirit* was a comedy classic that didn't need the Lunts to succeed.

In his memoir, *People in a Diary,* Sam Behrman skips over *I Know My Love*—with reason. His suffering over script changes in *The Pirate* was nothing compared to the battles over his adaptation of *Auprès de ma blonde,* Marcel Achard's vehicle for Pierre Fresnay and Yvonne Printemps. Behrman was trying to create complex characters; the Lunts, he charged, wanted only to be sympathetic.

The Theatre Guild originally intended *I Know My Love* for Helen Hayes. That made Lynn and Alfred want it badly. "We had read your play and had talked wildly and excitedly about it," Lynn wrote Behrman. ". . . Then we came home and were filled with a terrible depression and apprehension . . . the Guild having something so perfect for us and allowing somebody else to have it—that old vendetta. . . . Oh, darling, don't let anybody but us do it. I promise you we shall be doing it for years."

The Lunts took over Behrman's play, Alfred again directing, Jack Wilson co-producing. Sam had to submit every word to the stars. When he proposed coming to Genesee to work with them, Lynn cautioned, "Alfred is very, very tired," and allowed him one week. Alfred made constant demands. Sam simmered. But remembering the nightmare of Behrman's inability to revise *The Pirate,* Alfred's stomach tied in knots.

I Know My Love begins with the Chanlers' fiftieth wedding anniversary, then flashes back to their courtship and midlife crisis. The play gave the Lunts a chance to raid the makeup and costume boxes. Alfred acted young Tom Chanler with his scalp wrapped in fishnet tightened with a twisted pencil under a black wig, Lynn young Emily in a saucy red hat of her own creation.

Behrman thought the Lunts saw the play as a parable of their own marriage. People resent the Chanlers' closeness and constantly try to separate them. If so, the Lunts weren't thinking so much of Aleck's dislike of their sleeping together under his roof as of Noël's "If their whole-hearted engrossment in each other occasionally makes them a trifle remote from other people, so much the better." That was Noël with gloves on; he could call the Lunts' mutual absorption selfish. Lynn believed that people "resent our completeness"—Noël (who always had to be surrounded by retainers) among them.

That October, Alfred had a physical exam in Chicago with Dr. Edward Bigg, a friend of George Bugbee, and from then on their trusted doctor, who never asked a fee. Bigg, he wrote Behrman, "is anxious over my ever acting again, not because I'm a poor actor he swears, but because the result of the constant strain may pull me back into a long and painful existence—It is a chance & a decision I have to take & make—and I have decided—to continue on the stage." He went into rehearsals, therefore, determined to make *I Know My Love* conform exactly to what the public most appreciated from them.

Julie Harris auditioned for the ingenue. If Alfred was under the weather, he didn't show it. "He was so beautiful," said Harris. "And she wore a pale mink coat with a mink turban and little ivory Harlequin glasses. They were the personification of glamour." Harris didn't get the part, but became a star two years later in *The Member of the Wedding.* " 'They were two of the most beautiful people I've ever seen' is a line from *The Member of the Wedding,*" she added, "but it was really true about them. They were just perfection."

In February 1949 they kicked off *I Know My Love* triumphantly at the university theater in Madison, then moved to Minneapolis and St. Paul. But "at the end of the week," Lynn wrote Lady Juliet Duff, "Alfred complained bitterly of a pain in his stomach. We had him X-rayed, and they discovered an ulcer—very large and acute." They canceled the Milwaukee week and Alfred, "a screaming hysteric" over a mere blood test, checked into Passavant Hospital in Chicago.

"I'm quite capable of working," Alfred wrote Bob Sherwood, "but after looking at some X-rays I had (foolishly) taken in St. Paul the medical profession at large forced me into this ridiculous life. They want me to stay here for 3 weeks but I'm opening in St. Louis on Monday [March 21]. I feel no pain while I'm acting (transfer it to the audience I suppose) it's only when I'm not active that there's any discomfort. It's too bad, but let's face it, after all these years in the theater I've now become a hazard and a liability. It's the Goddam doctors who've done it. I want to get out of here and so I want things on the dot. I'm behaving rather like a fourth rate Woollcott but it works!" They opened in St. Louis on schedule.

Not only was *I Know My Love* the twenty-fifth play Lunt and Fontanne had acted for the Theatre Guild, but 1949 marked the silver anniversary of a partnership that had begun with *The Guardsman* in 1924. *Life* for November 7 featured them on its cover as "the world's greatest acting team," with a six-page inside spread. The Guild added *I Know My Love* to the silver plaque they had engraved with the titles of Lunt-Fontanne plays. Despite "vendettas," Langner and Helburn had always pampered their stars with gifts of dispatch cases, china, antique mirrors, telegrams, and flowers. No wonder. This year Alfred estimated they had given more than eight thousand performances for audiences totaling more than 1,250,000 people. Their partnership had well outlasted those of Henry Irving and Ellen Terry and Julia Marlowe and E. H. Sothern, until now the English-speaking theater's most famous acting couples.

Behrman expected things to simmer down as the company trouped west to California, but critics didn't much like his play, creating incessant demands for change from the stars. Yet he felt the Lunts had a "psychological block" whenever he tried to come to grips with the problems—and he was helpless because they were the managers. Alfred didn't feel sorry for Sam. "We have rehearsed constantly since you left," he wrote Langner, "and, I think, much to the good, as Jack [Wilson] will tell you. But these endless changes keep us on edge and I shall welcome a week when we can play it without eruptions in the script."

Jack Wilson and the Guild had their own problems. *I Know My Love* had a cast of twenty-one; theater costs were skyrocketing. "Everyone feels depression ahead; the stock market is in very bad shape; and while I do not want to be gloomy, conditions are very different from when *O Mistress Mine* opened with the theatre booming, and there was no difficulty in making money," wrote Langner, who encouraged doubling parts and playing Denver to pay for transporting the production to the West Coast. Alfred struggled to understand the new economics. In May in San Francisco they broke all records at the Geary, including their own for *O Mistress Mine;* in Portland, Oregon, hundreds were turned away. "I am very depressed that the profits are so small. We can't do more than sell out."

Alfred's precarious health and Lynn's determination that he not overwork created more problems. That July the Guild received a plea from Dr. Edward Bigg: "It would definitely be to his advantage . . . if the time of the New York opening could be extended to as late a date as possible. The rest in Wisconsin means a great deal to him."

Langner and Helburn groaned. Theatre Guild on the Air had just gone over to NBC and a new sponsor, U.S. Steel, guaranteeing them national publicity and countless plugs for the New York opening of *I Know My Love.* Lunt and Fontanne had promised to launch the NBC season. Now they were asking to postpone the radio broadcast, cut out-of-town tryouts, and come into New York late in the season, risking losing the Shubert Theatre. Moreover, when informed of the delay, Actors' Equity ruled that the company must be paid full salary—a total of $16,000—during the layoff.

Lynn didn't care. She had Larry Farrell canvass the company, who loyally agreed to accept $7.50-a-day maintenance pay from her personally. (She intended to be reimbursed.) She whisked Alfred away to northern Wisconsin for a guided fishing trip. She also demanded a vaca-

The Chanlers celebrate their fiftieth wedding anniversary in I Know My Love, *1949.*

tion in Maine after the radio broadcast and before opening out of town. (She liked to visit Elizabeth Arden's Maine Chance salon.)

As usual Lunt and Fontanne had their way. *I Know My Love* opened at the Shubert on November 2, 1949, to sold-out houses and frantic applause from deep-dyed fans. Critics found themselves trapped in the familiar dilemma of panning the play while praising the actors. Brooks Atkinson in the *Times* was most severe: "Although the Lunts are dazzling actors, it is difficult not to look at what they are playing." *I Know My Love* "has nothing to say and very little to contribute to entertainment. [It is] untidy in construction, cluttered with clichés and nonentities and deficient in wit." A kind of resentment was growing that Lunt and Fontanne could succeed so brilliantly while taking no risks.

John Mason Brown discounted the quality of the play: "No one needs to be reminded that, much as the theatre benefits from dramatic literature, it can thrive without it. Fine acting is capable of creating a satisfactory substitute for good writing. Actors of the Lunts' perfection endow shallow scenes with depth and make tarnished situations sparkle. Their faces do the work of words. Their voices, gestures, expressions, stance, make-up and costumes supply a self-sufficient vocabulary of their own." No wonder Alfred and Lynn telegraphed him: WILL YOU MARRY US AS WE LOVE YOU SO MUCH?

Possibly the most famous commentator on *I Know My Love* is J. D. Salinger's Holden Caulfield. "For one thing, they kept on drinking tea or some goddam thing all through the play. . . . Alfred Lunt and Lynn Fontanne were the old couple, and they were very good, but I didn't like them very much. They were different, though, I'll say that. They didn't act like people and they didn't act like actors. It's hard to explain."

That year Binkie Beaumont canceled a trip to the States because he was busy with John Gielgud's *The Lady's Not for Burning,* Irene Selznick's London production of *A Streetcar Named Desire,* and the possibility of Elia Kazan coming over to do *Death of a Salesman*—venturesome for conservative H. M. Tennent. In New York, T. S. Eliot's *The Cocktail Party* (Lynn thought it pretentious); *The Member of the Wedding; Come Back, Little Sheba;* and *The Madwoman of Chaillot* made serious statements.

But with *I Know My Love* Alfred and Lynn were laughing all the way to the bank. Certainly it was their least adventurous play. "I asked God for it to be a success," said Lynn, "but I didn't ask for *Abie's Irish Rose.*"

Anticipating a substantial New York run, they bought an elegant four-story brownstone "chock full of fireplaces" at 150 East End Avenue across the street from Gracie Square. Alfred drew up the remodeling plans, while the stage designer Stewart Chaney created an eighteenth-century setting in muted grays and yellows inspired by the set of *I Know My Love,* giving them a new excuse to plunge into antique shops and auctions for Regency commodes, Venetian torchères, and Louis XVI love seats. Lynn herself lined all the closets with quilted fabrics. *Ladies' Home Journal* gave them a state-of-the-art kitchen in exchange for photos and an interview. The day they actually paid for the house Lynn kept forgetting her lines. They were installed by the end of April, threw their first dinner party in May.

"The top room awaits its star guest, of course," Lynn wrote Noël. "You can almost see it palpitate. It overlooks the river and you can see the ships go up and down and hear the funnels toot in a lazy, sleepy way. The particular spot where we live is like a street in a country town, with little trees in front of our houses and on the sidewalk and a tiny park about the size of somebody's front garden, and then the river which you can almost reach out and touch. We have given the house our all and are now rather lying down and panting, so Jamaica will come as a most pleasant relief."

236 / DESIGN FOR LIVING

But they didn't visit Noël at his new hideaway at Blue Harbour in Port Maria. When *I Know My Love* closed on June 3, 1950, after 246 performances, Alfred's troublesome stomach made it wiser to head for Genesee, examined en route by Dr. Bigg.

Worn down by the Lunts' New York success, Behrman no longer made "all changes in bitter pain." *I Know My Love* had been tightened and clarified and now unspooled chronologically from courtship to golden wedding day. For the complexity Behrman had wanted, Lunt and Fontanne had substituted their uncanny feeling for the characters they played.

The 1950–51 tour was notable for sold-out houses and a run of bad luck: a robbery backstage in Hartford; a property man's wife knocked down in the street in Springfield; a brain concussion for Esther Mitchell, playing the maid, when the prop box fell on her head.

Then in Portland, Maine, Lynn tripped on the hem of her skirt coming out of their hotel, went sprawling, and broke her arm. Behind her, Alfred "gave a high strangled 'Oh!' and ran away." Lynn calmly bound up the arm in a scarf, took herself to a doctor, was jabbed with a local anesthetic, and went on that night with her arm in a sling.

"Brave little woman!" said Alfred, kissing her. "If I'd broken my arm there'd be no show."

"Did he get any black on me?" protested Lynn and sailed onstage. The arm was finally set next day in a plaster cast from fingers to just below the shoulder. After his initial panic, Alfred rallied, admitted Lynn:

He is very cross if I don't ask him to do things for me and when I do comes around me like a flailing windmill, knocks my arm, kicks my ankles and I dare not say a word or he is bitterly offended, and thinks he is no use. The other day he was putting a coat on me and twisted the elbow of the good arm so that he almost put that out of commission too. My ankles were both bruised from the fall and he loves to put my stockings on. But all is well so far except that the seams go round my legs like a corkscrew and I can hardly walk.

"Iron woman," wrote Edna Ferber. Alfred felt differently: "I find Lynn's behavior rather difficult to deal with. If she would only yell out and go into tantrums and complain, I would find it—curiously enough—a little easier to take." He should have heard her complain to the cast that the broken arm was "a buggered-up shit."

Lynn was cool about her health, but took good care of herself. Dr. Bigg made appointments for her in cities they toured, so that she had regular checkups, massages, and heat and hydrotherapy. She was indomitable and still doing neck stretches. No pencil-tightened hair-nets for Lynn. She and Mary Martin were considered the best makeup artists in the business, following Lynn's rule: "You make up for the orchestra, not the balcony."

In Pittsburgh thirty inches of snow cost them thousands of dollars. Their car was snowbound for a week; the train to Detroit crawled end-lessly through drifts. Scenery, costumes, makeup, and props never arrived for the Detroit opening, so Alfred did an *Our Town* Stage Man-ager and set the scenes verbally for an audience who felt it was having a cutting-edge experience.

In Cleveland Lynn's maid Alma became ill and had to be sent home. In Cincinnati another blizzard, in Dayton an ice storm, then a railroad strike, so their scenery had to go from Columbus to Toledo by truck and the company by bus. In their new maroon Cadillac they skidded on icy roads from Indianapolis to Louisville and back to Philadelphia.

In Washington, D.C., they were "stunned and brought low" by news of Ivor Novello's death. Back in Genesee, Lynn felt adrift. "We have never taken a whole season off since we began acting together. . . . This time we have no contract, no promises, no obligation to author, man-ager or anybody, and so we have decided to seize the opportunity and take a sabbatical year . . . and we are broken-hearted."

Larry Olivier was urging Alfred to do Christopher Fry's *Venus Observed,* but there was no part for Lynn. He did not, however, turn down Rudolf Bing, general manager of the Metropolitan Opera, who now asked him to direct a production.

CHAPTER FOURTEEN

The Met—Noël Encore—*Ondine:* 1951–1957

Interpreting Alfred's reluctance to direct *Così fan tutte* as respect for Mozart's genius, Rudolf Bing persuaded him that his "taste and elegance" and "supreme knowledge and experience" would make him the ideal director, as well as advance Bing's crusade to rejuvenate the Metropolitan Opera. He sent the conductor Fritz Stiedry to Buffalo to persuade him in person.

Alfred caught fire. "I think we should establish the fact that the opera is being sung by a troupe of singers in a little pavilion in a park beside a lake. . . . I think the dark woods and the little rococo baroque stage and the shimmering lake behind gives much of the feeling of *Così fan tutte.* Steps are good to make love on, believe it or not, excellent to die on. . . . I could not proceed unless I knew exactly how [*Così*] is to be set."

In spirit Alfred's set described Ten Chimneys, his scheme for *Così* the commedia dell'arte form he had used for *Shrew.* "You can establish an intimacy if the audience is immediately aware that the performers really are performers and in that way you can speak (or, rather, sing) directly to them, without added artificiality creeping in," he argued. ". . . Also the curious combination of the deeply tender and then suddenly satyric {sic} music can be so much more easily handled."

Mozart's combination of the tender and the satiric made *Così fan tutte* the ideal vehicle for Alfred to direct. It was Lunt and Fontanne's own stage style: passionate one moment, mocking passion the next. Innocent and knowing; highly stylized yet genuinely felt.

Lynn simmered. Alfred had sandwiched directing *Candle in the Wind* between runs of *There Shall Be No Night,* but now she had nothing to do but design and make stunning gowns on her Singer sewing machine. She tried to persuade Binkie to bring *I Know My Love* to London, but the Guild refused to lose money on the tumbling pound. "I shall be doing you out of a season's work," Lynn wrote Bessie Porter, "and that is very bad." She begged Terence Rattigan to "sit down at once and write that play you have in mind for us." She petitioned Noël: "We have no play in mind when this one peters out." She waited for the end of May when "sonny boy comes over the horizon."

Noël's Genesee visit sparked a play. The three cooked up a variation on his couple-switching *Private Lives.* Lynn would play a subtle, wise woman and Alfred a blunt, emotional man. It had worked in *The Guardsman, Reunion in Vienna, Design for Living, Amphitryon 38, The Pirate, O Mistress Mine,* and *I Know My Love.*

Sipping champagne under the crystal chandelier in the Swedish baroque dining room, the old pals didn't realize their magic show was out-of-date. Though he would triumph in personal appearances at Las Vegas, drama critics currently dismissed Coward as passé. And though Lunt and Fontanne could still sell a show, the theater was changing. When Brando read Coward's script of *Present Laughter,* he snarled, "Do you know that millions of people are starving in Europe and Asia?" The Lunts should have avoided Coward like the plague. And vice versa.

That summer Alfred committed *Così fan tutte* to memory. He assured his cast—Eleanor Steber, Blanche Thebom, Patrice Munsel, Richard Tucker, John Brownlee, and Frank Guarrera—that he was eager to work with them. Yet he was miserably apprehensive, telling Larry Olivier that accepting Bing's offer had been a "childish mistake."

"That Mr. Bing. He's one of the most fascinating and most amusing men who ever lived—and one of the most Machiavellian. I didn't want to do this; he made me do it. He has the charm of the devil."

Though *Così* would not have its premiere until December 28, they left for New York in early fall, Alfred wanting to be on-site. Interviewed in their "mirrored treasure-house of crystal, porcelains, rare pieces of glass, brass and furniture," Alfred kidded, "It's the first time that I've been without a job since 1912!" Chimed Lynn: "We have no plans, just nothing." Still, they refused to worry. They wanted to catch up on Broadway plays, visit Noël in Jamaica, and if no new play appeared, revive *The Guardsman, Caprice,* and *Reunion in Vienna.*

Alfred thought he should coach the singers four weeks minimum. In the end he was allowed seventeen hours in which to create a heavenly Mozart production—only the hardest thing to achieve on the operatic stage. He invited six actors to Gracie Square to help him block the action so that when he finally met with the singers on the roof stage of the Met he could guide them efficiently through the patterns. He quickly discovered he wasn't working with actors. "If you beat your breast as they sometimes do in opera," he told his divas, "I'll kill you." At night he would beat his own breast. "Oh, those singers can't act, they just can't act," he moaned to their guest Lady Juliet Duff. "What am I going to do?" He felt doomed.

As Bing had calculated, the media seized on Lunt at the Met. He was photographed rehearsing and interviewed widely about his conception of *Così fan tutte*—which, rare in any opera season, said the critics, had a consistent point of view. "When you eat fish, you want to know it's fish, not something else," explained Alfred. "I want Met audiences to know it's Mozart." Acting and decor must not overwhelm music, however: *Così* is "a sort of celestial revue, sung by uninhibited angels, a string of jewels, flashing their colors on a slender thread of unimportant plot."

He bought props with his own money—china and wineglasses that he hand-painted. He taught Eleanor Steber the gavotte. He taught Richard Tucker that more than one gesture was imaginable, and Patrice Munsel how to drink tea. Dark and attractive, Munsel caught on quickly. "Never has 'Despina' been sung as well and certainly never acted as well," he wrote William Le Massena, "nor will it be again." Finally Alfred himself agreed to set the period elegance he aimed for. Outfitted in a powdered wig, plum coat, knee breeches, silk stockings, and court pumps, he would enter and cross the stage, lighting "candles" with a long taper. He would then loudly clear his throat and exit.

ALL SUCCESS IN YOUR DUAL ROLE, telegraphed Terry Helburn and the Langners on opening night, THOUGH OF COURSE WE DON'T APPROVE OF YOUR ACTING UNDER ANOTHER MANAGEMENT. "God help me to stay awake!" muttered Lynn, dressing for the ordeal in black satin. She would suffer in Rudolf Bing's box.

Alfred coaches (left to right) Blanche Thebom, Eleanor Steber, and Patrice Munsel in the Met's 1951 production of Così fan tutte.

Raves greeted this *Così fan tutte.* Virgil Thomson in the *Herald Tribune:* "Not before at the Metropolitan Opera House have I seen an opera so completely planned from a visual point of view. . . . [Mr. Lunt] knew the opera and he knew the cast when he came to direct them. The result makes history." Olin Downes in the *Times:* "[Mr. Lunt's] production appears to us in every way to serve a double and profoundly artistic purpose. It is comprehending of Mozart, and it is in the truest sense a modern realization of a classic masterpiece."

In the *Saturday Review,* John Mason Brown devoted himself to Alfred:

> Mr. Lunt's brief crossing is more than a personal appearance. It provides as vivid an illustration as can be found of the gifts he possesses which have enabled him to blend theatre with opera and hence light up the whole performance of *Così fan tutte.* . . . To watch him enter, cross and exit is to sample the kind of lesson in acting which as a director he must have given his singers when he transformed them into players. . . . Then, suddenly, the little that is so much is over, and Mr. Lunt is gone. But his spirit, his manner, and his wonderfully gay comic touch remain, brighten-

ing at every turn and in beguiling ways the performance of *Così fan tutte* he has staged.

"Son," Alfred wrote Noël jubilantly, "This violet is now pre shrunk—I haven't an ounce of modesty left for *Così* is a smash hit and the reviews are unbelievably good and if I had more than the enclosed left I'd send them to you—particularly the *Tribune* which is headed 'Lunt makes history'!!!"

"Alfred's opera is the sensation of New York," agreed Lynn, "and everyone is talking of nothing else. After the difficulty and frustration & torture of directing—it is a lovely reward and he is very happy." Privately Lynn called it "his damn old *Così fan tutte*" and swore she'd divorce him if he did another opera. Alfred himself vowed he'd never direct opera again. He'd made two thousand dollars and sweat a million in blood and tears.

On February 5, 1952, Sonny Boy came over the horizon and read *Quadrille* to Lynn and Alfred. "Oh dear, dear, dear darling it's *got* to be awfully good and I *know* it is," Lynn had pleaded. Noël believed it was; and they did love it, except for the endless first scene between the second pair of lovers, when all they could think of was "When do WE come on?" Noël wanted to open *Quadrille* in England. Cecil Beaton would design the sets and Victorian costumes.

The discussion continued in February at Blue Harbour in Jamaica. Noël's homes were definitely not Ten Chimneys: little attempt at interior decoration, and "the food was awful, always covered in pickled walnuts. The desserts looked like they'd been made in toilet seat moulds." Noël's style was lounging naked next to the pool with a drink, chatting with equally naked guests—"Vivien draped over Larry's cock." The Lunts also stripped. "People find us ravishing to behold," a tanned Alfred reported, back in New York from "paradise."

Cecil Beaton came to dinner with "boundless enthusiasm." What fun for the four of them to be working on a play! No, said Lynn: "it will be a lot of hard work, anxiety, worry. We will very likely fight to death, we will hope to win through to success, but it won't be fun." They did have fun next day at the Metropolitan Museum researching 1866 costumes, then took their ideas to Madame Helene Pons, who made a corset for Lynn that nipped her waistline to twenty-five inches.

Alfred was crazy about the Victorian beards, top hats, and traveling cloaks.

Yet the Lunts were dissatisfied with the script. "I can tell you exactly where I mean the low dull spots occur," Alfred wrote Noël. "I don't want *more* lines but truer ones here & there. Does this destroy the placidity of your Jamaican holiday? I truly hope not. It's a glorious play—I just want it perfect."

Their delight in working with Noël again and the relief of having a new play made both Lynn and Alfred blind to the dead weight of much of Noël's text. Lines like "Please let me press my lips on yours, my darling," and "Ah, here is tea—thank heaven! I am quite prostrate," and "I have not the remotest idea. Is that not extraordinary?" must have been spoken rarely even in 1866. It would take every ounce of the Lunt-Fontanne magic to spin such stiff dialogue into gold. Style, of course, reflected content: this quadrille had been danced many times.

Arriving in London in April, Alfred and Lynn immediately plunged into theater—*The Importance of Being Earnest,* John Gielgud and Diana Wynyard's *Much Ado About Nothing,* Coward's *Relative Values*—and reunions with friends.

Again they had much more social life in England than in America. Noël was performing at the Café de Paris and there were gatherings with the Sherwoods, Douglas Fairbanks, Mary Martin, John Gielgud, Danny Kaye, Gene Kelly, Chips Channon, and Binkie Beaumont. Appearing in Shaw's *The Millionairess,* Katharine Hepburn lent them her car and chauffeur. Alfred cooked up storms for guests like Gielgud and Lady Juliet Duff: fish chowder, ham and spinach, sweet potatoes, beet salad, and caramel custard "over which we now sprinkle burnt almonds and toffee—a trick we learnt from Vivien Leigh."

In June they spent a weekend with Larry and Vivien at Notley Abbey, the thirteenth-century estate in Buckinghamshire Olivier had bought after his acclaimed 1945 movie *Henry V.* The seventy-acre grounds of Notley Abbey were thick with almond, plum, cherry, lime, and beech. There were lush gardens, five hundred rose bushes, a tennis court, farmland. Alfred and Larry immediately fell to discussing manures, seeds, compost, pigs, and Notley's cows—Ophelia, Titania, Cordelia, and Cleopatra. Like Alfred, Larry was thrifty. Both were passionately devoted to the theater and to their country estates. Unlike Alfred, Olivier was a cold man, took himself seriously, and was disappointed in his marriage.

The Gothic main house had twenty-two rooms. Courtesy of Vivien, guests enjoyed crackling fires in their bedrooms, favorite novels, a bud vase holding a flawless rose. Notley served four-course dinners with distinguished wines; afterward there were charades or cards in one of the three large living rooms. Vivien played manically, often drunk.

Lynn and Alfred must have been aware during this visit that Notley Abbey had become a living hell. Vivien had always been moody, insomniac, insecure. She had passionately loved Olivier, caressing him in letters to Lynn as "Larryboy." But her affection embarrassed Olivier, who retreated from her sexual demands. His frigidity and homosexual adventures drove her more deeply into depression and hysteria. That late winter she had had a nervous breakdown. She became manic-depressive and delusional for days in a row, after which she would emerge, exhausted but calm. Her dependency, anger, and fragility in turn exhausted her husband. Between 1951 and 1957, Olivier would appear only three times on the London stage, in contrast to 1950, when he had acted in thirteen plays, directed eight, and produced nine.

The Olivier-Leigh stage partnership also hadn't lived up to expectation. Meeting Lunt through Coward years before, Olivier had been overwhelmed by his passion for the theater. Soon he was calling Lunt "Master." "Alfred was the only American actor Larry met whom he felt inferior to." The lazy and uneducated young actor began to grasp that he too could achieve great heights. "Just think, Larry," Noël had told him, "you and Jill [Esmond, Olivier's first wife] could do for motion pictures what Alfred and Lynn have done for the stage—you could be a tremendously popular cinema team."

But Olivier wanted stage greatness. When he met the exquisite Vivien Leigh, his thoughts turned again to a Lunt-Fontanne type of partnership. Vivien's acting, however, was more suited to the screen; yet after they married, Hollywood vetoed a married couple making love as box-office poison. That left the stage, where, despite sensitivity and intelligence, Leigh could never match Olivier as Fontanne matched Lunt. The British critic Kenneth Tynan observed that Olivier deliberately limited his range when he played opposite Leigh. "Blunting his iron precision, levelling away his towering authority, he meets her halfway."

Doubtful whether the four openly discussed the problem. Though Vivien had confided to Lynn that she could tolerate Larry's homosexual affairs better than affairs with women, Larry tended to disappear at a hint of intimacy. They were still maintaining a facade. Yet in less than a year Vivien was in a mental home undergoing induced comas and Larry had gone to Italy. Alfred grieved for them both: poor Vivien, and Larry "so tired and inarticulate." He was to have directed them in a new Rattigan play. Larry was bitter: "Sweet Vivien and dirty me."

Coward was directing *Quadrille* "with acknowledgement to Alfred Lunt and Lynn Fontanne," to whom he also dedicated the play. Their reading had brought tears to Noël's eyes: "They are *great* actors." Rehearsals went well, the cast was excellent, Lynn and Alfred entrancing. Noël was in high spirits.

"How is it you're not harassed and pulling out your hair?" asked Cecil Beaton.

"It doesn't do any good and it's bad for the hair."

Quadrille premiered in Manchester on July 15, 1952. Beaton had been driven mad by postwar shortages of the materials he wanted for Lynn's costumes. Some fabrics had to be hand-loomed—then the loom broke down. Alfred complained that in his last-act suit he looked like "a distinguished pile of manure."

On opening night there were still calls of "Cecil! Cecil!" from the Lunts' dressing rooms.

"Darling, what about my wedding ring? Will you choose one because I can't wear this: it's so thin and modern."

"Cecil, this tie—it's a bit puny, isn't it? And how about this watch chain?"

"Darling, I wondered what you meant about my eyebrows being thicker?"

Alfred asked Cecil to sit with him in his dressing room because he was "lonely," but Cecil had no time. The opening was so supercharged he felt his hair standing on end.

Manchester gave them "endless curtain calls," and in Edinburgh the audience was "from heaven." Accompanying the tour, Beaton was amazed at the changes of pace and mood Alfred and Lynn invented for Noël's well-crafted play. He'd always thought Lynn "adorable" in her Empress Eugénie bustles and bonnet; onstage she became the consummate elegant beauty. As for Alfred—a genius.

A week before the London opening, the happy collaboration chilled. Gertrude Lawrence, Noël's longtime friend and stage partner, died in America at the age of fifty-four. Noël wept as he wrote a sentimental obituary for the *Times*. He included the statement "No one I have ever known, however brilliant and however gifted, has contributed quite what she contributed to my work."

Lynn had always been jealous of Lawrence. "I hate to seem such a sour puss," she'd written Noël after seeing Gertie in the smash hit *Lady in the Dark*, "but because you know I am really not, I shall confess it was the longest and worst acted part that I have ever seen in my life. Alfred . . . was waiting in the car when I came out. He asked me what it was like and all I could think of was, 'But, Alfred, she stinks.' " Which didn't stop Lynn from practicing the striptease Gertie had done to "The Saga of Jenny."

Now, though Noël's phone shrilled with sympathy calls, Alfred and Lynn did not ring. At rehearsals at the Phoenix on September 8—a theater that Noël and Gertie had opened in 1930 with *Private Lives*—they were gloomy and withdrawn. Lawrence was perhaps not the only tension. In May Coward had withdrawn from Transatlantic Productions, fracturing a business partnership of more than twenty years. Although Alfred and Lynn pulled themselves together a few days later to bake him a reconciliatory chocolate cake, tensions remained. For the first time the trio would not exchange first-night gifts.

Quadrille opened at the Phoenix on September 12 to an audience that included Douglas Fairbanks, Hermione Gingold, Syrie Maugham, Rex Harrison, Lilli Palmer, Constance Collier, and Zsa Zsa Gabor. Backstage, Michael Allinson, playing with the Lunts for the first time, was amazed to discover that "the two of them were so nervous they were positively shimmering—like a hot road!" Yet they sailed through the play flawlessly.

At the last curtain a green spotlight picked out Noël. He rose in his box, looking "like a Mongolian ghost in evening dress," and blew a kiss to Lynn, who in turn bowed low to the Master. Lovely applause, curtain calls, and a gala at Binkie Beaumont's following the performance. "Obviously a triumphant success," Noël recorded in his diary.

He woke next morning to virulent abuse.

"The text suggests that Mr. Coward was fatigued when he wrote it," wrote Ivor Brown in the *Observer*, while Beverly Baxter and Kenneth Tynan found *Quadrille* "devoid of wit" and "comedy gone flabby." Cecil Wilson of the *Daily Mail* said bluntly that no husband in his right senses would have run away from anyone so enchanting as Lynn Fontanne, making Coward's plot patently absurd. "Without the Lunts," said the *Daily Express*, "*Quadrille* would be a dull dance indeed."

Yet Coward had brought London the Lunts, always a matter for rejoicing. In Axel Diensen he had also created an American of dramatic substance. As the railroad magnate, Lunt was "gritty," "rasping," and "defiant," with fierce, anguished eyes and a voice "with the shrill urgency of a train." Again he did not seem to remember lines so much as create them. As for Lynn Fontanne, her playing was brilliant, tender, irresistible. *Quadrille* was a foursome, but "only as a two-some does it fascinate," concluded Ivor Brown.

Yet Lunt and Fontanne did not escape entirely. *Love in Idleness, I Know My Love,* and *Quadrille* were all below Rattigan, Behrman, and Coward's standards—because they had been written as vehicles for that phenomenon the Lunts. Kenneth Tynan had interviewed the legendary pair. Lynn was "wily and feline of tread" with "hooded eyes" and a "complacent mouth"—a sorceress packing "a large hip flask of the elixir of life." Lunt resembled "a polar bear, a bulky pet with kind eyes" and "gently smiling jaws." They were vivid, genial, vital. Yet, "I wish the Lunts would test themselves in better plays," continued Tynan. "I wish I even felt sure that they knew a good script when they saw one. As things are, they have become a sort of grandiose circus act; instead of climbing mountains, they are content to jump through hoops."

Quadrille was another hoop. Lynn Fontanne "was doing great honour to a feeble play. Her madcap Marchioness had the crackle and sheen of a five-pound note; her eyes mocked marvellously, her voice cut like a knife into wedding-cake, and the whole performance tinkled like crushed ice. Given one sprig of wit to adorn it, this would have been a rare bouquet; but wit was what Mr. Coward had neglected to provide."

In Noël's view, "The first night audience and all the critics were determined not to like it before the curtain went up." The West End was now dominated by "the Clever Ones" who considered Coward old hat. "I have seldom read such concentrated venom." But they hadn't liked his hit *Private Lives* either, he comforted himself, and *Quadrille* was virtually sold out until Christmas.

Griffith Jones played the Marquis of Heronden; Marian Spencer, Diensen's wife, Charlotte. Their bad notices gave Alfred and Lynn new ammunition for the cuts they'd been urging. Noël agreed about the actors: "I hated them so that I could barely sit still. I would gladly agree to cut *anything* that would shorten their time on the stage." But his writing was not at fault: "As played by Griff Jones [the Marquis] was a dull, meaningless bore but if played by an actor with humour and charm he would be neither meaningless, dull nor a bore. . . ."

Alfred and Lynn photographed by Cecil Beaton in Noël Coward's Quadrille *(1952).*

That December they played in fog that "filled the theatre like grey chiffon . . . we acted as though under the sea." Alfred ogled Christmas shop windows filled with turkeys, geese, duck, pheasant, lobsters, crabs, and oysters. They dined splendidly with Binkie on Christmas Day, but a New Year's Eve party which they hosted at Noël's studio was not much fun and they left early. In February 1953, Churchill came to see the play: this time no cigar. In March, according to Coward, Marian Spencer and Griffith Jones were still ineffective, Lynn superb, Alfred overplaying a bit (a temptation in a part whose key line was "Hell and damnation! Hell and damnation!"). Though they watched the coronation parade of Queen Elizabeth II from a club near the Dorchester, they missed some coronation excitement because they toured Ireland that summer to packed theaters. "Audiences really *scream* at the end of the play—never did I hear such a noise." They'd played sixty-five weeks abroad, had been in the British Isles eighteen months.

Noël saw the last performance at Streatham on September 12.

It was a fairly gruesome evening. Lynn was wonderful, Joyce [Carey] excellent and Griffith Jones and Marian Spencer dreadful. The real horror was Alfred, who overplayed badly. He crouched and wriggled and camped about like a massive *antiquaire* on [sic] heat. It is so depressing that such a really beautiful actor can go so far wrong. Between the two of them they have pretty well ruined the rest of the cast. If only, if only, they would let well alone. When I think of Alfred's original performance and compare it with what I saw last night, I feel the clammy touch of despair.

With Noël in the audience, a much younger Alfred as Mosca had suddenly leapt into bed with Volpone. If the camp antics were for his benefit, this time Noël was not amused. Conferring with Binkie about the American production, he agreed that his only choice was to keep as far away as possible. But he was bitter.

They are deeply concerned with only three things—themselves, the theatre (in so far as it concerns themselves) and food—good, hot food. Lynn has a strong character and is to be trusted. Alfred is frightened of everybody's shadow except, unfortunately, his own. He is weak, hysterical and not to be trusted on stage. On the other hand he has tremendous charm, great humour and is, or can be, an actor of genius. They are unique and valuable and far too complex to be managed in the same play. They love me very much and will listen to me with respect but after a while, with Alfred anyhow, the words of wisdom . . . are forgotten. It is very confusing and exceedingly irritating, especially because I love and admire them both so much.

"Noëlly is concerned with only three things," the Lunts might have said: "himself, the theater (in so far as it concerns himself) and sybaritic pleasures in hot climates. He is a snob, amazingly uncultured and plainly insecure. He loves us very much and will listen to us with respect, but after a while our words of wisdom are forgotten. It is very confusing and exceedingly irritating, especially because we love and admire him so much."

The days of young dreams of triumph seemed far away. After a two-week vacation in Paris, where Lynn bought clothes at Balmain, they did have an emotional farewell dinner with Noël at Binkie's on October 5 before sailing on the *Queen Elizabeth*. Yet they'd decided not to open *Quadrille* in New York until the following October. They were exhausted.

Hattie had "literally been dying for months," but on April 1, her ninety-first birthday, she began to recover. Still, when they returned they found her shockingly old. She still wore perky bows atop her white chignon; but she no longer baked pies, no longer devoured books. She was frail and walked with a cane. As Gus Eckstein observed, she was "exasperated at being old."

Alfred returned to the "goddam cook book." "I make recipes sound so dull and dreary—no aroma seems to come from the words," he complained to John Mason Brown. ". . . I manage to make it all sound so ominous like 'scalpel, gauge, scissors, cat gut!' " He did manage to inject touches of humor: "Using cheap wines in cooking is like attending an opera in an undershirt," or "A double-boiler is such a comfort," or "An egg always knows when you're treating it right." Yet he found writing down recipes heavy going. "What can you do? It's the same thing over and over. Put it in the oven. Take it out." Several publishers had asked for a cookbook and also the Lunts' memoirs, but he'd replied to Knopf and Henry Holt, "There is nothing in the world that Miss Fontanne and I want to do less than write about our lives."

In November Bob Sherwood wrote "with the devout hope" that Alfred might detach himself from his "drought-ridden acres" long enough to direct Giraudoux's play *Ondine* with Audrey Hepburn and Mel Ferrer. "I know you are tired and need and deserve a good spiritual rest—not a physical rest, because I am sure you are out with that watering can

morning, noon and night. . . . But I feel I owe it to this really great play
to try to persuade you. . . . It needs the *Così fan tutte* treatment in direction, and I know of only one living individual who can supply that."

For Alfred exhaustion was relative. Faced with nothing to do till
next October but keep Ten Chimneys going and rework *Quadrille,* he
accepted the Playwrights' Company's offer, happy to work again with
Sherwood, who would supervise the production. He would get $5,000,
a straight three percent of the gross, and expenses to $500.

Giraudoux had offered them the play sixteen years before, but at fifty
and forty-five, Lynn and Alfred had wisely refused the parts of the water
nymph and the prince. Now Lynn would co-direct, though without
credit. She would also work with Dickie Whorf on the costumes, again
uncredited. And she and Alfred would discuss the play endlessly. "We
go to bed with scripts in our hands."

Giraudoux's romantic mood play soon gripped Alfred. "I'm beginning to find *Ondine* almost too exciting to think about," he wrote Sherwood.

> It has problems, far more difficult than any play I know. If we
> could just find the right man to do the scenery! A combination of
> Cecil Beaton, Jo M[ielziner], Chagall, [Oliver] Messel . . . but
> how queer can you get! . . . The actors of course must have their
> feet on the ground but the scenery must literally ebb and flow.
> You must have music too, amplified—so that it comes from
> everywhere—a *quartet* like Ravel's Introduction for Harp &
> Strings & wood instruments—have you ever heard it—and one
> trumpet & percussion. *Five* Union musicians could do it. Anyway
> music—*you MUST have.*

Yet there was Hattie. He couldn't leave her alone, even with Jules,
whom she tolerated better than female help. He persuaded her to move
temporarily to Chicago, to be with Karin and close to Dr. Bigg. Ben
Perkins drove her away in the Cadillac, Alfred wondering whether she
would ever return to Genesee.

They had sublet their East Side town house, so in December they
rented an apartment in Manhattan, giving their telephone number to a
few intimates. Alfred was cutting a script that was much too talky for
Americans. On December 28 he appeared at rehearsals at the Forty-
sixth Street Theatre in an impeccably tailored suit, tie, and handker-

chief in his breast pocket. He and Lynn were always punctual, never took a drink before or during a performance, and did not tolerate lateness or alcohol. "We don't mind garlic or onion on the breath—but we do object to the smell of liquor!" He had an explosive temper and used it to effect. According to a young cast member, he drove actors as he drove himself:

> Lunt works us until we're ready to drop. The first week of rehearsal I think we all tried to see how much we could get away with. He wouldn't stand for it, wouldn't give an inch. He made his authority stick the first week—I've heard he handed in his resignation twice. While I wouldn't say he's a tyrant, he certainly is the boss and won't stand for any tricks or temper tantrums. . . .
>
> On the other hand, Lunt, though he can give you a raised eyebrow and a sharp reprimand that will make you wish you were dead, is just about the most wonderful audience an actor could want. He's a genuine appreciator. If you're having a good moment, he's so warm and generous in his praise that you forget all the times he's glared or made you feel like an ignorant slob by reading one of your speeches more beautifully than you know you could ever do it yourself.

Alfred and Lynn blamed films, television, radio—and the Method—for young actors' "ghost voices." *But they won't be able to* HEAR *you!*" thundered Alfred until the cast wanted to scream. He certainly didn't throw out the Method's creed of finding the inner truth of a character (it was his own method), yet realizing a moment of inner truth could carry an actor only so far. Unimpressed with many who auditioned, he had engaged experienced actors like William Le Massena, Alan Hewitt, and Edith King.

One actor was a problem. Fresh from an Academy Award for *Roman Holiday,* Audrey Hepburn had signed on condition her fiancé, Mel Ferrer, play the romantic lead. Hepburn, with her ballet training and gamine beauty, was ideal for Ondine. "She has such a clean neck!" exclaimed Lynn, ever conscious of chin lines. Ferrer was less talented and experienced, arrogant and insecure. He complained loudly about Lynn's presence at rehearsals and plainly considered Alfred over the hill. Alfred seethed.

Alfred was comforted by a note from Margaret Sullavan. "Until this afternoon I had always complained that I had never seen a really creative job of direction—one that made the play more exciting to watch than to read. The most one could hope for was that the director kept out of the way of the play, and arranged his actions and pace so that one was unaware of them. But on the run-through of *Ondine* this afternoon I was lost in admiration for you. Your contribution was greater than Giraudoux, to me; I am still spellbound, and at your feet." Maxwell Anderson also dropped in and went away inspired, reported Sherwood. "Max has been in a very despairing, defeated state of mind. . . . But what he saw of one rehearsal of *Ondine* has evidently revived his faith and his will to live and write." Lynn understood Anderson's despair: "My experience has taught me a surprising thing—surprising to me I mean—that most audiences do not hear the *writing* in a play now."

Embarrassed by her fiancé's hostility to Lynn, twenty-five-year-old Audrey Hepburn wrote her personally: "I am able to step out there with so much more happiness and confidence than ever before, thanks to your patient guidance and encouragement."

When *Ondine* opened in Boston on January 29, 1954, Ferrer had not improved. Playing the spoiled brat superbly, he openly sneered at Lunt's direction, demanded that his role be expanded, and threatened to quit the play and take Hepburn with him. Alfred offered to resign.

Sherwood stepped in. He refused to let Maurice Valency, the translator, alter the text, persuaded Alfred to stay, and calmed Hepburn's fears when she flew to New York to explain the dilemma of wanting to succeed without angering Ferrer. On February 5 Sherwood telegraphed Alfred:

I HAVE HAD A VERY USEFUL AND SENSIBLE TALK WITH AUDREY
HEPBURN AND AM GOING TO BOSTON TOMORROW SATURDAY
AFTERNOON TO DISCUSS WITH YOU VALENCY AUDREY AND
FERRER ANY POINTS THAT REMAIN IN DOUBT. . . . AUDREY SAID
TO ME THAT SHE COULD ASK NOTHING BETTER FOR HER
FUTURE CAREER THAN ALWAYS TO BE DIRECTED BY YOU AND I
TAKE THAT STATEMENT LITERALLY AS EVIDENCE OF HER
INTELLIGENCE.

Ondine opened in New York February 18 to an audience primed for a special event. It was not disappointed. At the post-play party a radiant Alfred accepted congratulations until a woman came up to him and

Audrey Hepburn and Mel Ferrer in Ondine, *directed by Alfred in 1954: "He held her like a potted palm."*

asked: "Did you learn anything from working with a movie star like Mel Ferrer?"

"Yes, madam," said Alfred between his teeth. "I learned that you cannot make a knight errant out of a horse's ass!"

But Alfred forgave more easily than Lynn. Years later he could shrug off the conflict with Ferrer, but Lynn always exploded when she remembered the movie star's refusal to take direction: "That wasn't jealousy, that was imbecility."

"No critic writing about *Ondine* has said enough, in my opinion, about Alfred Lunt," said Alan Hewitt. "He is the star of the show. Sets and costumes were designed according to his notions. Actors took their impulses from him. Author abided by his textual cuts. To put it mildly, he's a genius." Brooks Atkinson agreed: "As a work for the theatre, *Ondine* is perfect. . . . Under Alfred Lunt's skimming direction, it emerges as a fully wrought work of art composed of dialogue, music, pantomime and spectacle." Fortunately Alfred did not read Noël's diary entry: "*Ondine,* directed by Alfred [Lunt], ineffably dull but then it always was. . . . I fear my mind is ill-attuned to Gallic whimsy." Or Harold Clurman's open letter to Audrey Hepburn: "The production you shine in is expensive and old-fashioned fashionable; it is not creative."

Ondine played its limited run to full houses, making a clear profit of $40,000. But for Alfred the conflict with Ferrer had done permanent injury to the play. When he and Audrey Hepburn won Tonys for *Ondine,* Alfred asked Dickie Whorf to accept the award for him. "That beautiful play—half acted," he wrote Max Anderson. "Of *COURSE* some of it is dull—it's the man's play, you know, really, but who'd ever guess it?" Sherwood had his last word:

All the medals & praise in the world will never convince me that beautiful play comes off. Of course people are disappointed in the love story—*She* jumps on the hero's lap & he holds her like a potted palm—he sits beside her at the table & treats her like a tired waitress at Childs. Listen! If he played his scenes on top of her you'd have the feeling he was laying a corner stone. Personally I'd call the whole show a fucking failure . . .

CHAPTER FIFTEEN

American *Quadrille*
and a Pair of Mind Readers: 1954–1957

The Theatre Guild had no part in *Quadrille*. Apparently the Lunts considered the Guild's billing them for wigs for *I Know My Love* the last straw. If so, they didn't inform Helburn or Langner, both of whom still searched for plays and radio programs for their stars. Helburn learned from *Variety* that the Lunts were doing *Quadrille* without the Guild. But their exchanges remained impeccably cordial.

Noël and Alfred were loving sons. Noël's mum died that summer of 1954, reducing his patience for the *Quadrille* revisions Lynn kept urging. "I have racked my brains to try and think of ways of improving the play and it is no use, my original conception remains clear in my mind and I can't budge it." Lynn wanted Brian Aherne for the Marquis in America. "The only outstanding difference between Griff Jones and Brian Aherne," replied Noël, "is that Brian is less decorative and has adenoids." He had written *Quadrille* lovingly for Lynn and Alfred. Until "the Clever Ones" had got hold of it, they'd loved it too.

Apparently Lynn felt he was letting them down (and still hadn't forgotten Gertrude Lawrence). She sent him a cool note. Noël wrote Alfred after the successful Boston opening on October 14:

The only thing, of course, that saddens me a little is the inside feeling I have of stiffness between you and Lynnie and me.

Lynn's tart little note which started "Dear Noel" and finished "Love Lynn" was rather chilling which I presume it was intended to be. None of this can be explained satisfactorily until we meet but it certainly must be then. . . .

I expect to arrive in New York in the first week of December; I shall come and see the play the night I arrive and will expect to be asked to supper after the performance. No place cards will be necessary and if conversation should be a little stilted during the first part of the soiree I hope by the end of the evening Lynnie might be induced to call me "Noelie" on leaving and even perhaps to let me kiss her hand. Failing this, I shall be forced to goose you both thoroughly as I always have and always will.

> I am,
> Yours sincerely,
> Noël Coward

X X X X Fuck Fuck Fuck!

With LUNTS AND COWARD REUNITED ON B'WAY! fanfare, *Quadrille* opened at the Coronet in New York on November 3, 1954.

Alfred and Lynn came off brilliantly. The Lunts "are back again, as handsome and slick and gifted as ever," said John Chapman in the *Daily News.* "It is always a joy to observe them in action," agreed Richard Watts Jr. in the *Post,* "not only because they are masterly performers, but also because they bring such style and relish to everything they do."

Not Noël.

Brooks Atkinson mourned that the Lunts were not devoting their skills to Congreve or Wycherley. Walter Kerr dismissed *Quadrille* as "placid comedy." "Nobody, not even Noel Coward," said John Chapman, "seems to be able anymore to write a play for the Lunts." Richard Watts went so far as to speculate that the audience might have been better served if the Lunts read the telephone book.

Again an uneasy situation between the Lunts and a playwright, but Noël apparently had recovered his equilibrium. "[*Quadrille*] is very well done, mostly better than in London. Lynn and Alfred are superb, Edna [Best] brilliant and Brian Aherne passable."

The Lunts had fired their business manager, Larry Farrell, for drinking on the job. Now their production partner Jack Wilson was drinking heavily. A few years before, Alfred and Lynn had asked the New York lawyer Donald Seawell to take over their finances. Seawell had turned $200,000 in war bonds into a million dollars. "That's wonderful, Donnie," said Lynn. "Now make us another million." They now asked Seawell to dissolve the partnership, citing Wilson's incompetence. Though the Coronet was sold out every night, they were losing more than $5,000 a week and making $300 a week less than Brian Aherne.

Wilson fought back, blaming first the Lunts, then Seawell, for the rift. But when Seawell agreed to take over the production, the Lunts told him, "You let us know the minute the investors are paid back in full, and we're closing this play."

Strange, then, to find Noël recording in his diary that *Quadrille*'s closing on March 12 was "a sad blow and a very nasty little surprise." He had expected to recoup losses in Philadelphia and Chicago, but the Lunts refused. "Whether this is because they are old or cross or tired or just stubborn I don't know, probably all four." Was *Quadrille* really a bad play? "Perhaps the critics were right and I was wrong. I find this *dreadfully* hard to believe."

The *Quadrille* collaboration had been rocky from the beginning, but there were other reasons for closing the play. With soaring railroad costs, transporting Cecil Beaton's elaborate sets would be financially disastrous. Coward's bad notices pained Alfred, spoiling his pleasure in the play. And Alfred was again not well—in Passavant Hospital in Chicago, running a high temperature from "some infection," not allowing Lynn near him because "it's all too shaming." "Personally I think I've got MICE." Back at Genesee, to Russel Crouse, "I'm better, much better though I still look & move about like something from *Howdy-Doody. . . .* Lynn has been an angel & makes Florence Nightingale look like Sarah Gamp."

There was Hattie. In March she had fallen and broken her arm. Failing, she had vowed not to let go until Alfred finished the New York run of *Quadrille.* She managed to hold on until May 16, 1955, her "best beloved" at her side. "Oh God—oh God," she murmured before she died. She was ninety-three.

"She was a sweet bird. I loved her," said Ethel Brimmer, one of the hired help. Jane Doud, an artist friend of Hattie's, was sure that Alfred inherited his brilliance and style from his "vibrant, exciting mother." Hattie "possessed an extraordinarily sensitive perceptive and even critical mind," wrote Bob Sherwood. Sam Behrman had loved her: "I was conscious of a great and unforgettable personality as well as of a personal loss. I always loved to see Hattie and to talk to her—life was enhanced in her presence—and I grieve with you that she is gone. . . . I remembered so many things . . . her sailing from New York on the *Olympic.* . . . She looked around the great Palm Court and said, 'Well, I don't see anyone here from the Depot!'

"Dearest Alfred, you were a wonderful son to her and she took such joy in you and Lynn."

Hattie . . . Rejecting a minister's marriage proposal because *"You don't know me at all."* Naming her chickens for decapitated ladies like Anne Boleyn and Marie Antoinette. Photographed in the sleigh, a coat hanger stiffening her ermine scarf as though she were racing sixty miles an hour. Hattie and her young son entwined on couch pillows, peas in a pod. Hattie in handwriting only a loving son could decipher:

> *Where've you been?*
> *In my skin.*
> *I'll jump out*
> *An' you jump in.*

Distraught after her death, Alfred wanted to make a Viking funeral pyre: "I'm going to burn down the cottage!" "Don't," said George Bugbee, laying a quiet hand on his arm. "Karin and I might like to retire there. I'll keep it up."

There was another reason to close *Quadrille.* Howard Lindsay and Russel Crouse, the team responsible for *Arsenic and Old Lace* and the long-running *Life With Father,* had written a play about a pair of mind readers who use their trickery to escape the Communist regime in Prague.

Even though the Lunts had sworn they could *not* do another light comedy after *Quadrille,* Alfred had suggested the mind-reading act, Lynn the political intrigue. Alfred had never forgotten Harry and Emma Sharrock's mind-reading turn when he was playing vaudeville in

1916 with Lillie Langtry; he still treasured a photo signed "To Al, our legit friend." A draft completed, Lindsay and Crouse formally wrote Lynn and Alfred letters asking whether they would consider the parts of Essie and Rudi. YES, BUT NOT WITH ALFRED LUNT, Lynn wired. Alfred: YES, BUT NOT WITH LYNN FONTANNE.

Unlike their recently difficult collaborations, they enjoyed Lindsay, Crouse, and *The Great Sebastians* from the start. "Never in our long careers has a management treated us as you propose to do"—meaning that Alfred and Lynn were co-producers with script, cast, director, and designer approval. They immediately hired Bretaigne Windust to direct, and Lynn chose Mainbocher to design her gowns.

"We are very happy indeed—a little dizzy—rather frightened but happy," Alfred wrote Crouse; but—"the play MUST be a success." Lynn had been as urgent with Coward: "It's *got* to be awfully good." Their anxiety betrayed doubts about their aging collaborators but deeper doubts about their own continuing appeal in a culture now dominated by rock 'n' roll, tail fins, television, the Cold War, and Marilyn Monroe. The 1950 film *All About Eve* was already being called the last literate Hollywood movie, while Broadway itself offered only some twenty productions in 1955. The French pantomimist Marcel Marceau probably had the greatest artistic and financial success, while Katharine Cornell and Tyrone Power flopped in *The Dark Is Light Enough.*

"What would you like for dinner?" Alfred greeted Russel Crouse, come to discuss the play.

"I eat anything."

"Good, Benny shot some rabbits this morning. We'll have rabbit stew!"

Crouse paled. However, "Ten Chimneys was all I ever dreamed it to be," he wrote after four days with the Lunts. Lindsay and Crouse made several treks to Genesee Depot with their typewriters, each time offering a new draft which Alfred and Lynn amended with red pencil. Though all their "little words and tiny cuts" improved the text, the playwrights hinted strongly at the end of August that it was time to print parts for casting. One "tricksy" bit continued to worry Alfred: the mind-reading scene in which Essie in a "trance" sees that the Communist general really wants to flee Czechoslovakia. "If not done 'just so' it will be farcical & absurd. . . . Don't change a word. . . ." But his red pencil did not rest.

The pre-Broadway tour opened on November 3 in Wilmington,

Delaware. Despite a cast of twenty-one, *The Great Sebastians* was sheer Lunt and Fontanne, onstage constantly except for a seven-minute change. (Reporter: "What is the most difficult thing about acting?" Alfred: "Changing costumes.")

The play begins with a mind-reading act, Alfred actually going into the audience while Lynn as Essie in a white feathered turban sits blindfolded onstage receiving "psychic impressions." Most playgoers didn't guess the code: "And now, Madame" signaling a handbag; "Madame, can you tell me," a wristwatch; "Madame, may I have the pleasure?" the color blue. One difficulty: some people simply froze when Alfred approached them, averted eyes telegraphing "Don't pick on me." Yet he reveled in the act: he was back in vaudeville again, sandwiched between Fink's Mules and Burns and Allen, hitting every point on the nail, expertly milking the audience for one final round of applause.

D ear uncle and Lynn," Sydney Greenstreet had written in January 1954, "I'm still a pretty sick man. . . . Love, love, love, love, love, love." His death shortly after that note had deeply saddened Alfred and Lynn. Now, playing Philadelphia in mid-November, Alfred opened a telegram announcing the death of Robert Sherwood. He went alone to New York. There was a downpour the morning of Sherwood's funeral, reflecting his heartache. "Alfred Lunt gave a moving eulogy," Edna Ferber recorded in her diary.

Sherwood's death was as great a blow as the deaths of Aleck Woollcott and Graham Robertson—greater, because Sherwood had written three of their biggest successes. Ironically, he had been more inspired by Lunt and Fontanne than their closest friend, Noël: *Design for Living* was a classic, *Point Valaine* and *Quadrille* unworthy. Earlier that year Alfred had seen a revival of *Reunion in Vienna* and couldn't resist reminding Sherwood of past glories: "You should be very proud. The manner in which it was done I thought was 'dated' if that's the word to cover artificiality & a forced gayety that sounded nothing so much as like the man who sells Chevrolets for Dinah Shore. In fact a lot of it was acted with all the lightness of a fart. Never-the-less your part of it held up like Gibraltar." Equally, Sherwood's death now reminded Alfred and Lynn of past glories. No use pretending *The Great Sebastians* was *Reunion in Vienna, Idiot's Delight,* or *There Shall Be No Night.*

The Great Sebastians,
1956

The *Times* did not pretend. "As usual the Lunts are giving a bright performance in a dullish play," wrote Brooks Atkinson after the opening on January 4, 1956, at the ANTA (formerly the Guild) Theatre. ". . . Everything they do is meticulous, pertinent, fluent and funny. . . . Golly, what they could do if they selected a script as subtle and skillful as they are!" Watching the Lunts in *The Great Sebastians* was like hearing Toscanini conducting "Pop Goes the Weasel."

Lee Strasberg, guru of the Actors Studio, was fed up. "A man like Alfred Lunt has more equipment as actor and director than Laurence Olivier. But what do the Lunts do? Fool around with tired Noël Coward. What is their total impact? They make nice nostalgic pictures in the Sunday supplement. But what does Olivier do? He's got the Old

Vic to work with, and he is in a position to *create*." Tyrone Guthrie regretted "that the great talent, the unexcelled technique and unique partnership of these two players has been used to make so many beautiful but immemorable toys." A founder of the Group Theatre, Harold Clurman, washed his hands of the Lunts. The past ten years he'd scolded them for choosing trivial plays, but "I have come to think my carping was really beside the point. The Lunts want to be just what they are, either because they esteem their talent at exactly the level at which they employ it or because conditions peculiar to the American theatre make it more practical to conduct their career as they have."

Yet watching the Lunts also forcibly reminded Clurman that they were among the last of the older stars. The average age of "stars" these days was thirty—and in no way were they true stars. "What is truly alarming is that one is not sure that these gifted young people will be stars or even be in the theatre at all when they reach fifty. Our theatre is fast becoming a theatre of beginners."

Like drama critics before him, the agent Richard Maney mourned the death of the actor. Of nineteen actors nominated for Best Performance in a Play over the past nineteen years, only Alfred Lunt and Fredric March had won the Tony twice. Of the rest, four were British, eight on loan from Hollywood, two dead, two song-and-dance men, and José Ferrer hadn't appeared on Broadway since 1952 in *The Shrike.* Lunt, March, and Burgess Meredith were the residue, and of the three, only Lunt and Meredith were faithful. The moral of this "evil arithmetic"? An ingrate American theater was not only "false to its maids" but fatal to its male actors.

Whitney Bolton in the *Morning Telegraph* recognized the Lunts' rare star quality in the theater: "The plainest of stories in the hands of these . . . individuals becomes something with the shimmer of magic and the shine of heaven. The most commonplace line takes on polish and intent, the merest situation takes on stature and delight. Since most of us go to the theatre to be conned, it is lovely to be conned by experts." Walter Kerr in the *Herald Tribune* lauded the "magical, stage-struck" Lunts: "swirling drapes and flowing capes and flaring nostrils and, if circumstances permit, a variety of unplaceable accents." Maxwell Anderson thought the Lunts "fabulous, like Merlin and Vivian creating a world." Virgil Thomson went further: "The Sebastians are a dream of everything I adore on a stage, including the Lunts, completely happy-making, completely rewarding."

Brooks Atkinson had seldom pleased the Lunts, but then a critic who called Maurice Evans the greatest English-speaking actor had radical blind spots. Lynn took revenge. One night Rudi asked Essie to identify the newspaper in a man's pocket. "The *New York Times*," said Essie correctly, then broke up the audience by adding, "*Is* there such a paper?" But Lynn and Alfred's irritation with the critics was also irritation with themselves. *The Great Sebastians,* no matter how they protested, was "south of their heart's desire."

Few critics saw *The Great Sebastians* as a version of the Lunt and Fontanne marriage, though bits of dialogue came straight from their public repartee:

RUDI: In all our years together there has never been one thought of divorce.
ESSIE: Oh, no, never.
RUDI: Murder, yes!
ESSIE: Yes!
RUDI: But never divorce.

There were other similarities. The Great Sebastians are *not* mind readers, though they convince the public that Essie has psychic gifts. Similarly, Alfred and Lynn's marriage was apparently not sexual, though their passion onstage persuaded the public that they spent their lives stalking each other in bedrooms. "I don't understand you people!" mutters General Zandek in the play. "That's good!" says Essie. "That's very good!" says Rudi.

Alfred and Lynn did not want to be understood. As Kenneth Tynan put it, their onstage "sharply timed interplay with its false starts, hesitations and perennial mutual mockery" could be summed up "as a private joke on a public scale." Though not completely private. A stagestruck girl was gazing at a poster of *The Great Sebastians* outside the ANTA Theatre when an old Broadway character shuffled up. "Huh—the Lunts!" she muttered. "He sleeps with men, she sleeps with women!"

Like the Lunts, the Sebastians view every occasion as a performance. Sweeping into a room only to find it empty, they mourn a wasted entrance. They are so absorbed in their con they confuse it with reality. Their long kiss at the end of the play has nothing to do with passion, everything to do with transferring the escape key from Essie's mouth to

Rudi's. Yet though their public act is fake, Rudi and Essie's union is not. Apart from irritating each other as performers, they are deeply devoted and trust each other implicitly.

Still hurt about *Quadrille,* Noël criticized Alfred and Lynn's inability to forget play for reality. "Every time I saw the Lunts they would start talking about *The Great Sebastians* until I said, 'Listen, darlings, if I hear this damned play mentioned once more, I swear I'm going to knock your damned heads together until your brains rattle.' "

Years before, Charlie MacArthur had the same complaint. Outside the Lunts' door Charlie had sworn that if they talked shop he would rave on about his typewriter ribbon breaking in the middle of a paragraph. Says Helen Hayes, often catty about Lynn and Alfred in print: "We went inside and, by God, Alfred and Lynn launched right into their usual rigamarole about what had happened at their show that evening. The theatre was their life, and they scarcely knew what was going on in the outside world. We used to joke about their having no home life: between shows they were hung up in their dressing rooms in cellophane bags to keep the dust out."

The *Great Sebastians* ran 174 performances on Broadway, a comfortable success, then set off cross-country. "Somebody has to go on tour. We're bats, we're nuts, we have no sense at all." In Chicago they had good audiences at the Great Northern, a charming and very dirty old theater where, on opening night when the ventilation was turned on, so much soot flew down that "the audience went out looking like so many Dalmatian hounds." They never knew what to expect of Ben Astar, playing General Zandek: one act he was Andrew Carnegie, the next Fiorello La Guardia—until Lynn wondered when he was going to bring on the feathered fan. "No—we ain't bored!" But: "The reviews were so dreary—might have all been written by one tired, shabby *hack—so routine*—so dusty."

By mid-January 1957, they'd reached San Francisco, always their favorite American city to play. Many times they'd sat sipping drinks at the Top of the Mark overlooking the Golden Gate Bridge and the ocean beyond, talking theater with Sydney Greenstreet and Dickie Whorf, Alfred telling Lynn that Mrs. Siddons was right about Juliet, a woman of seventy could play her because Juliet was nothing but the wonderful lines. And now Lynn would be seventy this year, Alfred sixty-five. Cast members marveled at the difference between the tiny aging lady backstage and the star who sailed onstage. "You know, Alfred," Lynn would say, "we aren't artists—we're just terribly strong."

The theater had changed. They missed other road companies in San Francisco—"or anywhere else for that matter." Then too, "Apparently the day of light comedy is gone—one must wear a sexual hair shirt to stay on Broadway these days." As for the critics: "Any day now I expect to see the ads run 'Fucking fine play.' It's getting nearer & nearer every day." Yet Alfred's enthusiasm could not be destroyed. The theater was jammed, laughs from start to finish, thunderous curtain calls—and "we have *3 new sure fire laughs.* In Act I Scene II when I say to Essie—'You were good too' she says 'Go on, go on.' In Act II the Sergeant spills a little champagne & we rub it behind our ears for luck—and in Act II when the Sergeant is about to punch me on the nose I say 'Essie put down that inkwell' (& she does!). These don't sound convulsing on paper but they are on the stage!"

They came off the road to film *The Great Sebastians* for NBC Television. The *Journal-American* published an interview on March 27:

"It's frightfully difficult to lower your voice for somebody's parlor."

"I wonder what we'll look like."

"Immediately after our debut we shall get on a plane. That very night. In blackface, of course."

"You are talking too loud. You're projecting again."

"We've seen some of the plays we used to do on television."

"Like somebody using your own toothbrush."

"Our play has a beginning, a middle and an end. That's not art. Don't watch it."

"Don't say that, you basset hound."

"No makeup in this *wo-o-o-rld* could do anything for me."

"But you must admit, dear. Television is much more restful than acting."

Officially Alfred and Lynn admired television less than movies. Yet early that year, hearing that the *Hallmark Hall of Fame* was presenting *There Shall Be No Night* with Charles Boyer and Katharine Cornell, the Lunts had Donald Seawell phone Madeline Sherwood to say *they* wanted to do their play on television. This was not petty jealousy: simply as a professional courtesy, Lunt and Fontanne wouldn't dream of doing plays famously associated with Cornell, like *The Barretts of Wimpole Street.*

After *The Great Sebastians* aired on the ninety-minute *Producers' Showcase* April 2, 1957, they wanted rather less to do television than before. If they *had* rested instead of acting, their performances would not have appeared so high camp on the small screen. Clumsy editing didn't help; nor did the fact, as the *Times* observed, that the Lunts "had to race the clock to accommodate the plot," sacrificing the subtle interplay between them. The chief problem was, however, that the distance so essential to their art was shattered. They were prisoners of the close-up. The unforgiving camera was in charge. Close up, Lynn's "radar eyelashes" screamed fake. Close up, Alfred's jowls *were* decidedly basset-houndish. Close up, the long key-exchanging kiss seemed faintly obscene: these charming older people should be at home in their slippers in front of the fire. Their deft magic was all but destroyed.

Lunt chronicler George Freedley says their television debut "was hailed by all who saw the production." This does not quite square with the *Times*'s conclusion that *The Great Sebastians* was "a painful embarrassment" or *Variety*'s "one of the most abysmal productions yet to hit the television spec trail." Then again, George Cukor wrote the Lunts: "For the first time TV is what it ought to be thanks to you." Compared to much television fare, anything Lunt and Fontanne offered was superior. Yet, said Lynn, TV "completely disembowels us."

hope people don't get tired of us," Alfred had remarked back in 1951. "We've now been acting together longer, god knows, than most people have been alive." Six years later, on May 26, they celebrated their thirty-fifth wedding anniversary before sailing for England, where they intended to play *The Great Sebastians* in London. "There has been so much erroneous talk and so many rumours printed about when we were born and how old we are," Lynn at her most charming told George Freedley, "that I'd like to say one thing only—I wish I *had* been born on the day that I met Alfred and now I know I really *was* born then."

Their shipmates on the *Queen Elizabeth* included Noël Coward, Howard Lindsay and Dorothy Stickney, Madeline Sherwood, and Eddie

Fisher and Debbie Reynolds. "The Lunts are as sweet as ever," said Noël, but between Alfred, Lynn, and Madeline there was a momentary chill. "Oh, why did nobody tell me!" cried Madeline. "I wish I had had the sense to get in touch with you. . . . In a way, *There Shall Be No Night* belongs to you two. What can I do? I feel dreadful." There was no "in a way" about it, but Lynn and Alfred of course accepted her apology.

Increasingly relied upon by the Lunts, Donald Seawell was also onboard. During their post-*Sebastians* holiday at Genesee Depot he had brought them *The Old Lady Pays a Visit* (*Der Besuch der alten Dame*) by the Swiss dramatist Friedrich Dürrenmatt. The Guild had hoped Lunt and Fontanne might want this black comedy about a wealthy woman returning to her village for revenge upon the man who impregnated and abandoned her. Alfred and Lynn were impressed but didn't think the play quite their style. Besides, they were pledged to play *The Great Sebastians* for Binkie.

Yet all across the Atlantic they couldn't stop talking about Dürrenmatt's macabre tale of greed, menace, and murder.

CHAPTER SIXTEEN

The Visit: 1957–1960

I t's the saddest thing I've heard in years," said Alfred, interviewed by the London *Daily Mail* about the Oliviers' split. Vivien had sued Larry for adultery with Joan Plowright—not that she didn't have affairs of her own. "What can I say? What advice can I give him? . . . There's no formula. The recipe? We just love each other. And we're lucky. We're not difficult people to get along with. Our lives aren't violent—I couldn't bear it if they were."

Chips Channon had found them a house at 23 South Street in Westminster, overseen by their British secretary and gofer, Nancy Towle. During their stay Nancy would arrange cleaning, maintenance, bill paying, shopping, trains, appointments, packing. Lynn and Alfred were always well looked after.

Lunching with Seawell and Binkie Beaumont (drinking more heavily than usual), Alfred and Lynn kept talking about Dürrenmatt instead of Lindsay and Crouse. Binkie confided that the British director Peter Brook thought that with cutting and sharpening the play could be brilliant. Still the Lunts hesitated. After all, in Brook's words, it's the story of "this old woman who is very rich and she comes to Güllen [the word means 'shit' in Swiss dialect], a little town in Europe, and she has a black panther, an empty coffin, two American gangsters, two blind musicians, and she's prepared to pay a billion marks to get a man killed because thirty years before he had given her an illegitimate baby." But they agreed to meet with Brook.

The thirty-two-year-old director was currently hot, with distinguished stagings of *Venice Preserv'd, The Lark,* and *Titus Andronicus* to his credit, as well as productions in Moscow, Paris, and New York. This was different from nostalgia with Noël. And Lunt and Fontanne excited Peter Brook, who knew what they could do for a play. He would meet with Dürrenmatt. If the playwright agreed to cuts and changes, he would direct; if he directed, Lunt and Fontanne would sign. Seawell would break the bad news to Lindsay and Crouse.

Brook and Maurice Valency met Dürrenmatt in Paris that July 1957 to propose radical alterations. *The Old Lady Pays a Visit* had failed in Zurich and Paris; Dürrenmatt gave director and translator free rein. His final advice: "Claire is neither Justice nor Apocalypse, nor the Marshall Plan. Money has enabled her to act like the heroine of a Greek tragedy. Just play the foreground, and the background will take care of itself."

In the original, the cigar-smoking Claire Zachanassian is "a spitting, biting, ugly and hard old trull" with a wooden leg and an ivory hand—emphasizing that she seduces the town to murder with cash, not charm. Brook felt she should be played as a dazzling, impersonal force, only "twenty per cent witch," while Lynn, who thought Claire mad, argued for an injection of tenderness, grace, and style to balance and disguise her character from the town. She also insisted that Claire's age be changed from sixty-five to fifty. She wanted to give Claire a "rattlesnake beauty" and erotic menace the original visitor completely lacked.

Given their stars, Valency and Brook focused on the love story—for though Claire comes to kill Anton Schill, she has never stopped loving him. "I wanted the audience to feel that Claire and Schill were two comprehensible human beings whose actions were real and motivated," said Brook. In the original, Dürrenmatt explored the psychology of the townspeople. Valency substituted a ritualized dance of greed: citizens coming into Schill's store to charge expensive shoes, cigars, and brandy, until Schill realizes they are racking up credit against his murder. Yet Brook kept the Brechtian feel of an ensemble play, each actor combining to create, finally, the faceless inhumanity of a crowd.

Lynn and Alfred read Valency's adaptation and telephoned Donald Seawell to return from the States to London immediately. When he walked in the door they sat him down on a sofa. Lynn read the six women's parts, Alfred the twenty-six men's. "It was the finest performance of *The Visit* I've ever known," said Seawell. "I was so shattered when they finished reading it that I couldn't move."

Since Brook couldn't rehearse until November, Alfred and Lynn enjoyed a long vacation. They met Karin and George in Paris, where Karin shopped the lesser boutiques and George bought good suits but insisted Lynn be there for the final fitting because no one could match her eye. On the other hand, Lynn visited Antonio del Castillo of Lanvin-Castillo for Claire Zachanassian's six gowns, including her arrival outfit—dead red from cloche to cape to matching shoes and umbrella: like her red wig, a stunning contrast to the drab set of Güllen. Then a driver chauffeured them through Sweden, Denmark, Holland, and the French chateau country before Alfred and Lynn were driven on to Biot in the south of France—"incredible beauty."

In Paris in early August, Alfred and and Jules Johnson enrolled in a six-week course at the famed Cordon Bleu cooking school (while Lynn visited more couturiers). Alfred was proud of his Scandinavian cooking

Proud of their Cordon Bleu diplomas: Alfred and Jules Johnson in the kitchen of Ten Chimneys.

but wanted to master French refinements. He found himself taught by chefs who scorned American gadgets. "Egg whites are beaten by hand with a wire whisk or not at all. You beat and beat. . . . I don't understand why American cookbooks always state 'beat whites until stiff but still moist.' That's nonsense. We beat the daylights out of them and turned out the finest soufflés you've ever tasted." He and Jules earned highest marks; a proud Alfred would hang his framed Diplôme de Cuisine Bourgeoise et de Patisserie Courante in the kitchen at Ten Chimneys.

ynn has great stability; Alfred is mercurial," Brook decided. Brook himself was mercurial. "The Lunts were able to hold me down. They would say, 'You've done something good, let's save it.' " Certainly the Lunt and Fontanne he directed were not the despots who had ruled their own productions. "Alfred and I have been directing each other for over thirty years," said Lynn. "You know, we never really trusted anyone else, but he's the first we really trust when it comes to taste. He appeals to the actor's imagination—the area where the actor is a specialist—and that's why we're so excited about him."

Still, they were in charge of their own parts. Lynn decided that Claire Zachanassian must be smiling but remote as an idol, emphasizing her aloofness from the town. As Schill, Alfred felt his clothes must reflect the economic and moral poverty of Güllen. Back in London, he scoured stalls in the Portobello Road for a secondhand suit, old hat, torn shirt, and darned socks. (The shirt and socks wouldn't show, only help him live the part.) As with Bluntschli's uniform, he further aged the jacket and pants by weathering them outdoors. Jules dipped the shirt in water once a week and squeezed it gently since it would fall apart if washed.

"Directing Lunt is a revelation," Brook acknowledged. "You can't imagine the countless tiny details that Alfred puts into a performance. This may sound like finicky acting but these painstaking details make up an enormous conception. It is like one of Seurat's pointillist paintings. Each little dot is not art, but the whole is magnificent."

It was Tennent's bad decision to advertise Dürrenmatt's nightmare as high comedy and open at the Theatre Royal in the resort city of Brighton on Christmas Eve. "An audience of uncles and aunts, already full of port, nuts and good cheer, virtually in paper hats, assembled to see the Lunts," Brook reported gloomily. "They had made up their minds that this would inevitably be a sweet tale of candles and champagne, carrying a nostalgic reassurance that the aristocratic virtues of elegance and taste still rule the world. Instead, they got a bitter and important play about the evasions and dishonesty of provincial minds."

At intermission patrons dragged their children out of the theater or took refuge at the bar. The last curtain, falling on the corpse of Alfred Lunt being carted away, so depressed the remaining audience that they stalked out in angry silence. It didn't help that in the following week a woman in the front row expired with a death rattle like Schill being throttled by the citizens of Güllen or that another patron was stricken with a heart attack during the performance. Instead of braces of game and bottles of scotch at the stage door, Alfred and Lynn opened violent letters. "This is an evil play; it will never get to London," predicted an actress in the company.

Suddenly the London theater Tennent had booked was "unavailable," so the company went on to Blackpool and Stratford-on-Avon, where they "introduced a completely new version of the play with much less text and more action; Lynn went on trembling, but came off convinced that the new version was better than the old."

In Dublin in February 1958 Alfred and Lynn enjoyed fog, sleet, snow, icy roads, a strike, and a freezing stage. "Audiences superb but shocked," Alfred wrote Nancy Towle—generous since they were playing to half-filled houses. "It's the coffin," the box-office manager explained: Catholics didn't like the coffin. Watching a melancholy performance, Roger Stevens, a director of the Producers Theatre, which was backing the play with Tennent, decided, "This show'll be a sensation in New York."

Stevens was so impressed with *The Visit* (its final name) that he finally chose to bring it to New York for a gala reopening of the old Globe Theatre under a new name: the Lunt-Fontanne. The idea had been suggested by Chuck Bowden, now a producer, when Stevens told him he'd like to present the Lunts with a Georgian tea service in gratitude for their work. Ten Chimneys bulged with Georgian tea services. "Give them a theater," said Bowden.

On February 16 Lynn and Alfred were interviewed by two-way radio from Dublin about the signal honor of having a New York theater named for them. They were, of course, grateful and delighted. Privately, however, Alfred wrote Alan Hewitt: "I wonder if this is the play to open a grand new theater? It's so sordid—half the audience hates it, and they will feel the same in New York." Yet Roger Stevens was convinced *The Visit* would succeed in New York, if only because for years the critics had been begging Lunt and Fontanne for an important play. Alfred was his usual pessimistic self and muttered about retiring.

Finally, in Edinburgh, audiences and press were enthusiastic—ten curtain calls. But Edinburgh was an exception. Most audiences wished to see neither *The Visit* nor the Lunts in it. It was a play, Kenneth Tynan wrote that March in the *Observer,* "as lurid and unsparing as a Daumier cartoon." Provincial audiences were "chilled and affronted." Their idols the Lunts had betrayed them.

Though they still believed intensely in *The Visit,* Alfred and Lynn were not sorry to end the tour. They sent instructions to Nancy Towle: Get rid of house as soon as possible. Pack sheets and pillowcases. Deposit checks. ("Do I have enough in the bank to pay the tailor?") Buy cheap locker trunk from railroad lost and found. Pack trunks by night of March 15. Reserve room at Southampton. ("How much salary do we owe you?") With the combined efforts of Jules and Nancy, Alfred and Lynn sailed for home on March 20, Alfred fretting about *The Visit* in New York every wave of the way.

Anxiety perhaps helped trigger a severe sinus infection that landed Alfred in a hospital in New York. It would take months, he wrote Nancy Towle gloomily, for him to recover. Chest and stomach pain also bothered him during rehearsals at the New Amsterdam Roof Theater on Forty-second Street. Eric Porter, Peter Woodthorpe, and five other English actors came with Lunt and Fontanne to New York; but most of the large cast was new, and Brook continued to retune staging and business. Alfred and Lynn closeted themselves with Brook at lunch, sharing sandwiches brought in a picnic basket and dissecting the play.

Brook found the second act difficult to direct. It begins with a confident Schill the most popular man in town and burgomaster-elect. Gradually, horrifyingly, he discovers that his friends want him killed for Claire Zachanassian's billion marks. Suddenly he is a beast at bay. His first instinct is to flee, but menaced by a crowd at the station, he fears it will strike if he tries to board the train. At the end he submits: "This is my town. This is my home. I've changed my mind. I'm staying." The challenge for Brook was to demonstrate Schill's subtle evolution from confidence to resignation while not slowing the pace of the play.

They opened out of town at the Shubert in Boston on April 9 to an audience that loved and hated it. During the Boston run, Brook discovered that Alfred was always thinking, thinking. As he passed his dressing room one night, Alfred beckoned. "There's something I want to try tonight," he said. "But only if you agree. I went for a walk on the Common this afternoon and found these." He held out some pebbles in his palm. "That scene where I shake out my shoes . . . and nothing falls out. So I thought I'd try putting the pebbles in. Then when I shake my shoe they'd drop—and you'd hear the sound. What do you think?" Brook liked the idea. Alfred's face lit up. Then he studied the stones again. "You don't think that it might be better with just one?"

Alfred also added an effective piece of stage business in Act Two when the crowd closes ominously around Schill at the station:

At first I sort of used to lie there. . . . And then one night in Boston it occurred to me that a man like Schill—all sorts of men, in fact, if they were dreadfully frightened, if they knew in short order they would face being murdered—would be frightened out of his wits. In this condition Schill would either vomit or mess his pants. So, one night, I leaned over and retched. Peter—my back was to the audience, I had turned away—came up afterward and said, "Did you vomit?" and I said, "Yes." And he said, "Oh, I like it."

The only problem was that once he started retching Alfred found it hard to stop and the spasms tired him. Yet he was proud of his innovation. "It has never been done before," he told Larry Olivier. "Yes, it has," Olivier reminded him. "You did it in *Elizabeth the Queen.*" Alfred, the trendsetter. Today, particularly in movies, vomiting is almost as obligatory as the scene in a men's urinal.

In Act Two Claire Zachanassian sits on a balcony smoking a cigar, gazing impassively at the tragedy unfolding below. Primarily Lynn used the time to observe Alfred. "Why are you throwing in so many ohs and ahs and Gods before you speak?" she said, confronting him after a performance. "Why do you do that—to give yourself leverage?" When Alfred gave a bad performance—nervously forcing, overprojecting— "it is not such a pleasant home life," he admitted. Alfred was the kind of actor who could go overboard. Lynn seldom did.

The Visit opened the new Lunt-Fontanne Theatre at 205 West Forty-sixth Street on May 5, 1958. A delightful drawing by Don Freeman shows Helen Hayes tossing a bouquet to the Lunts from the window of her theater across the street, singing, "Oh, the towering feeling, just to be on the street where you live." The Helen Hayes is a bijou; the Lunt-Fontanne, a luxurious tribute to stars: powder-blue walls, ceiling graced with the largest mural in New York, gilt scroll and feather moldings, cushy seats, crystal chandeliers, plush blue carpets—"as soft as a theater can be," said Walter Kerr. At the dedication ceremony on Friday, May 3, 1958, Helen Hayes bravely declared that the new Lunt-Fontanne Theatre "commemorates the moment when the two most beautiful people in the world become the most beautiful theater in the world." Larry Olivier sent orchids to Lynn "on this wonderful occasion—the opening of your special house" and "my love and my loving wishes and homage to my beloved master—LUNT."

Dürrenmatt might have been amused that his ruthless exposure of bourgeois corruption debuted in New York as a Lunt-Fontanne gala. A carpet was laid across Forty-sixth Street for first-night arrivals. In the lobby Ambassador and Mrs. Henry Cabot Lodge, Anita Loos, Bette Davis, the John D. Rockefellers, Spyros Skouras, Mary Martin, Paulette Goddard, Beatrice Lillie, and Ginger Rogers scintillated and sipped champagne. A first-night audience is always more interested in itself

Anton Schill and Claire Zachanassian in Dürrenmatt's chilling The Visit *(1958)*

Lynn, Alfred, and Helen Hayes celebrate the opening of the Lunt-Fontanne Theatre in New York, May 5, 1958.

than in the play, and this one chattered ruthlessly as the curtain rose on the citizens of Güllen. The actors tried to talk over the buzz—a losing battle until Alfred slouched on in his dirty shirt, sluggish suspenders, and worn shoes. Shock waves cut through the house. "From that time on," said John Randolph, a young Method actor playing the Police Chief, "the silence was deafening."

At the end of the play the townspeople close in on Schill. He sinks to his knees; his killers surround him. "Oh, God . . . oh, God," cries Schill—Hattie's dying words, uttered by Alfred in Hattie's tone.

Dressed in black mourning, Claire Zachanassian approaches. "Uncover him." She sighs. "Cover his face." Her retinue carries the coffin shoulder-high, she follows, they board the train. The crowd onstage gazes after the train in total silence. The mesmerized audience was still. Then it took one deep collective breath and shattered that silence with roars of applause that surged on and on.

People jammed backstage to talk about the play. Most felt like Anita Loos: "my mental solar plexus was hit such a blow that I am still staggering." "Horrible, horrible, horrible!" said Alice Roosevelt Longworth with relish. Then Lynn and Alfred went on to the Grand Ballroom of the Astor Hotel for the Lunt-Fontanne Ball for the Benefit of the Mary MacArthur Memorial Fund. (Helen and Charlie MacArthur had lost their only daughter to polio some years before.) Theaters out, actors currently on Broadway swelled the crowd: Larry Olivier, Ingrid Bergman, Dorothy McGuire, Alan Bates, Henry Fonda, Ralph Bellamy, Richard Burton. A champagne supper followed a cocktail reception. Mary Martin, chair of the Memorial Fund and one of the Lunts' favorite people, sang to Lynn and Alfred. Mayor Robert Wagner read a City of New York citation. Helen Hayes and Robert Dowling presented an award to the Lunts for their support of the fund. A Grand Cotillion followed, then Alfred and Lynn led the dancers onto the floor to a specially composed Lunt and Fontanne waltz. As the Duchess of

Mary Martin visits backstage at the New York production of The Visit.

Kent said to a woman who told her she'd be dining soon with the Lunts: "Ah, then you will be with real royalty." Alfred, tired and unwell, was thinking of home and bed.

Critics had been waiting ten years to applaud Lunt and Fontanne in an important play. *The Visit,* wrote Walter Kerr in the *Tribune,* "is as hard as the nails in the coffin that waits patiently in the wings for a victim all night." Said Brooks Atkinson: "After squandering their time on polite trivialities for a number of years, Alfred Lunt and Lynn Fontanne are appearing in a devastating drama. . . . Our two most gifted comic actors look like our most gifted dramatic actors."

In the Sunday *Times* Atkinson explored their acting further:

When Miss Fontanne makes her entrance . . . her familiar combination of irony and grandeur promises another evening of witty entertainment. But that is not what she has in mind. The grandeur becomes power. The coolness disguises ferocity. Reserved, detached, elegant, responsive, intelligent, Miss Fontanne gives a superb performance that is meticulously planned but marvelously spontaneous on the stage.

As the aging, limp, helpless grocer, Mr. Lunt gives a brilliant performance, particularly in the scenes in which the author does not give him much to say. For Mr. Lunt is the master of wordless eloquence. When the grocer is trying to leave town Mr. Lunt vividly describes his lonely terror in a memorable pantomime at the railroad station. . . . The grocer's silent submission, his inner pride revealed against the final act of outward obedience are infinitely moving in the theatre, not because the author has stated them, but because Mr. Lunt has imagined them and knows how to transfer them to the imagination of the audience.

CERTAINLY THERE HAVE BEEN NO THEATRE NOTICES LIKE THAT, telegraphed Edna Ferber, SINCE BOOTH SHOT LINCOLN.

Because of its supposedly limited appeal, *The Visit* had been booked into the Lunt-Fontanne for only nine weeks, yet long lines formed next day snapping up tickets for the run. "$52,000 a week," Alfred wrote Nancy Towle, "can't believe it." Since the Lunt-Fontanne was pre-booked, the production would be moved to the Morosco after a vacation break. "We were evicted from our own theater," said Lynn.

Throughout the run, stomach spasms plagued Alfred, so that he was often forced to improvise a hurried exit, inventing a line to explain Schill's absence as he disappeared. One of his eyes also was giving him trouble. He had long had exotropia ("walleye": the pupil turning outward), but now controlling his left eye became more difficult. As usual Lynn was in good health, but she had begun to forget the occasional line, so that Alfred had to cover for her. Then in late June an acute stomach spasm sent him again to New York Hospital. "This has been a degrading (not to say humiliating) experience for me," he wrote Bob Downing. "To be hauled out of a theater at half hour is about as low as an actor can get."

For the second time in forty-six years Alfred Lunt was replaced by an understudy, the unenviable John Wyse. "I really believe people come to see Alfred, not me," worried Lynn, and in fact the box office fell from $50,000-plus to $38,000 during the week Alfred missed performances. Lynn hated acting without him. Yet the fact that *The Visit* wasn't automatically canceled like other Lunt-Fontanne vehicles was a tribute to Dürrenmatt's play and the enthusiasm of a public awaiting Lunt's return.

After the run, Genesee Depot worked its magic. Alfred made cherry jam, deadheaded geraniums, picked beans, and experimented with new recipes for the cookbook that Knopf wanted to publish. He liked to work furiously, then sit back and admire the order created out of chaos. "I get great pleasure from the pattern and the color of the row. They look sort of like green Knights Templar walking along." Lynn as usual felt left out when they didn't have a play together. "I don't know which is more distracting," she wrote Nancy Towle: "when Mr. Lunt is ill or when he is quite well again." To John Mason Brown, Alfred poured out his love for the simple life: "It is so *exciting* here. I sometimes can hardly bear it—new vegetables for dinner—trees being pruned like mad—hen houses painted . . . dairies . . . greenhouses. The place is a vision of glory. And how can one be so consciously happy every minute."

Yet he went willingly back to work. After performances in Boston and New Haven, *The Visit* opened at the smaller Morosco Theatre on August 20, 1958, again to full houses. Alfred was bemused at the demand for matinee tickets. "Rows of women watching this macabre play about a rich widow willing to pay for the murder of her girlhood betrayer. I have wondered: is the matinee business so sensational because secretly most women yearn to be rich enough to buy the murder of some man they detest? It's possible. Women can harbor dark thoughts and yearnings, I know." Lynn went further. "Women are the most cruel and remorseless of all breathing creatures."

Though *The Visit* was selling out, the Producers Theatre announced a closing date of November 29 because it was bringing in a new play, *The Cold Wind and the Warm*. Used to controlling their runs, Lynn and Alfred felt baffled, particularly since the Producers Theatre did not seem eager to have them tour. After *The Visit* won the Drama Critics Circle Award for best foreign play, a tour was arranged, though not until ten months after the November closing. Not since their "sabbatical" in 1951-52 would Alfred and Lynn have so much time at Genesee.

Louise had often visited Hattie when the Lunts were away. When they were in residence, she stayed pretty much alone in the big house on Highway D with its long, lonely drive. Her children had moved out; her husband, Jack Greene, had business elsewhere. On May 20, 1959, she jumped from a second-story window onto the stone patio below. She lived five days at the Waukesha Hospital before dying of chest and spinal-cord injuries. The newspaper report avoided the word "suicide," but for years Louise had been depressed and filled with, in Alfred's words, "dark thoughts and yearnings." She was fifty-six years old. Alfred wrote to and talked about Karin often; he seldom mentioned Louise, and if he wrote, his letters apparently have not survived. She is the only family member not buried in the Milwaukee Forest Home Cemetery Lunt plot.

The Lunts began the tour of their "shocker" in Wilmington, Delaware, on September 16, 1959, but *The Visit* did not alienate audiences outside New York as expected. Thomas Gomez was back with the Lunts playing the Burgomaster, big as a house because Hollywood wanted him to play fat villains. On this tour Alfred and Lynn flew between Philadelphia, Washington, Los Angeles, and San Francisco, very unlike the days when Alfred used to sit up half the night on the train jawing with the company.

Playing seventeen cities across the country, *The Visit* broke box-office records for a nonmusical. "If we could have played one-night stands, we could have stayed out for years and years," said Alfred. Yet heavy production costs and salaries for thirty-two cast members made both one-night stands and big profits impossible.

A few found *The Visit* too violent. In Cleveland, a note: "Dear Mr. and Mrs. Lunt: I saw your play. It was well acted, as is always the case with you. But it made me quite ill and I am going straight to bed." In Washington, as the townspeople closed about Schill, a woman at the back of the orchestra began screaming, "If you're going to kill him, bring down the curtain!" Ushers hauled her away. Still, nothing to compare with the poison-pen letters they'd had in Brighton.

he Visit returned to the New York City Center for two weeks, again breaking house records. Maurice Valency came to the play again. "You've both of you refined and sharpened the characterizations to the point where the play is an absolutely unforgettable masterpiece of production. I have never seen anything better in my lifetime and don't expect to." He pleaded with Alfred and Lynn to extend the run: there was an unprecedented demand for tickets; it would be "a long time before anything like this play, and such acting, is seen again in New York."

Lewis Funke, drama editor of the *Times,* interviewed Alfred in his cheerless dressing room before a performance. Wrapped in an old blue robe, he is busily applying hair black and eyebrow pencil with the help of Jules. Funke notes a silver pig salt shaker among the pots and jars. A good-luck charm given to him during the London run of *Reunion in Vienna,* Alfred explains. He and the pig haven't parted company since.

He is upset that the week's take has been $49,730 instead of $50,000—"Broke our hearts." Good business must mean people love the Lunts? "No, no. It is the play. Don't kid yourself." Again the compulsive perfectionism: "I mean you never give a satisfactory performance from the time you start. Something always goes wrong."

The next day Funke interviews both Alfred and Lynn in their Upper East Side home. He decides that the living room has "a certain impersonality," notes that the exquisitely groomed Lynn quickly checks her face in a mirror before making an entrance. During the interview Lynn vies with Alfred for equal time:

"Now wait a minute, Alfred dear."

"Did I spoil your story?"

"Yes, you did. You going to do that? You want to tell the story?" Lynn is the more competitive because, as she often says, "Oh, Alfred always knows everything." She wants to prove she knows something too.

These days Lunt and Fontanne are inevitably quizzed about the

Method. Their answers are always sensible. "We had a boy in this company [John Randolph]—a Method boy. He was marvelous." They also love Tennessee Williams's *The Rose Tattoo,* pure Method. If an actor is gifted, that gift will emerge, no matter the means. Maureen Stapleton, Geraldine Page, Eli Wallach, and Ben Gazzara will be good actors no matter what their training. "I've seen some beautiful acting from those young ones, superb," says Alfred. No good actor is bound by theories or rules. Lynn's Methodist maid was right. Finding herself on Sunday in Genesee Depot with only Saint Paul's Catholic Church to attend, "Oh, that doesn't bother me," she said. "We're all heading for the same place." So with acting. "We're all just heading for the same place."

When John Randolph was eighty-three Studs Terkel asked him about acting with Alfred Lunt. For Randolph *The Visit* was like yesterday. Schill at the station with his suitcase, running for his life: "In the middle of one performance, a matinee, an actor got in his way by mistake and touched him. Lunt screamed. That sent chills down your spine. It was the most horrifying thing, his fear."

Then there was the performance when, coming to sit on the bench next to the Police Chief, Alfred stumbled. "Oh, Jesus Christ! And he falls into my arms. Now I did the only natural thing. I didn't want him to get hurt—he's Alfred Lunt! He falls into my arms and he starts to play with my lapel. He says, 'Is it to be now?' I'll tell you something: all you know is that, Holy Shit, you can't even imagine a thing like that. 'Is it going to be now?' like a baby. And from then on, every night he did that."

At the end, "what happens is that he falls on the ground, his back is to us and we see his feet kicking out as they come in on him, like a wounded animal, he's kicking and he's scared." (Lynn called it "Alfred's Actors Studio ending.") "What you hear is the pounding of his legs. And they were choking him. They were killing him."

Alfred tells Lewis Funke he's tired.

"That isn't true," contradicts Lynn quickly.

"Yes. At the end, when I have to stamp my feet. You know, when they strangle me—and it is a very bad position. . . . It is damned uncomfortable. Hard. And some nights, I just can't stamp my old feet. They won't stamp. I am too damned tired."

Says Randolph: "I'll always remember working with Alfred Lunt as the greatest fucking experience of my life. When he died on that stage, you knew that was it."

Most apprehensive about *The Visit* in London," Alfred and Lynn sailed on the *Queen Elizabeth,* arriving in Southampton on May 30, 1960, and in London staying at the Savoy, with Nancy Towle again in charge of maintenance. After two and a half years *The Visit* had found a London venue.

The Royalty was a new theater, built into an office block in Kingsway, north of Drury Lane—the first new theater in central London in thirty years. The theater is always "dying"; certainly in these years "the foundations of the West End stage appeared to be cracking." H. M. Tennent produced one banal drawing-room comedy after another. "Binkie," said Noël, "is obviously losing his mind." Inaugurating the Royalty as it had the Lunt-Fontanne, *The Visit* therefore had a great deal riding on its success. That's why the first-night crowd on June 23, 1960, was particularly spectacular: the Duchess of Kent, Princess Alexandra, Richard Attenborough, Dame Sybil Thorndike, Sir Lewis Casson, Anna Neagle, Jean Simmons, Robert Mitchum, Stanley Holloway, Julie Christie—and Binkie, backing the play with Two Arts Ltd.

With a fine supporting cast, notably George Rose as the Burgomaster, *The Visit* finally found an audience in England. Audience and critics were dazzled. "This is brilliant," said Bernard Levin in the *Daily Express,* "—triumph, triumph, triumph," while Robert Muller in the *Daily Mail* wrote simply: "A stupendous evening." The *Financial Times* praised Peter Brook, whose genius was to have "caught the curious, removed unreal tone of voice of the expressionist play, and to have kept it absolutely consistent throughout the evening." Kenneth Tynan lauded Dürrenmatt's play as a "lacerating assault on greed" but also as satire on bourgeois democracy: the killing of Anton Schill "monstrously unjust and entirely democratic."

The actor Donald Sinden was "bowled over" by the Lunts. Here was "a totally new dimension in acting." Sinden had "never encountered such 'Truth'; such apparent underplaying. To 'throw away' a line to the point of danger: Such precision: Such 'reserve.' Oh! I could go on and on: the deer in the garden/forest scene . . . I looked over my shoulder to see where it had gone! Such orchestration."

Startling, then, after all the praise, to read in *Plays and Players:* "I think the Lunts are a bag of tricks." To critic Peter Roberts, Lunt and Fontanne stood at the opposite pole to contemporary American Method actors. Moreover, the Lunts' plays were "brilliant rubbish." (Equally startling to be informed over the BBC that according to Lee Strasberg, "The Lunts *are* the Method.")

Yet for a few viewers and scholars of Dürrenmatt and Brook, Lynn Fontanne less realized the original macabre spirit of *The Visit* than Alfred Lunt, playing Claire Zachanassian "less as a Medea-figure, an implacable goddess of fate, than as a recognizable, plausible, and potentially sympathetic woman who has been wronged." The Castillo wardrobe was partly at fault—and Lynn for choosing it. Alfred's performance was truer to Dürrenmatt's conception: the metamorphosis of a venal shopkeeper into a man who achieves moral greatness by accepting his guilt and doom. According to the dissenters, Brook and Fontanne had commercialized Dürrenmatt. For the majority, however, Fontanne's glamour made Claire Zachanassian the more chilling. Here was a woman with everything—money, beauty, suitors, power—who still demanded blood.

The Visit was booked for eight weeks and ran for twenty. Compared with their usual London whirl, Lynn and Alfred had relatively little social life during its run. Noël was occupied with Princess Margaret and Tony Armstrong-Jones, Dickie Mountbatten, the Duchess of Beccleuch, and the wedding of the Duke of Kent, where the Queen and Prince Philip were charming. Still, they dined with Binkie, Chips, Lady Juliet Duff, and other old friends. But as Alfred explained, *The Visit* was "a tough play to do and we find now that we can only go out on Sundays; a real deprivation. . . ."

When they sailed from England on November 27 they had little, if any, idea that they would not perform on a stage again. A reporter asked whether they were thinking of retiring.

"No," said Alfred.

"Just let us have one flop," said Lynn the practical, "and the audiences will retire us."

Yet in retrospect the finale of *The Visit* seems prescient. "Is it to be now?" Schill whispers. "Naturally, now," answers the Police Chief. It may not have seemed inevitable, but it was now more than natural that the careers of two people who between them had worked 103 years in the theater should be drawing to an end.

It was inevitable, too, that nine months later the Royalty was turned into a cinema, and that in 2001 *The Visit* became an American musical.

CHAPTER SEVENTEEN

"When a Good Play Comes Along": 1960–1970

Alfred and Lynn returned to Genesee Depot. Edna Ferber appreciated the "fine feeling of serenity and contentment" of their rural Christmas card, "but I decided that I'd discount fifty percent of that and put it down to a Lunt-Fontanne performance."

Like Claire Zachanassian with Güllen, Lynn had always been aloof with Genesee. People said that when she was driven through town she looked neither right nor left. On the other hand, like Schill, Alfred mixed with the locals—*was* a local. Occasionally he could be found at the town hall Friday nights square-dancing to the fiddlin' of Texas Slim and His Buckaroos. He liked to drop into Stag's Tavern for a beer. (One day tourists came in looking for Ten Chimneys. Stag gave lengthy misdirections. When they'd gone, he winked at the silver-haired man nursing his beer at the bar. "That 'bout right, Alfred?") It was Alfred who chatted up the villagers when he collected mail, Alfred who talked tractors with the local John Deere dealer, Alfred who baked bread and Swedish cookies for area charity events. He was irrepressibly friendly. Hitching a ride one day on a snowplow, he kept the driver company for hours up and down the snowy roads. That evening the driver mentioned his passenger. *"Alfred Lunt?"* shrieked his wife. "My god, what did you *talk* about?" Her husband shrugged. "Man stuff."

A small group of Alfred's friends was disintegrating. That year

Edward Harris Heth's House on the Hill burned to the ground. His friend William Chauncey took an apartment and Heth began to rebuild. But the next year Chauncey would commit suicide, and two years later in 1963 Heth himself died of an overdose of tranquilizers. Their deaths left Alfred without the support of artistic friends in the area. But losing one's friends is a fact of growing older. Alfred and Lynn drew closer.

She had her little excursions. Ben Perkins would drive her into Waukesha to the Singer Sewing Center, where she would buy fabrics for her many projects. When she had her hair done at Gertrude Perkins's La Belle Salon in Waukesha, Gert would close the shop all afternoon to treat her famous customer's hair with a Roux oil bleach of two parts gold #1 to one part drab #2, followed by Roux shampoo tint #106½. But she did not go out much on her own, and even at Ten Chimneys "she mainly stuck in the house," as James Butler, a yard worker, put it.

Of course Lynn and Alfred went out together. One destination was the Little Shop in Milwaukee, specializing in restoring antique furniture. They would come in disguised in big heavy Russian-looking coats with high fur collars, knowing exactly what they wanted. Enid Anderson, the owner, quickly discovered that though Lynn had a great sense of style, Alfred stage-managed Ten Chimneys. And the Lunts did love disguise, going into Waukesha in summer outfitted like rustics in blue denim, red bandannas, and straw hats—"You couldn't miss them." Sarah Connor, an area resident, remembers stepping into an elevator at McCoy's department store:

> There was a very small person in the left corner dressed in complete army camouflage: field hat covering her hair, shirt, and pants tucked into army boots! In amazement I asked a clerk, "Who was that?" She replied, "Oh, that's Lynn Fontanne. She frequently will wear a disguise so people won't notice her." I rather like to think that Ms. Fontanne was playing out a humorous little adventure. I felt we were in a play scene together. My part was to enter the elevator and look surprised. I hope I did all right!

They had come home to Genesee with "no plays, no plans," yet in the summer of 1961 Alfred accepted Roger Stevens's offer to direct Samuel Taylor's "joyous shout of defiance" *First Love*, starring as mother and son the famous German actress Elisabeth Bergner and Hugh O'Brian, television's Wyatt Earp.

Before they left for New York, Lynn, wearing a jet-spangled black dress, accepted the Gimbel's Fashion Forum Award for fashion eminence on the stage. "I've never been so thrilled before," she announced. "Not even a stage success has pleased me more. I always think people may consider me empty-headed because I love clothes so much," she added unguiltily. The award acknowledged her creativity: she did not just wear clothes, she helped design them, couturiers like Molyneux, Mainbocher, and Castillo following her instructions. Peter Brook had been delighted with her outfits for *The Visit*. The better the actress, he believed, the more thought she gives to what she wears onstage.

"I've had rather a weary time of it," Alfred wrote Bob Downing from New York, "and if the play is a success I shall be happy. It's been tough. 41 scenes & 2 leading ladies." Unfortunately, Alfred could not be happy about *First Love*. Elisabeth Bergner acted so slowly and inaudibly that she had to be replaced by Lili Darvas. Forty-one scenes on an essentially bare stage confused audiences. Despite "expert direction" (the *Times*), "the play I fear is not a success—too bad as it had much good in it—but apparently not enough." *First Love* closed after twenty-four performances. Hugh O'Brian's friendship was a bonus.

While the Lunts were in New York, Natasha Wilson had found Jack dead in his bedroom. "What a hideous, foolish waste of life!" sighed Noël, reflecting that for the past ten years Jack had been "a trouble and a bore to himself and to everyone else." Noël was in New York for the production of *Sail Away* (Lynn and Alfred saw it three times in Boston); on November 25 they had discussed Jack and much else over a dinner lasting almost five hours. "We wandered back and forth happily over the forty-one years we have known and loved one another and it was altogether enchanting and, above all, comforting. Lynn looks marvellous and Alfred much better than he has looked for years. They are a fabulous couple."

Guthrie McClintic also died in 1961, and Katharine Cornell never acted again. In her dedication, she had been Lunt and Fontanne's chief American rival. Robert Sherwood once compared Cornell's, Hayes's, and Lunt and Fontanne's attitudes toward the theater. Cornell tended it like "a vestal virgin guarding a sacred flame." For Hayes the theater was "an Everest to a professional mountain climber." As for the Lunts, they had "a plain, simple, childish relish" for everything theatrical. Despite

Alfred's nerves, Sherwood had never known anyone who enjoyed acting more. In contrast, Cornell claimed she never drew an easy breath while she was working.

That year, 1962, Donald Seawell approached the English playwright Enid Bagnold, author of the successful *Chalk Garden* and a new play called *The Chinese Prime Minister*. "Go visit the Lunts," he advised. Terrified of planes, Bagnold flew into "O'Hara," where on July 19 Alfred, "immensely elegant, looking thirty," met her in the car with chicken sandwiches and whisky. He escorted her onto the grounds of Ten Chimneys and there were Lynn and the actress Cathleen Nesbitt elegant in lawn chairs on the grass, gowned for evening with false eyelashes exuberantly in place. Overweight, exhausted, and exalted, Enid had to be put to bed.

The Chinese Prime Minister was not mentioned for three days, while Bagnold nervously noticed piles of unopened scripts lying about. Finally they invited her to read it aloud. They liked it, yet Alfred thought his part not important enough. "Looking back on it now I understand perfectly that they didn't deal in yes or no," said Bagnold. Besides, "They have exhausted fame. They don't want it any more. At least one of them doesn't. The other very nearly hides it."

Which one still wanted it? Lynn, of course, who'd told Bessie Porter "I expect to be on the stage until I am ninety," and Aleck, "I hope to be like Mrs. Fiske and spend my old age doing one night stands." It was Alfred who had found himself more tense onstage with every passing year, Alfred who insisted he'd rather be weeding than acting. Lynn would listen without comment, but Enid understood. Lynn had been deprived of acting—"about which you never say a word."

What Alfred and Lynn did deal in was hospitality. Picnic baskets of lunch to eat in picturesque spots all over the estate. Swims in the pool with the sound of apples falling. Fires in the cool house even in summer. Dressing for dinner. Cocktails in the big drawing room. Lynn "liked a brandy old Fashioned," said Richard Perkins, Ben's nephew, who mixed drinks in a white jacket—and she sometimes asked for a third. "From now on," Alfred had told him, "you only serve Lynnie two drinks and if there's a problem, come and see me." But Richard could never say no to Miss Fontanne and sneaked her a third when she wanted it.

She had trained him how to announce dinner from the top of the stairs. He must say, "Madam, dinner is served" but not until he had made eye contact. "And she would let me stand at attention for five, ten minutes and meanwhile Jules is in the kitchen pulling his hair out." Dinner itself was leisurely and rich: crown roast, veal Parmesan, lots of buttery dishes, liqueur desserts "you could get drunk on." Lynn would ring a little bell for service. She instructed the waitpeople never to interrupt, however, if anyone was telling a story. Richard noted that with guests the Lunts always talked as though they were onstage. People would fall silent anyway whenever Lynn spoke, "because it was such a beautiful voice. It took up the whole room." Richard didn't mind Lynn's rules but considered Alfred "a bastard to work for"—finicky and demanding.

After dinner there were cards or television or talk or Alfred would ask Lynn to model her latest creation. "He did his best to make her shine." Lynn would appear on the steps leading down to the drawing room in a black silk suit with braided jacket that she had just finished—hat, gloves, handbag, shoes perfectly matching—make a little pirouette, and descend. "She glided round the room," said Cathleen Nesbitt, "the skirt swaying gracefully, a top model from Paris, wearing the latest Balmain."

What guests appreciated most about Ten Chimneys, however, was not feeling like visitors: Lynn and Alfred absorbed guests into the life of the household. Enid Bagnold confessed she loved "everything to do with both your lives. It makes a kind of glitter. *Tiffany*-lives but not made with cold jewels." She adored "the beautiful indulgence" they showed each other. "Alfred watches you, Lynn, with such pride." She loved their playful give-and-take, Lynn snatching a story away from Alfred, Alfred indulgently yielding it to her. "*They* were a play, a new one. Ah, if only I could do that!"

In January 1963, Lynn and Alfred went to New York. Noël was there. They had begged him to write a farewell play for them and he'd murmured that he had an idea. "You know," said Alfred, "we thought he was writing a play for us, and instead he was writing three for himself"—*Song at Twilight.* So they went to current plays: *Beyond the Fringe, A Man for All Seasons, Oliver!* "They were thrilled. They go to the theatre so seldom, it was taking the kiddies to the panto."

Until February 10, 1963, Sarah Bernhardt had been the only actress officially invited to the Players Club in Gramercy Square. That night Lynn Fontanne entered the male precinct with Alfred for a Pipe Night in her honor. Howard Lindsay was the master of ceremonies for a distinguished crowd that included Sir John Gielgud, Sir Ralph Richardson, Russel Crouse, Peter Ustinov, and Marc Connelly. George Burns gave the keynote speech. Long in awe of the Lunts, he had been won over when, appearing unexpectedly with Carol Channing at the Burnses' house for dinner, Alfred hit Gracie with a line from Burns and Allen's first vaudeville act: "I'm glad I'm dizzy boys like dizzy girls and I like boys and you must be glad I'm dizzy because you're a boy and I like boys!" But Alfred and Lynn could hardly have been grateful for Burns's hilarious speech, which went on interminably—about himself. ("When do WE come on?!")

Finally, Burns wound up. "Lynn, if you're thinking of getting rid of that straight man you've been using, I've got a trunkful of stuff. . . . What a team we'd make—Lynn Fontanne and George Burns. You'll notice, of course, that I'm even giving you top billing." The rest of the speakers remembered who was being honored. "We have some good performers," said Ralph Richardson. "But America has something greater—America has the Lunts." Lynn and Alfred spoke briefly and eloquently and Lynn presented the club with a reading desk that had belonged to Sarah Siddons.

In May 1963 they filmed James M. Barrie's *The Old Lady Shows Her Medals* for CBS, a play they had done on radio for the Theatre Guild in 1952. Lunt and Fontanne had been especially invited for this eighteenth and last Guild production sponsored by U.S. Steel. Alfred introduced the play and narrated, Lynn played the Cockney charwoman "Mrs." Dowey, Donald Madden the World War I soldier she pretends is her son, with old friends Cathleen Nesbitt and Romney Brent as a neighbor and a minister.

Lynn considered Barrie's one-act "really nauseating" and vowed to blast every trace of sentimentality out of Mrs. Dowey. They came to rehearsal bringing their lunch, eager to work, yet still found television acting disappointing. "It's like a rehearsal—no audience," Lynn complained. Alfred's performance lasted only about four minutes but seemed to him like four hours. "I stand there and talk to a big black box, but it does not respond," he complained to the *Times*. "At least I'd like to see a couple of eyes."

Lynn's seventy-five years alone—the bags under her eyes, her arthritic hands—helped desentimentalize Mrs. Dowey. More arresting was the spiritual truth she brought to the role. The Lunts called Donald Seawell their son; they'd considered themselves Montgomery Clift's real parents; they'd invented a pretend son as a serious game. In *The Old Lady Shows Her Medals* Mrs. Dowey persuades a soldier on leave to adopt her; when he is killed in action, his medals come to her as though she had been his real mother. "By nothing more than a lovely smile," wrote Jack Gould in the *Times*, "she made the years fade away from the spinster's face and totally involved the spectator in the woman's joy of having a lifelong dream come true." A sentimental judgment. Lynn's raspy Cockney and straight back make Mrs. Dowey a feisty old girl, as flirtatious as she is motherly. Above all she is proud of a son who gives her status; she too is doing her bit for Britain. Alfred is distinguished and charming as the narrator, but *The Old Lady Shows Her Medals* is Lynn's show all the way.

Prior to filming Barrie, they had gone to Greece to film *Athens: Where the Theatre Began*—chiefly as compensation for a trip around the world that Alfred had canceled as too expensive. CBS would pay all their expenses. "I thought, why not?" said Alfred. "Greece is a lovely place."

Envious of Jacqueline Kennedy, who had shown off the White House on TV, the Queen of Greece wanted to show off the Coliseum. Since no one could touch the royal body, it took two weeks to mike and film her. The Lunts, Rosemary Harris, Alfred Drake, Donald Madden, and a randomly recruited bimbo hung around. Alfred developed a tormenting sty and couldn't get a grip on his lines.

Rosemary Harris recalls a horrifying lunch break when the Lunts disappeared into their trailer while Lynn's unintentionally miked voice reverberated among the entire cast outside. "I'm shocked, I'm furious! How could you let me down like that? Either you know your lines by tomorrow or we're leaving!" The Lunts were so unhappy with the film that they tried to buy it from CBS, but it was shown on September 11, 1963. "It was," says Harris, "a *strange* experience."

That May Enid Bagnold came to dinner in New York with Roger Stevens. *The Chinese Prime Minister* had not been resolved.

"You know," said Alfred, on his feet, into the part, "—if we *were* doing this play I would want to play Bent, not the husband."

Lynn leaned over to Enid. "Don't build hopes, darling," she whispered. "He'll reverse it in the morning." She was talking to herself as much as to Enid. Enid had written the part of a seventy-year-old actress with Lynn in mind. Lynn wanted to play it.

Alfred did reverse. "What the devil comes between you and the white paper?" he asked Bagnold, still dissatisfied with his character. Jules took up Bagnold's cause: "Write *another*," he pleaded. "Write with *two* parts. Write so they can *act together*."

But the Lunts were constantly turning down plays: *The Madwoman of Chaillot, Buried Alive, Poor Brinsley, The Marriner Method, Dear Liar, Bashful Genius, Exit the King*. In print it was always "We can't do it"; but in fact Lynn could not overcome Alfred's reluctance to return to the theater, stronger than her fear of failing memory. Edward Albee tried for years to get them to play *A Delicate Balance*, not understanding why they refused.

Financially, too, they did not need the theater. In June 1965, the market value of Alfred's investment portfolio was $712,390; Lynn's, $749,890 (Donald Seawell called her "the financial wizard of the Lunt

Alfred and Lynn with Queen Mother Elizabeth at Noël's house in Jamaica, March 1965

family"). Lynn also had thousands of dollars' worth of furs and jewelry. They owned Ten Chimneys and a New York City house. There was no practical need.

Instead of acting they flew to Jamaica on February 18, 1965, to visit Noël at his retreat on Firefly Hill. He took Lynn out to show her with pride the spectacular view of the Blue Mountains like an amphitheater sloping downward to a crescent of silver sand and the Caribbean. Lynn was unimpressed. "It looks like a bad matinée with rows and rows of empty seats." The big event was the visit of the Queen Mother, accompanied by security agents and police. Noël's fish mousse collapsed at the last minute, so he had to make an iced soup to be served with curry in coconut shells followed by strawberries and a rum cream pie. The lunch went off beautifully, with the Queen Mum radiating charm and Alfred, Cole Leslie, and Noël slaves at her feet. Noël asked Alfred to direct a revival of *Design for Living* in New York, but Alfred turned him down.

The years of honors, which never compensated for the work that earned them, had begun and would continue. In the 1950s New York University and Dartmouth granted them Doctorates of Humane Letters, Dartmouth noting that "what the Lunts have joined together Dartmouth will not set asunder." Russell Sage College honored Lynn and Emerson College (where Alfred had attended classes randomly for a few months) named this "Magnificent Actor, Devoted Patron of the Arts, Beloved Friend of the Theatre Audience" a Doctor of Laws. Yale, Temple, and Brandeis honored both Lynn and Alfred in 1964, the Art Institute of Chicago in 1966, Smith in 1968, UCLA in 1972. From Wisconsin alone came honorary degrees from the University of Wisconsin, Carroll College, Aquinas College, Beloit College, and Marquette University, as well as the first Governor's Award. (Returning to Carroll after fifty years to speak to the Drama Society, Alfred charmed a cheering student crowd.) They were made life or honorary members of the Actors' Fund, the Drama Teachers Association, the Press and Union League Club of San Francisco, the Wisconsin Idea Theatre, and the American Institute of Interior Designers.

A 1966 dinner given them at Lawrence College by the Wisconsin Academy of Sciences, Arts and Letters sums up the honors scene. Ben in chauffeur's livery drove them to Appleton, where at a hotel they were met by James and Marilyn Auer, who would take them on to a cocktail party. Alfred unfolded himself from the front seat of the Mercedes, helped Lynn out of the back. "Benny, you are free," said Lynn majestically. They climbed into the Auers' small green Rambler, which Lynn professed to find charming. At the cocktail party Lynn accepted a millimeter of scotch and clicked open a double lorgnette to peer at the guests. Auer discovered Alfred had a mnemonic system for remembering names: he kept referring to their host, Professor Cloak, as Mr. Overcoat. The women flocked about Alfred. At the dinner he accepted the award and spoke. Lynn had refused to speak, but then as Alfred talked she thought of something she wanted to say and was terribly annoyed when he didn't turn it over to her. Otherwise they were gracious and charming and departed in the Mercedes on the dot.

The highest American civilian honor is the Presidential Medal of Freedom. On September 14, 1964, Alfred and Lynn attended a noon ceremony in the East Room of the White House to receive jointly the gold medal. The "wise and modest Lunts," as George Jean Nathan called them, wondered why they were being honored—was it mere longevity?—and hovered beyond camera range until President Lyndon B. Johnson pulled them toward him. With twenty-eight other honorees, including Dean Acheson, John L. Lewis, Walter Lippmann, John Steinbeck, Carl Sandburg, T. S. Eliot, Walt Disney, and Helen Keller—they heard that they had "made man's world safe, his physical body more durable, his mind broader, his leisure more delightful, his standard of living higher and his dignity important. They are the creators; we are the beneficiaries."

Later in 1964, another recognition: the publication of theater writer Maurice Zolotow's biography *Stagestruck: The Romance of Alfred Lunt and Lynn Fontanne.* Though they shied from writing their own lives, Alfred and Lynn had given Zolotow hours of taped interviews; the biography was immediate, lively, packed with anecdotes, popular. What Lunt and Fontanne actually revealed about themselves, except indirectly, however, was predictably discreet—yet "the biography did not please them."

Zolotow was excited when Richard Burton and Elizabeth Taylor expressed interest in making a movie of *Stagestruck* because they had always wanted to be another Lunt-Fontanne in witty vehicles like *The Guardsman* and *Reunion in Vienna.* The plan fell through—perhaps just as well, since Lynn disliked Taylor's acting. When Noël had visited in

1963 she sent him and Alfred alone to Milwaukee to see *Cleopatra.* "Miss Fontanne would not partake of it," said Richard Perkins, the driver. (Alfred and Noël enjoyed the film.)

Their next NBC television appearance earned them National Academy of Television Arts and Sciences Awards for Excellence. That summer they had been working on the script of *The Magnificent Yankee,* Emmet Lavery's play about the life and marriage of Oliver Wendell Holmes when he takes up his position on the Supreme Court. (Louis Calhern and Dorothy Gish had done *The Magnificent Yankee* on Broadway in 1946, Calhern and Ann Harding the movie in 1950.) The Lunts made it clear to the author and the director, George Schaefer, that by rehearsals in December they expected the cast to be word perfect.

Rehearsals turned out to be a dream. Partly it was the cooperation of the Lunts: "Please remember one thing—you *can't* give us enough direction." Partly it was George Schaefer, who never allowed the camera to intrude on a scene, restoring the stage to the actors. "One day for blocking, three days for taping," said the happy Lavery, "and through it all a sense of style and joy. . . . I kept watching the Lunts between takes. . . . Never out of breath, never rushed. Always at ease, always willing to share a little talk but always in character. They never let go of the pace, the rhythm of the scene to which they were returning." Still, their perfectionism was never satisfied. "Once a scene is taped, there it is, recorded forever," said Alfred. "In the theater, there always is the chance to better it."

An estimated fourteen million TV sets were tuned to the *Hallmark Hall of Fame* on January 28, 1965—far more people than Lunt and Fontanne had acted to in their combined lives. (At least seven million saw the rerun in 1966.) *The Magnificent Yankee,* said the critics, was television showing how good it could be when it wanted to. The Lunts had simply taken over the characters, giving beautifully seamless performances as Fanny and Oliver Wendell Holmes. "Absolutely superb," Noël recorded in his diary. "The best acting possible. They are both incredible."

Melvyn Douglas and their good friend Joan Crawford accepted their Emmys while Alfred and Lynn watched the ceremony at Ten Chimneys. The phone rang after the telecast. "It was a long show," Alfred told a reporter from the Milwaukee *Sentinel,* ". . . and it's way past our bedtime." Still, he admitted, "We were awfully damned pleased." Actually, Lynn had not been happy with her appearance on the small screen. "I didn't like myself." They installed their Emmys on either side of the fireplace in the drawing room.

Would *A Patriot for Me* and *The Killing of Sister George* be plays for us?" Lynn wrote Nancy Towle, now working in theatrical management. "When is Terence Rattigan going to write us a play?" Rather than Broadway or the West End, however, Alfred returned to the Metropolitan Opera. Since Lynn hated being an opera widow, he advised George Schaefer that she was free.

Rudolf Bing had been trying for years to tempt Alfred back to the Met, first for *The Barber of Seville* and then for *Don Giovanni: Barber* "wants your elegance, your wit and grace, your style and flair for that period." In 1965 Alfred did direct a revival of *Così fan tutte,* with Richard Tucker in his original role and Leontyne Price, Roberta Peters, and Donald Gramm. He had all the problems of getting enough time with the singers he'd faced in the original. (This time he refused to light candles as a footman.) "One of the highlights of my career has been to have the pleasure of working with you on *Così,*" wrote Peters. ". . . Thank you from the bottom of my heart for just being you."

Now he and Cecil Beaton were talking sets and costumes for a production of *La traviata.* Beaton wanted "a very agreeable baudiness [sic] in Act One, with ladies straddling chairs and flaunting lots of leg. In the bucolic Act Two, Violetta in simple white muslin but Flora's ball in every shade of red, with Violetta dazzling in scarlet. Alfred agreed. He wanted Joan Sutherland for Violetta; Rudolf Bing persuaded him Anna Moffo was sexier. Alfred agreed on the sex. "After all, she's a Parisian whore, and the person she was based on, Alphonsine Plessis, had so many lovers . . . that she died of overwork at the age of twenty-three."

But many of his inspirations for Moffo and Robert Merrill had to be scrapped, because opera must be acted on the notes. "You don't really direct an opera, it directs you. . . . The music doesn't stop, and by the time Miss Moffo was doing all those nice pieces of business I'd invented for her, the music would have been in the middle of the next aria." Moffo said she appreciated his guidance:

He directs by casting a spell. . . . He sort of shrugs, or smiles in a strange way at you, and then maybe stands or sits to illustrate something, and he doesn't expect you to copy it, but in some mysterious way he gets across to you how he thinks you should do it. The most important thing he did for me was to show me that in certain passages I was moving around too much—my hands, my body—for no reason. . . . I never realized before how strong, how very strong it is to stand still like a statue, and that you can act even when standing still.

Opening on September 22, 1966, in the Met's new Lincoln Center home, *La traviata* was not a triumph for Alfred like *Così*. Moffo did not "melt" him, notices were decidedly mixed, and he had worked "under exceedingly difficult and trying circumstances," as Bing himself admitted—among them Sunday rehearsals and no time or place to make the staging right. The *Times*'s "very fine production" seemed to damn with faint praise.

Lynn had accepted George Schaefer's invitation to film *Anastasia* for television. Playing the Dowager Empress, she acted against an actress with qualities of sensitivity and control she hadn't experienced since Uta Hagen. Julie Harris was as disciplined as Lunt and Fontanne: "She's an important actress already and I think her importance will grow because—besides being highly intelligent—she has no bad habits. She doesn't drink, or do anything to excess." (Lynn's invariable advice to actresses: "Never have more than two drinks a day.") Still, Lynn outdisciplined Harris, arriving an hour before rehearsals. Her stamina at seventy-eight was daunting: she was the driving (and driven) force at rehearsals, persuading actors to go over and over the lines. Inviting Julie to East End Avenue for lunch on their day off, she turned a chicken sandwich into another rehearsal. She wasn't just worried about her memory. As Julie Harris said of the last day of shooting, "We were still taping at midnight, and she seemed just as fresh then as when she started at nine in the morning. Her attitude was just, 'Well, when do we begin the next scene?' "

Another reason Lynn rehearsed so devotedly was that a decade earlier Helen Hayes had played the Dowager Empress in a film of *Anastasia* that won Ingrid Bergman an Academy Award. ("I thought it had a bad script," said Lynn.) Lynn would never have acted opposite an actress as dominating as Bergman, never consented to be a foil—and she certainly intended to better Hayes's performance. Lynn's Empress commanded her scenes from the beginning, a regal, lonely matriarch comforting Julie Harris's vulnerable child.

Anastasia was telecast on NBC March 17, 1967, but Milwaukee's

WTMJ chose to air the Wisconsin state high school basketball tournament instead. Channel 18 carried the show, but the Lunts didn't have UHF. At their call, Channel 18 technicians rushed out and erected special antennas. Fontanne and Harris both were nominated for the outstanding single performance by an actress but lost the Emmy to Geraldine Page. *Anastasia* was the last appearance of Lynn Fontanne on any stage.

've ceased to be interested in dressmaking," Lynn wrote Nancy Towle from Genesee that December. "What I shall take up next to occupy my time I don't know. I have to start another career as a painter or a writer—always assuming I have the talent which I don't think I have." She felt at loose ends. "Mr. Lunt and I want a young man to write a play for us. We are dying to do an original play," Lynn told a reporter, speaking for herself.

People seemed "to be dropping like flies" around them: Lady Juliet Duff, Dickie Whorf, Montgomery Clift, only forty-five. Suicidal, his face ruined by an auto accident and plastic surgery, openly gay, heavily into drugs and alcohol, Monty had become a problem the Lunts couldn't handle. They stopped asking him to their New York house, though he didn't stop thinking about them. Reading Noël Coward's explanation of Alfred's angst in Zolotow's biography—"Alfred's wretchedness is genuine, it is a nervous reaction for trying too hard for perfection"—the wretched Clift burst into tears. They had last met in Paris, where he was filming *The Young Lions.* Nervous and excited in the company of his idol, he drank too many martinis at dinner and in the elevator afterward collapsed against Alfred. His slurred apologies only further disgusted Lunt, who couldn't tolerate drunkenness in an actor. They never saw him again.

Unlike Lynn, Alfred was busy, busy. They were adding a bedroom, bathroom, shower, laundry, and garage to the cottage for Karin and George in anticipation of his retirement, and Alfred was painting Swedish murals in the hall and staircase—"my Sistine Chapel." For the next three years he worked on the cottage despite trauma with his eyes. Doctors believed the problem was due to neglected glaucoma. "My left eye is now gone completely," he wrote Nancy Towle. He worried about being able to "cook by ear." "Just remember," said Noël, "when you cook whitefish don't serve it on a white platter." They were injecting alcohol behind the eye to kill the pain, his right eye was "a triangle of cataracts," and he wore a black patch to disguise the fact he could no longer control his migrating left eye. He dictated all letters now and could no longer read: no alcohol injection could kill *that* pain—though he had a great actress to read aloud to him. "I still see a great deal more than I want to sometimes," he wrote his old friend Kenneth Conant.

Sadly, Karin did not live to move into the cottage. More than Alfred, she had always been frail, infections seriously weakening her heart. In 1970 she was faced with uprooting their comfortable, independent life in Chicago to move back to Wisconsin—not to a childhood home but to the cottage on Alfred and Lynn's famous estate. The stress of George's retirement and breaking up their home may well have exacerbated a constitutional weakness. Dr. Bigg recommended open-heart surgery; Karin did not survive the operation. Eventually George moved into the cottage, well aware how essential he would become to Alfred and Lynn's well-being. The perceptive Enid Bagnold had found Karin "strange and unusual." Certainly she was the half-sibling closest to Alfred. "We are still stunned by my sister's death," he wrote Bob Downing. "We can't believe it."

Carl Sederholm had died in February 1970 of an apparent heart attack, survived by a second wife, Delores, after his marriage to Patricia ended in divorce. Over the years he had bought thirty-one new Chevrolets from his friends the Koefflers in Mukwonago, all of them green. There was a stability about Carl after all. As the only sibling not sharing a love of theater, music, cooking, antiques, or decorating, he had remained aloof from the drama of Ten Chimneys. He and Alfred were too different to be close.

Alfred and Lynn went to New York to receive a special citation on April 19, 1970, "to the outstanding couple of the American stage for a lifetime of contribution to theater" on NBC's telecast of the Tony Awards. The newly knighted Noël also received a special award, as did Joseph Papp, founder of New York's free outdoor Shakespeare Festival, and Barbra Streisand as "performer of the decade." ("That woman's ego will get in the way of her life," Lynn said of Streisand.)

Two months before, they'd had more fun live on *The Dick Cavett Show* with Sir Noël, on the occasion of a Broadway revival of his *Private Lives*. Though Alfred agonized as usual, one problem was real. Because of the eye patch he was unsure of his movements. He and Lynn arrived hours early to rehearse the seemingly casual moment when Noël stands up to welcome "my two most beloved friends, Lynn and Alfred." What they could not have anticipated was the applause that greeted them as they entered—a prolonged drumroll of affection that crescendoed as the audience rose to its feet shouting "Bravo! Bravo!" Lynn accepted the long ovation like a queen, Alfred with lower lip trembling.

Young but unafraid, Dick Cavett is a ringmaster handling three tigers. Noël, a mandarin with hooded eyes, seldom moves out of double entendre. Cavett: "What can you do now as a knight that you couldn't do before?" "It's what I *can't* do now that I'm a knight." When Alfred in a dark blue suit and Lynn in a full-length sable coat, sable hat, red dress, and pearls join Cavett and Coward, Alfred immediately launches into a flirtatious tease about Cavett having taken off his shirt on TV— "virginal and timid but not coy"; then Lynn goes on to deplore young actors now having to strip for auditions. "We lowered this show right to the ground," laughs Alfred with satisfaction.

Alfred the Overwrought appears the most calm. Throughout the show Lynn clenches and unclenches her gloved left hand while Noël fidgets with tie knot, earlobes, cigarettes. They talk among themselves with an intimacy the public is not supposed to understand. "Alfred

In 1970 Alfred and Lynn celebrate Noël's winning a Tony Award at the Pyranees Restaurant in New York; Walter Matthau and Julie Andrews pay homage; Cary Grant is at Alfred's left.

wanted to be an acrobat," says Noël with a small smile, "—and to a large extent succeeded." "I paid for everything," says Lynn, referring to *Dulcy* days—"*and went on doing so.*" But they also rely on safe stories they've enjoyed telling for years. *Design for Living* might have happened yesterday.

The three old pals were an enormous coup for Cavett, underlined when he gravely thanked Sir Noël at the end for having stood in for comedian Soupy Sales. Letters poured in from across the country. "I've never seen one show produce that kind of marvelous reaction," said Cavett. "It just kept coming. . . . It thrilled not only the people who . . . knew the Lunts and Coward, but also my youngest viewers, some of whom couldn't have told you exactly who the Lunts and Coward were the day before."

Then they flew back to Milwaukee and were met by Benny in the big black Mercedes that Hallmark had given them in appreciation for *The Magnificent Yankee* and settled down in front of the fire to tea and scones brought by Jules.

"I was *awful* on the show. Tongue-tied!"

"No, no, no."

"Yes. Did you hear me apologize afterward to Cavett for not holding up my end? I let him down terribly."

"No, no no. *I* was awful. I couldn't think of anything but getting Noëlly to tell those silly old stories."

"Oh, Noëlly was very, very good. But I failed us all miserably."

"No, no. Do you think I showed too much knee?"

"Knee? No. But my face looked like a discarded douche bag."

CHAPTER EIGHTEEN

The Best Revenge: 1971–1983

Not far from Chicago," wrote critic Claudia Cassidy, "in a highly personal Petit Trianon . . . the Lunts are up to an old trick. They are giving what may be their finest performance. Actually they are waiting for a play. But they are waiting in the high style of Alfred Lunt and Lynn Fontanne. . . ." Waiting for a play had become a reflex, though in 1971 they did consider making a television film of Ferber and Kaufman's *The Royal Family*. But Universal and NBC could not find enough sponsors—a blessing given the improbable casting of the Lunts, Edward G. Robinson, Mia Farrow, and Danny Kaye.

Rather they felt free to travel. They began spending February and March at the Beachcomber in Naples, Florida, where they saw old friends like Kit Cornell, her companion Nancy Hamilton, and Joan Crawford. They visited Noël at Les Avants in Switzerland, his tax-evasion chateau high above Montreux on Lake Geneva. Charlie and Oona Chaplin were guests during the Lunts' stay as well as Viscount Earl Louis Mountbatten, so often in Noël's company. He found the Lunts "absolutely charming." And they spent weeks in New York at 150 East End Avenue.

Alec Guinness, who revered Alfred as an actor, visited them there. Alfred, Lynn informed him, was cooking. Guinness found him in the kitchen in a towering white chef's hat, Hispanic girls holding bowls of mushrooms and herbs. "Alfred took a handful of mushrooms and cast them in a pan on the cooker as if making a brilliant exit line." Herbs followed. "Let's leave it to the girls," he said, whipping off his chef's overall. In the living room they sipped martinis. Guinness was so mesmerized by Lynn's reddish-black hair "scraped off her forehead and the sides of her head and screwed up to form a sort of Thai temple . . . bound round with beautiful tortoiseshell and heavy gold" that he remembered nothing of Alfred's dinner. Lynn admired Guinness, especially his brilliant work in the movie *Kind Hearts and Coronets.* Guinness admired Alfred: "He was not only a marvellous, tremendously professional actor, but a man of gentle courtesy and understanding; his philosophical courage when his sight began to fail was truly impressive."

Nineteen seventy-two turned out to be a year of change, of retrenching. Jules's heart had been tricky for years. In May Alfred found him unconscious on the floor, having collapsed from a heart attack (or a diabetic stroke; accounts vary). He recovered in a Chicago hospital, then returned to Los Angeles after thirty-three years of devotion as wig washer, makeup artist, valet, cook, and companion. "Mr. Lunt and Jules, I think, were very close," said Arlene Dable, who also cooked and waited at Ten Chimneys. "Miss Fontanne and Jules were more on a business-type basis."

There is an unlikely ending to the Lunt-Jules story, corroborated, however, by at least four people: that Jules came back to Ten Chimneys saying, "You know, my white friends here in Genesee treated me better than my friends in California," and that Alfred and Lynn refused him the house. In former days, when his duties were finished, Jules had taken his flashlight and walked over to Ben and Gert's for a glass of wine and TV. Now he was forced to ask the Perkinses to take him in. Lynn tended to be distant with the help, but it's hard to imagine Alfred refusing Jules his old room off the kitchen. Jules was "a nice, nice man," said Catherine Gavigan, Ben's sister-in-law.

Stella Heintz from nearby Wales took over as cook and resented the Lunts from the beginning because they required her to live in and sometimes canceled her day off. Lola Parton, "a gem from the Depot," was now in charge of laundry and housekeeping.

Shortly after Jules was hospitalized, Alfred and Lynn celebrated their fiftieth wedding anniversary—though Alfred made Lynn take back the

$600 couture dress she'd bought at Saks for the occasion. Ronald Bowers, as assistant buyer at Saks, remembers her coming in wearing a pink suit that looked like a Chanel and eventually choosing a $125 floor-length beige chiffon with tiny ruffles around the collar and sleeves. She looked about sixty-five and made the dress look like a million. "You can't buy style," thought Bowers. They celebrated May 26 quietly with George Bugbee, who came down from the cottage in formal attire for the occasion. George felt trapped by the Lunts' standing invitation to rich meals eaten in candlelit splendor with waitstaff standing by; he'd rather scramble himself an egg up at the cottage. But he was a gentleman and almost always obeyed the summons, praying dinner wouldn't be rabbit in cream or braised tongue.

President Richard Nixon sent them a telegram: "Your unique careers have been enriched by the most precious blessing any two people could ask for: a truly happy marriage." The Lunts consented to be interviewed about their anniversary, but not photographed: "I've seen enough pictures of old mushrooms in your newspaper." How, asked reporters, had they managed to stay married fifty years? "When we were acting, I always thought of him as another person and he thought of me as another person," said Lynn. "I had a new lover every night, and so had he." Alfred said, "She gets a salary, I get a salary. She pays for her things, I pay for mine. . . . There's none of that stupid haggling about money."

Perhaps John Mason Brown said it best. "Everybody knows that the Lunts have been liberated, not fettered, by their union. Their marriage bonds have set them free, entitling them to audacities beyond the reach of unwedded performers. . . . The justification of freedom is not freedom itself but the uses to which it is put. . . . Their performances are glorious games of give-and-take in which there is no jealousy in the giving and only generosity in the taking." In fifty years the Lunts had gained more fame, more notoriety, and more press coverage for their hallowed marriage than any star could possibly attract for a mere divorce.

On June 11 they were guests of honor in Hollywood for a Dinner Dance and All-Star Tribute hosted by the American National Theatre and Academy (ANTA) at the Beverly Hilton. Arriving, they looked all their eighty and eighty-five years, Alfred in dark glasses (no patch: an operation in 1970 had been partly successful), Lynn small and bent as they were seated at a table with Governor Ronald and Nancy Reagan and their dear friend John Gielgud. "They seemed transformed," how-

*Christmas greeting from
Alfred and Lynn*

Merry Christmas

LYNN FONTANNE
ALFRED LUNT

ever, during the show in their honor, laughing and applauding Jack Benny, George Burns, and the vaudeville soft shoe of Jack Albertson and Buddy Ebsen, laced with clips from *The Guardsman,* their silent films and home movies. Edward G. Robinson, Fred Astaire, Henry Fonda, Tony Randall, Agnes Moorehead, Lauren Bacall, Gregory Peck, Carroll O'Connor, Shelley Winters, and Carol Burnett were among the stars cheering the presentation to the Lunts of the first National Artists Award of the United States of America. Donald Seawell presented it, citing Noël Coward's famous observation: "The Lunts are the greatest monsters in the history of show business because they demand from everyone a degree above perfection that only they could achieve."

"I'd like to tell some stories that will offset some of the lovely things said about us tonight," said Lynn, beautiful again.

"I don't think we deserve all this kindness and generosity," agreed Alfred. "I think your imagination has run away with you. Most of what we achieved depended on playwrights. That's the trouble with the theater today—not enough good playwrights. Actors are dying to work if only they could find the words to say."

Not only the theater but New York had deteriorated. "When we were there last February and last spring," Alfred had written Robert Downing in 1970, "we truly had no desire ever to return." Now they decided to sell 150 East End Avenue. This also meant selling its fabulous antiques; and their old friend and colleague Charles Bowden made the arrangements with Sotheby Park Bernet. Louis XVI beechwood settees, Regency games tables, and George II mahogany chests were marked at prices ($375, $2,000, $800) that today seem giveaway. Some antiques and household items were donated to charity. Sydney Luria, the new owner of 150 East End Avenue and the lawyer who had drafted the Lunts' final will, purchased $4,800 worth of furniture. Personal treasures were shipped home to the Depot.

Alfred and Lynn had taken Stella Heintz with them to help with packing and last-minute entertaining. A guest she remembered was Joan Crawford. "Now, don't you look at her," Lynn instructed. "You don't look at Joan." Joan brought her vodka in her purse, but Stella served more, and since Miss Crawford stayed a long time, Alfred was tipsy when she left. "She was quite a woman," said Stella.

The Lunts had bought the house for $40,000 during the run of O Mistress Mine; they sold it for $125,000—dividing the proceeds as usual. Its sale confirmed their retirement at last.

Still divesting, that fall of 1972 they offered twenty-five wooded acres for parkland abutting twenty-seven acres already optioned by the Depot. The proposed park created a small-town controversy, but finally the town board accepted their offer and on July 4, 1975, at a public ceremony, Alfred and Lynn presented eighteen acres (twenty more in 1977) to Genesee. The mike failed before and after speeches but, knowing who was boss, not during theirs. At one point Lynn forgot what she was going to say and appealed to Alfred. "I never know what she's going to say," he protested. The sun got in their eyes, but they charmed the crowd.

Donating the acres introduced them to the town chairman, Clarence Bundy, who drove a Rolls-Royce and owned businesses in Genesee. Despite their "just folks" act, Bundy learned that Lynn and Alfred could be quixotic. Alfred called once during an ice storm: "I want electricity!" Bundy rounded up the biggest generator he could find, then discovered they had left for a Milwaukee hotel. Opening the door after asking him over, Alfred would roar, "What are *you* doing here?" Yet they were friendly and spent many evenings in the Bundys' hilltop home outside of town. Bundy felt at ease with the Lunts, yet always conscious that they were working him like an audience. Christmas Eve at Ten Chimneys became a command performance. Dorothea Bundy was never invited, but Clarence obediently showed up for tea and crumpets as Lynn poured milk and tea simultaneously in the British manner from the Georgian silver service given them by Larry and Vivien.

Clarence Bundy's girls, who worked downtown, kept him up-to-date on the Lunts' famous guests. But the Depot was aware of the celebrities who arrived in chauffeured cars or were met by Ben and staff at the Milwaukee airport. Kitty Carlisle came with her handsome bandleader. Gwen Verdon slept eighteen hours and departed refreshed. Merle Oberon entered in high style with a companion. "These movie stars," marveled Stella Heintz, "got such young men and they're old." Unfortunately, Oberon ate too much of Alfred's rich food and spent a tortured night, not improved when Alfred greeted her with a breakfast tray next morning. Laurence Olivier came to visit his Beloved Celestials, but was so infirm (the help noted) that he couldn't put on his shoes. Hugh O'Brian came and gave everybody the Wyatt Earp grip.

Helen Hayes visited several times a year, often staying for a week, attending Catholic services at Saint Paul's. In 1968 she had had one of her best parts in many years in *The Show-Off,* and in Chicago Alfred and Lynn had led a standing ovation. She turned to the other actors. "Do you see? Alfred is standing for *me*!" (Afterward Lynn said accusingly, "That isn't acting. That's *memory.* Memory!") But Helen was disillusioned with the theater. "I've no acting plans," she wrote the Lunts in 1970. "Theatre without you and Larry and Kit and Noël doesn't invite me even for a short visit. It all seems rather drab and flat. . . . Here in New York the new theatre seems to confuse heaviness with sincerity and drabness with truth. I starve for one play with *flair.*"

Helen was very popular with the Depot—except with Ben's nephew Richard, because she never spoke to him on trips back and forth to the airport. One time Clarence Bundy's daughter didn't recognize her when she came into the shop where she worked to buy a small gift for the Lunts and refused to cash her check. (The great lady cashed it next door.) But that was not as disconcerting as, according to Stella Heintz, Lynn's behavior to her guest:

"Mrs. Lunt couldn't handle Helen Hayes. She was Mr. Lunt's girl-friend before Lynn came to this country. When she was playing Milwaukee she'd come to stay at the Lunts and she'd go to a Chicago hotel, Mrs. Lunt, and stay there in Chicago until Helen Hayes left." Stella admitted they spent time together in the summer. "But when she was ready to leave, you'd think that Mrs. Lunt would come down from upstairs to say goodbye? She made believe she was sick. Oh, she was terrible. But Helen Hayes was a grand person. She was very fine."

This is undoubtedly some truth mixed with distortion. Heintz insists Lynn was rude to Helen Hayes, and Lynn was indeed upset once when Helen arranged with Alfred to visit without telling her. But it's hard to believe that Helen Hayes would have returned regularly to Ten Chimneys had Lynn's behavior been overtly hostile. Hard to believe she would have written warmly of four days in Genesee Depot "with you two angelic, funny people."

Apparently, however, Alfred could pull the same tricks. Lillian Gish came for a few days, was given dinner but told by Lynn next morning that she would have to leave because Alfred was sick. Stella Heintz again: "He just played sick. And so she had to go home."

A good friend these years was Carol Channing, the six-foot-one bombshell of *Gentlemen Prefer Blondes* and *Hello, Dolly!* Alfred and Lynn went down to Chicago to see her solo show and "had a Hell of an evening. She is really a marvel and curiously can get away with—well, let us say 'murder' . . . but she is never tasteless, no matter what she does. I think it's because of her innate goodness, and underneath it all she is a damned fine actress. Lynn says she's a real 'rabble rouser.' The audience loved everything she did, everything she wore and didn't wear, and we happened to be a member of that audience." Carol returned the compliment: "Alfred is so handsome, the first time I met him I was dumbstruck."

Carol became a repeat visitor to Ten Chimneys, particularly at Christmas and New Year, when she arrived with her husband, Charles Lowe, and lots of trunks. "She was as nutty in person as she was on stage or television," said Richard Perkins. One year she showed up with cases of zucchini: "That's all she ate was this zucchini and nothing on it, not even salt." Other times she brought rattlesnake and buffalo meat, which didn't amaze Lynn as much as her eating eight apples in one evening. "Genesee Depot is to performers what the Vatican is to Catholics," said Channing. "It's my home—I'm complete there. The Lunts are where we all spring from. We all have the same disease, only ours isn't as strong as theirs."

Guests these years were amused by Winnie, the big black poodle who slept at the foot of Lynn and Alfred's bed every night, and by Walter, the Toulouse goose. More aggressive than ten watchdogs, Walter had a crush on Lynn, loathed everyone else, particularly Alfred. One afternoon when Lynn and Joan Crawford were sitting in lawn chairs and Alfred was bent over a flowerbed nearby, Walter attacked his rival. Joan and Lynn dissolved in laughter. "Oh," gasped Lynn, "I finally understand Alfred's joke about the athletic goose who made the broad jump." Walter was so aggressive that a large raccoon finally eliminated him from duty; but while Walter's love affair with Lynn lasted, it was intense.

Many distinguished guests were not celebrities. Enid Bagnold, Deems Taylor, Brenda Forbes, Cathleen Nesbitt, and Cecil Beaton aroused little curiosity. Of the celebrities Van Johnson was the hands-down favorite. Everybody loved the freckle-faced actor who invariably wore red socks. The Bundy girl in the gift shop was so starstruck by his presence that she kept wrapping string around his purchase until it looked like a beehive. He was a big man with a big appetite. Stella Heintz was about to remove the rest of the apple pie she'd just served when Johnson said, "Just set that there." Amazed, Lynn watched him devour the whole thing.

Stella Heintz was a keen but hostile observer, one of the few people uncharmed by the Lunts. "Oh, that damn house," she said. Every lamp was broken, curtains hadn't been washed in thirty years, Alfred was tight as a fist with money even though she was getting only $250 a month with room and board. Lynn left big messes when she arranged flowers in the sink and paraded around upstairs without clothes. Particularly she hated Alfred interfering in her kitchen.

"Are you *sure* you followed the recipe?"

" 'Yes, Mr. Lunt.' But I never did."

The Lunts sent her to Dr. Bigg in Chicago for her sciatica, but still worked her hard—no dishwasher, lots of stairs. "The help was dirt under the Lunts' feet," she complained. She thought Alfred acted gay and insisted that her Waukesha doctor, Dr. Smerl, had told her Alfred was gay: he'd studied such things. And Lynn flirted with the guests. "I want to tell you something—that Genesee don't care much for the Lunts. Well, they lived such a closed life, and they didn't want nobody to know anything, and they didn't need the Genesee people at that time, so most of the people won't have a thing to do with them."

Jules, who had always cared for them so well, died the winter of 1972–73. On March 23, 1973 the once-brilliant impresario Binkie Beaumont was found dead of alcohol and disappointment. Alfred and Lynn were in London at the time. "I don't want to come to London anymore now that Binkie's dead," said Alfred. Lynn's sister Antoinette was ill, further distressing them. Old friends remained: John Gielgud, Cecil Beaton, Joyce Grenfell, Jamie and Yvonne Hamilton, Larry. Vivien had died in 1967 of tuberculosis, a photograph of the handsome young Larry by her bedside. Larry had married Joan Plowright ("Wheelbarrow," Vivien called her) in 1961 and started a new family—Richard, Tamsin, and Julie Kate: "I dote on them and am butter in their wicked small hands." But Olivier was far from well and frantically making movies because "mountainous debts were piling 'Pelleas on Melisande.' "

Noël died three days after Binkie, on March 26, in Jamaica, and was buried on the grounds of Firefly, his house overlooking Blue Harbour. Alfred and Lynn did not attend the private ceremony. Their last long time together had been the week Noël spent in 1966 recuperating from a gallbladder operation at Ten Chimneys. He noticed that Alfred and Lynn bickered more now that they weren't acting. But they plied him with grilled steaks, ham, and chocolate pudding, and the rest and tender care sped his recovery, as did Lynn bringing in his tray wearing an apron and turning round to flaunt a bare behind. When he died, they had been friends for fifty-two years. "It does get better and more fun, doesn't it, as the years go on?" Lynn had written Noël in 1937. For the most part it had.

Alfred's pain and discomfort during the last years of his life were matched only by his stoicism. Not that he didn't complain humorously to friends. In 1973 he was operated on for an aneurysm. "You *must* save him," said Lynn. That same year he was again in Northwestern Hospital in Chicago for major exploratory surgery because doctors hadn't liked the look of some X rays. Lynn stayed at the Ambassador Hotel to be near him. (An Ambassador bellman once put his hand on Lynn's shoulder: the Lunts avoided the hotel for ten years.) "Hated every moment of every day I was there," he wrote Bob Downing. ". . . Those dreadful, slippery, cold, hard X-ray tables, and they twist you into the most terrible, painful positions—over and over again. If they had photographed me I bet I spelled J-E-S-U-S." By November he was able to walk to and from his front gate. "I have the most terrible scar you ever saw running right down the front of me . . . and now that it is stitched, I must say it looks as though I've got on a pair of corsets of Lillian Russell's."

His eyes continued to deteriorate: the reflection of snow in the kitchen or drawing room blinded him; he couldn't watch television, though he still painted. Ironically, he was taking only three medications—Synthroid, Zyloprim, and maramide—while the healthier Lynn took eleven, including Bartropin, Dialose, Hygroton, and belladonna.

What was remarkable these years was his poise, his good nature, his refusal to discuss his poor health or let it dull his zest for life. He'd stopped smoking. He continued to dress impeccably in jackets, slacks, and ascots and in black tie for dinner. (A charity group in Milwaukee, opening a donated package, took out a suit. "This must belong to Alfred Lunt," said a volunteer. "No one else in Wisconsin wears tailoring like this.") Formal dinners were waited on by a new employee, fourteen-year-old Brent Fintel, in white shirt, white jacket, black bow tie, and black trousers. Alfred continued to cook on Stella Heintz's day off, occasionally substituting Stouffer's beef stroganoff for his own mouthwatering creation. He continued to work in his greenhouse and keep the arrival court spotless—or instructed others how to do it. One of the help just swept the dirt down the drive. "No, no, no, no, no! You've got to pick that dirt up."

Encouraged by Helen Hayes, who had become a "cruise bum," they sailed on the *Kungsholm* in January 1974 for a world cruise that would take them around Africa to India, Singapore, Thailand, Hong Kong, Taiwan, Japan, and Honolulu. The Seawells saw them off with a case of champagne and a floral arrangement with a red balloon floating above. "Oh," said Lynn, "Alfred's aneurysm." Alfred had booked a table for two and a secluded stateroom because they didn't want to meet people. By the second day out he was the life of the party.

Back at Genesee, because he couldn't read or watch TV, he listened to the *Milwaukee Journal* radio station, WTMJ. He became a fan of Gordon Hinckley's household-hints program called *Ask Your Neighbor,* followed Bill Carlsen's weather reports, and particularly admired Jim

*Alfred and Lynn
at Ten Chimneys*

Irwin, WTMJ's "Voice of the Green Bay Packers." (Lynn did her best to understand baseball and "finally I realized that the gentleman holding the bat is antagonistic to the gentleman throwing the ball.")

A friendship developed with Jim and Gloria Irwin and their children, Anne and Jay, with whom Lynn became "truly enamored." The Lunts were thrilled to be invited to the Irwins' home in Whitefish Bay to meet their WTMJ colleagues. (They ate pizza for the first time.) The Irwins visited Ten Chimneys, Alfred zooming their picnic lunch down to the Studio in his new electric golf cart; and they all enjoyed the Brookfield Zoo, where Lynn adored the baby hippo. On the way back

Alfred did his imitation of a coop of chickens clucking "That Old Black Magic," which had everyone rolling in the aisles. The Irwins also took Lynn and Alfred to the revue *Oh, Coward!* with Patricia Morison at the Performing Arts Center. "Oh, my, wasn't that thrilling!" exclaimed a woman as the Lunts went by.

More typical was the young usher asked to identify the famous couple. "I've heard of them, of course. But I'm afraid they were before my time." Insulated as they were, the Lunts still faced these moments of shock as their names receded from the public. Handing a ticket across the counter at the Milwaukee airport, Lynn realized her name meant nothing to the young woman. "You don't know who the Lunts are? And you're from Wisconsin? Shame on you!" Once she asked wistfully, "Do you think we still have a public?"

If Alfred had a premonition he would soon die, it was the day he bent over to pick runner beans and discovered he couldn't straighten up again. The cane he tried to support himself with sank into the damp ground; he lay in the garden two hours before he was found. He knew he was due to go back to the hospital in August and also knew that he would not survive another operation. He asked Donald Seawell to make provisions for Lynn's care after his death.

One day Helen Hayes's phone at Nyack rang. It was Alfred.

"I have to tell you, Helen, that I've been laughing for a good hour about you and me. I've been recalling some of our times in *Clarence,* and laughing so hard that I had to call and tell you. You know I can't see anymore. I can't read or play cards or watch television. I'm tired of the radio programs, and I can't stand rock music. My cooking has gone to pot because I can't see the ingredients. But I found out what I like to do. . . . I just sit and remember."

One conflict was resolved. "Mr. Lunt would always try to get up before I did," said Stella Heintz, "and that irked me because I felt fixing breakfast was my job. So this particular morning I says, 'I can't take this no more.' 'Oh,' he says, 'then you'll have to quit.' " After breakfast Lynn came and said, "You go now and apologize to Mr. Lunt." But Stella figured she had nothing to apologize for and packed her bag. "I didn't know he had cancer, and I didn't know he was ill," she explained. "I'd have never left." Alfred wasn't sorry; he called her brew "coffee you could walk on."

Sometimes Alfred could forget his physical discomfort in the kitchen. He invented a new dish with leftover chicken; when he baked a cake he forgot the pain. But on July 11 George Bugbee wrote Alan Hewitt, actor and friend, "Alfred currently is very uncomfortable with pain most of the time. He is to go back to the hospital about the first of August. Just what is ahead is not clear."

On July 21, 1977, Alfred complained to Lynn that the pain was bad. Dr. Bigg told her to call an ambulance immediately. Alfred didn't want to leave Ten Chimneys. "I'm going to die in it," he'd vowed to John Hale long ago. Lynn insisted. This time she did not go with him, because Dr. Bigg considered her too frail.

Alfred was diagnosed with prostate cancer. Doctors recommended surgery. Carol Channing called him before the operation. "Of course, they all know me at this hospital," he told her cheerfully. "I left my liver on the second floor, my aorta on the fourth floor, my kidneys on the fifth floor. . . . I feel right at home. After all, most of me is here."

He was not released yet. They operated twice within a week, and then, as the cancer continued to spread, again on August 1. The following day George Bugbee drove Lynn to Northwestern Memorial Hospital, where she held her unconscious husband's hand for two hours before returning to Genesee. When a call came recommending still another operation, Lynn and George refused to allow the indignity. Alfred Lunt died alone at 4:05 a.m. on Wednesday, August 3, 1977, just short of his eighty-fifth birthday.

On Friday, August 5, at 7:59 p.m., all Broadway theaters dimmed their lights for one minute except the Lunt-Fontanne, which blazed. The passing of no other twentieth-century American stage actor—not Cornell, Hayes, or Fontanne herself—would mean as much to the theater as the death of Alfred Lunt. "Make it an obituary to a god, not a man," said one Broadway producer. Or to a monstre sacré—that gifted, driven creature whose passions torment and elate not only himself but all who cannot attain his vision.

"The outstanding actor of the post-Barrymore generation was Alfred Lunt," said Harold Clurman. "He was all fluid feeling, intuitive understanding, a certain softness together with quirky humor. . . . The span between his comedy performance in *The Guardsman* and the agony he conveyed in *The Visit* describes the breadth of his talent." Almost: Clarence, the Southern poet in *Robert E. Lee,* and Tom Prior in *Outward Bound* were also outstanding performances. It is true that Alfred Lunt dominated Broadway—and American theater—from the opening of

The Guardsman on October 13, 1924, to March 20, 1960, when *The Visit* ended its New York run.

The flag outside the Genesee Depot post office flew at half-mast. An invited group attended the funeral in Forest Home Cemetery in Milwaukee. Escorted by Donald Seawell, taking a seat between George Bugbee and her old friend Gustav Eckstein, Lynn in a black lace mantilla looked like a tragic Goya *madre.* Seawell spoke briefly: "We are witnessing the end of an era in the English-speaking theater. . . . Nothing I may say . . . can do justice to that noble spirit. How often . . . shall we recall, with happiness, Alfred's many-faceted genius, his gentle humor, his quiet dignity, his devotion to work and perfection. . . ."

Lynn did not attend the actual burial. At Ten Chimneys, stoic as always, she raised a glass of champagne to the guests and said, simply, "To Alfred." Winnie the black poodle trotted unhappily among the guests looking for her tall friend.

On tour in Michigan, Larry Olivier chartered a plane and flew to Genesee the day after the funeral to be with Lynn. Hundreds of telegrams and letters poured into Ten Chimneys. "Oh, you're so afraid of gushing," wrote Helen Hayes, "but we won't see his likes again in my time, I'm sure. As an actor or a man. He was exceptional." "Thank God I came out to lunch that day," said Van Johnson simply. Brooks Atkinson wrote the tribute in the *Times,* which had run a front-page story on Alfred's death: "Joy was his overwhelming gift to the stage."

Hard to believe that fragility kept Lynn at Ten Chimneys while Alfred was dying. She was eighty-nine, true; but she was not ill, ate well, and rode an exercise bike thirty minutes a day. More likely she declined to face the ultimate crisis after the endless crises she'd coped with for so many years.

Lynn said many things after Alfred's death, but one of the first things she did was let her mahogany hair go white. It was such a relief, she said, not to have to lie any longer. The local papers, however, had been printing their correct ages for years. Perhaps Lynn had not read those bits aloud to Alfred. Yet surely he knew. He probably loved her being older; it gave him power; and, too, he had a taste for older women. She said, "Toward the end he was in a lot of pain, so it really was a great relief." At first relief seemed to be the dominant emotion; then calm, because, as she said, "I will soon be joining him." Later she would say, "I miss him every second of every day. Right now, if he were still alive, he would be making our spring garden. It was one of our happiest times of the year."

She admitted frustrations. She would like to have played the poet Elizabeth Barrett Browning, but Katharine Cornell had co-opted *The Barretts of Wimpole Street*. She would like to have acted *The Magnificent Yankee* on Broadway, not on TV. She would love to have played Portia, and Catherine of Aragon in *Henry VIII*. She had rarely spoken out before about her preferences, but it is notable that all these plays had superb parts for Alfred.

A few weeks after Alfred's death she flew to England with Donald Seawell, sitting up all night because their original flight was canceled. Yet the night of their arrival, on August 25, they went to see *The King-fisher* with Ralph Richardson and Celia Johnson (Celia Johnson had profoundly impressed Lynn in Noël's film *Brief Encounter*). The audience cheered Lynn that night and at every play they attended. At Drury Lane, Prince Charles insisted she sit in the Royal Box. (She found him charming, delightful, and well informed.) She waved and bowed to the audience in the theater where she had made her debut seventy-two years before in the pantomime *Cinderella*.

The cheers and the tributes in the press for the Lunts—John Gielgud wrote a feeling letter to the *Times* about a perfection "which we can never hope to see again"—could not mask her disappointment, however, at not having been made a dame of the British Empire. "They thought I was American. But I was always British. I would have cherished the award."

Karin's daughter Suzanne Knapp flew over to England to help her aunt with personal attentions like dressing and answering phones and notes. When they returned in September, Lynn asked that the memorial services to Alfred planned in her absence be canceled. As she wrote Alan Hewitt, "It's time we stopped crying."

Back at Ten Chimneys, Lynn settled into a routine. Mrs. Miller was the new cook, Harriet Owens Lynn's secretary, Richard Perkins drove her, Brent Fintel moved in because she was afraid to be alone, and the practical Suzanne visited more often than she had while Alfred was alive. Lynn had breakfast at eight in the library—tea, a poached egg, waffles or butter-soaked toast. She now sat in Alfred's tall wing chair to the left of the fireplace. The library, with its portraits, and Alfred's leather-bound books gold-stamped with his name, and the photograph of Alfred, Lynn, and Noël, was her favorite room. About ten a.m. George Bugbee came down from the cottage to greet her and play cards in front of the fire.

"Lynn was amazing about cards. Her favorite game was Sugar and Spite, one step above Old Maid. We played it endlessly and though she was extremely intelligent I could never convince her that chance was the big factor. She truly believed that she could win intellectually, despite the odds."

After cards, Lynn went up to her dressing table with its mirror framed in lights and glass flowers and spent a long time fixing her hair, doing throat exercises, and applying eyelashes. When she had finished dressing, she walked Winnie up and down the long drive. Sherry, then lunch at one, then a nap. Then the exercise bicycle. Late afternoons were for select visitors, dictating letters, or driving out on errands in the big tan Buick LeSabre with leather-and-walnut interior. "Towards the later years," said Richard Perkins, "we would be on our way to Waukesha and she'd say 'Richard, where are we going?' " He'd remind her and she'd say, "Oh, yes, yes. Carry on, carry on." Dinner was served in the Flirtation Room or Yellow Room in front of a fire on a tray, George usually joining her. A little television—she loved *Upstairs, Downstairs* and *Police Woman*—hands of double solitaire, a Barbara Cartland or Dickens novel, then he would kiss her goodnight.

As soon as George left she would ring for Brent Fintel. "Come along, Brent." Together they went from room to room, turning on the lights. "Sometimes she would open closet doors, sometimes she would have me peek under the beds with the bedspread up and look and while we're doing this she would tell me of the Boston Strangler and how this Strangler hid in closets or under beds." She made Brent sleep across the hall in the Helen Hayes Room so that he could guard her door.

By now Ben Perkins, more than fifty years at Ten Chimneys, spent a lot of time with his feet up in the furnace room, though he'd come round to see what was wanted. Fintel was obviously the young man to watch Lynn. George Bugbee offered him Jules's apartment rent-free. "I think Mr. Bugbee must have known that it wasn't going to be too much longer for Miss Fontanne."

Paranoia, the companion of senile dementia, tormented Lynn more and more. Chuck Bowden, a friend since they'd given him a small part in *The Taming of the Shrew,* came to Genesee. At dinner in the formal dining room, Lynn clutched his hand across the table. "Chuck, three people are watching me out there. I see their faces in the window. I'm so afraid." Chuck covered her cold hand with his. "Only three, Lynnie? And you so beloved and so famous? There must be thousands out there loving and applauding you."

Chuck came quite often, once escorting Lynn into Milwaukee to see Hume Cronyn and Jessica Tandy in *The Gin Game.* "She came in on Chuck's arm: a small, fragile widow with white hair who, while retaining all her charm and vitality of spirit, seemed to have shrunk from her compelling stage presence." Cronyn reminded her that he had auditioned between a matinee and evening performance for *The Sea Gull* but Alfred had turned him down. Lynn smiled: Alfred should have been resting, not auditioning. When they left she "paused in the dressing room doorway, put her hand on mine and said: 'Mr. Cronyn, Alfred made a great mistake.' "

She still fought being a prisoner of Ten Chimneys—always Alfred's more than hers, and now that he was gone it was haunted. In April 1978 she paid a three-week visit to New York, staying with Dorothy Stickney and seeing Lawrence Langner's wife, Armina Marshall (Langner had died in 1962). When they went to see Carol Channing in *Hello, Dolly!* Armina was amazed that the once tall and regal Lynn just vanished into her seat. Helen Hayes came to a gathering; they realized that every woman there had lost her husband.

Anita Loos dropped in for a cup of tea to tell about the theft of Charlie Chaplin's corpse. A cemetery had not wanted a "Jewish Communist" buried in its ground; his coffin had been dug up and deposited at Oona's door and what was poor Oona to do . . . ? The women were sighing when Lynn interrupted with charming concern: "And how *is* deah Charlie?"

Her vagueness made it necessary for her niece Suzanne to accompany her last visit to London in 1978. She stayed at the Dorchester and was photographed as a beautiful woman in ropes of pearls and growing-out white hair who admitted to eighty-six. She did confess to Sheridan Morley that she couldn't do *The Royal Family* because it took her three days to learn three lines, previously the work of an hour. "Still, I feel fine and it really hasn't been a bad life, now, has it?"

Understatement had no place at the dinner she threw at the Dorchester for remaining friends. The company toasted the absent—Noël, Binkie, Ivor, Graham, Clemence Dane—then settled down to toasting Lynn and Alfred with Veuve Cliquot. John Gielgud wrote his thanks:

> What a sumptuous occasion. What a Lucullean Fest, and such a gathering of dear faithful friends, and all contrived and organised by your radiant and unchanging self. . . . How we all loved to be at your table . . . the joy of thinking what happiness you gave us all in your unforgettable years with Alfred. I'm sure he and Binkie and Noël were all hovering about with loving wings and blessing you with the comradeship and *hard work* of all the years you labored together to bring so much happiness and fun to so many different lives. . . . You are a great lady, an unmatched actress, and a most dear friend.

She would make other public appearances. Early in 1980, Donald Seawell, now publisher of the *Denver Post* and president of the Denver Center for the Performing Arts, persuaded her to present an ANTA National Artist Award to Henry Fonda. Accepting the award, Fonda, weeping, murmured elegantly, "I never dreamed that the reigning greatest lady of the theater would lay this on me."

George Schaefer, director of *The Magnificent Yankee* and a good friend, had persuaded Lynn to make *The Lunts: A Life in the Theater,* a four-hour conversation edited to one hour by her friend Gloria Irwin, for PBS. She felt safe talking with Schaefer at Ten Chimneys, flirting with him, singing snatches of old music-hall songs, reliving some of the great triumphs, though always modestly. She was worried about her face on camera, however—"lots of wrinkles around the mouth"—but more worried about her memory; and Schaefer had to prompt her throughout as she blotted her mouth anxiously with a handkerchief. Yet her smile was as enchanting as ever and the white hair softened her strong-boned face. Schaefer was frankly worshipful: Alfred Lunt, he said, was the greatest man he had ever known and *There Shall Be No Night* the finest evening in the theater. Most effective, perhaps, was the clip from *Anastasia,* Lynn's last film, ending with Lynn walking out of the room shutting double doors behind her, "the perfectly symbolic ending to a matchless career."

Watching the telecast on June 21, 1980, Helen Hayes cheered when

Lynn broke into a music-hall song: "You are an ever-lasting wonder." "What a treat to hear that lovely voice," wrote Madeline Sherwood. "No one was ever so beautiful, so elegant, so glamorous, so sexy as you are on the glorious TV," wrote Ruth Gordon. ". . . Last night you were queen of all the actresses who ever lived." Hundreds wrote thanking Lynn Fontanne for giving them another unforgettable performance.

Lynn next flew to Washington to receive a Kennedy Center Honor for the Performing Arts on Sunday, December 7, the day after her ninety-third birthday. Leonard Bernstein, James Cagney, Agnes de Mille, and Leontyne Price were fellow honorees. It was a two-day bash, the cultural swan song of the departing Carter administration, played to a chiefly Democratic crowd. At the State Department dinner on Saturday, Lynn wore a raspberry chiffon dress and gold coat, her white hair

At the Kennedy Center Honors, December 7, 1980. Left to right: Leonard Bernstein, Agnes de Mille, Leontyne Price, James Cagney, Lynn Fontanne, Eleanor Mondale, Vice President Walter Mondale

piled atop her head. She smiled graciously as she received the broad collar of multicolored ribbons caught by a heavy gold medal; but then she smiled graciously throughout the entire festivities, seldom knowing a name. At the Kennedy Center itself Beverly Sills and Jason Robards led two thousand in singing "Happy Birthday" as Lynn, seated next to President Jimmy Carter in his box, glowed like a jewel. Lunt and Fontanne were lauded as the greatest acting team in the history of the theater, artists who had set a performance standard for American actors throughout the twentieth century. Said Robards in his speech: "Alfred Lunt and Lynn Fontanne worked together on the stage nearly every day for decades with a dedication to the theater matched only by their devotion to one another." "I'm bedazzled," said Lynn.

The staff at Ten Chimneys came and went, many unsung, like Melana, Lynn's faithful personal maid in her last years. Martha Roland was assigned to Lynn from the caregiving agency Midwest Medical, staying four nights a week. The ever-efficient George Bugbee had set up the schedule, as he made up the menus, according to Lynn's wishes. He also instructed Martha about the proper distance to maintain between herself and her employer. At first Martha did gauche things like answering "You're welcome." George took her aside. "When Miss Fontanne thanks you, you don't say 'You're welcome.' She's acknowledging your service and that's the end of it." At first Martha was both cook and nurse, then just a nurse as Lynn became more fragile. But the actress still dominated the stage: "I would have to stand down below the staircase and listen to see when the door would open and then she would make her entrance and come down the stairway, and by that time I would light the fire. . . . She always looked like a shining star, you know, and the way she came down the staircase . . . with such grace and her head was high and she was perfectly groomed, and it was just a pleasure."

Helen Hayes still could create friction. Lynn was sure Helen didn't like her because when she visited she "was paying all her attention to George Bugbee." (George called Helen "an Irish charmer.") Katharine Hepburn came to Ten Chimneys in 1982. The seventy-five-year-old actress had the limousine drop her at the back entrance of the property and came striding down the winding road in hiking boots and britches, swinging a walking stick she'd picked up on the way—a "Hey, I'm arriving!" attitude, said Martha Roland. Lynn and Hepburn squared off, continued Roland, in an "I'm somebody, too" kind of way. That day she witnessed a Fontanne victory at the table when Lynn graciously presented the dish of lemon meringue pie to Hepburn. Martha understood. It was a hell of a mess getting out that first piece of pie. Let Hepburn take the dive.

"What a real thrill it was to see you in your beautiful house which I've heard so much about," Hepburn wrote afterward. "It's indeed lovely—And so are you—unique creature—lovely to look at—& such a wonderful atmosphere you create around you—I must say you lifted my spirits. . . . Please thank George Bugbee—he was sweet—& tell him that the whole adventure gave us a real thrill & that certainly includes the sandwiches & the lemon pie!"

have no fears. I don't think I'll ever die," Lynn told an interviewer in 1981. But eventually she gave up walking out into the courtyard with Martha Roland and could no longer be persuaded to ride her exercise bike. She answered few letters and sometimes forgot she was in the

Lynn and Alfred

middle of a game of solitaire. Larry Olivier continued to phone but all they said, as far as Martha could hear, was "Darling, darling, darling, darling." Sometimes she stood at the threshold of the steps leading down into the drawing room, lost in memories of the past until Martha led her away.

One evening in May 1983 Lynn collapsed as she was taking her medicine. She was taken to Waukesha Hospital for X rays, but had broken no bones. Back at Ten Chimneys she was put to bed. She got up as usual the next day, but within weeks she no longer wanted to come downstairs. On the night of July 29 both George Bugbee and Martha Roland realized she was dying and stayed at her bedside until she fell asleep. The next morning Brent Fintel saw the ambulance and knew Mrs. Lunt was dead at ninety-five. Martha had nursed many Alzheimer's patients. She marveled how Miss Fontanne maintained her dignity and reserve right until the end.

She was buried beside her soul mate, Alfred, at Forest Home Cemetery, Donald Seawell again giving the eulogy. People commented on the appropriateness of the weather: rain, lightning, and thunder when Alfred was buried; a calm, sunny day for Lynn. Dramatics for Alfred Lunt, yes; but to pursue the Romantic fallacy, Lynn's day should have been elegantly gray, crystal clear, fragrant with lilacs and yellow primroses, a little chilly—an English day.

The inscription on the Lunt memorial reads: "Alfred Lunt and Lynn Fontanne were universally regarded as the greatest acting team in the history of the English-speaking theater. They were married for fifty-five years and were inseparable both on and off the stage."

The names of major correspondents, biographers, and interviewers are abbreviated:

AL	= Alfred Lunt
LF	= Lynn Fontanne
HS	= Harriet Sederholm
RBW	= Ray Bennett Weaver
NC	= Noël Coward
AW	= Alexander Woollcott
GR	= Graham Robertson
RS	= Robert Sherwood
LL	= Lawrence Langner
MZ	= Maurice Zolotow
JB	= Jared Brown
THG	= Thomas H. Garver
MP	= Margot Peters

I have regularized some punctuation and spelling in the letters of AL and LF for clarity. Newspaper theater reviews not endnoted appeared the day after the given opening (or on the Monday following a Saturday opening). I have identified quotations from magazines and newpapers to the best of my ability, given the fact that many clippings in the Billy Rose Theater Collection of the New York Public Library (BRTC), the Covent Garden Theatre Museum, Ten Chimneys, and the Lunts' personal scrapbooks at the BRTC and the Wisconsin Historical Society (WHS) lack source and/or date.

PROLOGUE

3 "You both ennobled": Kitty Carlisle Hart to LF, n.d., but August 1977, on the occasion of AL's death.
"a symbol for": Edna Ferber to the Lunts, September 18, 1940.

3 "Brilliant and heavenly": John Gielgud to the Lunts, June 3 [no year].

"I thank God": Raymond Massey to LF, August 4, 1977.

"God-given understanding . . . the Best Artists": Thornton Wilder to AL and LF, February 5, 1942, and September 15, 1933.

"Absolutely superb": NC, *Diaries,* February 15, 1965, 592.

CHAPTER ONE • LYNN'S WAY: 1887-1919

In LF's childhood Woodford Bridge was a small village divided east-west by a railroad line, the west side being the better side of town. The house was at 6 Station Terrace. Station Terrace is now renamed and the house, renumbered as 96, is currently Tony Haywood, Bookmaker; but through the efforts of Roger Frederick Fisher (LF was Mr. Fisher's father's second cousin), a pavement plaque now marks the building as LF's birthplace. I am extremely grateful to Roger Fisher and to Patricia Burnell, another cousin of LF's, for information about her childhood that helps set the record straight. (The Fontannes, for instance, did not live in London's East End, as *Stagestruck* has it.)

Roger Fisher obtained LF's birth certificate for me from the Family Records Centre, London, confirming she was born December 6, 1887, as Lillie Louise. He also helpfully located the birth certificates of LF's sisters, Mai Ellen (1882), Antoinette Mary (1883), and Frances Emma (1884). Frances presumably died young, since LF rarely mentions her.

Ms. Burnell has researched LF's mother's family, discovering the Irish great-grandmother from a titled Irish family who eloped with a soldier, had a baby daughter, was returned to her family, and gave the baby up to foster parents. This daughter, Sarah Ann Barnett, was LF's grandmother. LF's parents' marriage certificate from August 1, 1881, is in WHS: her father was twenty-six years old, occupation "plaister founder"; her mother, Frances Ellen Thornley Barnett (Jacob Barnett was her stepfather), was twenty-two.

5 "I will be a mother": quoted in MZ, *Stagestruck,* 11.

6 "ring out like a bell": MZ, quoting Antoinette Fontanne Keith, *Stagestruck,* 12.

"She had climbed" . . . "I never shall": Patricia Burnell, quoting Antoinette Fontanne Keith, letter to MP, October 31, 2000.

7 "I was a very noisy": MZ, *Stagestruck,* 12.

"I demand to know": Patricia Burnell to MP, October 31, 2000.

8 "her little circle": quoted from T. Edgar Pemberton, *Ellen Terry and Her Sisters,* in Joy Melville's *Ellen and Edy,* 121.

"Do something!": LF talked about her meeting with Ellen Terry to MZ and to George Schaefer for the TV program *The Lunts: A Life in the Theater,* March 7, 1980.

"No, don't say it": MZ, *Stagestruck,* 13.

9 "Must get Lynn": quoted in Tom Prideaux, *Love or Nothing,* 261.

10 "That's all": MZ, *Stagestruck,* 14.

"I thought to myself": JB, *The Fabulous Lunts,* 35.

"kept these men": JB, *The Fabulous Lunts,* 35.

"He'd be waiting": MZ, *Stagestruck,* 15. Since they are based on later reminiscences, LF's whereabouts in London these early years are hard to chronologize. MZ and JB give differing accounts. LF connects Byrne waiting for her on Battersea Bridge with her residence in Down Street, Mayfair, off Piccadilly. She recalled living in Pimlico when she applied to Beerbohm Tree for *Edwin Drood.* When she lived with Antoinette in a small flat in Chelsea (JB, 35) is unclear. One certain dating of an address is LF's letter to Ellen Terry of June 11, 1910, from 37 Lambs Conduit Street in Holborn, apparently their only surviving communication.

11 "Dear Miss Terry": LF to Ellen Terry, June 11, 1910.

"I'm on the stage": LF interviewed by Bunny Raasch, Milwaukee Channel 12, WISN, July 30, 1981.

12 "Oh, places with": MZ, *Stagestruck,* 16.

"Both *belles laides*": John Gielgud to MP, January 7, 1997.

"Lynn Fontanne": London *Times,* November 2, 1914.

13 "Why, she's as shy": Marguerite Courtney, *Laurette,* 158–59.

14 "I got it finally": MZ, *Stagestruck,* 22.

"Gawd A'mighty": Marguerite Courtney, *Laurette,* 159.

15 "She was a young": Guthrie McClintic, *Me and Kit,* 155–56.

16 "I'm sure": MZ, *Stagestruck,* 27.

"very fast, very brightly": MZ, *Stagestruck,* 28.

17 "knew the plots": Guthrie McClintic, *Me and Kit,* 170.

"goodbye, Juliet": Helen Hayes, *On Reflection,* 122.

"Shakespeare has been": quoted in Guthrie McClintic, *Me and Kit,* 170.

"She was sometimes": Marguerite Courtney, *Laurette,* 160.

18 "I think we can skim": Scott Meredith, *George S. Kaufman and His Friends,* 58.

"I gave it everything": MZ, *Stagestruck,* 30.

"a notable young actress": *New York Times,* September 17, 1918.

CHAPTER TWO • ALFRED'S WAY: 1892–1919

Born in 1830, one of five sons of Nathaniel and Sallie (Griggs) Lunt, Alfred Lunt Sr. came to Wisconsin from Orono, Maine, around 1855. (The family had originally come to America from London in 1634.) He became part-owner of a logging and lumber business centered at Phillips, Wisconsin, and was a member of the Great Weyerhauser Lumber Syndicate. The Briggs family—Daniel, Mary, and their children, William, Achsah, and Harriet—came to Wisconsin from Maine in a Conestoga wagon and settled in Hortonville. Alfred Lunt hired William Briggs as his foreman and became interested in Harriet Washburn Briggs through the humorous letters she wrote her brother. Harriet had attended Lawrence College and was a schoolteacher. Born in 1862, she was thirty-two years younger than Lunt, whom she married in 1882. A daughter, Inez, died in 1891, the year before Alfred David Lunt's birth on August 12, 1892. (Some documents and news clippings give his second name as David, some as Davis.) For some reason Hattie always insisted Alfred was born on August 19; his birth certificate confirms August 12. Alfred Lunt Sr. died after a series of strokes on November 30, 1894. Photographs of their Milwaukee home show a large, impressive house. (Grand Avenue began as Spring Street and eventually became Wisconsin Avenue.) I am indebted to some unpublished pages called "The Lunt Connection," written by one of Achsah Briggs Tipler's four sons (probably the youngest, Perry), and to the research into Lunt family history of Verna Schmidt.

20 "How are the children?" AL to HS, Milwaukee, October 5, 1905. AL is visiting the Austin family while Hattie is away: "When are you coming home?"

21 "I drew all": *The New Yorker,* January 11, 1947, covering AL's display of toy theaters at the Museum of the City of New York.

"Alfred always stood": May Massee, Columbia Oral History interview.

"I wasn't good": JB, *The Fabulous Lunts,* 18.

"Well, I walked away": Alexander Woollcott, "The Actor from Genesee Depot," *McCall's,* April 1929. Lunt was coached in Wolsey's speech by a family friend, a lawyer named Chavannes with a local reputation as a good speaker. Lunt calls his nurse Cathy; in contemporary sources she is Cassie.

22 "If Alfred dies": MZ, *Stagestruck,* 34. Zolotow's biography doesn't often give sources for quotes.

23 "The saddest thing has happened": AL to Kenneth Conant, Helsingfors, August 19, 1909. Alfred always maintained Dr. Sederholm died in his sleep, though depression over losing his wife's money makes suicide not impossible. This year AL and Ray and Andrew Weaver put enormous effort into designing props, costumes, sets, and posters for a three-act play, "very morbid but vital." They adapted *The Greater Love* from James Lane Allen's *The White Cowl.* Unfortunately, none of them could write dialogue; the play was never produced at Carroll.

"Audiences could not": *Racine Journal,* n.d. AL performed these enormously popular sketches from 1909 to 1911. On August 2, 1910, at Genesee Depot, an ad proclaimed "Big entertainment—dance, 2 bands, Coney Island Red Hots. Oh! Boy Alfred Lundt [sic] & other big attractions!"

"Carroll 13": AL to HS, 104 East Avenue, Waukesha, October 20, [1909?].

"Oh, I would give": AL to HS, 104 East Avenue, Waukesha, October 21, 1909.

"Just *rooms* full": AL to HS, 104 East Avenue, Waukesha, December 18, 1909.

"selfish" . . . "borrowed out of": AL to HS, 104 East Avenue, Waukesha, December 18, 1909. The Swedish relatives in Finland are rather shadowy: Alfred refers to "Foster Matte" (Matilda), Hanna, Elsa, and the boys.

24 "dearest of sons": HS to AL, Järvelä, Finland, March 25, 1910. Many letters over the years from HS to AL survive—vigorous, funny, gossipy, often poetic.

"My best friend": AL to May Rankin, Järvelä, Finland, August 16, 1910.

"Matilda told Mother": AL to RBW, August 27, 1910.

"Hurrah Hu-Ray": AL to RBW, September 1, 1910. Dr. Rankin, president of Carroll College, had died August 16. Alfred sent May Rankin condolences from Finland, with news that he and Ray Weaver were hard at work on a play, *The Greater Love.*

"three-elm institution": George Bugbee, *Reflections of a Good Life,* 1.

"that weird household": AL to RBW [February 8, 1916].

"In God's name": MZ, *Stagestruck,* 36. "Hattie's boarding house" in Waukesha can be confusing. The Waukesha City Directory (Waukesha Historical Museum) lists both Alfred and Hattie living at 101 Hartwell Avenue in 1911–1912; they moved in 1910, too late to be listed. These, then, are the years of AL running the boardinghouse. After AL left Carroll College in 1912, Harriet W. Sederholm is listed as living at 113 East Avenue in Waukesha from

1913 to 1917. In 1917 the Bankes sisters, artists, lived with her, so she was still in the boarding business.

"We don't have one penny": George Bugbee to MP, October 17, 1985.

"Those who enjoy": Handbill in the archives at Ten Chimneys.

25 "Working like fury": AL to Kenneth Conant, October 15, 1911.

"It was a faculty concert": Letter from Mrs. R. M. Fairleigh to Alexander Woollcott, quoted in Woollcott's "The Haunted House of Lunt," *Vanity Fair,* March 1929.

"Rehearsals all last week": AL to HS, 104 East Avenue, Waukesha, June 3, 1910. Alfred also loved shopping for himself, Hattie, and the children, once with Ray Weaver running into a sale in Milwaukee: "Both of us had a peach of a time, watching the scrambling & grabbing and all that goes with a bargain sale. We wondered if the women didn't have to go into 'training' to be able to 'tear' about as they do. I got something for every one. . . ." AL to HS, June 3, 1910.

26 "Dearest Beloved": AL to HS, New York, April 8, 1917.

"My heart leaps": AL to RBW, n.d. With letters to RBW from Boston but possibly written earlier at Carroll College.

27 "the prettiest black haired": AL to RBW, Chippewa Falls, April 2, 1911.

"The only women": AL to RBW, July 22 [1914], written on a trip to Europe when he became friendly with several attractive married women.

"I wish they wouldn't": AL to HS, 548 Columbus Avenue, Boston [October 3, 1912]. During his years in Boston, Lunt stayed at various addresses. There is a photo of him at the Savoy Hotel on Columbus Avenue doing laundry in his room. And Kenneth Conant writes mysteriously of them sharing a suite in a private dormitory "courtesy of the McDonnell family of Buffalo" during 1913–1914. He often ate at Smith's Basement Dining Room, $4.50 a week for three meals a day.

"Tomorrow I register": AL to RBW, 548 Columbus Avenue, Boston, September 23, 1912. The address of Emerson College was 130 Beacon Street; AL enrolled September 24, 1912.

"Not a particularly satisfying": AL to RBW, September 30, 1912.

"I rise at 7:30": AL to RBW, October 10, 1912.

28 "went to sleep": AL to HS, October 3, 1912.

"Honestly Ray I don't": AL to RBW, October 18, 1912.

"I honestly am": AL to RBW, October 25, 1912.

29 "unquestionably the finest": AL to RBW, January 26, 1913.

"I just want": AL to RBW, January 8, 1913. The letter protests that AL does not deserve RBW's love; AL is not what RBW thinks him.

30 "It's *cruel*": AL to RBW, December 14, 1912.

"What do we know": AL to RBW, Thursday, n.d. [1913?].

"height, voice, appearance": AL to RBW, December 30, 1912.

"Yes! . . . I have decided": AL to RBW, January 8, 1913.

"to die there and then": AL to RBW, June 21, 1914.

"Such confusion": AL to RBW, St. Petersburg, July 7, 1914.

31 "one enormous room": The description of an early visitor quoted in *Ten Chim-*

neys: Historic Site Analysis and Preliminary Master Plan, 1–4. George Bugbee
gives the local builder as a Mr. Monty. Cathleen Nesbitt also describes the original house in *A Little Love and Good Company,* 243.

32 "He was, in my opinion": Howard Lindsay, "Lindsay and Crouse and the Fabulous Lunts," *Good Housekeeping,* February 1956.

"Shades of Edwin Booth!": AL to RBW, Chicago, Sunday, 1915.

"dreadfully miscast" . . . "I blush": AL to HS, New York, 444 West 22nd Street,
Saturday, June 13, 1917, and Albany, Wednesday, April 11, 1917.

HERE'S TO YOU: HS to AL, August 19, 1915. Though his birth certificate gives
August 12 as his birthday, Hattie insisted AL was born on August 19.

"Oh, the spirit": AL to RBW, Sunday [August 8, 1915].

33 "about eight feet": Howard Lindsay, "Lindsay and Crouse and the Fabulous
Lunts," *Good Housekeeping,* February 1956.

"This, I never": AL to Arnold Johnson, Naples, Florida, February 22, 1971.
Johnson had asked Lunt to explain why Margaret Anglin had been forgotten as
an actress.

"I asked you": AL to HS, Friday [n.d.], probably late fall of 1915 or 1916.

34 "Miss Anglin is": AL to RBW, Sunday [August 8, 1915].

"It was late": AL, "Twenty-Six Weeks in Vaudeville—Learning Things I Have
Never Forgotten," *Billboard,* December 26, 1936.

35 "I adore her . . . She's brilliant": AL to RBW, Thursday [November 9, 1916].

"I have decided": AL to HS, Hotel Radisson, Minneapolis, Monday [December
4, 1916]. AL's ambivalent attitude toward Mrs. Langtry is expressed in a poem:

> *Mrs. Langtry, in the best of sashes*
> *Every evening turns to "Ashes."*
> *Many times the house grows chilly.*
> *But no one dares to poke the Lillie.*

GLADLY, BUT NOT: Howard Lindsay, "Lindsay and Crouse and the Fabulous
Lunts," *Good Housekeeping,* February 1956.

"Yes do enlarge": a composite of letters from AL to HS of Tuesday [February 14,
1917?], April 26, 1917, and May 11, 1917. Letters to HS show AL to have
been in New York that spring, at several addresses, one William Hurlbut's
1840 house where "The Night Before Christmas" had been written, sharing
quarters with someone he calls "The Pup" (I have been unable to identify this
person). He met Marie Doro, who wanted to do a film with him, saw Geraldine Farrar in *Madama Butterfly* and Nazimova "in a terrible play," *'Ception
Shoals.*

36 "he was involved": Bill Bryson, *The Lost Continent,* 113.

"I should serve": AL to HS, Providence, Rhode Island, April 25, 1917.

"so boiling mad" . . . "great husky brute" . . . "I leave Carl": AL to HS, Providence, April 26, 1917, and Sunday [April 8, 1817].

"tall gangly" . . . "Oh! Alfred": Cathleen Nesbitt, *A Little Love and Good Company,* 113.

"walked away with": H. H. Ryan, unidentified clipping in the Lunt-Fontanne
Collection [August 20–27, 1917].

37 "I didn't say": MZ, *Stagestruck,* 47.

"Not since I": AL to HS, Stratford House, 11 East Thirty-second Street, Saturday [November 6, 1917].

BE GLAD . . . "lost the job": interview with William Pronold, longtime Genesee Depot resident, June 18, 1998.

"You could buy": MZ tells the story in *Stagestruck,* 48.

38 "Lunt's got his own": Booth Tarkington to George C. Tyler, October 22, 1918, in *On Plays, Playwrights, and Playgoers,* 6.

"He's going to": quoted in James Woodress, *Booth Tarkington,* 211.

"Of course I am": AL to HS, St. Louis, Monday [November 1918].

CHAPTER THREE • DULCY MARRIES CLARENCE: 1919-1922

39 "Who was *that?*": The story of the Lunts' meeting has been told many times in many ways. MZ says in *Stagestruck* (50) that LF asked to be introduced to AL at a rehearsal of *Clarence* at the New Amsterdam Theatre. JB says the play was *Made of Money* and that Toler said of Lunt's voice: "That young man's voice is literally a gift from heaven. A voice like that can't be acquired. You have to be born with it." JB also has AL falling backward down the stairs (80). No one seems to be sure who said "He certainly fell for her," though MZ believably credits Kaufman. LF in an interview with George Schaefer said that she met AL at a rehearsal of *A Young Man's Fancy,* and though LF was ninety-three at the time, MP goes with LF. A year later she told Bunny Raasch that AL hadn't yet arrived at the theater; she was sitting on a chair facing a little door; he came through that door and, falling down three steps, landed at her feet. (No mention of his voice.) The meeting is also discussed by Lawrence Lader, "Lunt and Fontanne: First Family of the Theatre," *Coronet,* June 1948; Mary B. Mullett, "Jealous? We Should Say Not!" *American Magazine,* December 1928; and Ada Patterson, "The Guardsman and His Wife: Tea-Time at the Lunts—An Intimate Study of a Happy Stage Marriage," *Theatre Magazine,* March 1925.

"to look presentable": MZ, *Stagestruck,* 50.

40 "rather picturesque": undated, untitled article in Robinson Locke scrapbook, BRTC.

"Lynn Fontanne is a joy": AL to HS, Washington, Sunday [n.d.].

"*is* a queer guy": Booth Tarkington to AL, July 16, 1919.

41 "*No stress on points*": Booth Tarkington to George Tyler, n.d., in *Plays, Playwrights, and Playgoers,* 16.

"This is the best": Booth Tarkington to George Tyler, February 13, 1919, in *Plays, Playwrights, and Playgoers,* 7.

"It's a harness": Booth Tarkington to AL, August 12, 1919.

42 "I suppose it must": MZ, *Stagestruck,* 60. MZ's account of Lynn's arrival has her coincidentally running into Alfred, Hattie, and Karin on a train coming back from the circus in Milwaukee, Karin blowing up balloons, Hattie wearing Alfred's straw hat, everyone boisterous and hysterical. A good story. What seems certain is that because of a mixup in dates at the telegraph office LF arrived a day before she was expected. George Bugbee, Karin's husband, told me in an interview on October 17, 1985, of Hattie's original jealousy of LF,

confirmed by LF in the interview with Bunny Raasch. Laurette Taylor writes of
it in "Lynn Fontanne," *Town and Country,* August 1942.

44 "Mr. Alfred Lunt": Alan Dale, *New York American,* September 22, 1919.

"I should have": AL to James Woodress, February 27, 1954, quoted in *Booth Tarkington,* 211.

45 "Write it on": Alexander Woollcott, *New York Times,* September 22, 1919.

"awkward, skinny creature": Helen Hayes, quoted in Kenneth Barrow, *Helen Hayes,* 64.

46 "I didn't *handle*": Bunny Raasch interview, Milwaukee Channel 12, WISN, July 30, 1981.

"love and longing" . . . "Dear heart . . . love without end": AL to HS, Washington, D.C., Sunday [1919]; Thursday [n.d.]; Ithaca, New York, May 7 [1917].

"He'd make a terrible": MZ, *Stagestruck,* 66.

"Wait, wait" . . . "Just having Alfred": MZ, *Stagestruck,* 66.

"I was torn": Helen Hayes, *On Reflection,* 100–101.

47 "If you really": Tyler to AL, November 6, 1920.

"give you a real": Arthur and Barbara Gelb, *O'Neill,* 649.

48 "Knoblock is awfully": LF to George C. Tyler [May 1920].

"contemplated a matrimonial": AL to George C. Tyler, November 19, 1920.

"pure Kaufman": Howard Teichmann, *George S. Kaufman,* 83.

49 "The intelligent people": Booth Tarkington to John Peter Toohey, February 22, 1921, in *Plays, Playwrights, and Playgoers,* 46.

"Lynn Fontanne wants": Leslie Howard to Adrian Brunel, quoted in Leslie Ruth Howard, *A Quite Remarkable Father,* 67.

50 "When I say": George C. Tyler to AL, New Amsterdam Theatre Building, New York, February 5, 1921.

"Much disappointed": Booth Tarkington to George C. Tyler, February 6, 1921, in *Plays, Playwrights, and Playgoers,* 44.

"Did you and Alfred": LF interviewed by Bunny Raasch, Milwaukee Channel 12, WISN, July 30, 1981.

"a scraggy, friendly": Noël Coward, *Present Indicative,* 97.

"particularly attractive": Philip Hoare, *Noel Coward: A Biography,* 95–96. Hoare also quotes an unnamed contemporary that AL was "a bit of a freelancer sexually" these days—rather unsatisfactory as evidence.

51 "a lovely companion!": George Schaefer interview, *The Lunts: A Life in the Theatre,* PBS, March 7, 1980.

"happy delirium": AL to NC, London, n.d. Written much later, but a sample of the only-half-kidding intimacy of the three.

52 "From these shabby": Noël Coward, *Present Indicative,* 136–7.

"We drifted in": Noël Coward, *Present Indicative,* 137.

53 "thin as toothpicks" . . . "Tell Lynn": Howard Lindsay, "Lindsay and Crouse and the Fabulous Lunts," *Good Housekeeping,* February 1956.

54 "Darling, of course": Noël Coward, *Present Indicative,* 138.

55 "You worked too hard": JB, *The Fabulous Lunts,* 101–02.

"stayed up late": Billie Burke, *With a Feather on My Nose,* 199. Billie Burke says that AL and LF were married by a parson before the matinee in Atlantic City, that AL's voice failed him, so that he was barely able to mutter "yes" and couldn't say a word during the matinee performance. Neither AL nor LF ever mentioned an Atlantic City wedding.

55 "has to have *remarkable*": Booth Tarkington to AL, March 11, 1922.

56 "Let's get married": LF and AL reminiscing on their fiftieth wedding anniversary, *Milwaukee Journal,* May 26, 1972; also reported variously by MZ, JB, and many other sources. Some say that LF had forgotten her purse, so that each witness was asked to contribute a dollar. LF says very definitely on ABC's *The Dick Cavett Show* (February 10, 1970) and during the interview with Bunny Raasch (July 30, 1981) that she paid for the license.

"When we got back": LF, interview with George Schaefer for *The Lunts: A Life in the Theater,* PBS, March 7, 1980.

57 "She was a bit": LF interviewed by Bunny Raasch, Milwaukee Channel 12, WISN, July 30, 1981.

58 "It must have been odd": Enid Bagnold, *Autobiography,* 255.

"Lynn was intensely": Laurette Taylor, "Lynn Fontanne," *Town and Country,* August 1942.

"never seemed to have": Maurice Zolotow's daughter, Crescent Dragonwagon, to MP, April 12, 2000.

"We were friends" . . . "Never had the time": LF to Bunny Raasch, Milwaukee Channel 12, WISN, July 30, 1981.

CHAPTER FOUR • ENTER THE GUARDSMAN: 1922-1925

59 "Next time you": "They Glory in a Rustic, High-Style Hideaway," *Life,* July 26, 1963.

"It must be": quoted by Lesley, Payn, and Morley in *Noel Coward and His Friends,* 104.

"largely unaccountable" . . . "gifted grotesques" . . . "a shy, repressed" . . . "a funny, gawky" . . . "felt sorry for": Robert Sherwood, "The Lunts," in *The Passionate Playgoer,* 79–81.

60 "Oh, my dear": Marguerite Courtney, *Laurette,* 263.

61 "I was fascinated": S. N. Behrman, *People in a Diary,* 86–87.

"I made a mess": *Milwaukee Journal,* May 11, 1923.

62 "Lynn and Alfred": Laurette Taylor, "Lynn Fontanne," *Town and Country,* August 1942.

63 "Isn't she a *dream!*" "Mr. and Mrs.," *Time,* November 8, 1937. LF said later (*Theatre Arts,* November 1936) that she once had a very bad costume part to play. "I went to the Metropolitan and saw all the Peter Lylys. I copied one person exactly, down to the jewelry. My make-up and my appearance were so startling that the part made quite an impression. But that was only trickery."

"She's the only woman": Laurette Taylor, "Lynn Fontanne," *Town and Country,* August 1942.

"vulnerability that was": Harold Clurman, *Collected Works,* 279.

"The neck and shoulders": John Gielgud quoting LF to MP, January 7, 1997.

64 "Anyone who can't": quoted in Cathleen Nesbitt, *A Little Love and Good Company,* 214.

64 "Married to perhaps": Howard Lindsay, "Lindsay and Crouse and the Fabulous Lunts," *Good Housekeeping,* February 1956.
   "In *In Love*": Noël Coward, *Present Indicative,* 174.

65 "Great fun altering" . . . "utterly futile" . . . "reduced to a jelly": Leslie Howard, *Trivial Fond Records,* 41.
   "Lunt is one": Helen Ormsbee, *Backstage with Actors,* 260–1.

66 "Never mind, darling": Noël Coward, *Present Indicative,* 175.

67 "Success of play": Leslie Howard, *Trivial Fond Records,* 41. Howard reported dozens turned away at some performances, but by April there were rumors of the play closing and Howard took a $50-a-week cut in pay.
   "in a dirty": Murdoch Pemberton, "The Daddy of Sunday Painters," *The New Yorker,* July 11, 1925. Pemberton's profile mentions as students "Alfred Lunt and Leslie Howard, widening their scope of art."
   "begin to ponder": Leslie Ruth Howard, *A Quite Remarkable Father,* 90.
   "For chrissake, Mr. Lunt": quoted in MZ, *Stagestruck,* 86.
   "Something told me": Theresa Helburn, quoted in MZ, *Stagestruck,* 97.

69 "Captain Molyneux is an *artiste*": quoted in JB, *The Fabulous Lunts,* 125.

70 "a mysteriously ugly": AL quoted in MZ, *Stagestruck,* 103.
   "We couldn't even" . . . "If we run": quoted in George Freedley, *The Lunts,* 33.
   "Saw Lee": Theresa Helburn, *A Wayward Quest,* 92.
   "We had terrible" . . . "You can't play": *Actors Talk About Acting,* Part II, 16.

71 "They sat facing": Richard Boeth, "Alfred the Great," *Newsweek,* August 15, 1977.
   "arid, without the": Howard Lindsay, "Lindsay and Crouse and the Fabulous Lunts," *Good Housekeeping,* February 1956.

72 "It's the cruellest": MZ, *Stagestruck,* 105.
   "What we wanted": Theresa Helburn, *A Wayward Quest,* 71. Rollo Peters and Augustin Duncan were original members of the board of managers, but resigned, to be replaced by Theresa Helburn and Maurice Wertheim. Twenty years later, Langner and Helburn were running the Theatre Guild themselves.
   "The play really": Montgomery Davis, artistic director of the Milwaukee Chamber Theatre, to MP, March 2001.

CHAPTER FIVE • PURE GOLD: 1925-1929

77 "wear extraordinary things": George Bernard Shaw to Alma Murray, March 30, 1894, in *The Collected Letters of Bernard Shaw,* vol. 1, 422.
   "His Bluntschli was": LL, *The Magic Curtain,* 214.
   "I have seen": quoted in Theresa Helburn, *A Wayward Quest,* 157.
   "But I am only putting on": quoted in MZ, *Stagestruck,* 108.

78 "The big wind": Helen Hayes, *On Reflection,* 147.
   "a perpetual amateur": Theresa Helburn, *A Wayward Quest,* 246.
   "quick as a knife" . . . "mentally slow": *The Noel Coward Diaries,* 220.

79 "Hurt by nature": Howard Teichmann's words in *Smart Aleck,* 113.
   "What are the chances": LF to AW, Genesee Depot [summer 1934].
   "As far back": Helen Hayes, *On Reflection,* 89.

"There's no reason" . . . "Many of Laurette's" . . . "In later years": Marguerite Courtney, *Laurette*, 303, 172.

80 "broken soul" . . . "stumbling about" . . . "They were six": Laurette Taylor, "Lynn Fontanne," *Town and Country*, August 1942.

"Art theater, my foot": quoted in MZ, *Stagestruck*, 129.

81 "Goddammit, Lynn": quoted in MZ, *Stagestruck*, 115.

84 "Copeau could not": Harold Clurman, *Collected Works*, 890. Lawrence Langner tells in *The Magic Curtain* (219) of a final contretemps between Alfred and Copeau at the dress rehearsal. Copeau was not satisfied with the scratch on Alfred's cheek; he wanted "a big large wound right across your cheek, at once!" Alfred disappeared and twenty minutes later appeared with a huge, gaping, gangrenous-looking wound. "We will have no wound at all!" said Copeau. Alfred left the stage and reappeared later with "a fair to middling scar." "I've made a compromise," he said, giving Copeau a lesson in how to handle American actors.

85 "Oh, Alfred, we can't": quoted in MZ, *Stagestruck*, 121.

86 "casual, only sporadically" . . . "I suppose" . . . "I'd not had" . . . "had the audience" . . . "shafted a light": S. N. Behrman, *People in a Diary*, 78–80.

"was the luckiest thing": S. N. Behrman, *People in a Diary*, 81.

87 "bidding for the laughter": AW, "The Haunted House of Lunt," *Vanity Fair*, March 1929.

88 "Oh, boy, he": *Actors Talk About Acting*, Part II, 25.

89 "Remember during": paraphrased from conversation reported by Arthur and Barbara Gelb, *O'Neill*, 649. "When I went into *Strange Interlude*, O'Neill asked me if I remembered a conversation we'd once had during the production of *Chris*, when I told him that I wished someone would write a play exposing possessive mothers, showing how some of them ruin their children's lives. 'This is it!' O'Neill said, pointing to a script of *Interlude*."

"did not cherish": Arthur and Barbara Gelb, *O'Neill*, 649.

"He's not as great" . . . "Even if" . . . "Play it as I": LF in interview with George Schaefer, March 7, 1980.

"When I tell you": LF to Kurt Weill, Minneapolis, October 17 or 18, 1939.

90 "In the seventh": Noël Coward, tape-recorded interview of LF and AL by MZ.

"a six-day": quoted in Arthur and Barbara Gelb, *O'Neill*, 649.

91 "sexy games" . . . "blue in the face": Cheryl Crawford, *One Naked Individual*, 40.

"Suicidal, desperate": Theresa Helburn, June 4, 1956, unpublished Lunt-Fontanne–Theatre Guild papers. Helburn considerably modified her opinion of Lynn in her memoir, *A Wayward Quest*.

92 "There are many": LL, *The Magic Curtain*, 217.

93 "You want to pack": A six-stanza poem published in Ring Lardner's column "Ring's Side" in the *Morning Telegraph*, January 16, 1929.

CHAPTER SIX · MERGER: 1928–1931

94 "By spreading out": LL, *The Magic Curtain*, 243.

96 "Twenty-five hundred": quoted in George Freedley, *The Lunts*, 54.

97   "No, we never": *Actors Talk About Acting,* Part II, 34.

"Just because we": LF quoted in "The Actor Attacks His Part: Lynn Fontanne and Alfred Lunt," *Theatre Arts,* November 1936.

"Lynn is the lantern": Laurence Olivier quoting Constance Collier in *Confessions of an Actor,* 110.

"Lunt? He's indistinguishable": Richard Maney, *Fanfare,* 285.

"rather sadly, that Alfred": Joan Plowright (Olivier's third wife), *And That's Not All,* 42.

"It is the play": Lucius Beebe, "At Breakfast with the Lunts, Lynn, Alfred," *New York Herald Tribune,* February 15, 1931.

98   "We rehearse at": Djuna Barnes, "Lord Alfred and Lady Lynn," *Theatre Guild Magazine,* March 1930.

"Husbands and wives": Theresa Romberg to Theresa Helburn, n.d.

"Please don't tell": quoted by Ashton Stevens in the *Chicago Herald-Examiner,* April 10, 1931.

"We rehearse together": Djuna Barnes, "Lord Alfred and Lady Lynn," *Theatre Guild Magazine,* March 1930.

"Isn't it nice": quoted widely, based on a famous Helen Hokinson cartoon in *The New Yorker.*

"How can any": quoted in LL, *The Magic Curtain,* 394.

"I was a ten months": quoted in MZ, *Stagestruck,* 87.

"blackguarding and scandalizing": Louise Scott to AL and LF, January 30, 1929.

99   "Stay out of it": Cheryl Crawford, *One Naked Individual,* 37.

"I have *never* felt": "Theatre Lovers Analyse Marriage," *Ocean Times,* May 8, 1930.

100   "Oh, sir, they boos": Wilson McCarty, "The Lunts Meet the 'Gods,' " *New York Times,* June 30, 1929.

101   "sardonic and laid back": John Gielgud to MP, January 7, 1997.

"It's not acting": quoted in Lawrence Langner, *The Magic Curtain,* 394.

"He's all pink": reported in the *Pittsburgh Sun Telegraph,* dateline London, July 1929.

"The character was" . . . "They won't like me": S. N. Behrman, *People in a Diary,* 87, 88.

102   "Six weeks' rest": *Milwaukee Sentinel* [n.d. but summer 1930].

103   "It seemed as though": Theresa Helburn, *A Wayward Quest,* 190.

104   "She conveys cross-grained": Mary Cass Canfield, "Lynn Fontanne: An Appreciation," *New York Times,* January 18, 1931.

105   "It's on my heart": letter in the Theatre Guild files, signed only "Yours, Hi," dated December 11, 1930, during the run of *Elizabeth the Queen.*

106   "Now let's not": quoted from "Are Lynn and I Actors? I'm Not Sure," *Milwaukee Journal,* April 29, 1931.

107   "Though they didn't": Ginger Rogers, *Ginger: My Story,* 94.

"You did it on purpose": Bob Thomas, *Thalberg,* 181.

"Oh, it seems": a composite version of a true story, as confirmed by AL, that was told and retold (and printed) so often no one really knows the original, which was probably fairly basic until Alexander Woollcott began to elaborate.

108   "a joke that became": James Harvey, *Romantic Comedy in Hollywood,* 66.

"I knew exactly": undated interview [early 1970s?] at Ten Chimneys, unpublished, by Ruth Hamilton.

"But these are all": Bob Thomas, *Thalberg,* 181.

"Our stay so": AL to Maxwell Anderson, July 11, 1931.

CHAPTER SEVEN • A GOOD DEPRESSION: 1931–1933

111 "apprehensions from which": Preface to *Reunion in Vienna* (New York: Charles Scribner's Sons, 1932), xvi.

114 "A queer thing": RS, "The Lunts," *The Passionate Playgoer,* 82–83.

115 "How's the press": a reconstruction from Bob Sherwood's account in "The Lunts" (84) and current reviews.

116 "it's so awfully": LF to NC, June 11 [1932].

"When your grandchildren": AW to AL, December 14, 1931, *The Letters of Alexander Woollcott,* 102.

"Oh, she's failing beautifully": AL's reminiscences taped by Karin's husband, George Bugbee, n.d.

118 "We don't need": Carolyn Every, "Home Life of the Lunts," *Wisconsin Magazine of History,* Spring 1983. AL's coffee and fish recipes are also from this source, as is LF's posing for Adam and Eve and the cape episode.

"a feisty old bat" and following quotes: Carolyn Every interviewed by MP, June 18, 1998.

119 "I'm pretty fed up": AL to Robert Sherwood, September 7, 1932.

"It was like acting": AL and LF, interviewed by Ashton Stevens, "Clothes or 'Unclothes' Topic of Actorview with Lynn and Alfred," *Chicago American,* November 5, 1932.

121 "NOËL: I shall never": Unpublished "Design for Rehearsing" by NC, 12 pages, a spoof of their rehearsals for *Design for Living.*

122 "They were *my* silk" . . . "I'm all for having": Ashton Stevens interview, *Chicago American,* November 5, 1932.

123 "How do you like": William Pronold, interviewed by MP, June 13, 1998.

"Do you like": LF quoted in "Lunts Celebrate 50th Anniversary," *Milwaukee Journal,* May 26, 1972.

"Yes, of course": NC quoted by Sheridan Morley in an interview with MP, December 4, 2000. Alfred had a history of male relationships, said Morley— without naming names. When Morley interviewed the Lunts in Genesee Depot for his biography *A Talent to Amuse,* he found them extremely guarded about NC.

"suggested a few": quoted in Sheridan Morley, *A Talent to Amuse,* 215.

125 "I suppose if your house" . . . "Oh, Noëlly, I": NC quoting LF on *The Dick Cavett Show,* February 10, 1970.

126 "Beside the young": David Carb, "Seen on the Stage," *Vogue,* March 1933.

127 "I can see": George Jean Nathan, "The Theatre," *Vanity Fair,* April 1933.

"Oh, nothing of": AL to RBW, January 1933.

"I found the play": Simonson to AL, January 25 [1933], the day after the opening.

127 "Nothing either of you": NC quoting LF on *The Dick Cavett Show,* February 10, 1970.

128 "Lynnie, Lynnie": quoted in F. Beverly Kelley, *It Was Better Than Work,* 222. In Atlanta AL also went to a circus performance. Eight of the elephants had grazed on chemically poisoned grass and were dying, and Alfred wept openly.

129 "In *Design for Living*": NC, *Present Indicative,* 175.

CHAPTER EIGHT • LONDON—A FLOP—A HIT: 1933-1936

130 "I hope you know": George Bugbee, *Recollections of a Good Life,* 31.
"the goddamn son": AL to AW, Monday [July 1933?].

131 "In these days" . . . "Positively Russian": LF in the *New York Herald Tribune,* September 14, 1933.
"We would like": LF to AW, May 9 [1933].
"First they wouldn't": *New York Herald Tribune,* September 14, 1933.

132 "Moscow has completely": AL to AW, Berlin, October 16, 1933.
"It's bleak" . . . "Never laughed so" . . . "harp, wig": AL to AW, Paris, December 1, 1933.

133 "I hope you will not": AL to RS, January 7 [1934].
"No, not at all" . . . "Lecherous mountebank!": AL to AW, March 29, 1934.
"I suppose you know": LF to AW, March 31, 1934.

134 "from his bed and board": AW to AL and LF, February 1, 1934, *The Letters of Alexander Woollcott,* 128–31.
"You see—until": GR to the Lunts, Sandhills, Witley, Surrey [April 1934]. A flurry of letters back and forth initiated their friendship. GR had a house in Kensington; they visited him there, but chiefly at Sandhills, with its accompanying house, Redlands, which GR rented. GR had felt that *Reunion in Vienna* would fail in London because RS was hardly known in England.
"I don't wonder": GR to Kerrison Preston, February 5, 1934.

135 "You gave me": AL to GR, June 20, 1934.
"We are mad": LF to AW, September 17, 1934.
"shy and sweet": LF to AW, London, March 31, 1934.

136 "our greatest joy": AL to AW, March 29, 1934.
"I can't grow": AL to AW, September 29 [1934].
"a divine gait": LF to NC, Genesee Depot, August 30, 1934. LF named the horse David after Alfred (though his second name is often given as Davis) and the Prince of Wales (later King Edward VII).
"I hope to God": AL to NC, Genesee Depot, August 16, 1934. Larry Farrell typed many of AL's letters, as Carolyn Emery did LF's.
"You can emerge": LF to AW [1934].
"It was very sad": AL to AW, New York, Friday [1934].
YOU USED TO: Ethel Barrymore to AL, June 13, 1934.
"The saxophone was": AL to AW, September 29 [1934].

137 "When I played": MZ, *Stagestruck,* 201.
"Alfred had rehearsed": LF to NC, May 19, 1949, after reading Coward's autobiography *Present Indicative:* "I took umbrage . . ."

"The play got panned": AL to LL, January 20, 1935.

138 "You are the first": JB, *The Fabulous Lunts,* 219.

"was neither big": NC, *Future Indefinite,* 327.

"I wish Bob": AL to GR, July 19 [1935].

"a lovely idea": AL to GR, July 19 [1935].

139 "one of the hollowest" . . . "Personally": "Theatre Letter," *University,* July 1933.

140 "a fairy-tale quality": LF to GR, November 11, 1935.

141 "Pots and pans": AL to AW, July 31, 1935.

143 "Petruchio suddenly collapsed": G. B. Stern, . . . *And Did He Stop and Speak to You?,* 77.

"She is not written": "The Actor Attacks His Part," *Theatre Arts Monthly,* November 1936.

"with a shrew": John Anderson, *Evening Journal,* November 1, 1936.

145 "I can learn" . . . "a neat little": AL to NC, Wednesday, September 11 [1937]. AL delayed telling NC about joining the board, unsure of his new partner's reaction; finally sent a brief cable. NC's answering cable was "too long"; AL reassured NC that he was free to leave the board if serving interfered with Transatlantic Productions.

"a trenchant silence": LF to GR, New York City, November 11, 1935. AW adored the cape, had a hat made to go with it. "It has changed the darling into a sinister foreign gentleman with great hidden sources of fascination," LF told GR, March 11, 1936.

146 "the old flapdoodle": AL to RS, quoted in John Mason Brown, *The Worlds of Robert Sherwood,* 325.

"passionately anti-war": LF to GR, March 11, 1936.

CHAPTER NINE • *IDIOT'S DELIGHT* AND
AMPHITRYON: 1936-1938

147 "Oh dear, now": LF to GR, October 14, 1935.

"You could put us": AL to RS, quoted in John Mason Brown, *The Worlds of Robert Sherwood,* 325.

148 "I never play": Morton Eustis, "The Actor Attacks His Part," *Theatre Arts Monthly,* November 1936. AL spent an hour before each performance slicking his hair and face with grease to get the Harry Van effect. "Perhaps it's foolish. I could go out with hardly any make-up and get away with it. But it wouldn't be the same thing."

"forced bravado" . . . "the look you see": John Mason Brown, *The Worlds of Robert Sherwood,* 325.

"sort of average-looking": Milton Berle, *Milton Berle,* 205–6.

149 "I like it better": LF to GR, Washington, March 11, 1936.

"like lying on": LF to GR, April 4, 1936.

"Now let's try it": Richard Whorf to Elliot Norton, reported to MP in a telephone interview of November 30, 2000. Whorf was a fellow Bostonian and knew Norton well.

150 "He irritated me": LF to George Schaefer, *The Lunts: A Life in the Theater,* PBS, March 7, 1980.

"Lynn Fontanne was": MP telephone interview with Elliot Norton, November 30, 2000.

151 "Oh, shit": John F. Wharton, *Life Among the Playwrights,* 17.

"We will not give": quoted in JB, *The Fabulous Lunts,* 234.

"We gave a performance": LF to GR, Washington, March 11, 1936. The *Washington Post* singled out British-born Sydney Greenstreet, a cast member "whose local performances always have betrayed such perfected artistry, so complete a command of both comedy and the serious aspects of drama and so persuasive a quality of personal charm that it seems fitting to celebrate him briefly in these Sabbath remarks."

"The Great Flood": GR to Kerrison Preston, *Letters from Graham Robertson,* 351.

152 "Theater is more": AL quoted in the *Boston American,* Monday, November 16, 1936.

"howls and insults": LF to GR, April 4, 1936.

153 "un-American": Clayton Hamilton, a longtime Pulitzer juror, quoted in the *World-Telegram* of May 5, 1936.

"Dear Bob": AL to RS [May 1936].

154 "Each piece" . . . "and why not": LF to GR, April 4, 1936.

"the orchestra playing" . . . "Why would anyone": quoted in Julie Gilbert, *Ferber,* 367, 272.

"Goddam kidney" . . . "my face does grow": AL to AW, Tuesday [summer 1936] and July 20 [1936].

"half orgy, half": S. N. Behrman to AW, n.d.

"I do hope" . . . "People who came": AL to RS, September 2, 1936. Sherwood objected that making Irene a Cockney would not work naturally. Lynn differed and wrote the following scene:

IRENE: I suppose many people in Paris are now being killed.

WEBER: I suppose so, unless the Italians bungle it.

IRENE: Perhaps your sister, Madame d'Hilaire, and her darling little children, ils sont tous morts.

WEBER: I wish you wouldn't speak French, Irene. Your Russian is bad enough.

IRENE: [*in broad Cockney*]: And my Cockney is the worst of all; both for your sake and for mine, perhaps I had better not talk at all.

WEBER: For you, Irene, that would be impossible.

IRENE: I could sing. [*Singing like a street singer*] If those lips could only speak, and those eyes could only see, and those beautiful golden tresses [*shaking her blonde hair*]—

WEBER: [*All through this song is saying to Irene reprimandingly until he rises to a last loud*] Irene!

LF to RS, September 1, 1936. Not a bad scene ("Alfred thinks my writing is tremendously in your own vein"), and it gave Lynn a chance to sing one of the

Cockney street songs she loved; but RS did not use it in the published *Idiot's Delight.*

"the actor is not": "The Actor Attacks His Part," *Theatre Arts Monthly,* November 1936.

155 "People who came": AL to RS, September 2, 1936.

"*Family Album,* delightful": LF to GR, October 15–November 22, 1936. Uncommonly direct, LF wrote NC frankly that she disliked the first play, *We Were Dancing:* "I am certain that when you read it again you will hate it and very probably replace it, and I hope you do." Philadelphia, September 15 [1936].

"I have often wondered": Peter Daubeny, *Stage by Stage,* 53.

156 "I am inarticulate": reported by Ashton Stevens, *Chicago American,* April 15, 1937. AL and LF suffered acute moments of stage fright offstage. That Christmas, 1936, they tried five times to record on a phonograph disc their major scene from *Idiot's Delight* for GR but got into "such a cold sweat of nerves and fright that we couldn't get through it." LF to GR, February 2, 1937.

"If you play": adapted from a letter from AW to Gustav Eckstein, May 19, 1937.

157 "I saw *Sappho*": front-page story in the *Omaha World-Herald,* May 18, 1937.

"You couldn't be": S. N. Behrman, *People in a Diary,* 91.

"to impel the dramatist": Donald Inskip quoting Giraudoux in *Jean Giraudoux,* 117.

158 "Ladies and gentlemen": George Freedley, *The Lunts,* 72.

159 "Oh, yes, it's the best": quoted by S. N. Behrman, *People in a Diary,* 92.

"the tiniest capillary": S. N. Behrman, *People in a Diary,* 91.

"All right, let's" (and following): "A Play in the Making," *Theatre Arts Monthly,* December 1937.

160 "It was a brilliant": LF to NC, November 11, 1937.

161 "spirited Aphrodisiantics": *Time,* November 8, 1937.

"an enchanting and iridescent": AW to GR, March 1938.

"all charm, gentle": LF to NC, November 11, 1937.

"possibly more satisfying": Donald Inskip, *Jean Giraudoux,* 161.

"the matchless Lunts" . . . "Lynn Fontanne and": Elaine Barrie, *All My Sins Remembered,* 218.

162 "one obvious Lunt-Fontanne": LF to NC, October 22, 1939.

"I think that if": AL to Charles Dornbusch, November 19, 1937.

CHAPTER TEN • SEARCHING: 1938-1940

164 "Why should all": AL quoting Thomas Gomez and commenting himself in a letter to Robert Downing, Ten Chimneys, May 17, 1974.

"I have never seen": AW to GR, March 1938.

166 "Our souls get stronger": AL to LL, n.d.

"Today is the Great": quoted in *Letters from Graham Robertson,* 390. GR's further comments in this chapter on the first night of *Amphitryon,* NC, and the Lunts are from the same source, 355–401.

167 "Bravo! Speech!": LF to AW, London, June 23, 1938.

"Miss Fontanne acts": "Mr. and Mrs. Lunt in London," unidentified article used for publicity for the run of *Amphitryon* at the Pabst Theatre, Milwaukee, week of March 27, 1939.

169 "I really don't care": LF to Lady Sibyl Colefax, New York, March 7, 1947.

"a sandwich and a seat": LF to AW, London, June 23, 1938.

"This may sound bizarre": AW to GR, March 1938.

"You are fond": GR reminiscing in a letter to Kerrison Preston, August 28, 1941, *Letters of Graham Robertson,* 467.

170 "much too exciting": AL to Warren Munsell, Hango, Finland, August 1, 1938. The Guild constantly sent LF and AL new scripts; they searched for them as well.

"What shall we do" . . . "or there was hell" . . . "all cottony" . . . "I don't have to": Donald Buka to MP in telephone interview, March 25, 2001.

171 "No mother could": LL, *The Magic Curtain,* 395.

"Hattie doesn't bother": LF to AW, October 13, 1938.

"We sat around": THG interview with Copeland Greene, nephew of John Greene, Louise's husband, July 9, 1998.

"completely foul": AW to LF, August 2, 1939.

"a tragic topic": LF quoting Karin Bugbee in a letter to Karin, August 13, 1941.

172 "[Your family] have": Ben Perkins to AL, n.d., a three-page, single-spaced letter to Alfred about the tensions among his family and staff: "I am sad and unhappy."

"sang Christmas carols": LF to AW, January 18, 1939.

"discoursing beautifully": LF to AW, December 31, 1938.

173 "I love Genesee": Gustav Eckstein to LF, College of Medicine, University of Cincinnati [1938–1939?]. Eckstein came often for Christmas. Harpo Marx suggests his popularity when he wrote AW on July 7, 1939: "My idea of a perfect [Neshobe] island: Alice [Duer Miller], the Kaufmans, Neysa, Eckstein, [Charles] Lederer, your boyfriend from Washington [Jo Hennessey] and the [Howard] Dietzes."

"Alfred and I": LF to Tottie Harwood, Oakland, California, November 27, 1939.

"I have read": AL to LL, Los Angeles, December 12, 1939.

"A producer always" . . . "I've been seducing you": quoted from MZ, *Stagestruck,* 202. Howard Lindsay himself and his wife, Dorothy Stickney, played the leads in the original production.

174 "Lynn, you would make": quoted from MZ, *Stagestruck,* 202, though mistakenly calling the part LF refused "Miss Prism," a character in *The Importance of Being Earnest.*

"Well to hell": LF to AW, Washington, November 7, 1938.

"used to be entirely": GR quoting Behrman and LF in a letter to Kerrison Preston, December 12, 1929, in *Letters from Graham Robertson,* 422–23. He adds: "That she has only been playing it 'right' for five or six performances after playing it wrong for two years won't worry her at all." Robert Sherwood always considered it Alfred's play. "I'm very fond of Ray and he's a fine actor," he said when Raymond Massey was going to bring *Idiot's Delight* to London, "but I don't want to see anyone but Alfred as Harry Van." *Letters from Graham Robertson,* 380.

"You have never seen": AL quoted in Morton Eustis, "Lunts in Dixieland," *Town and Country,* August 1939. Eustis was killed in France in World War II. "We saw him always when he had leave here," AL wrote HS in 1944 from London. "Such a good friend, he was."

"drenched alternately": This and the following quotes are from Eustis, "Lunts in Dixieland," *Town and Country,* August 1939.

175 "Jo wants to marry": MP interview with James Auer, arts critic for the *Milwaukee Journal-Sentinel,* and a friend of the Hagens.

"promising" . . . "in love or some God damn": LF to AW, January 18, 1939.

176 "Prettiest kitchen": AL to AW, *Aquitania,* August 14 [1938].

"Alfred was hands on" . . . "something different": John Hale to MP, June 13, 1998.

177 "we adore it": AL to AW [spring 1939].

"And if you see": Kurt Weill to Lotte Lenya, Lys Symonette and Kurt Kowalke, editors and translators, *Speak Low: The Letters of Kurt Weill and Lotte Lenya,* 337.

"A wonderful night's": Edna Ferber's diary, quoted in Julie Gilbert, *Ferber: A Biography,* 319.

"that certain Genesee quoi": my husband Peter Jordan's felicitous pun.

178 "Well, bake, dig": S. N. Behrman to AL, September 17, 1939.

179 "The more I think": AW to AL, June 6, 1939.

"Well, my darlings": the story of NC's phone call and the Lunts locking the Studio comes from Christine Plichta, docent at Ten Chimneys. Almost four years later, on April 23, 1943, LF writes to Karin Bugbee, "The only thing I regret deeply, but of course it cannot be helped, is the studio. But we will have the gramophone in the little house, I expect, and can hold our family parties there." A less dramatic explanation for the locked studio is James Gray's: "When Ben needed more room for his hay, Alfred Lunt gave up his studio, had the piano moved to the house and his miniature theaters packed away": "Ten Chimneys," *Pine, Stream and Prairie,* 308.

181 "whoopsing across the country": LF to NC, Omaha, October 22, 1939.

"Ladies and gentlemen": quoted in JB, *The Fabulous Lunts,* 273, based on the account of William Le Massena, who, with persistence, won the part of the Pedant.

"It was a night": Louise Marston, *Wisconsin State Journal,* October 10, 1939. The Lunts performed October 9, 10, and a matinee and evening performance on the 11th. For this tour Harry Wagstaff Gribble directed; Claggett Wilson did production and costumes; Carolyn Hancock, settings.

182 "by far the most": "The Lunts and the Theatre Guild," a press release in the Beinecke Library's collection of Lunt-Fontanne–Theatre Guild papers, Yale University.

"assembled casts that few": Guthrie McClintic, *Me and Kit,* 315.

"Alfred, it's so dear": Donald Buka to MP in telephone interview, March 25, 2001.

183 "The blaze of excitement": LF to GR, quoted in a letter to Kerrison Preston, March 23, 1940, in *Letters from Graham Robertson,* 435.

"suitors caught bringing": John Mason Brown, *The Ordeal of a Playwright,* 65.

CHAPTER ELEVEN • *THERE SHALL BE NO NIGHT: 1940–1942*

185 "Donald, I don't": Donald Buka to MP, telephone interview, March 25, 2001.

186 "Look what the wind": Mrs. John Steinbeck, present at the audition, remembers AL's exclamation, quoted in Patricia Bosworth, *Montgomery Clift,* 76.

"That's the boy": cited in Robert La Guardia, *Monty,* 32.

187 "Don't work for money" . . . "Noël Coward" . . . "Alfred taught me": *Montgomery Clift,* 79, 84. Bosworth's biography is unfortunately without sources; yet given Alfred's paternal feelings for Clift, the warning seems in keeping.

"very sloppy": quoted in John Mason Brown, *The Ordeal of a Playwright,* 67.

"something more": John Wharton, *Life Among the Playwrights,* 91–92.

"exquisitely": John Mason Brown, *The Ordeal of a Playwright,* 67.

188 "sweet, dear": LF to AW, May 13, 1940.

"She tactfully shooed": AW to GR, November 20, 1940, in *The Letters of Alexander Woollcott:* 261–62.

190 "never been so happy": telegram from AL to AW, April 7, 1940.

"It is with considerable": AL to Theresa Helburn and LL, May 25, 1940, but not sent until June 4.

191 "You can take it": Howard Teichmann, *Smart Aleck,* 269.

"The Lunts will occupy": n.d., quoted from *Smart Aleck,* 179. The original members of the island-owning club were Woollcott, Alice Duer Miller, Beatrice Kaufman, Ruth Gordon, Neysa McMein, Harold Guinzburg, George Backer, Raoul Fleischmann, Howard Dietz, and Ray Ives. Memberships were bought and sold but never numbered more than ten.

"morose gaiety": AW to AL, July 21, 1942.

"I like her": LF to AW, July 31, 1940. Dinah Sheean was the daughter of the actress Gertrude Elliott and niece of the more famous Maxine Elliott. Bringing over the Redgraves involved signing papers of sponsorship but not financially supporting the family.

192 "as though I were" . . . "important not only": Edna Ferber to AL and LF, September 18, 1940.

"I reject most": Edna Ferber to AL, September 21, 1940.

"That horrible, horrible Lindbergh": LF to LL, April 24, 1941. Kathleen Norris, a currently popular novelist.

"if there is a troupe": AW to GR, November 20, 1940, in *The Letters of Alexander Woollcott,* 261–62.

193 "notoriously anti-war": AL to RS, December 27, 1940.

"First of all": LF to RS, Genesee Depot, May 31, 1941.

194 "rather amusing, considering": LF quoted by GR to Kerrison Preston, June 13, 1941, *Letters from Graham Robertson,* 462–63.

"[Franchot] Tone would be": AL to Maxwell Anderson in a series of letters from May to September 1941 dated chiefly by day of the week, first from Genesee Depot, then, after July 21, from 130 East Seventy-fifth Street, New York.

195 "wearing crepe": LF to AW, August 20, 1941.

"That man doesn't": John Wharton, *Life Among the Playwrights,* 119.

"Lynn could always": Theresa Helburn, "Temperaments—Actors vs. Authors," June 4, 1956, notes for *A Wayward Quest* in the Theatre Guild papers.

"nervous as a cat": LF to GR, September 8, 1941.

196 "flopped and the awful": LF to NC, Richmond, Virginia, October 25, 1941.

"They certainly left me": AL to John C. Wilson, Richmond, Virginia, October 25, 1941.

"I thought possibly": AL to LL, Durham, North Carolina, October 28, 1941. In response, LL assured AL that his direction was not at fault: "Nobody seems to blame the production, the acting or the scenery, but places it squarely on the play itself."

"What else can Finland": AL to Maxwell Anderson, letter fragment [1942].

197 "has been the greatest": AL to Theresa Helburn, Wichita, Kansas, December 12, 1941.

"Alfred is blissful": LF to GR, Genesee Depot, January 12, 1942.

"Your mother is": Ben Perkins to AL, November 25, 1941.

"I think it": LF to GR, Genesee Depot, January 12, 1942.

198 "We want to do": LF to NC, August 19, 1941.

CHAPTER TWELVE • A VERY GOOD WAR: 1942-1945

199 "They have nothing" . . . "He is really": Lotte Lenya to Kurt Weill, [March 13, 1941], *Speak Low,* 311.

200 "chief cook": AW to AL, May 26, 1942.

"my pride and joy": LF to AW, April 24, 1942.

"There are many" . . . "The perfectly poached": from AL's unpublished cookbook at Ten Chimneys. One of his students was his sister Karin Sederholm Bugbee, a talented and perfectionist cook.

201 "First it's an interesting": Lotte Lenya to Kurt Weill, [April 10, 1942], *Speak Low,* 321.

"No, no, she wouldn't": Kurt Weill to Lotte Lenya, [April 5 1942], *Speak Low,* 317.

"The Lunts are awful fakers": Kurt Weill to Lotte Lenya, [April 13, 1942], *Speak Low,* 325. Weill and Lenya enjoyed exploiting any professional jealousy between Helen Hayes and the Lunts, Weill noting with satisfaction that Alfred quickly changed the subject when told how wonderful Hayes's recent recordings were.

"[Sam] has finished rewriting": Kurt Weill to Lotte Lenya, [April 30, 1942], *Speak Low,* 243. Lenya retaliated with further insults: the Lunts were scared, jealous, untrustworthy, "two old Possart"—poseurs.

"Berrie should know": LF to Kurt Weill, n.d., Lyceum Theatre, Minneapolis.

202 "But he warned me" . . . "that female impersonator": Kurt Weill to Lotte Lenya, [May 15, 1942], *Speak Low,* 354.

"We wanted Kurt Weill": LF to AW, May 1942.

"is a genius": Ruth Gordon to AW, "Home," Friday [n.d.].

"I hate to see": LF to GR, NYC, December 10, 1942. Robert Downing also had left and William Le Massena would be drafted mid-tour.

"He is really brilliant": LF to GR, New York, December 10, 1942.

203 "divine colored people": LF to AW, September 15, 1942.

203 "a very dull girl": LF to GR, New York, December 10, 1942.

"mostly over Behrman's": LF to NC, New York, December 8, 1942.

"I get more": Charles Laughlin, *J. Scott Smart,* 23.

"a soft, kind" . . . "though that part": LF to GR, New York, December 10, 1942.

"I shall never" . . . "like a skin-tight": GR quoting Hamish Hamilton in a letter to Kerrison Preston, September 21, 1942, *Letters from Graham Robertson,* 493.

204 "Jack has become": LF to NC, NYC, December 8, 1942.

"our strange disturbing": LF to AW, July 13, 1942.

"a passionate defender": Lloyd Paul Stryker, attorney and a classmate of AW's at Hamilton, quoted in *Smart Aleck,* 315.

"our dreadful loss": Telegram from LF to Sibyl Colefax, January 27, 1943.

"I feel . . . as if": LF to NC, New York, December 8, 1942.

205 "shaken up like": AL to HS, London, June 18, 1944.

"bounced out of bed": LF to Karin Bugbee, January 6, 1941.

206 "It's something we've": AL to HS, Hotel St. Regis, New York, September 8, 1943.

"all arse": AL to to "Darlings" (Karin & George?), April 24, 1944. The Lunts sub-let their apartment at 130 East Seventy-fifth Street to the consul from Brazil and his wife and had to vacate September 1. They stayed at the St. Regis while waiting ("booted and spurred") for passport clearance and travel permits, amusing themselves by buying antiques to furnish Karin and George Bugbee's new apartment in Chicago, where George now worked in hospital administration. They sent their current maids, Alma and Lotte, to help Hattie at Genesee; Jules evidently stayed in New York. (JB says he was in Genesee.) Alfred sent George Bugbee $12,000 to be used at his discretion for Ten Chimneys in their absence. He worried till the last moment that something would stop their going. "If we are prevented from leaving these shores," he wrote RS in dead earnest, "I shall become a cook! In the Merchant Seaman canteen, I learned yesterday that a school has opened for training ships cooks, a four week's course. . . ." [August 1943].

"a very old New England" . . . "an enchanting city": AL to HS, Lisbon, September 23 {1943}.

"a wonderful boy" . . . "so like Sydney": LF to RS and MS, Savoy Hotel, London, October 11, 1943.

"Would you like": Muriel Pahlow to MP, January 19, 2001.

207 "We saw the searchlights": LF to RS and MS, Savoy Hotel, London, October 11, 1943.

"not silly any more": LF to Karin Bugbee, London, January 10, 1944. Karin and George sent the Lunts endless packages during the war at their request: tea ("for God's sake lots"), jams and jellies, pâté, Bisquick, slippers, Elizabeth Arden face powder, adhesive tape, Lextron and Multicebrin pills, socks, professional eyebrow pencil, stockings, etc.

"Personally I'd rather": LF to HS, London, October 10, 1943.

"We had a delightful": GR to Kerrison Preston, October 15, 1943, *Letters from Graham Robertson,* 506.

"a tremendous success": LF to GR, November 14, 1943.

208 "And the W.C.": AL to "Dearest All," Edinburgh, November 25, 1943.

"thrilling for us": AL to HS, Savoy Hotel, London, December 19, 1943.

"It was the most amazing": quoted in Richard Huggett, *Binkie Beaumont,* 314.

"seemed to weep": AL and LF quoted in Lloyd Lewis, "With the Lunts It's Time for Comedy," *New York Times Magazine,* November 11, 1943.

209 "Alfred was so overcome": LF interviewed by Bunny Raasch, Milwaukee Channel 12, WISN, July 30, 1981.

"A buzz bomb hit": Clifton Daniel, "With the Lunts on the (Buzz-Bombed) Road," *New York Times Magazine,* February 4, 1945.

"Now you'll know": quoted in Richard Huggett, *Binkie Beaumont,* 315.

210 "We were afraid": Clifton Daniel, "With the Lunts on the (Buzz-Bombed) Road," *New York Times Magazine,* February 4, 1945.

"There is something": AL to HS, April 24, 1944.

"We are much safer": AL to HS, April 7, 1944.

211 "seen and worshiped": Laurence Olivier, *Confessions of an Actor,* 110.

"We had a heavenly": AL to HS, Savoy Hotel, London, [April 8?] 1944.

"I had a high old": AL to "Darlings," July 21, 1944.

212 "Oh, Larry and Vivien": John Wharton, *Life Among the Playwrights,* 164.

"It seems incredible": AL to HS, June 8, 1944.

"a boon and a blessing": quoted by GR to Kerrison Preston, August 25, 1944, *Letters from Graham Robertson,* 513.

213 "superb picture": AL to George Bugbee, July 3, 1944.

"One or two": AL to George Bugbee, Maidenhead, July 3, 1944.

"I hope they": AL to HS, Maidenhead, July 25, 1944.

"Sometimes Lynn has" . . . "I didn't realize": quoted in Geoffrey Wansell, *Terence Rattigan,* 142.

214 "Alfred's way of rehearsing": Geoffrey Wansell, *Terence Rattigan,* 143.

"must be acted": AL to GR, Manchester, August 17, 1944.

"with his patriotic": Geoffrey Wansell, *Terence Rattigan,* 144.

215 "Lynn's performance is": AL to Theresa Helburn, Savoy Hotel, London, April 19, 1945.

"My god but": AL to George Bugbee, Liverpool, November 30, 1944.

"gave the impression": Peter Daubeny, *My World of the Theatre,* 41.

216 "I did the whole": AL to HS, Lyric Theatre, London, April 2, 1945.

"my great gift": AL to HS, March 12, 1945.

"That night all": LF to GR, Lyric Theatre, May 11, 1945.

217 "If it's true": interview with Beverly Nichols, *Sunday Chronicle,* December 31, 1944.

218 "If you can": AL quoted in Richard Huggett, *Binkie Beaumont,* 319. They played *Love in Idleness* in Paris (staying at the Hotel Ritz) from June 24 to July 10; then left for Bad Kissingen, where they played for the Ninth Air Force, then to Kassel, then Bayreuth—six weeks in all. As AL reported to HS, there were loads of old friends about—Laurence Olivier, Bob Hope, Beatrice Lillie, Marlene Dietrich, Jack Benny. Binkie Beaumont thought the Lunts were competitively inspired to entertain the troops when Katharine Cornell and her company passed through London in 1944, triumphant with their success playing the "Foxhole Circuit."

CHAPTER THIRTEEN • COMFY LAURELS: 1946-1951

219 "Sitting in a theater": Dan H. Laurence to MP, April 15, 2000.

221 "that peculiar alternation": *The New Yorker,* February 2, 1946.

"A cat could not": John Mason Brown, "Reunion in New York," *Saturday Review of Literature,* February 16, 1946.

"was a far better": LL, *The Magic Curtain,* 394.

222 "Do you think": Ward Morehouse, a friend as well as a Broadway critic, interviewed AL and LF for the *Evening Standard,* June 23, 1945.

"Needless to say": LL to AL and LF, June 14, 1945.

"downright stupidity": LF to AW, Los Angeles, February 27, 1941.

"We are just": LF to GR, New York, March 23, 1946.

"Why were you": AL to NC, New York, October 15, 1946.

223 "everybody got rather drunk": LF to Juliet Duff, January 5, 1946.

"My weekend at Genesee": Terence Rattigan to AL and LF, June 4, 1946. AL and LF had passed on to Terence Rattigan as an idea for a play a clipping from an American newspaper about a midshipman at a naval training school threatened with expulsion because of stealing. Rattigan used the idea: *The Winslow Boy* became his greatest success. In this same letter Rattigan says that Paulette Goddard almost stole the show with a brilliant tiara, that he thought the play a failure and went out for "four enormous zonks," returned to find *The Winslow Boy* a success. Now business "almost up to *Love in Idleness.*"

"more trouble than": LF to Molly Humphrey, May 14, 1946.

DEAR LITTLE GRAY HAIRED: quoted in a letter from AL to RS, May 5, 1948, typical of the genre "done with the deepest satire on both our parts."

224 "Sound your horn": Peter Daubeny's delightful account of visiting Genesee Depot in 1946 in *Stage by Stage,* 56–62.

225 "Certainly Rattigan had": Howard Barnes, *New York Herald Tribune,* February 3, 1946.

"the best actors": Dick Van Patten to Michael H. Drew, *Milwaukee Journal,* quoted to THG, May 25, 1999.

"the child is killing" . . . "fatter and oh": LF to GR, NY, July 8, 1946.

"Alfred is blissful": LF to "Darling" [Karin Bugbee], Empire Theatre, February 9, 1946. The Swedish cook didn't last long: "We kicked her out. She was a beast," LF told Vivien Leigh November 25, 1946. Their new cook was "a lovely, large colored lady named Johanna, whose father was a French chef."

"A.L. has the nicest": Joyce Grenfell to Virginia Graham, June 21, 1946, *Joyce and Ginnie,* 145.

226 "Whenever he hears": LF to GR, Savoy Hotel, n.d. [1944?].

"I worked my Goddam": AL to RS, December 26, 1946.

227 "Why I'm doing it": "A. Lunt, Impresario," *Cue,* December 21, 1946. The exhibit ran from December 17, 1946, until March 1947 and included costume plates, uncut theater sheets, and drawings for the theater by artists such as William Blake and the Cruikshanks. AL shared his passion for miniature theaters with Charles Dickens, Robert Louis Stevenson, Bernard Shaw, and John Gielgud. His collection was reputedly the largest in the world.

227 "I hate music!": John Gielgud quoting LF to MP, January 7, 1997.

"Poor darling": LF to Lady Sibyl Colefax, New York, March 7, 1947.

"I designed both": LF to Sibyl Colefax, New York, March 7, 1947.

"thin as a pencil": LF to Antoinette Keith, March 10, 1947.

"escaped from Dachau": LF to Vivien Leigh, February 8, 1947.

228 "modest, gay, witty": John Mason Brown to LF, May 5, 1947. "I was overjoyed to have Robeson there," wrote JMB. "He made it magnificently American."

"nothing short of stunning": LF to Binkie Beaumont, April 4, 1947. With separate financial accounts, AL and LF had been investing for years, chiefly in E bonds. They also invested in theater productions. There were hard feelings when the Guild, considering *Oklahoma!* a risk, refused to let them invest in what was an immediate smash hit. In April 1947, the Guild allowed LF to invest in two percent of the British rights to *Oklahoma!,* particularly since the Guild had made a considerable profit from *O Mistress Mine.* "We feel that [allowing LF to invest] will greatly strengthen our relationship with the Lunts," said LL.

"I have just discovered": LF to Antoinette Keith [1947]. Antoinette had married Thomas Neville Keith, but her marital status is uncertain. In 1946 she had "two miserable rooms" at 2 Derby Street, Mayfair (LF to Sophie King, September 3, 1946).

"no story, no situations": LF to RS, June 1947.

"you concentrate on": John Wharton quoting RS in *Life Among the Playwrights,* 163.

"I can only tell you": AL to RS, Ten Chimneys, August 2, 1947.

229 "terribly happy" . . . "He and she": LF to GR, Ten Chimneys, August 2, 1947.

"I should have": quoted in Jonathan Croall, *Gielgud,* 335.

"It's been a perfectly": AL to LL and Armina Marshall, Geary Theatre, San Francisco, April 28, 1948. According to AL, his illness began with a Virus X bug that quickly went to his kidney. As a testimony to the Lunts' enormous popularity, the Lunt-Fontanne Collection has letters from managers all over the country begging them not to cancel and financially ruin their theater seasons.

230 "I hate Brecht": Michael H. Drew, "Fabulous Lunts and Their Friends Find Tranquility at Ten Chimneys," *Milwaukee Journal,* February 20, 1967.

"We had read your play": LF to S. N. Behrman, March 31, 1948.

231 "Alfred is very, very": LF to S. N. Behrman, May 20, 1948.

"If their whole-hearted": NC, *Present Indicative,* 175.

"resent our completeness": LL to AL and LF, April 29, 1949, quoting LF's remark to him apropos Coward.

"is anxious over": AL to S. N. Behrman, Ten Chimneys, November 3, 1948.

"He was so beautiful": quoted in JB, *The Fabulous Lunts,* 327.

232 "at the end": LF to Lady Juliet Duff, March 1949.

"a screaming hysteric": LF to Roger Quilter, December 13, 1946.

"I'm quite capable": AL to RS [Chicago, circa March 15, 1949].

233 "We have rehearsed": AL to LL, Geary Theater, San Francisco, May 4, 1949.

"Everyone feels depression": LL to AL and LF, August 4, 1949. A separate financial drain was the $200-a-week salary of the British actor Geoffrey Kerr, playing Alfred's brother, Frederic Chanler. When LF was negotiating with Binkie

Beaumont in the spring of 1950 to bring *I Know My Love* to London, Beaumont stressed that he was looking for a new play for the Lunts with a small cast.

"I am very depressed": AL to LL, Mayfair Theatre, Portland, Oregon, May 13, 1949.

"It would definitely": Dr. Edward Bigg to LL, July 5, 1949. On July 14, Dr. Bigg drafted a more convincing letter, arguing that AL had been under "medical management" throughout the tour.

234 "No one needs": John Mason Brown, *Saturday Review,* December 3, 1949.

235 WILL YOU MARRY: AL and LF to John Mason Brown, November 30, 1949.

"I asked God": LF to Hugh Beaumont, New York, February 16, 1950.

"chock full": LF to Hugh Beaumont, December 12, 1949.

"The top room": LF to NC, Shubert Theatre, NYC, May 1, 1950.

236 "all changes in": LF to Antoinette Keith [1950].

"gave a high": LF to Antoinette Keith, Toronto, November 13, 1950.

"Brave little woman": quoted by Gaye Jordan, telephone interview with MP, May 15, 2001.

"He is very cross": LF to NC, New Nixon Theatre, Pittsburgh, November 21, 1950.

"Iron woman": Edna Ferber to AL and LF, July 8, 1951.

"I find Lynn's behavior": AL in a joint letter to Victor Wittgenstein, Antoinette Keith, John Wilson, Karin Bugbee, Hattie Sederholm, Theresa Helburn, Lawrence Langner, Hugh Beaumont, Ashton Stevens, and Edward Molyneux, Montreal, Quebec, November 6, 1950.

237 "stunned and brought": LF to NC, Erlanger Theatre, Buffalo, New York, March 27, 1951.

"We have never": LF to Winifred Ashton (Clemence Dane), Philadelphia, February 17, 1951.

CHAPTER FOURTEEN • THE MET—NOËL ENCORE—*ONDINE:*
1951-1957

238 "taste and elegance": Rudolf Bing to AL at the Statler Hotel, Buffalo, New York, March 23, 1951.

"I think we should": AL to Rudolf Bing, Buffalo, New York, March 28, 1951.

239 "I shall be doing": LF to Bessie Porter, February 6, 1951. Beaumont's chief objection seemed to be to *I Know My Love*'s large cast, or so he said, promising at the same time to look for an "entrancing" new play for them with fewer actors. Quite probably LF's demand that actors like Glenn Anders and Jules Johnson, AL's valet, be imported turned off Beaumont. LF had seriously been counting on a London production.

"sit down at once": LF to Terence Rattigan, April 4, 1947.

"We have no": LF to NC, January 13, 1951.

"sonny boy comes": LF to NC, March 27, 1951.

"childish mistake": AL to Laurence Olivier, August 1951.

"That Mr. Bing" . . . "mirrored treasure-house": Ward Morehouse, "The Lunts of Gracie Square," *New York World Telegram,* October 19, 1951.

240 "If you beat" . . . "When you eat": Howard Taubman, "Inescapable Stamp of the Lunt Style," *New York Times Magazine,* January 27, 1952.

"a sort of celestial": quoted in JB, *The Fabulous Lunts,* 379.

"Never has 'Despina' ": quoted in JB, *The Fabulous Lunts,* 380.

"God help me": LF to NC, New York, December 14, 1951.

242 "Son, This violet": AL to NC, New York, January 6, 1952.

"Alfred's opera is": LF to HS [late December 1951 or early 1952]. That season's final performance of AL's *Così fan tutte* took place on February 9, 1952. NC saw *Così fan tutte* that night: "Alfred's production brilliant but I hate Mozart and I loathed the libretto": *Diaries,* 189.

"his damn old *Così*": LF to NC, New York, December 15, 1951.

"Oh dear, dear": LF to NC, New York, December 15, 1951.

"When do WE": a paraphrase of LF's "when *were* we to come on" to NC, Ten Chimneys, n.d. [but summer 1954, before the New York opening of *Quadrille*]. But as LF said, they had objections from the beginning: "When you first read the play—we both felt there was something wrong with the first scene." NC had no idea of their objection, reporting them ecstatic, grateful, and sweet.

"the food was" . . . "Vivien draped": Philip Hoare, *Noël Coward: A Biography,* 397, 399.

"it will be a lot": quoted in Sheridan Morley, *Noël: A Talent to Amuse,* 356.

243 "I can tell you exactly": AL to NC, New York, April 3, 1952.

"over which we now sprinkle": AL to HS, London, December 2, 1952.

244 "Alfred was the only" . . . "Just think, Larry": quoted from Thomas Kiernan, *Sir Larry,* 80, 79.

"Blunting his iron": Kenneth Tynan, *Curtains,* 10.

245 "so tired and inarticulate": AL to RS, March 23, 1953.

"Sweet Vivien": Laurence Olivier to "Our darling Lynnie," Italy, n.d. [1953]. Olivier discusses his filmed *Hamlet*—soon he'll be boring about 200 million people; Ralph Richardson is still "banging away"; their new "whitest hope" is Alec Guinness in *Richard II.* He says that he and Vivien hope to live up to Lunt and Fontanne, "but we can't feel quite ready for that just yet."

"They are *great*": NC, *Diaries,* 193.

"How is it" . . . "a distinguished pile of manure": Cecil Beaton, "Diary of a Designer," *Theatre Arts,* November 1954, 95.

"Darling, what about": quoted from Cecil Beaton, *Self Portrait with Friends,* 248.

"endless curtain calls": AL to HS, Manchester, July 18, 1952.

"from heaven": AL to HS, Edinburgh, August 1, 1952. The Lunts called many audiences "the best in the world," but San Francisco and Edinburgh share the prize as the cities most mentioned.

246 "I hate to seem": LF to NC, October 25, 1941.

"the two of them": quoted in "The Human Side of the Stars" by Elliot Norton, the Boston theater critic [no source, 1952?].

"like a Mongolian ghost": Beverly Baxter in the London *Sunday Express,* September 14, 1952.

247 "wily and feline" . . . "I wish the Lunts" . . . "was doing great honour": The

description of the Lunts appears in a clipping from an unidentified British magazine, partly included in Cecil Beaton and Kenneth Tynan, *Persona Grata,* 44, 43, the source of "I wish the Lunts."

247 "The first night audience": NC to LF, Venice, August 10 [1954].

"I hated them": NC to LF, Venice, August 10 [1954]. LF did not mind Jones and Spencer as much as Joyce Carey, a close friend of Noël's, acting in *Quadrille.* At one performance a small couch pillow stuck to LF's bustle when she rose, exciting unintended laughter as she walked around the stage throughout the scene. Carey saw it but did nothing. "I will never work with her again," said LF. Nearly two years later the Lunts were still arguing about the opening scene between the Marquis of Heronden and Charlotte Diensen, Alfred urging that the Marquis be clearly in love with Charlotte so that his and Lynn's last scenes would be more effective. Coward correctly argued that the Marquis was in love only with himself.

248 "filled the theatre": AL to HS, 38 Chapel Street, London, December 13 [1952].

249 "Audiences really *scream*": AL to HS, August 21, 1953. The Lunts fell in love with Ireland: "great *hedges* of fuchsias," dogs everywhere, and gorgeous horses. While playing in Dublin they stayed in a cottage outside town and were royally entertained by people like Lady Dufrin and Lady Londonderry.

"It was a fairly": NC, *Diaries,* September 13, 1953, 219.

"They are deeply concerned": NC, *Diaries,* September 17, 1953, 220.

250 "literally been dying": AL to John Mason Brown, Belfast, August 8, 1953.

"exasperated at being old": Gus Eckstein to LF, November 23, 1952.

"goddam cook book": AL to John Mason Brown, August 18, 1951; but AL was still compiling recipes.

"There is nothing": AL to Keith W. Jennison of Henry Holt, February 19, 1946.

"with the devout hope": RS to AL, November 4, 1953.

251 "I'm beginning to find": AL to RS, November 11, 1953. AL rejected Rolf Gérard, who had set *Così,* because his color was inclined to be "dirty."

"We don't mind garlic" . . . "Lunt works us": quoted by MZ in "Alfred Lunt, Director," *Theatre Arts,* April 1954.

252 "She has such a clean": LF to Gay(e) Jordan Elwell, who played Angelique in *Ondine:* telephone interview with MP, May 15, 2001.

"Until this afternoon": Margaret Sullavan to AL, Friday [January 1954]. Sullavan was currently appearing in Rattigan's *The Deep Blue Sea.*

253 "Max has been": RS to LF, February 10, 1954. Anderson now undertook to write a play for the Lunts about an older Elizabeth I. LF gently refused the play: his writing was magnificent but she felt his Elizabeth I was the same character she had played in *Elizabeth the Queen,* only older, and therefore no challenge.

"My experience has": LF to Maxwell Anderson, Ten Chimneys, n.d.

"I am able": Audrey Hepburn to LF, February 24 [1954].

"Did you learn": John Wharton, *Life Among the Playwrights,* 225.

254 "That wasn't jealousy": LF on tapes made by MZ for *Stagestruck,* 1964.

"No critic writing": letter to the *Boston Herald,* February 8, 1954.

255 "*Ondine,* directed by": NC, *Diaries,* March 29, 1954, 233. To date on this New York visit NC had seen seventeen shows.

"The production you shine in": reprinted in Harold Clurman, *Lies Like Truth,* 96.

"All the medals": AL to RS, June 2, 1954.

CHAPTER FIFTEEN • AMERICAN *QUADRILLE* AND
A PAIR OF MIND READERS: 1954-1957

256 "I have racked": NC to "Darling Grandma and Grandpa," June 26, 1954.

"The only outstanding": NC to LF, August 10, 1954.

257 "The only thing": NC to AL, October 25, 1954.

"[*Quadrille*] is very well": NC, *Diaries,* December 1, 1954, 254.

258 "That's wonderful, Donnie": Donald Seawell to MP, January 10, 2002. Seawell tells that when he asked the Lunts to make their wills, they couldn't comprehend that two would be needed, having automatically thought that they would go together.

"You let us know": quoted in JB, *The Fabulous Lunts,* 345.

"a sad blow": NC, *Diaries,* March 10, 1955, 257.

"some infection" . . . "Personally I think": AL to RS, Passavant Hospital, March 24, 1955.

"I'm better, much better": AL to Russel Crouse, Ten Chimneys, April 12, 1955.

"She was a sweet": Ethel Brimmer interviewed by THG for Ten Chimneys, August 26, 1999.

259 "possessed an extraordinarily": RS to AL, June 12, 1955.

"I was conscious": S. N. Behrman to AL, Monte Carlo, June 1, 1955.

"I'm going to burn": George Bugbee to MP, October 17, 1985.

260 "Never in our long" . . . "We are very happy": AL to Howard Lindsay and Russel Crouse, Ten Chimneys, July 20, 1955.

"What would you": Lunt biographer MZ tells the rabbit story about himself arriving at Ten Chimneys (*Milwaukee Sentinel,* June 13, 1979); but others, like Crouse and Sherwood, also claimed to have been welcomed with rabbit.

"Ten Chimneys was all": Russel Crouse to AL and LF, July 11, 1955. "And you have always been more than anyone could dream you to be," he added.

"little words" . . . "If not done": AL to Howard Lindsay and Russel Crouse, September 11, 1955.

261 "Alfred Lunt gave": quoted in Julie Gilbert, *Ferber: A Biography,* 147.

"You should be very proud": AL to RS, Ten Chimneys, April 14, 1955. On November 18 and December 31, 1951, AL had appeared on the Ed Sullivan show, *Talk of the Town,* to honor Sherwood, along with colleagues like Helen Hayes, Raymond Massey, and Humphrey Bogart. At the same time Alfred turned down directing Sherwood's *Small War on Murray Hill* and acting in it: "Don't want to do another comedy," but chiefly he believed he couldn't do a British general. Alfred recommended Angela Lansbury for Mrs. Murray. The death of AL and LF's close friends is also a deprivation for the biographer: with Woollcott, Robertson, Lady Sibyl Colefax, Sherwood, and Hattie gone, the Lunts' significant correspondence shrinks drastically.

262 "A man like Alfred": Toby Cole and Helen Frich Chonoy, *Actors on Acting,* 607,

described as Strasberg's "reputed comment." Also quoted by Frederic Morton, *Esquire,* December 1954.

263 "that the great talent": Tyrone Guthrie, "Greatness in the Theatre," *Horizon,* January 1961. Though writing five years after *The Great Sebastians,* Guthrie must have considered it a more fragile toy than *The Guardsman,* which he cites.

"I have come to think": Harold Clurman in *The Nation,* reprinted in *Lies Like Truth,* 270.

"evil arithmetic": Richard Maney, *Fanfare,* 285–86.

"fabulous, like Merlin": Maxwell Anderson to AL and LF, April 18, 1956.

"The Sebastians are": Virgil Thomson to AL, January 7 [1956]. Thomson had composed the music Alfred found so central to *Ondine.*

264 "south of their heart's": Richard Maney's opinion in *Fanfare,* 286.

"sharply timed interplay": Cecil Beaton and Kenneth Tynan, *Persona Grata,* 43.

"Huh—the Lunts": interview with James Auer, arts critic of the *Milwaukee Journal-Sentinel,* November 21, 2001; the incident happened to his wife.

265 "Every time I saw": MZ, *Stagestruck,* 4, and MZ tapes.

"We went inside": Helen Hayes, *My Life in Three Acts,* 106.

"Somebody has to go": AL quoted by Ward Morehouse, *New York World Telegram,* June 3 [1951].

"the audience went" . . . "No—we ain't" . . . "The reviews were": AL to Russel Crouse, Chicago, November 1 and 6, 1956.

266 "You know, Alfred": AL quoting LF in a letter to RS of October 4, 1953.

"or anywhere else" . . . "Apparently the day": AL to Robert Downing, San Francisco, January 15, 1957.

"Any day now": AL to Robert Downing, Ten Chimneys, April 5, 1955.

"we have 3": AL to Russel Crouse, San Francisco, January 14, 1957.

267 "was hailed by all": George Freedley, *The Lunts,* 83.

"For the first": George Cukor to the Lunts, April 2, 1957.

"I hope people": interview with Ward Morehouse, *New York World-Telegram,* June 3 [1951].

"There has been so much": George Freedley, *The Lunts,* 84.

268 "Oh, why did": Madeline Sherwood to AL and LF, February 4, 1957; but since she apologized to the Lunts again on board the *Queen Elizabeth,* she perhaps used similar words.

CHAPTER SIXTEEN • *THE VISIT: 1957-1960*

269 "this old woman": MZ, *Stagestruck* (262), quoting Moss Hart, to whom Brook gave this apparently preposterous plot summary of a Lunt-Fontanne play.

270 "Claire is neither": quoted in J. C. Trewin, *Peter Brook: A Biography,* 115.

"a spitting, biting" . . . "twenty per cent": Albert Hunt and Geoffrey Reeves, *Directors in Perspective: Peter Brook,* 33.

"I wanted the audience": quoted in Albert Hunt and Geoffrey Reeves, *Directors in Perspective: Peter Brook,* 34.

271 "It was the finest": Donald Seawell to MP, December 6, 2001.

272 "Egg whites are": AL interview by Craig Claiborne in New York during the run of *The Visit,* n.d., source unknown.

"Lynn has great" . . . "Directing Lunt is": interview with Peter Brook quoted from Randolph Goodman, *Drama On Stage,* 404, 405. Goodman's discussion of *The Visit* (378–423) is the best single source on the play.

"An audience of uncles": Peter Brook, *The Shifting Point,* 36. For the pre-London tour the title was changed to the meaningless *Time and Time Again,* which did not help the production.

273 "This is an evil": Mary Lynn, stage manager for *The Visit,* quoted in Randolph Goodman, *Drama On Stage,* 410.

"introduced a completely": interview with Peter Brook, quoted in Randolph Goodman, *Drama On Stage,* 404.

"Audiences superb but": AL to Nancy Towle, Dublin, February 10, 1958. The Lunts spelled her name alternately "Nancy" and "Nancie," and even Ms. Towle varies her signatures.

"Give them a theater": quoted in JB, *The Fabulous Lunts,* 408, also the source of AL's letter to Alan Hewitt, 408–9.

274 "Do I have": excerpts of letters from AL and LF to Nancy Towle, Edinburgh, February 24, 1958, and Newcastle-on-Tyne, where the tour concluded, n.d.

275 "At first I" . . . "It has never" . . . "Why are you": quoted in Lewis Funke and John E. Booth, *Actors Talk About Acting,* 23–25.

277 "From that time": quoted in JB, *The Fabulous Lunts,* 416.

278 "my mental solar plexus": Anita Loos to AL and LF, June 20, 1958.

279 "$52,000 a week": AL to Nancy Towle, May 26, 1958. *The Visit* broke all house records for a drama.

"We were evicted": LF to James Auer, quoted in interview with THG for Ten Chimneys, December 12, 1998.

280 "This has been a degrading": AL to Robert Downing, New York Hospital [week of June 23, 1958]. A special benefit performance for the Actors' Fund of America had been scheduled for June 29, 1958: "And I feel particularly upset about cancelling the Fund performance on Sunday." The benefit was eventually given at a matinee on August 21, 1958.

"I get great pleasure": "They Glory in a Rustic High-Style Hideaway," *Life,* July 26, 1963.

"It is so *exciting*": AL to John Mason Brown, n.d. [but 1960s].

"Rows of women": AL and LF interviewed by Whitney Bolton, *New York Morning Telegraph,* September 17, 1958.

281 "If we could have played" . . . "Dear Mr. and Mrs.": quoted in Randolph Goodman, *Drama On Stage,* 401.

282 "If you're going to kill": interview with AL at Carroll College, 1973.

"You've both of you": Maurice Valency to AL, March 9, 1960.

"Broke our hearts": This and the following quotations are from Lewis Funke and John E. Booth, *Actors Talk About Acting,* 15–46.

283 "In the middle": Studs Terkel, interview with John Randolph, *The Spectator,* 133–34.

284 "Most apprehensive": AL to Robert Downing, Ten Chimneys, n.d. [May 1960].

284 "the foundations of the West End": J. C. Trewin, *Peter Brook: A Biography,* 115.

"Binkie is obviously": Noël Coward, *Diaries,* June 4, 1960, 472.

"bowled over": Donald Sinden to "Dear greatly admired both," January 1, 1972. Sinden's letter also refers to *There Shall Be No Night* and *Love in Idleness.*

"I think the Lunts": "Truth, Tricks or Technique," *Plays and Players,* August 1960.

285 "The Lunts *are*": interview with AL and LF on the BBC *Radio Newsreel,* June 2, 1960. LF says that they had Method actors in *The Visit* in New York and when they asked Lee Strasberg in what category to put the Lunts, he made that reply.

"less as a Medea-figure": Edward Trostle Jones, *Following Directions,* 61.

"a tough play to do": AL to Robert Downing, who was visiting in London, August 6, 1960.

"Just let us": quoted in Randolph Goodman, *Drama On Stage,* 401.

CHAPTER SEVENTEEN • "WHEN A GOOD PLAY
COMES ALONG": 1960-1970

286 "fine feeling": Edna Ferber to AL and LF, December 26, 1959, but a response that could have been made to any number of the photographs of Ten Chimneys the Lunts regularly sent.

287 "You couldn't miss them": Arlene Dable, cook and table waitstaff at Ten Chimneys, to THG, September 23, 1998.

"There was a very small": Sarah L. Connor to THG, April 19, 1999.

"no plays, no plans": quoted by Ward Morehouse, "Lunt and Fontanne Are Enjoying Life of Ease," *New York World Telegram,* April 25, 1961.

288 "I've never been so thrilled": quotes from the *Milwaukee Journal* and *Milwaukee Sentinel,* May 14 and September 23, 1961.

"I've had rather" . . . "the play I fear": AL to Robert Downing, New York, December 17, 1961, and Ten Chimneys, January 6, 1962.

"What a hideous": NC, *Diaries,* November 2, 1961, 485.

"We wandered": NC, *Diaries,* November 27, 1961, 488.

"a vestal virgin": Robert Sherwood, "The Lunts," *The Passionate Playgoer,* 83.

289 "immensely elegant" . . . "Looking back": Enid Bagnold, *Autobiography,* 252–62.

"I expect to be": LF to Bessie Porter, October 22, 1941.

"I hope to be": LF to AW, December 30, 1940.

"about which": Enid Bagnold to LF, June 30, 1970.

"liked a brandy": THG interview with Richard Perkins, August 2, 1998.

290 "you could get drunk": THG interview with Arlene Dable, September 28, 1998.

"because it was such": THG interview with Thomas Bugbee, who also waited table for the Lunts, September 20, 1998.

"He did his best": THG interview with Winifred Eschweiler, February 23, 1999.

"She glided round": Cathleen Nesbitt, *All My Friends,* 245.

"everything to do" . . . "the beautiful indulgence": Enid Bagnold to the Lunts, August 6, 1966, and August 5, 1962.

"*They* were a play": Enid Bagnold, *Autobiography,* 256.

"You know, we thought": AL to James Auer, quoted in THG's interview with Auer, December 12, 1998.

"They were thrilled": NC, *Diaries,* February 4, 1963, 527.

291 "Lynn, if you're thinking": quoted in George Burns, *Living It Up,* 134. A two-disc recording of the February 10, 1963, Pipe Night was made privately for the Players Club.

"really nauseating": LF to George Schaefer, *The Lunts: A Life in the Theater,* PBS, March 7, 1980.

"I stand there" . . . "I thought, why not?": AL quoted in the *New York Times,* May 17, 1963.

292 "I'm shocked" . . . "It was a *strange*": Rosemary Harris to MP at Ten Chimneys, April 13, 2002.

"You know, if we *were* doing" . . . "What the devil": Enid Bagnold, *Autobiography,* 256.

293 "Write *another*": Jules Johnson to Enid Bagnold, May 30, 1963.

294 "It looks like": quoted in Graham Payn, *My Life with Noel Coward,* 204.

295 "the biography did not": George Bugbee, *Reflections of a Good Life,* 107.

296 "One day for blocking": Emmet Lavery, "Some Notes on Two-Piano Music," ANTA Souvenir Booklet, 1972.

"Once a scene is taped": AL quoted in the *Milwaukee Journal* (January 25, 1965).

"Absolutely superb": NC, *Diaries,* February 14, 1965, 592. AL and LF arranged a showing for Noël, Katharine Cornell, Nancy Hamilton (Cornell's partner), Carol Channing, and Cole Leslie.

297 "I didn't like myself": quoted in the *New York Times,* January 20, 1965.

"Would *A Patriot*": LF to Nancy Towle, Ten Chimneys, March 30, 1966. Both plays had homosexual themes.

"wants your elegance": Rudolf Bing to AL, February 9, 1953. AL had agreed to do *Così* in 1964, then was unwell.

"One of the highlights": Roberta Peters to AL, February 6, 1965.

"a very agreeable": Cecil Beaton to AL, June 10, 1964. This *Traviata* had been in the works a long time.

"After all, she's" . . . "You don't really" . . . "He directs": MZ, "When a Broadway Star Stages an Opera," *New York Times,* October 9, 1966.

298 "under exceedingly difficult": Rudolf Bing to AL, October 11, 1966. Bing's letter (and AL's payment) was delayed because of "pressure" on management. Cecil Beaton, the designer, commented in his *Diaries:* "Messages had been left for me at the hotel, and before I had unpacked an excited Alfred Lunt was on the line. Could we go immediately to the opera house? . . . The old problems arose: not much money; little rehearsal time; and too many productions in too short a time. But Alfred, smelling of beer, said his piece, and apologized for talking too much. He is sweet and understanding and a good man, and I pray to God that I will always love him" (370). The Lunts gave Beaton a dinner that night with Truman Capote, the Joe Alsops, and Madeline Sherwood.

298 "She's an important": LF quoted by Joanne Stang in the *New York Times,* March
    12, 1967.

    "We were still taping": quoted in JB, *The Fabulous Lunts,* 441.

299 "I've ceased to be": LF to Nancy Towle, Ten Chimneys, December 9, 1966, and
    January 3, 1967.

    "Mr. Lunt and I": quoted in the *Waukesha Freeman,* October 7, 1965.

    "My left eye": AL to Nancy Towle, March 27, 1968.

    "Just remember": quoted in F. Beverly Kelley, *It Was Better Than Work,* 222.

    "a triangle" . . . "I still see": AL to Kenneth Conant, February 4, 1970.

300 "We are still stunned": AL to Robert Downing, Ten Chimneys, October 12,
    1970. Both Karin and Carl were buried in the Lunt plot in Forest Home Ceme-
    tery in Milwaukee.

    "That woman's ego": quoted by John McMillan, friend of Ms. Channing, to MP,
    July 17, 2000. Carol Channing and the Lunts went to hear Streisand at Mr.
    Kelly's early in her career.

302 "I've never seen": quoted from the *Waukesha Freeman,* May 23, 1970, and *Cavett,*
    305. The *Dick Cavett Show* with the Lunts was broadcast on ABC February 10,
    1970; it was repeated by popular request on June 1, 1970. Brian Bedford and
    Tammy Grimes, who won a Tony for her current role in *Private Lives,* also
    appeared on February 10 and sang Coward selections. AL and LF were fans of
    Cavett and had asked the actress Leueen McGrath to introduce them.

    "I was *awful*": AL did apologize profusely after the show to Dick Cavett for not
    contributing more. He also complained on occasion to Laurence Olivier that his
    face looked like a discarded douche bag. The rest of the conversation is a rea-
    sonable (I trust) guess.

CHAPTER EIGHTEEN • THE BEST REVENGE: 1971–1983

303 "Not far from Chicago": Claudia Cassidy, "A Visit with the Lustrous Lunts,"
    Chicago Tribune Magazine, June 25, 1967.

    "absolutely charming": Lord Mountbatten to Noël Coward, September 27,
    1971.

304 "Alfred took a handful": Alec Guinness, *A Positively Final Appearance,* 112–13.

    "Mr. Lunt and Jules": THG interview with Arlene Dable, September 23, 1998.
    Ms. Dable also cooked for George Bugbee at the cottage.

    "a nice, nice man": THG interview with Catherine Gavigan, January 16, 1999.
    Gavigan, Arlene Dable, John Hale Jr., and Stella Heintz, the Lunts' cook,
    among others, all talked about the Lunts not wanting to put Jules up when he
    returned. Stella Heintz: "He came at tea time and they wouldn't let him in—
    they wouldn't give him tea. He had to go on back home again. Back over to
    Ben's—over to the Perkins'."

305 "You can't buy style": Ronald Bowers to MP, telephone interview, April 16,
    2001.

    "Your unique careers" . . . "I've seen enough" . . . "When we were": quoted from
    "Lunts Celebrate 50th Anniversary," *Milwaukee Journal,* May 26, 1972.

    "I had a new lover": LF to Ruth Hamilton, unpublished interview, n.d.

"Everybody knows that": John Mason Brown, "Seeing Things," *Saturday Review,* December 3, 1949, and February 16, 1946.

"They seemed transformed" . . . "I'd like to tell" . . . "I don't think": "Stars Turn Out to Honor the Lunts," *Milwaukee Journal,* June 12, 1972. LF and AL insisted on taking George Bugbee's nephew Thomas to the ceremony, and introduced him to all the stars. "I mean, I'm just going 'holy cow,' " said the awed Thomas, then an economics major at the University of California.

307 "When we were there": AL to Robert Downing, Ten Chimneys, November 21, 1970.

"Now, don't you look": Stella Heintz to THG, August 2, 1998.

"I never know": reported in the *Waukesha Freeman,* July 5, 1975.

308 "I want electricity" . . . "What are *you*": Clarence Bundy to MP, April 4, 2000.

"These movie stars": THG interview with Stella Heintz, August 2, 1998.

"Do you see?": Kenneth Barrow, *Helen Hayes,* 182–83.

"I've no acting": Helen Hayes to LF and AL, September 7, 1970.

309 "Mrs. Lunt couldn't": THG interview with Stella Heintz, August 2, 1998.

"with you two": Helen Hayes to AL and LF, December 10, 1971.

"had a Hell": AL to Robert Downing, Ten Chimneys, July 19, 1973. The Lunts' friendship with Channing had begun back in 1949 with the casting of *Gentlemen Prefer Blondes*. Channing was not thought right for the role; the author, Anita Loos, asked AL and LF's opinion. They quizzed Channing an hour about the part of Lorelei Lee and were so impressed that they put money into the show.

"She was as nutty": THG interview with Richard Perkins, August 2, 1998.

"That's all she ate": THG interview with Stella Heintz, August 2, 1998.

310 "Just set that" . . . "Oh, that damn" . . . "Are you *sure*" . . . "The help was": Stella Heintz, interview with MP, March 28, 2000.

"I want to tell": Stella Heintz to THG, August 2, 1998.

311 "I dote on them": Laurence Olivier to "Glorious Beloved Supremes," July 11, 1970.

"mountainous debts": Laurence Olivier to AL, September 16, 1975.

"It does get better": LF to NC, November 11, 1937.

"Hated every moment": AL to Robert Downing, Ten Chimneys, September 4, 1973, and November 14, 1973.

312 "I have the most terrible": AL to Romney Brent, November 10, 1973.

"Oh, Alfred's aneurysm": Donald Seawell to MP, January 10, 2002.

313 "finally I realized": quoted from THG's interview with Jim and Gloria Irwin, March 2, 1999.

314 "I've heard of them": Jay Joslyn, "Theatrical Majesty Keeps Spotlight Shining on Lunts," *Milwaukee Sentinel,* January 31, 1975.

"I have to tell you": quoted in Helen Hayes, *My Life in Three Acts,* 107.

"Mr. Lunt would always": Stella Heintz to MP, March 28, 2000.

"coffee you could": British friend Arthur Marshall to AL, quoting AL, February 9, 1973.

315 "Alfred currently is": quoted in Alan Hewitt's unpublished "Farewell to Alfred Lunt," August 7, 1977.

315 "I'm going to die": Jim Auer quoting John Hale, THG interview, December 12, 1998.

"Of course, they": quoted in JB, *The Fabulous Lunts,* 455.

"The outstanding actor": Harold Clurman, *Collected Works,* 936.

316 "We are witnessing": Donald Seawell, "For Alfred," unpublished tribute, August 5, 1977.

"Oh, you're so": Helen Hayes to LF, n.d. but shortly after AL's death on August 3, 1977.

317 "I will soon": LF to Jim and Gloria Irwin, quoted in their interview with THG, March 2, 1999.

"I miss him": quoted in the *Milwaukee Journal,* April 24, 1978.

"They thought I": LF interviewed by Bunny Raasch, Milwaukee Channel 12, WISN, July 30, 1981.

"It's time we stopped": LF to Alan Hewitt, November 10, 1977.

318 "Lynn was amazing": George Bugbee to MP, October 16, 1985.

"Towards the later": Richard Perkins to THG, August 2, 1998.

"Come along, Brent": Brent Fintel to THG, July 7, 1998.

319 "Chuck, three people": Charles Bowden, his unpublished pages of a visit to Ten Chimneys.

"She came in": Hume Cronyn, *A Terrible Liar,* 137.

"And how *is*": Helen Hayes, *My Life in Three Acts,* 105.

320 "What a sumptuous": John Gielgud to LF, October 16, 1978.

"I never dreamed": quoted in the *New York Times,* January 4, 1980.

"the perfectly symbolic": Michael H. Drew in the *Milwaukee Journal,* June 20, 1980. *The Lunts: A Life in the Theater* was produced by PBS and shown on WMVS-TV, Milwaukee's Channel 10, on June 21, 1980.

321 "You are an": Helen Hayes to LF, June 26, 1980.

"No one was ever": Ruth Gordon to LF, June 26, 1980.

322 "Alfred Lunt and": reported in the *New York Times,* December 8, 1980.

"I would have to stand": Martha Roland, interview with THG, July 27, 1999.

"was paying all her attention": Winifred Eschweiler to THG, February 23, 1999. Winifred's husband was an architect who handled several projects at Ten Chimneys.

323 "What a real": Katharine Hepburn to LF, May 17, 1982. Presumably "us" refers to the limousine driver, who may have been entertained by Ben Perkins.

"I have no fears": LF interviewed by Bunny Raasch, Milwaukee Channel 12, WISN, July 30, 1981.

Bagnold, Enid. *Autobiography (from 1889)*. London: Heinemann, 1969.

Bankhead, Tallulah. *Tallulah: My Autobiography*. Chicago: Sears Readers Club, 1952.

Barrow, Kenneth. *Helen Hayes: First Lady of the American Theatre*. Garden City, N.Y.: Doubleday, 1985.

Beaton, Cecil, and Kenneth Tynan. *Persona Grata*. New York: G. P. Putnam's Sons, 1954.

———. *Self Portrait with Friends: The Selected Diaries of Cecil Beaton, 1926–1974*, ed. Richard Buckle. London: Weidenfeld and Nicolson, 1979.

Behrman, S. N. *People in a Diary*. Boston: Little, Brown, 1972.

Berle, Milton (with Haskel Frankel). *Milton Berle: An Autobiography*. New York: Dell, 1974.

Blum, Daniel. *A Pictorial History of the American Theatre, 1900–1956*. New York: Greenberg, 1950.

Bosworth, Patricia. *Montgomery Clift: A Biography*. New York: Harcourt Brace Jovanovich, 1978.

Brook, Peter. *The Empty Space*. Harmondsworth: Penguin, 1968.

———. *The Shifting Point: Theatre, Film, Opera, 1946–1987*. New York: Harper and Row, 1987.

Brown, Jared. *The Fabulous Lunts: A Biography of Alfred Lunt and Lynn Fontanne*. New York: Atheneum, 1986.

Brown, John Mason. *The Worlds of Robert E. Sherwood: Mirror to His Times, 1896–1939*. New York: Harper & Row, 1962.

———. *The Ordeal of a Playwright: Robert E. Sherwood and the Challenge of War* (with *There Shall Be No Night*). New York: Harper & Row, 1970.

Bugbee, George. *Recollections of a Good Life: An Autobiography*. Chicago: The Hospital Research and Educational Trust, 1987.

Burke, Billie. *With a Feather on My Nose*. New York: Appleton, Century, Crofts, 1949.

Burns, George. *Living It Up, or They Still Love Me in Altoona!* New York: G. P. Putnam's Sons, 1976.

Cavett, Dick, and Christopher Porterfield. *Cavett*. New York: Bantam, 1974.

Clurman, Harold. *All People Are Famous.* New York: Harcourt Brace Jovanovich, 1974.

———. *The Collected Works of Harold Clurman,* ed. Marjorie Loggia and Glenn Young. New York: Applause Books, 1994.

———. *Lies Like Truth.* New York: Grove Press, 1958.

Cole, Toby, and Helen Krich Chinoy. *Actors on Acting.* New Revised Edition. New York: Crown Publishers, 1970.

Courtney, Marguerite. *Laurette.* New York: Atheneum, 1968.

Coward, Noël. *Diaries,* ed. Graham Payn and Sheridan Morley. London: Weidenfeld and Nicolson, 1982.

———. *Future Indefinite.* Garden City, N.Y.: Doubleday, 1954.

———. *Present Indicative.* Garden City, N.Y.: Doubleday, Doran, 1937.

Crawford, Cheryl. *One Naked Individual: My Fifty Years in the Theatre.* Indianapolis: Bobbs-Merrill, 1977.

Croall, Jonathan. *Gielgud: A Theatrical Life, 1905–2000.* New York: Continuum, 2001.

Cronyn, Hume. *A Terrible Liar: A Memoir.* New York: William Morrow, 1991.

Daubeny, Peter. *My World of the Theatre.* London: Jonathan Cape, 1971.

———. *Stage by Stage.* London: John Murray, 1952.

Denison, Michael. *Double Act.* London: Michael Joseph, 1985.

Eustis, Morton. "The Actor Attacks His Part." *Theatre Arts Monthly,* November 1936.

Every, Carolyn. "Home Life of the Lunts." *Wisconsin Magazine of History,* Spring 1983.

Eyre, Richard, and Nicholas Wright. *Changing Stages.* San Francisco: Bloomsbury Press, 2000.

Farago, Ladislas. *Patton: Ordeal and Triumph.* New York: Ivan Obolensky, 1964.

Freedley, George. *The Lunts.* New York: Macmillan, 1958.

Funke, Lewis, and John E. Booth, eds. *Actors Talk About Acting.* New York: Avon Books, 1961.

Gelb, Arthur, and Barbara Gelb. *O'Neill.* New York: Harper & Row, 1973.

Gilbert, Julie Goldsmith. *Ferber: A Biography.* Garden City, N.Y.: Doubleday, 1978.

Goodman, Randolph. *Drama on Stage.* New York: Holt, Rinehart and Winston, 1961.

Gray, James. "Ten Chimneys," in *Pine, Stream & Prairie.* New York: Alfred A. Knopf, 1945.

Grenfell, Joyce. *Joyce and Ginnie: The Letters of Joyce Grenfell and Virginia Graham,* ed. Jane Hampton. London: Hodder and Stoughton, 1997.

Guinness, Alec. *A Positively Final Appearance.* London: Hamish Hamilton, 1999.

Hart, Moss. *Act One: An Autobiography.* New York: Random House, 1959.

Harvey, James. *Romantic Comedy in Hollywood: From Lubitsch to Sturges.* New York: Alfred A. Knopf, 1987.

Hayes, Helen (with Katherine Hatch). *My Life in Three Acts.* New York: Harcourt Brace Jovanovich, 1990.

——— (with Sanford Doty). *On Reflection.* New York: M. Evans, 1968.

Helburn, Theresa. *A Wayward Quest: The Autobiography of Theresa Helburn.* Boston: Little, Brown, 1960.

Hoare, Philip. *Noël Coward: A Biography.* London: Sinclair-Stevenson, 1995.

Howard, Leslie. *Trivial Fond Records,* ed. Ronald Howard. London: William Kimber, 1982.

Howard, Leslie Ruth. *A Quite Remarkable Father.* New York: Harcourt Brace, 1959.

Huggett, Richard. *Binkie Beaumont: Eminence Grise of the West End Theatre, 1933–1973.* London: Hodder & Stoughton, 1989.

Hunt, Albert, and Geoffrey Reeves. *Peter Brook.* Cambridge: Cambridge University Press, 1995.

Inskip, Donald. *Jean Giraudoux: The Making of a Dramatist.* London: Oxford University Press, 1958.

Kelley, F. Beverly. *It Was Better Than Work.* Gerald, Missouri: The Patrice Press, 1982.

Kiernan, Thomas. *Sir Larry: The Life of Laurence Olivier.* New York: Times Books, 1981.

Kurtz, Maurice. *Jacques Copeau: Biography of a Theatre.* Carbondale: Southern Illinois University Press, 1999.

La Guardia, Robert. *Monty: A Biography of Montgomery Clift.* New York: Arbor House, 1977.

Langner, Lawrence. *The Magic Curtain.* New York: E. P. Dutton, 1951.

Laughlin, Charles. *J. Scott Smart a.k.a. The Fat Man.* Portsmouth, N.H.: Three Faces East Press, 1994.

Lesley, Cole, Graham Payn, and Sheridan Morley. *Noel Coward and His Friends.* London: Weidenfeld and Nicolson, 1979.

Lindsay, Howard. "Lindsay and Crouse and the Fabulous Lunts." *Good Housekeeping,* February 1956.

Lunt, Alfred. "An Editorial." *Theatre Arts,* February 1950.

———. "Twenty-Six Weeks in Vaudeville—Learning Things I Have Never Forgotten." *Billboard,* December 26, 1936.

Maney, Richard. *Fanfare: The Confessions of a Press Agent.* New York: Harper, 1957.

McClintic, Guthrie. *Me and Kit.* Boston: Little, Brown, 1955.

Meredith, Scott. *George S. Kaufman and His Friends.* Garden City, N.Y.: Doubleday, 1974.

Morella, Joseph, and George Mazzei. *Genius and Lust: The Creativity and Sexuality of Cole Porter and Noel Coward.* New York: Carroll & Graf Publishers, 1995.

Morley, Sheridan. *A Talent to Amuse: A Biography of Noël Coward.* Garden City, N.Y: Doubleday, 1969.

Mosel, Tad, with Gertrude Macy. *Leading Lady: The World and Theatre of Katharine Cornell.* Boston: Little, Brown, 1978.

Nesbitt, Cathleen. *A Little Love and Good Company.* London: Faber & Faber, 1975.

Nolan, Libbie Faulkner. "Lunt-Fontanne: Magic Names in American Theatre." *Landmark,* Special Lunt-Fontanne Issue, Autumn 1981.

Olivier, Laurence. *Confessions of an Actor.* New York: Simon & Schuster, 1982.

Oppenheimer, George, ed. *The Passionate Playgoer: A Personal Scrapbook.* New York: The Viking Press, 1958.

Ormsbee, Helen. *Backstage with Actors.* New York/London: Benjamin Blom, 1938 (reissued 1969).

Payn, Graham, with Barry Day. *My Life with Noël Coward.* New York: Applause, 1994.

Plowright, Joan. *And That's Not All.* London: Weidenfeld & Nicolson, 2001.

Robertson, Graham. *Letters from Graham Robertson,* ed. Kerrison Preston. London: Hamish Hamilton, 1953.

Rogers, Ginger. *My Story.* New York: Harper Collins, 1991.

Schanke, Robert A., and Kim Marra, eds. *Passing Performances: Queer Readings of Lead-*

ing Players in American Theater History. Ann Arbor: University of Michigan Press, 1998.

Spoto, Donald. *Laurence Olivier: A Biography.* London: Harper Collins, 1991.

Tarkington, Booth. *On Plays, Playwrights, and Playgoers: Selections from the Letters of Booth Tarkington to George C. Tyler and John Peter Toohey, 1918–1925,* ed. Alan S. Downer. Princeton: Princeton University Library, 1959.

Taylor, Laurette. "Lynn Fontanne." *Town and Country,* August 1942.

Teichmann, Howard. *George S. Kaufman: An Intimate Portrait.* New York: Atheneum, 1972.

———. *Smart Aleck: The Wit and World of Alexander Woollcott.* New York: William Morrow, 1976.

Terkel, Studs. *The Spectator: Talk About Movies and Plays with the People Who Made Them.* New York: The New Press, 1999.

Thomas, Bob. *Thalberg: Life and Legend.* Garden City, N.Y.: Doubleday, 1969.

Trewin, J. C. *Peter Brook: A Biography.* London: Macdonald, 1971.

Trostle Jones, Edward. *Following Directions: A Study of Peter Brook.* New York: Peter Lang, 1985.

Tyler, George C., with J. C. Furnas. *Whatever Goes Up: The Hazardous Fortunes of a Natural Born Gambler.* Indianapolis: Bobbs-Merrill, 1934.

Tynan, Kenneth. *Curtains: Selections from the Drama Criticism and Related Writings.* New York: Atheneum, 1961.

Wansell, Geoffrey. *Terence Rattigan.* London: Fourth Estate, 1995.

Weill, Kurt, and Lotte Lenya. *Speak Low (When You Speak Love): The Letters of Kurt Weill and Lotte Lenya,* ed. and trans. Lys Symonette and Kim H. Kowalke. Berkeley and Los Angeles: University of California Press, 1996.

Wharton, John F. *Life Among the Playwrights: Being Mostly the Story of The Playwrights Producing Company, Inc.* New York: Quadrangle, 1974.

Woodress, James. *Booth Tarkington: Gentleman from Indiana.* Philadelphia: J. B. Lippincott, 1954.

Woollcott, Alexander. *The Letters of Alexander Woollcott,* ed. Beatrice Kaufman and Joseph Hennessey. New York: The Viking Press, 1944.

Zolotow, Maurice. *Stagestruck: The Romance of Alfred Lunt and Lynn Fontanne.* New York: Harcourt, Brace & World, 1964.

This chronology is revised and expanded from George Freedley's *The Lunts* (1958), Alan Hewitt's "Two Careers Become One" (souvenir program of the American National Theatre and Academy tribute to the Lunts) (ANTA, 1972), and Phillip M. Runkel, "Alfred Lunt and Lynn Fontanne: A Bibliography" (1978).

LYNN FONTANNE: THEATER

1905 Appeared in *Cinderella,* December 26, Theatre Royal, Drury Lane, London.

1906 Toured in James M. Barrie's *Alice Sit-by-the-Fire.*

1906–1908 Walked on in Alfred Sutro's *The Bond of Ninon,* Savoy Theatre; *Edwin Drood,* His Majesty's Theatre; and Booth Tarkington's *Monsieur Beaucaire,* Lyric Theatre, London.

1909 Began tour on January 4 as Rose Carlisle in *Lady Frederick* by Somerset Maugham at the Theatre Royal, Bristol (dir. Percy Hutchinson) and as Joyce in the curtain raiser *The Peacemaker.*

December 11. Appeared in *Where Children Rule* by Sydney Blow and Douglas Hoare, Garrick Theatre, London (dir. Charles Rock).

1910 March–May. Toured as Harriet Bludgeon in *Mr. Preedy and the Countess* by R. C. Carton (dir. Weedon Grossmith).

June 23. Lady Mulberry in *Billy's Bargain* by Weedon Grossmith, Garrick Theatre, London (dir. Weedon Grossmith).

September–October. Appeared in Montreal and Washington, D.C., with Weedon Grossmith as Harriet Bludgeon in *Mr. Preedy and the Countess;* then at Nazimova's 39th Street Theatre, New York City, beginning November 7 for twenty-four performances.

1911 February 22. Gwendolyn in the curtain raiser *The Young Lady of Seventeen* by Charles Brookfield, Criterion Theatre, London (dir. Weedon Grossmith); production transferred to the Vaudeville Theatre in May.

September 8. Mrs. Gerrard in curtain raiser *A Storm in a Tea-Shop* by Stafford Hilliard, Vaudeville Theatre, London, through January 1912.

1912 February–May. Toured as understudy in *Baby Mine* by Gertrude Mayo (dir. Weedon Grossmith).

1913 January–May, August–December. Toured as Gertrude Rhead in *Milestones* by Arnold Bennett and Edward Knoblock.

1914 April 23. Liza and Mrs. Collisson in *My Lady's Dress* by Edward Knoblock, Royalty Theatre, London (dir. Frank Vernon).

October 31. Gertrude Rhead in revival of *Milestones,* Royalty Theatre, London (dir. Frank Vernon).

1915 February 11. Nurse in *Searchlights* by Horace Annesley Vachell, Savoy Theatre, London (dir. Holman Clark).

May 30. The Governor's sister in *The Terrorist* by Laurence Irving, Playhouse, London (dir. Edith Craig).

July 2. The Maid in *A War Committee* by Edward Knoblock, one-act for a charity matinee, Haymarket Theatre, London.

July 12. Ada Philbeam in *How to Get On* by Edward Knoblock, one-act in variety program, Victoria Palace, London (dir. Norman McKinnel).

December 29. A Pleiade in *The Starlight Express* by Algernon Blackwood and Violet Pern, music by Edward Elgar, Kingsway Theatre, London (dir. Lena Ashwell).

1916 March. Winifred in *The Wooing of Eve* by J. Hartley Manners, Lyceum Theater, Rochester, NY (dir. J. Hartley Manners).

November 27. Olive Hood in *The Harp of Life* by J. Hartley Manners, Globe Theatre, New York (dir. J. Hartley Manners); 136 performances into 1917.

1917 March 27. Princess Lizzie in *Out There* by J. Hartley Manners, Globe Theatre, New York (dir. J. Hartley Manners).

November 9. Winifred in *The Wooing of Eve* by J. Hartley Manners, Liberty Theatre, New York (dir. J. Hartley Manners).

December 31. Miss Perkins in *Happiness* by J. Hartley Manners, Criterion Theatre, New York (dir. J. Hartley Manners).

1918 April 5. Bianca in *The Taming of the Shrew* and Nerissa in *The Merchant of Venice,* special matinee with Laurette Taylor, Lyric Theatre, New York.

May 20. Mrs. Rockingham in *A Pair of Petticoats* by Cyril Harcourt, Bijou Theatre, New York (dir. Cyril Harcourt). Replaced Laura Hope Crews.

September 9. Mrs. Glendinning in *Someone in the House* by Larry Evans, Walter Percival, and George S. Kaufman. Knickerbocker Theater, New York (dir. Frederick Stanhope).

1919 Anna Christopherson in *Chris* by Eugene O'Neill, Nixon's Apollo Theater, Atlantic City, and (March 15) Broad Street Theater, Philadelphia (dir. Frederick Stanhope).

April 29. Zephyr in *One Night in Rome* by J. Hartley Manners, Garrick Theatre, London (dir. J. Hartley Manners). Opening-night riot postponed premiere until May 3.

1921 August 13. Dulcinea in *Dulcy* by George S. Kaufman and Marc Connelly, Frazee Theatre, New York (dir. Howard Lindsay); 246 performances into 1922.

1923 August 6. Ann Jordan in *In Love with Love* by Vincent Lawrence, Ritz Theatre, New York (dir. Robert Milton); 128 performances into 1924.

1926 November 15. Eliza Doolittle in *Pygmalion* by George Bernard Shaw, Guild Theatre, New York (dir. Dudley Digges); 143 performances.

1928 January 30. Nina Leeds in *Strange Interlude* by Eugene O'Neill, John Golden Theatre, New York (dir. Philip Moeller); 428 performances.

ALFRED LUNT: THEATER

1912–1915 Castle Square Theater, Boston. *The Aviator; Such a Little Queen; The Man of the Hour; All the Comforts of Home; Madame X; Rip Van Winkle; The Bishop's Carriage; The Little Minister; The Three Musketeers; Othello; Hamlet; A Midsummer's Night Dream; She Stoops to Conquer; Mice and Men; The Gingerbread Man; Believe Me, Xantippe; Damon and Pythias; Soldier of Fortune; Darling of the Gods; The Fires of Fate; The Man from Home; The Fourth Estate; A Comedy of Errors; Get-Rich-Quick Wallingford; Julius Caesar; The Butterfly on the Wheel; Held by the Enemy; The Royal Mounted; Two Flags; A Temperance Town; We the People; Miss Pocahontas; Babes in the Wood; Blue Jeans; Over Night; The Traveling Salesman; Mrs. Wiggs of the Cabbage Patch; The Mind the Paint Girl; Hawthorne of the USA; The Great Ruby; A New Farce; The Crisis; The Deep Purple; The Ghost Breaker; A Midnight Bell; Granstark; The Girl of the Golden West; Arizona; Snow White; The Triple Tie; Ready Money; The Thief; Paid in Full; Kindling; Common Clay; The Ne'er-Do-Well; Nearly Married; Maggie Pepper.*

1915 July. Joined Margaret Anglin's company in Chicago for tour to California as J. Courtland Redlaw in *Beverly's Balance* by Paul Kester.

August 14. First of four Saturday-night performances at the Greek Theater, Berkeley, in *Iphigenia in Aulis* (Messenger), *Medea* (Reveller), *Electra* (Messenger); on September 4 steps into the role of Achilles in *Iphigenia* (dir. Gustav von Seyffertitz, Margaret Anglin).

September. Touring in *Beverly's Balance* into 1916.

1916 June 5. Le Beau and Jacques de Boys in *As You Like It*, with Margaret Anglin, Municipal Open Air Theater, Forest Park, Saint Louis.

August. John Belden in *Her Husband's Wife* in vaudeville, Philadelphia and Washington, with Laura Hope Crews.

September 10. Began vaudeville tour with Lillie Langtry as Eric Huntsdowne in *The Eleventh Hour*, Orpheum Theater, San Francisco.

November 12. With Lillie Langtry as Fred Fowler in *Ashes*, Orpheum Theater, San Francisco; then touring into 1917.

1917 May. Toured as Colonel J. N. Smith with Margaret Anglin in *Green Stockings* by A. E. W. Mason, playing the Standard Theatre, New York, for one week beginning May 14. New York debut.

August 29. Trillo in *The Pirate* by Ludwig Fulda (trans. Louis N. Parker), stock engagement at Pabst Theater, Milwaukee (dir. George Foster Platt).

October 17. Claude Estabrook in *Romance and Arabella* by William Hurlbut, with Laura Hope Crews, Harris Theatre, New York (dir. George Foster Platt); 29 performances.

1918 Toured with Alexandra Carlisle as George Tewkesbury Reynolds III in *The Country Cousin* by Booth Tarkington and Julian Street.

1919 June 2. Billy Capron in *On the Hiring Line* by Harvey O'Higgins and Harriet Ford, George C. Tyler Stock at National Theater, Washington, with Emily Stevens and Helen Hayes.

September 20. Title role in *Clarence* by Booth Tarkington at Hudson Theatre, New York, with Helen Hayes (dir. Frederick Stanhope); into 1920.

1920–1921 Toured in *Clarence.*

November 7. Ames in *The Intimate Strangers* by Booth Tarkington, Henry Miller's Theatre, New York, with Billie Burke (dir. Ira Hards); 91 performances and tour.

1922 September 20. Count Alexandre de Lussac in *Banco* by Alfred Savoir (adapt. Claire Kummer), Ritz Theatre, New York (dir. Robert Milton); 69 performances.

1923 November 20. David Peel in *Robert E. Lee* by John Drinkwater, Ritz Theatre, New York (dir. Robert Milton); 15 performances.

1924 January 7. Tom Prior in *Outward Bound* by Sutton Vane, Ritz Theatre, New York (dir. Robert Milton); 144 performances.

1926 October 11. Emperor Maximilian in *Juarez and Maximilian* by Franz Werfel, Guild Theatre, New York (dir. Philip Moeller); 48 performances.

November 29. Babe Callahan in *Ned McCobb's Daughter* by Sidney Howard, John Golden Theatre, New York (dir. Philip Moeller); 132 performances into 1927.

1928 January 9. Marco Polo in *Marco Millions* by Eugene O'Neill, Guild Theatre, New York (dir. Rouben Mamoulian); 92 performances.

April 8. Mosca in *Volpone* by Ben Jonson in Stefan Zweig's version, Guild Theatre, New York (dir. Philip Moeller); 46 performances.

ALFRED LUNT AND LYNN FONTANNE: THEATER

1919 June 9. Daniel Hardy and Mary Blake in *Made of Money* by Porter Emerson Browne and Richard Washburn Child, George Tyler Stock Company, National Theater, Washington, D.C. First appearance together.

June 16. Pickering and Mary Darling Furlong in *A Young Man's Fancy,* George Tyler Stock Company, National Theater, Washington.

1922 With Laurette Taylor, as Charles II and Lady Castlemaine in *Sweet Nell of Old Drury* by Paul Kester, 48th Street Theatre, New York (dir. J. Hartley Manners); 35 performances.

1924 October 13. The Actor and the Actress in *The Guardsman* by Ferenc Molnár, Garrick Theatre, New York (dir. Philip Moeller); 248 performances into 1925.

1925 September 14. Bluntschli and Raina in *Arms and the Man* by George Bernard Shaw, Guild Theatre, New York (dir. Philip Moeller); 180 performances into 1926.

1926 January 25. Juvan and Stanja in *Goat Song* by Franz Werfel, Guild Theatre, New York (dir. Jacob Ben-Ami); 58 performances.

April 26. Mr. Dermott and Laura in *At Mrs. Beam's* by C. K. Munro, Guild Theatre, New York (dir. Philip Moeller); 59 performances.

1927 January 3. Dmitri and Grushenka in *The Brothers Karamazov* by Jacques Copeau and Jean Croue after Feodor Dostoyevsky, Guild Theatre, New York (dir. Jacques Copeau); 56 performances.

April 11. Clark Storey and Mrs. Kendall Frayne in *The Second Man* by S. N. Behrman, Guild Theatre, New York (dir. Philip Moeller); 44 performances.

September 12. Opened tour of *The Guardsman* and *The Second Man* at Hanna Theater, Cleveland.

September 26. *Pygmalion* added to repertoire in Chicago, Studebaker Theater, with Lunt as Henry Higgins.

October 31. *The Doctor's Dilemma* by George Bernard Shaw added to repertoire in Chicago, Studebaker Theater, Lunt and Fontanne as Louis Dubedat and Jennifer Dubedat (dir. Dudley Digges).

November 21. Louis Dubedat and Jennifer Dubedat in *The Doctor's Dilemma,* Guild Theatre, New York; 115 performances.

1928 December 31. Albert von Eckhardt and Ilsa von Ilsen in *Caprice* by Sil-Vara (trans. and dir. Philip Moeller), Guild Theatre, New York; 186 performances.

1929 June 4. *Caprice,* St. James's Theatre, London. Lunt's first London appearance, Fontanne's first there as a star.

December 23. Raphael Lord and Ann Carr in *Meteor* by S. N. Behrman, Guild Theatre, New York (dir. Philip Moeller); 92 performances.

1930 November 3. Essex and Elizabeth I in *Elizabeth the Queen* by Maxwell Anderson, Martin Beck Theatre, New York (dir. Philip Moeller); 147 performances.

1931 November 16. Rudolph Maximillian von Hapsburg and Elena Krug in *Reunion in Vienna* by Robert E. Sherwood, Martin Beck Theatre, New York (dir. Worthington Miner); 264 performances.

1932 Fall tour of *Reunion in Vienna.*

1933 January 24. Otto and Gilda in *Design for Living* by Noël Coward, Ethel Barrymore Theatre, New York (dir. Noël Coward); 135 performances.

1934 January 3. *Reunion in Vienna,* Lyric Theatre, London; Lunt's first official designation as director.

1935 January 16. Stefan and Linda in *Point Valaine* by Noël Coward, Ethel Barrymore Theatre, New York (dir. Noël Coward); 55 performances. (Earlier tryout at Colonial Theatre, Boston.)

April 22. Petruchio and Katharina in Shakespeare's *The Taming of the Shrew,* Nixon Theater, Pittsburgh (dir. Harry Wagstaff Gribble), and subsequent spring tour.

September 30. *The Taming of the Shrew,* Guild Theatre, New York; 129 performances, followed by short tour.

1936 March 24. Harry Van and Irene in *Idiot's Delight* by Robert E. Sherwood, Shubert Theatre, New York (dir. Bretaigne Windust); 300 performances.

1937 Cross-country tour of *Idiot's Delight.*

November 1. Jupiter and Alkmena in *Amphitryon 38* by Jean Giraudoux (adapted by S. N. Behrman), Shubert Theatre, New York (dir. Bretaigne Windust); 153 performances. (Earlier tryout at Curran Theater, San Francisco, and tour.)

1938 March 28. Trigorin and Madame Arkadina in *The Sea Gull* by Anton Chekhov (adapted by Stark Young), Shubert Theatre, New York (dir. Robert Milton); 41 performances.

May 17. *Amphitryon 38* at the Lyric Theatre, London.

Fall. Toured the United States in *Idiot's Delight, Amphitryon 38,* and *The Sea Gull* into spring 1939.

1939 Toured the United States in *The Taming of the Shrew* (dir. Harry Wagstaff Gribble).

1940 February 5. One-week benefit of *The Taming of the Shrew* at the Alvin Theatre, New York, for the Finnish War Relief.

March 29. Kaarlo and Miranda Valkonen in *There Shall Be No Night* by Robert E. Sherwood, Alvin Theatre, New York (dir. Alfred Lunt); 181 performances.

November. Toured the United States in *There Shall Be No Night* into spring 1941.

1941 October 15. Toured the United States in *There Shall Be No Night* until the attack on Pearl Harbor forced closing on December 18.

1942 November 25. Serafin and Manuela in *The Pirate* by S. N. Behrman, based on the play by Ludwig Fulda, Martin Beck Theatre, New York (dir. Alfred Lunt and John C. Wilson); 177 performances.

1943 December 15. Karilo and Miranda Vlachos in revised version of *There Shall Be No Night,* Aldwych Theatre, London (dir. Alfred Lunt); until July 1944. (After November 1 Liverpool opening.)

1944 December 20. Sir John Fletcher and Olivia Brown in *Love in Idleness* by Terence Rattigan, Lyric Theatre, London (dir. Alfred Lunt); until June 23, 1945. (After tryout in Liverpool, November 27.)

1945 Summer. Toured *Love in Idleness* for Allied troops on the Continent.

December 20. *O Mistress Mine* (retitled version of *Love in Idleness*) begins tryout run in Toledo.

1946 January 23. *O Mistress Mine,* Empire Theatre, New York; 452 performances through 1947.

1947–1948 Toured United States in *O Mistress Mine.*

1949 February 22. Thomas and Emily Chanler in *I Know My Love* by S. N. Behrman, adapted from Marcel Achard's *Auprès de ma blonde,* spring tryout tour beginning in Madison, Wisconsin, Wisconsin Union Theater (dir. Alfred Lunt).

November 2. *I Know My Love,* Shubert Theatre, New York; 246 performances.

1950–1951 Toured the United States in *I Know My Love.*

1952 September 12. Axel Diensen and the Marchioness of Heronden in *Quadrille* by Noël Coward, Phoenix Theatre, London (dir. Noël Coward, with acknowledgment to Lunt and Fontanne). (After tryout in Manchester, July 15; subsequently toured until September 12, 1953.)

1954 November 3. *Quadrille,* Coronet Theater, New York; 150 performances. (After tryout in Boston, October 14.)

1956 January 4. Rudi and Essie Sebastian in *The Great Sebastians* by Howard Lindsay and Russel Crouse, ANTA Theatre, New York (dir. Bretaigne Windust); 174 performances. (After tryout in Wilmington, Delaware, November 3, 1955.)

1956–1957 Toured the United States in *The Great Sebastians.*

1957 December 24. Anton Schill and Claire Zachanassian in *Time and Time Again* by Friedrich Dürrenmatt, adapted by Maurice Valency, tryout at Theatre Royal, Brighton (dir. Peter Brook). Tour canceled in March 1958.

1958 May 5. *The Visit* (*Time and Time Again*) inaugurates the Lunt-Fontanne Theatre, New York. (After Boston tryout, April 9.)

August 20. *The Visit* reopens after a summer break, Morosco Theatre, New York; 189 performances total at Lunt-Fontanne and Morosco.

1959 September 16. Begin national tour of *The Visit.*

1960 March 8. Return engagement of *The Visit* for two weeks at the New York City Center.

June 23. *The Visit* opens the new Royalty Theatre, London; 148 performances.

ALFRED LUNT AS DIRECTOR ONLY

1941 October 22. *Candle in the Wind* by Maxwell Anderson, Shubert Theater, New York, with Helen Hayes.

1951 December 28. *Così fan tutte* by Mozart, Metropolitan Opera House, New York, with Eleanor Steber, Blanche Thebom, Patrice Munsel, Richard Tucker, Frank Guarrera, John Brownlee. (Lunt walked on as a footman.)

1954 February 3. *Ondine* by Jean Giraudoux, adapted by Maurice Valency, 46th Street Theater, New York, with Audrey Hepburn and Mel Ferrer.

1961 December 25. *First Love* by Samuel Taylor, based on *Promise at Dawn* by Romain Gary, Morosco Theater, New York, with Lili Darvas and Hugh O'Brian.

1965 Revival of *Così fan tutte,* Metropolitan Opera House, New York, with Leontyne Price, Roberta Peters, Rosalind Elias, Richard Tucker, Theodor Uppman, Donald Gramm.

1966 September 22. *La traviata* by Verdi, new Metropolitan Opera House, New York, with Anna Moffo, Bruno Prevedi, Robert Merrill.

LUNT AND FONTANNE IN FILMS

1923 Lunt in *Backbone,* with Edith Roberts (dir. Edward Sloman), for Distinctive Pictures.

Lunt in *The Ragged Edge,* with Mimi Palmeri (dir. Albert Parker), Distinctive Pictures.

1924 Lunt and Fontanne in *Second Youth,* with Jobyna Howland, Walter Catlett (dir. Albert Parker), Distinctive Pictures.

1925 Lunt in *Sally of the Sawdust,* with W. C. Fields and Carol Dempster (dir. D. W. Griffith), United Artists.

Fontanne in *The Man Who Found Himself,* with Thomas Meighan, Virginia Valli, Frank Morgan (dir. Alfred E. Green), Famous Players–Lasky.

Lunt in *Lovers in Quarantine,* with Bebe Daniels (dir. Frank Tuttle), Famous Players–Lasky.

1931 Lunt and Fontanne in *The Guardsman,* with Roland Young, ZaSu Pitts, Maude Eburne (dir. Sidney Franklin), Metro-Goldwyn-Mayer.

1943 Lunt and Fontanne as themselves in *Stage Door Canteen,* with Katharine Cornell, Tallulah Bankhead, Katharine Hepburn (dir. Frank Borzage), United Artists.

LUNT AND FONTANNE ON RADIO

1940 October 13. Fontanne reading Alice Duer Miller's "The White Cliffs of Dover," NBC Blue Network; repeated live October 27.

1945 September 30. Lunt and Fontanne, *The Guardsman.* This and the following radio programs were broadcast for *The Theatre Guild on the Air* (CBS, NBC, ABC).

December 2. Lunt and Fontanne, *Elizabeth the Queen.*

December 9. Lunt in *Ned McCobb's Daughter,* with Shirley Booth.

1946 February 3. Lunt in *The Second Man,* with Peggy Conklin and Jessie Royce Landis.

March 3. Lunt in *The Show Off* by George Kelly.

March 31. Fontanne in *Strange Interlude,* part 1, with Walter Abel.

April 7. Fontanne in *Strange Interlude,* part 2.

June 2. Lunt and Fontanne in *Call It a Day* by Dodie Smith.

1947 January 5. Lunt and Fontanne in *The Great Adventure* by Arnold Bennett.

1949 January 9. Lunt and Fontanne in *O Mistress Mine.*

November 20. Lunt and Fontanne in *The Great Adventure* (repeat).

1950 September 24. Lunt and Fontanne in *There Shall Be No Night.*

1951 October 21. Lunt and Fontanne in *Pygmalion.*

1952 January 6. Lunt and Fontanne in *I Know My Love.*

February 3. Fontanne in *The Old Lady Shows Her Medals* by James M. Barrie, Lunt as narrator.

LUNT AND FONTANNE ON TELEVISION

1957 April 1. Lunt and Fontanne in *The Great Sebastians* on *Producers' Showcase* (dir. Franklin Schaffner), NBC.

1963 June 12. Fontanne in *The Old Lady Shows Her Medals,* Lunt as narrator, *U.S. Steel Hour* (dir. Tom Donovan), CBS.

September 11. Lunt and Fontanne as narrator-guides in *Athens—Where the Theatre Began,* with Alfred Drake, Rosemary Harris, Donald Madden (dir. Tom Donovan), CBS.

1965 January 28. Lunt and Fontanne in *The Magnificent Yankee* by Emmet Lavery, *Hallmark Hall of Fame* (dir. George Schaefer), NBC.

1966 February 3. Repeat of *The Magnificent Yankee.*

1967 March 17. Fontanne in *Anastasia* by Guy Bolton, with Julie Harris, *Hallmark Hall of Fame* (dir. George Schaefer), NBC.

1970 February 10. Lunt and Fontanne on *The Dick Cavett Show,* with Noël Coward (dir. David Barnhizer), ABC; repeated June 1.

April 19. Lunt and Fontanne appear on the live telecast of the Tony Awards to receive special citations for their long service to the theater (dir. Clarke Jones), NBC.

1980 March 7. Fontanne interviewed by George Schaefer at Ten Chimneys for *The Lunts: A Life in the Theater* (dir. George Schaefer), PBS.

1981 July 30. Fontanne interviewed at Ten Chimneys by Bunny Raasch for *The Bunny Raasch Special,* Channel 12, WISN, Milwaukee.

LUNT AND FONTANNE RECORDINGS

N.D. Lunt and Fontanne interviewed by Lewis Funke and John E. Booth for *Actors Talk About Acting,* Dramatic Publishing Company, 33⅓ rpm.

N.D. *Stars Over Broadway: Previously Unreleased Performances,* Star-Tone Records, 33⅓ rpm; includes excerpt from *There Shall Be No Night.*

1941 April. Fontanne reading "The White Cliffs of Dover," music composed by Frank Black, album released by RCA Victor.

1963 February 10. Lunt and Fontanne honored at "Pipe Night at the Players." 33⅓ record available only from the Players Club. Other speakers include Howard Lindsay (Pipemaster), George Burns, Marc Connelly, John Gielgud, Ralph Richardson, and Peter Ustinov.

INDEX

PERMISSIONS ACKNOWLEDGMENTS

Grateful acknowledgment is made to the following for permission to reprint previously published and unpublished material:

Alan Brodie Representation Ltd: Excerpts from *Design for Rehearsing* by Noël Coward. Copyright © The Estate of Noël Coward. Reprinted by permission of Alan Brodie Representation Ltd., 211 Piccadilly, London W1J 9HF.

Crescent Dragon Wagon: Excerpts from *Stagestruck* by Maurice Zolotow. Reprinted by permission of Crescent Dragon Wagon.

The Estate of Edna Ferber and Julie Gilbert: Excerpts from *Ferber: A Biography* by Julie Gilbert. Excerpts from the letters of Edna Ferber to Alfred Lunt and Lynn Fontanne. Reprinted by permission of the Estate of Edna Ferber and Julie Gilbert.

Philip Langner: Excerpts from *The Magic Curtain* by Lawrence Langner; *A Wayward Quest* by Theresa Helburn and a portion of a letter between Lawrence Langner and Alfred Lunt. Reprinted by permission of Philip Langner.

Dan H. Laurence: Excerpt from a postcard about Alfred Lunt and Lynn Fontanne. Reprinted by permission of Dan H. Laurence.

Methuen Publishing Limited: Excerpts from *Autobiography* by Noël Coward. Copyright © The Estate of Noël Coward. Reprinted by permission of Methuen Publishing Limited.

University of California Press: Excerpts from *Speak Low (When You Speak Love): The Letters of Kurt Weill and Lotte Lenya* edited and translated by Lys Symonette. Copyright © 1996 by Kurt Weill Foundation for Music, Bettelheim. Reprinted by permission of the University of California Press.

A NOTE ON THE TYPE

The text of this book was set in Garamond No. 3. It is not a true copy of any of the designs of Claude Garamond (ca. 1480–1561), but an adaptation of his types, which set the European standard for two centuries. It probably owes as much to the designs of Jean Jannon, a Protestant printer working in Sedan in the early seventeenth century, who had worked with Garamond's romans earlier, in Paris, but who was denied their use because of Catholic censorship. Jannon's matrices came into the possession of the Imprimerie nationale, where they were thought to be by Garamond himself, and were so described when the Imprimerie revived the type in 1900. This particular version is based on an adaptation by Morris Fuller Benton.

Composed by North Market Street Graphics,
Lancaster, Pennsylvania

Printed and bound by Berryville Graphics,
Berryville, Virginia

Designed by Iris Weinstein